DICTI

HUMAN

PERSONNEL MANAGEMENT

SECOND EDITION

658.3

Dictionary of Accounting ISBN 0-948549-11-4
Dictionary of Agriculture, 2nd ed ISBN 0-948549-27-0
Dictionary of Automobile Engineering ISBN 0-948549-78-5
Dictionary of Banking & Finance ISBN 0-948549-66-1
Dictionary of Business, 2nd ed. ISBN 0-948549-12-2
Dictionary of Computing, 2nd ed. ISBN 0-948549-51-3
Dictionary of Ecology & Environment, 3rd ed ISBN 0-948549-44-0
Dictionary of Government and Politics ISBN 0-948549-74-2
Dictionary of Hotels, Tourism, Catering ISBN 0-948549-05-X
Dictionary of Human Resources & PM, 2nd ed ISBN 0-948549-40-8
Dictionary of Information Technology, 2nd ed ISBN 0-948549-79-3
Dictionary of Law, 2nd ed. ISBN 0-948549-88-2
Dictionary of Library & Information Mgmnt ISBN 0-948549-33-5
Dictionary of Marketing, 2ns ed. ISBN 0-948549-68-8
Dictionary of Medicine, 2nd ed. ISBN 0-948549-73-4
Dictionary of Multimedia ISBN 0-948549-36-X
Dictionary of Printing and Publishing ISBN 0-948549-69-6
Dictionary of Science & Technology ISBN 0-948549-09-2
 ISBN 0-948549-67-X

(see back of this book for full title list and information request form)

Also Available

Workbooks for teachers and students of specialist English:

Check your
Vocabulary for Law ISBN 0-948549-62-9
Vocabulary for Computing ISBN 0-948549-58-0
Vocabulary for Medicine ISBN 0-948549-59-9
Vocabulary for Business ISBN 0-948549-72-6
Vocabulary for Hotels & Tourism ISBN 0-948549-75-0

DICTIONARY OF
HUMAN RESOURCES &
PERSONNEL MANAGEMENT

SECOND EDITION

A. Ivanovic MBA
P.H. Collin

PETER COLLIN PUBLISHING

First published in Great Britain 1988
as Dictionary of Personnel Management
Second edition 1997

published by
Peter Collin Publishing Ltd
1 Cambridge Road, Teddington, Middlesex, TW11 8DT

British Library Cataloguing-in-Publication Data

A catalogue record for this book is available from the British Library

ISBN 0-948549-79-3

Text computer typeset by Create Ltd. Bath

Printed by WSOY, Finland

Cover artwork by Gary Weston

PREFACE TO FIRST EDITION

This dictionary provides the user with a comprehensive vocabulary of terms used in personnel management. It covers all aspects of the subject, including recruitment and selection, assessments, payment systems, dismissals and other items of industrial relations.

The main words are explained in simple English, and, where appropriate, examples are given to show how the words are used in context. Quotations are also given from various magazines and newspapers, which give an idea of how the terms are used in real life. The supplement at the back of the book gives various documents which may act as useful guidelines as to how a company's own documents can be constructed.

PREFACE TO SECOND EDITION

Terminology changes rapidly, and this second edition includes a variety of new terms and expressions which have come into use since the first edition was published. We have also included a selection of new examples and quotations from recent magazines.

Also included is a pronunciation guide for the main entry words.

Aa

AA = ATTENDANCE ALLOWANCE

ability [ə'bɪlɪti] *noun* capacity *or* power to do something; *ability to sell is essential for the job*

able ['eɪbl] *adjective* capable *or* working well; *she's a very able manager*

◊ **able-bodied** ['eɪbl'bɒdɪd] *adjective* with no physical handicap; *both able-bodied and handicapped people may apply for the job; the work is strenuous and only suitable for the young and able-bodied*

abroad [ə'brɔːd] *adverb* to or in another country; *he worked abroad for ten years; the chairman is abroad on business; half of our profit comes from sales abroad*

absence ['æbsəns] *noun* not being at work; not being at a meeting; *occasional absence from work is not a valid reason for dismissal; he was asked to explain his repeated absences from work;* **in the absence of** = when someone is not there; *in the absence of the chairman, his deputy took the chair;* **leave of absence** = being allowed to be absent from work; *he asked for leave of absence to visit his mother in hospital;* **unauthorized absence from work** *or* **absence without leave** = being away from work without permission and without a good reason

◊ **absent** ['æbsənt] *adjective* not at work; not at a meeting; *he was absent owing to illness; ten of the workers are absent with flu; the chairman is absent in Holland on business*

◊ **absentee** [æbsən'tiː] *noun* person who is absent; worker who stays away from work for no good reason

◊ **absenteeism** [æbsən'tiːɪzəm] *noun* habit of staying away from work for no good reason; *there is a high level of absenteeism in the company; low productivity is largely due to the high level of absenteeism; from now on absenteeism will be penalized; absenteeism is high in the week before Christmas; the rate of absenteeism or the absenteeism rate always increases in fine weather* (NOTE: no plural)

ACAS ['eɪkæs] = ADVISORY, CONCILIATION AND ARBITRATION SERVICE

accept [ək'sept] *verb* **(a)** to take something which is being offered; **to accept delivery of a shipment** = to take goods into the warehouse officially when they are delivered **(b)** to say 'yes' *or* to agree to something; *to accept an offer of employment; she accepted the offer of a job in Australia; he accepted £2000 in lieu of notice*

◊ **acceptable** [ək'septəbl] *adjective* which can be accepted; *the terms of the contract of employment are not acceptable to the candidate*

◊ **acceptance** [ək'septəns] *noun* **acceptance of an offer** = agreeing to an offer; **to give an offer a conditional acceptance** = to accept provided that certain things happen *or* that certain terms apply; **we have his letter of acceptance** = we have received a letter from him accepting the offer; **acceptance sampling** = testing a small part of a batch to see if the whole batch is good enough

access ['ækses] **1** *noun* **to have access to something** = to be able to obtain *or* reach something; *he has access to large amounts of venture capital;* **access time** = time taken by a computer to find data stored in it (NOTE: no plural) **2** *verb* to call up (data) which is stored in a computer; *she accessed the address file on the computer*

◊ **accession** [æk'seʃn] *noun* joining an organization

◊ **accession rate** [æk'seʃn 'reɪt] *noun* **(a)** percentage of employees in an organization who have joined it during a particular period of time **(b)** rate of pay for employees when first hired; *after the first year, pay went up considerably despite the low accession rate; the accession rate depends on whether the entrants are skilled or unskilled*

accident ['æksɪdənt] *noun* something unpleasant which can be caused by carelessness *or* which happens by chance (such as a plane crash); *the safety inspector was looking for possible causes of accidents; accidents with machinery are not common here; how much compensation will the factory workers receive for the accident?;* **industrial accident** = accident which takes place at work; **accident book** = book in which details of accidents at work are noted down; **accident frequency rate** = number of accidents involving injury *or* death during a specified number of man-hours; *the accident frequency rate has risen since the new machinery was installed;* **accident insurance** = insurance against loss of earnings in the event of a serious accident; **accident-prone worker** = worker who is more likely to have accidents than other workers

> COMMENT: fatal accidents, and accidents which cause major injuries, or which prevent a worker from working for more than three days, must be reported to the Health and Safety Executive

◊ **accidental** [æksɪ'dentl] *adjective* happening by chance, not done intentionally; *accidental destruction of the computer files*

accommodation [əkɒmə'deɪʃən] *noun* lodgings *or* a place to live; *the company provides accommodation facilities for workers; visitors have difficulty in finding hotel accommodation during the summer; they are living in furnished accommodation;* **accommodation address** = address used for receiving messages but which is not the real address of the company (NOTE: no plural in GB English, but US English can have **accommodations**)

◊ **accommodate** [ə'kɒmədeɪt] *verb* to provide someone with a place to live in; *the company accommodates its employees near their workplace*

accord and satisfaction [æ'kɔːd n sætɪs'fækʃn] *noun* (i) payment by a debtor of (part of) a debt; (ii) the performing by a debtor of some act or service which is accepted by the creditor in full settlement, so that the debtor can no longer be sued

accordance [ə'kɔːdəns] *noun* **in accordance with** = in agreement with *or* according to; *in accordance with your instructions we have deposited the money in your current account; I am submitting the claim for damages in accordance with advice from our legal advisers*

◊ **according to** [ə'kɔːdɪŋ 'tʊ] *preposition* as stated or shown by (someone); *the computer was installed according to the manufacturer's instructions*

◊ **accordingly** [ə'kɔːdɪŋli] *adverb* in agreement with what has been decided; *we have received your letter and have altered the contract accordingly*

account [ə'kaʊnt] **1** *noun* **(a)** record of money paid *or* owed; *please send me your account or a detailed or an itemized account;* **expense account** = money which a businessman is allowed by his company to spend on travelling and entertaining clients in connection with his business; *he charged his hotel bill to his expense account* **(b)** customer who does a large amount of business with a firm; *he is one of our largest accounts; our salesmen call on their best accounts twice a month;* **account executive** = employee who looks after certain customers *or* who is the link between certain customers and his company **(c)** the **accounts of a business** *or* **a company's accounts** = detailed record of a company's financial affairs; **to keep the accounts** = to write each sum of money in the account book; *the accountant's job is to enter all the money received in the accounts;* **annual accounts** = accounts prepared at the end of a financial year; **management accounts** = financial information (sales, expenditure, credit, and profitability) prepared for a manager so that he can take decisions; **profit and loss account** = accounts for a company with expenditure and income balanced to show a final profit or loss; **accounts department** = department in a company which deals with money paid, received, borrowed or owed; **accounts manager** = manager of an accounts department; **accounts payable** = money owed by a company; **accounts receivable** = money owed to a company **(d)** **bank account** *or* *US* **banking account** = arrangement to keep money in a bank; *building society account; savings bank account; he has an account with Lloyds; I have an account with the Halifax Building*

Society; her salary is paid directly into her account; to take money out of or to withdraw money from your account; **budget account** = bank account where you plan income and expenditure to allow for periods when expenditure is high; **current account** *or* **cheque account** *or US* **checking account** = account which pays no interest but from which the customer can withdraw money when he wants by writing cheques; **deposit account** = account which pays interest but on which notice usually has to be given to withdraw money; **joint account** = account for two people; *most married people have joint accounts so that they can each take money out when they want it;* **savings account** = account where you put money in regularly and which pays interest, often at a higher rate than a deposit account; **to open an account** = to start an account by putting money in; *she opened an account with the Halifax Building Society;* **to close an account** = to take all money out of a bank account and stop the account; *he closed his account with Lloyds* **(e)** notice; **to take account of inflation** *or* **to take inflation into account** = to assume that there will be a certain percentage inflation when making calculations **2** *verb* **to account for** = to explain and record a money deal; *to account for a loss or a discrepancy; the reps have to account for all their expenses to the sales manager*

◊ **accountability** [əkaʊntə'bɪlɪti] *noun* being accountable *or* responsible

◊ **accountable** [ə'kaʊntəbl] *adjective* (person) who has to explain what has taken place *or* who is responsible for something; *if money is lost, the person at the cash desk is held accountable; the group leader will be held accountable for the actions of the group* (NOTE: you are accountable **to** someone **for** something)

◊ **accountancy** [ə'kaʊntənsi] *noun* work of an accountant; *he is studying accountancy or he is an accountancy student* (NOTE: no plural)

◊ **accountant** [ə'kaʊntənt] *noun* person trained in keeping *or* drawing up accounts *or* arranging systems of accounts; person who keeps a company's accounts *or* person who advises a company on its finances *or* person who examines accounts; *the chief accountant of a manufacturing group; I send all my income tax queries to my accountant; the accountant has shown a sharp variance in*

our labour costs; **certified accountant** = accountant who has passed the professional examinations and is a member of the Association of Certified Accountants; *US* **certified public accountant** = accountant who has passed professional examinations; **Chartered Accountant** = accountant who has passed the professional examinations and is a member of the Institute of Chartered Accountants; **cost accountant** = accountant who gives managers information about their business costs; **management accountant** = accountant who prepares financial information for managers so that they can take decisions

◊ **accounting** [ə'kaʊntɪŋ] *noun* work of recording money paid, received, borrowed or owed; *accounting machine; accounting methods or accounting procedures; accounting system;* **accounting period** = period usually covered by a firm's accounts; **cost accounting** = preparing special accounts of manufacturing and sales costs; **current cost accounting** = method of accounting which notes the cost of replacing assets at current prices, rather than valuing assets at their original cost (NOTE: no plural)

accreditation [əkredɪ'teɪʃn] *noun* process of certifying the competence of a person in a certain area; **accreditation of union officials** = official recognition by a company that certain workers are representatives of a trades union and are treated as such by the company

accredited [ə'kredɪtɪd] *adjective* (agent) who is appointed by a company to act on its behalf

accrual [ə'kruːəl] *noun* gradual increase by addition; **accrual of interest** = automatic addition of interest to capital; **accrual rate** = rate at which an employee's pension increases as each year of service is completed, so forming the basis for calculating his or her pension

◊ **accrue** [ə'kruː] *verb* to increase gradually by addition; *interest accrues from the beginning of the month*

accurate ['ækjurət] *adjective* correct; *the sales department made an accurate forecast of sales; we need an accurate copy of the plan*

◊ **accurately** ['ækjurətli] *adverb* correctly; *the second quarter's drop in sales was accurately forecast by the computer*

accuse [ə'kjuːz] *verb* to say that someone has committed a crime; *she was accused of stealing from petty cash; he was accused of industrial espionage* (NOTE: you accuse someone **of** a crime or **of** doing something)

achieve [ə'tʃiːv] *verb* to succeed in doing something *or* to do something successfully; *he has achieved his long-term training objectives; the company has achieved great success in the Far East; we achieved all our objectives in 1985*

◊ **achievement** [ə'tʃiːvmənt] *noun* success *or* something that has been achieved; **achievement test** = test designed to measure the skills which someone is currently using (as opposed to an aptitude test, which measures the skills a person could use in the future) (NOTE: also called **attainment test**)

◊ **achiever** [ə'tʃiːvə] *noun* person who is successful *or* who tends to achieve his or her objectives; *it was her reputation as an achiever that got her the management post;* **high achiever** = person who achieves more than he or she expects; **low achiever** = person who does not do as well as expected

across-the-board [ə'krɒsðə'bɔːd] *adjective* applying to everything *or* everyone; *an across-the-board wage increase; there will be a wage increase of 10% across-the-board; the new payment scheme applies across-the-board*

act [ækt] **1** *noun* **(a)** law passed by a parliament which must be obeyed by the people; *GB* **Companies Act** = Act which rules how companies should do their business; **Data Protection Act (1984)** = Act of Parliament which prevents the use of details of person which are stored in a database for others uses than that for which the record was originally made; **Finance Act** = annual Act of Parliament which gives the government power to raise taxes as proposed in the budget; **Health and Safety at Work Act** = Act which rules how the health of workers should be protected by the companies they work for **(b)** **act of God** = something you do not expect to happen, and which cannot be avoided (such as storms *or* floods) **2** *verb* **(a)** to work; *to act as an agent for an American company; to act for someone or to act on someone's behalf;* **to act as someone** = to do someone's job while he is away; *she will act as marketing manager while Mr Smith is on holiday* **(b)** to do something; *the board will have to act quickly if the company's losses are to be kept to a minimum; the lawyers are acting on our instructions;* **to act on a letter** = to do what a letter asks to be done

◊ **acting** ['æktɪŋ] *adjective* working in place of someone for a short time; *acting manager; the Acting Chairman*

◊ **action** ['ækʃən] *noun* **(a)** thing which is done; process of doing something; **to take action** = to do something; *you must take action if you want to improve productivity;* **action learning** = learning by doing *or* participating in an activity; **Action Programme** = EU initiative containing various draft directives to implement the Social Charter; **actions short of dismissal** = ways of disciplining a worker who has committed an offence, which stop short of dismissing him (demoting him, removing privileges, etc.) **(b)** **direct action** = strike or go-slow by the workforce; **to take industrial action** = to do something (usually to go on strike) to show that you are not happy with conditions at work **(c)** case in a law court where a person or company sues another person or company; **to take legal action** = to sue someone; *action for damages; action for libel or libel action; to bring an action for damages against someone;* **civil action** = case brought by a person *or* company against someone who has done them wrong; **criminal action** = case brought by the state against someone who is charged with a crime

◊ **actionable** ['ækʃnəbl] *adjective* (writing *or* speech *or* act) which could provide the grounds for bringing an action against someone; *was the employer's treatment of the employee actionable?*

◊ **active** ['æktɪv] *adjective* working *or* busy; **active partner** = partner who works in the company; *an active demand for out product; oil shares are very active; an active day on the Stock Exchange*

◊ **actively** ['æktɪvli] *adverb* in a busy way;

the company is actively recruiting new personnel

◊ **activity** [æk'tɪvəti] *noun* **(a)** being active *or* busy; things which are being done; *a low level of business activity; there was a lot of activity on the Stock Exchange;* **activity chart** = plan showing work which has been done so that it can be compared to the plan of work to be done; **monthly activity report** = report by a department on what has been done during the past month; **activity sampling** = observation of tasks and their performances, carried out at random intervals; *activity sampling was carried out to see how fast the machinists worked* (NOTE: no plural) **(b)** thing which is done; *out-of-work activities*

ad [æd] *noun* = ADVERTISEMENT

adaptable [ə'dæptəbl] *adjective* being able to change working practices; being able to change from job to job

add [æd] *verb* **(a)** to put figures together to make a total; *to add interest to the capital; interest is added monthly;* **added value** = amount added to the value of a product or service, being the difference between its cost and the amount received when it is sold (wages, taxes, etc., are deducted from the added value to give the retained profit); *see also* VALUE ADDED **(b)** to put things together to make a large group; *we are adding to the sales force; they have added two new products to their range; this all adds to the company's costs* = this makes the company's costs higher

◊ **add up** ['æd 'ʌp] *verb* **(a)** to put several figures together to make a total; *to add up a column of figures;* **the figures do not add up** = the total given is not correct **(b)** to make sense; *the complaints in the letter just do not add up*

◊ **add up to** ['æd 'ʌp tʊ] *verb* to make a total; *the total expenditure adds up to more than £1,000*

◊ **adding machine** ['ædɪŋ mə'ʃiːn] *noun* machine which adds *or* which makes additions

addition [ə'dɪʃən] *noun* **(a)** thing or person added; *the management has stopped all additions to the staff; we are exhibiting several additions to our product line; the marketing director is the latest addition to*

the board **(b)** in **addition to** = added to *or* as well as; *there are twelve registered letters to be sent in addition to this packet* **(c)** putting numbers together; *you don't need a calculator to do simple addition*

◊ **additional** [ə'dɪʃənl] *adjective* extra which is added; *additional costs; additional charges; additional clauses to a contract; additional duty will have to be paid;* **additional award** = extra payment ordered by an industrial tribunal to a dismissed worker if his company refuses to reinstate him; **additional voluntary contributions** (**AVCs**) = extra payments made voluntarily by a worker to a pension scheme (on top of the normal contributions, up to a maximum of 15% of gross earnings)

address [ə'dres] **1** *noun* details of number, street and town where an office is or a person lives; *my business address and phone number are printed on the card;* **accommodation address** = address used for receiving messages but which is not the real address of the company; **cable address** = short address for sending cables; **forwarding address** = address to which a person's mail can be sent on when they move house or office; **home address** = address of a house or flat where someone lives; *please send the documents to my home address;* **address list** = list of addresses; *we keep an address list of two thousand contacts in Europe* **2** *verb* **(a)** to write the details of an address on an envelope, etc.; *to address a letter or a parcel; please address your enquiries to the manager; a letter addressed to the managing director; an incorrectly addressed package* **(b)** to speak; *to address a meeting*

◊ **addressee** [ædre'siː] *noun* person to whom a letter *or* package is addressed

◊ **addressing machine** [ə'dresɪŋ mə'ʃiːn] *noun* machine which puts addresses on envelopes automatically

adequate ['ædɪkwət] *adjective* large enough; **to operate without adequate cover** = to act without being completely protected by insurance

ad hoc ['æd 'hɒk] *Latin phrase meaning* 'for this particular purpose'; **an ad hoc committee** = a temporary committee set up to study a particular problem; **an ad hoc decision** = a decision taken to solve a particular problem

◊ **adhocracy** [æd'hɒkrəsi] *noun* management which works by taking short-term decisions, but fails to make long-term plans

adjourn [ə'dʒɜːn] *verb* to stop a meeting for a period; *to adjourn a meeting; the chairman adjourned the meeting until three o'clock; the meeting adjourned at midday*

◊ **adjournment** [ə'dʒɜːnmənt] *noun* act of adjourning; *he proposed the adjournment of the meeting*

adjudicate [ə'dʒuːdɪkeɪt] *verb* to give a judgement between two parties in law; to decide a legal problem; *to adjudicate a claim; to adjudicate in a dispute;* he was adjudicated bankrupt = he was declared legally bankrupt

◊ **adjudication** [ədʒuːdɪ'keɪʃən] *noun* act of giving a judgement *or* of deciding a legal problem; **adjudication officer** = official who decides whether someone is qualified to receive benefit; **adjudication order** *or* **adjudication of bankruptcy** = order by a court making someone bankrupt; **adjudication tribunal** = group which adjudicates in industrial disputes

◊ **adjudicator** [ə'dʒuːdɪkeɪtə] *noun* person who gives a decision on a problem; *an adjudicator in an industrial dispute*

adjust [ə'dʒʌst] *verb* to change something to fit new conditions; *to adjust prices to take account of inflation; prices are adjusted for inflation*

◊ **adjuster** [ə'dʒʌstə] *noun* person who calculates losses for an insurance company; **average adjuster** = person who calculates how much of an insurance is to be paid

◊ **adjustment** [ə'dʒʌstmənt] *noun* act of adjusting; slight change; *tax adjustment; wage adjustment; to make an adjustment to salaries; adjustment of prices to take account of rising costs;* **automatic wage adjustment** = automatic increase in wages in line with the cost of living; *one of the attractions of the job in a time of rapid inflation, was the automatic wage adjustment attached to it;* **average adjustment** = calculation of the share of cost of damage or loss of a ship

◊ **adjustor** [ə'dʒʌstə] *noun* = ADJUSTER

admin ['ædmɪn] *noun (informal)* **(a)** work of administration, especially paperwork; *all this admin work takes a lot of my time; there's too much admin in this job; admin costs seem to be rising each quarter; the admin people have sent the report back* **(b)** administration staff; *admin say they need the report immediately*

administer [əd'mɪnɪstə] *verb* to organize *or* to manage *or* to direct the whole of an organization *or* part of one; *it will be the personnel manager's job to administer the induction programme*

◊ **administration** [ədmɪnɪ'streɪʃən] *noun* **(a)** direction *or* control *or* management of a whole organization *or* part of one; *he has a qualification in business administration;* **the expenses of the administration** *or* **administration expenses** = costs of management, not including production, marketing or distribution costs **(b)** person *or* group of people who manage *or* direct an organization; *it is up to the administration to solve the problem, not the unions* **(c)** running of a company in receivership by an administrator appointed by the courts

◊ **administrative** [əd'mɪnɪstrətɪv] *adjective* referring to administration; *administrative details; administrative expenses*

◊ **administrator** [əd'mɪnɪstreɪtə] *noun* **(a)** person who directs the work of other employees in a business; *after several years as a college teacher, she hopes to become an administrator* **(b)** person appointed by a court to administer a company which is insolvent

admonish [æd'mɒnɪʃ] *verb (formal)* to give a warning *or* reprimand; *the workers were admonished by the manager for careless work*

advance [əd'vɑːns] **1** *noun* **(a)** money paid as a loan or as a part of a payment to be made later; *bank advance; a cash advance; to receive an advance from the bank; an advance on account; to make an advance of £100 to someone; to pay someone an advance against a security; can I have an advance of £50 against next month's salary?* **(b)** **in advance** = early *or* before something happens; *to pay in advance; freight payable in advance; price fixed in advance* **(c)** early; *advance booking; advance payment; you must give seven days' advance notice of withdrawals from the account* **(d)** increase;

advance in trade; advance in prices **2** *verb* **(a)** to lend; *the bank advanced him £10,000 against the security of his house* **(b)** to increase; *prices generally advanced on the stock market* **(c)** to make something happen earlier; *the date of the AGM has been advanced to May 10th; the meeting with the German distributors has been advanced from 11.00 to 09.30*

◊ **advancement** [æd'vɑːnsmənt] *noun* promotion; *the only way to get advancement in this company is through further training; the job is attractive because of the potential for advancement*

advantage [əd'vɑːntɪdʒ] *noun* something useful which may help you to be successful; *fast typing is an advantage in a secretary; knowledge of two foreign languages is an advantage; there is no advantage in arriving at the exhibition early;* **to take advantage of something** = to use something which helps you

adverse ['ædvɜːs] *adjective* unfavourable; **adverse action** = personnel decision which has unfavourable consequences for employees; *the new bonus system was considered adverse action by underachievers in the organization;* **adverse impact** = undesirable and unexpected results of an action; *offering bonuses only for very high productivity rates had an adverse impact, discouraging rather than motivating workers*

advertise ['ædvətaɪz] *verb* to arrange and pay for publicity designed to help sell products *or* services *or* to find new employees; to announce that something is for sale *or* that a job is vacant *or* that a service is offered; *to advertise a vacancy; to advertise for a secretary; to advertise a new product*

◊ **ad** [æd] *noun* *(informal)* = ADVERTISEMENT *we put an ad in the paper; she answered an ad in the paper; he found his job through an ad in the paper;* **classified ads** *or* **small ads** *or* **want ads** = advertisements listed in a newspaper under special headings (like 'property for sale', 'jobs wanted'); *look in the small ads to see if anyone has a computer for sale;* **coupon ad** = advertisement with a form attached, which is to be cut out and returned to the advertiser with your name and address for further information; **display ad** = advertisement which is well designed to

attract attention; **open ad** = advertisement for a job where the applicant can apply to the employer directly, without having to go through a third party, such as an agency

◊ **advert** ['ædvɜːt] *noun GB (informal)* = ADVERTISEMENT

◊ **advertisement** [əd'vɜːtɪsmənt] *noun* notice which shows that something is for sale *or* that a service is offered *or* that someone wants something *or* that a job is vacant, etc.; *to put an advertisement in the paper; to answer an advertisement in the paper;* **classified advertisements** = advertisements listed in a newspaper under special headings (such as 'property for sale' or 'jobs wanted'); **display advertisement** = advertisement which is well designed to attract attention; **advertisement manager** = manager in charge of the advertisement section of a newspaper

◊ **advertiser** ['ædvətaɪzə] *noun* person *or* company which advertises; *the catalogue gives a list of advertisers*

◊ **advertising** ['ædvətaɪzɪŋ] *noun* business of announcing that something is for sale *or* of trying to persuade customers to buy a product or service; *she works in advertising; he has a job in advertising; advertising agent; advertising budget; advertising campaign;* **advertising agency** = office which plans, designs and manages advertising for other companies, such as recruitment advertising; **advertising manager** = manager in charge of advertising a company's products; **advertising rates** = amount of money charged for advertising space in a newspaper *or* advertising time on TV; **advertising space** = space in a newspaper set aside for advertisements; **to take advertising space in a paper** = to put an advertisement in a newspaper (NOTE: no plural)

advice [əd'vaɪs] *noun* **(a)** **advice note** = written notice to a customer giving details of goods ordered and shipped but not yet delivered; **as per advice** = according to what is written on the advice note **(b)** opinion as to what action to take; **to take legal advice** = to ask a lawyer to say what should be done; *the accountant's advice was to send the documents to the police; we sent the documents to the police on the advice of the accountant or we took the accountant's advice and sent the documents to the police* (NOTE: no plural)

advise [əd'vaɪz] *verb* **(a)** to tell someone what has happened; *we are advised that the shipment will arrive next week* **(b)** to suggest to someone what should be done; *we are advised to take the shipping company to court; the lawyer advised us to send the documents to the police*

◊ **advise against** [əd'vaɪz ə'genst] *verb* to suggest that something should not be done; *the bank manager advised against closing the account; the personnel manager advised against dismissing the staff without notice*

◊ **adviser** *or* **advisor** [əd'vaɪzə] *noun* person who suggests what should be done; *he is consulting the company's legal adviser;* **financial adviser** = person *or* company which gives advice on financial problems for a fee

◊ **advisory** [əd'vaɪzəri] *adjective* which advises; acting as an adviser; *he is acting in an advisory capacity;* **an advisory board** = a group of advisers; **advisory arbitration** = arbitration which recommends a solution to a dispute, but is not binding on either party; *the two parties resorted to advisory arbitration to avoid the legal process; though the two parties had agreed to advisory arbitration, neither of them agreed with the recommendation*

◊ **the Advisory, Conciliation and Arbitration Service (ACAS)** British government service which arbitrates in disputes between management and employees

> COMMENT: ACAS has three roles: it will conciliate in a dispute if asked; it advises employers, unions, workers on matters concerning industrial relations; it arbitrates in cases where industrial disputes cannot be settled inside the company's own grievance structure

affect [ə'fekt] *verb* to cause some change in *or* to have a bad effect on (something); *the new government regulations do not affect us; the company's sales in the Far East were seriously affected by the embargo*

affidavit [æfɪ'deɪvɪt] *noun* written statement which is signed and sworn before a solicitor and which can then be used as evidence in court

affiliated [ə'fɪlieɪtɪd] *adjective* connected with *or* owned by another company; *one of our affiliated companies;* **affiliated societies** = non-profit-making organizations which exist to provide financial support to members and their families in sickness and old age; **affiliated trade unions** = trade unions which are members of a larger organization, such as a national association

affirmative [ə'fɜːmətɪv] *adjective* meaning 'yes'; **the answer was in the affirmative** = the answer was yes

◊ **affirmative action** [ə'fɜːmətɪv 'ækʃən] *noun US* providing opportunities for disadvantaged groups, such as ethnic minorities, women, the disabled, etc.; *the special training sessions for handicapped workers are part of company's affirmative action policy;* **affirmative action group** = group of people who are eligible for *or* need affirmative action; *people in affirmative action groups get special consideration when applying for local government jobs;* **affirmative action program** = programme to avoid discrimination in employment; **affirmative recruitment** = recruitment which gives special consideration to applicants from affirmative action groups (NOTE: the GB equivalent is 'equal opportunities')

> COMMENT: affirmative recruitment is usually carried out by central or local government organizations

afford [ə'fɔːd] *verb* to be able to pay *or* buy; *we could not afford the cost of two telephones; the company cannot afford the time to train new staff* (NOTE: only used after **can, cannot, could, could not, able to**)

AFL-CIO ['eɪef'el 'siːaɪ'əʊ] = AMERICAN FEDERATION OF LABOR - CONGRESS OF INDUSTRIAL ORGANIZATIONS an organization linking US trade unions

after-hours ['ɑːftə'aʊəz] *adjective* **after-hours buying** *or* **selling** *or* **dealing** = buying *or* selling *or* dealing in shares after the Stock Exchange has officially closed for the day

◊ **after-sales service** ['ɑːftəseɪlz 'sɜːvɪs] *noun* service of a machine carried out by the seller for some time after the machine has been bought

◊ **after-tax profit** ['ɑːftətæks 'prɒfɪt] *noun* profit after tax has been deducted

against [ə'genst] *preposition* relating to *or*

part of; *to pay an advance against a security; can I have an advance against next month's salary? the bank advanced him £10,000 against the security of his house*

age [eɪdʒ] *noun* number of years someone has lived; **age bracket** *or* **age group** = group of people of about the same age; *the 25-30 age group;* **age limit** = oldest age at which someone can be offered a job; *there is no age limit for this post; the post has an age limit of 35;* **minimum age** = the lowest age at which someone can be employed (13 in a few types of employment, but 16 is the legal minimum); **retirement age** = age at which a worker can retire on full pension (in the UK usually 65 for men and 60 for women, though it is illegal to discriminate between the two)

◊ **ageism** [ˈeɪdʒɪzm] *noun* unfair discrimination against older people

agency [ˈeɪdʒənsi] *noun* **(a)** office *or* job of representing another company in an area; *they signed an agency agreement or an agency contract;* **sole agency** = agreement to be the only person to represent a company *or* to sell a product in a certain area; *he has the sole agency for Ford cars* **(b)** office *or* business which arranges things for other companies; **advertising agency** = office which plans *or* designs and manages advertising for companies; **employment agency** = office which finds jobs for staff; **news agency** = office which distributes news to newspapers and television stations; **travel agency** = office which arranges travel for customers; **agency labour** = staff supplied by an employment agency; *US* **agency shop** = provision that requires non-union employees to pay union dues if they are part of a bargaining unit

agenda [əˈdʒendə] *noun* list of things to be discussed at a meeting; *the conference agenda or the agenda of the conference; after two hours we were still discussing the first item on the agenda; the secretary put finance at the top of the agenda; the chairman wants two items removed from or taken off the agenda*

agent [ˈeɪdʒənt] *noun* **(a)** person who represents a company *or* another person in an area; *to be the agent for IBM;* **sole agent** = person who has the sole agency for a company in an area; *he is the sole agent for Ford cars;* **agent's commission** = money

(often a percentage of sales) paid to an agent **(b)** person who is formally acting on behalf of employees *or* a union; *management would only discuss the new payment scheme with agents officially representing the workers; certain workers were selected as agents to voice the grievances of the men and women on the shop floor* **(c)** person in charge of an agency; **advertising agent; estate agent; travel agent; commission agent** = agent who is paid by commission, not by fee; **forwarding agent** = person *or* company which arranges shipping and customs documents; **insurance agent** = person who arranges insurance for clients; **land agent** = person who runs a farm *or* a large area of land for the owner **(d)** *US* **(business) agent** = chief local official of a trade union

aggrieved [əˈgriːvd] *adjective* upset and annoyed; **the aggrieved party** = the person who has a grievance

AGM [ˈeɪdʒiːˈem] = ANNUAL GENERAL MEETING

agree [əˈgriː] *verb* **(a)** to approve; *the auditors have agreed the accounts; the figures were agreed between the two parties; we have agreed the budgets for next year; the terms of the contract are still to be agreed* **(b)** to say yes *or* to accept; *it has been agreed that the lease will run for 25 years; after some discussion he agreed to our plan; the bank will never agree to lend the company £250,000; we all agreed on the plan* (NOTE: to agree **to** *or* **on** a plan) **(c)** **to agree to do something** = to say that you will do something; *she agreed to be chairman; will the finance director agree to resign? he agreed to advise the company at a fee of £25,000 a year*

◊ **agree with** [əˈgriː wɪð] *verb* **(a)** to say that your opinions are the same as someone else's; *I agree with the chairman on the subject of redundancies* **(b)** to be the same as; *the auditors' figures do not agree with those of the accounts department*

◊ **agreed** [əˈgriːd] *adjective* which has been accepted by everyone; *he refused to pay the agreed amount; the new secretary was appointed on agreed terms; the agreed terms of employment are laid down in the contract*

◊ **agreement** [əˈgriːmənt] *noun* spoken *or* written settlement between people *or* groups; contract between two parties which explains how they will act; *an agreement on strikes between unions and management; a no-strike agreement has been signed; an unwritten or verbal agreement; to draw up or to draft an agreement; to break an agreement; to sign an agreement; to witness an agreement; an agreement has been reached or concluded; to reach an agreement or to come to an agreement on prices or salaries; an international agreement on trade; to sign a collective wage agreement;* **blanket agreement** = agreement which covers many different items; **collective agreement** = agreement on salaries, working conditions, etc., negotiated through collective bargaining; **exclusive agreement** = agreement where a company is appointed sole agent for a product in a market; **framework agreement** = draft of the main points of an agreement, with further details to be added later; **gentleman's agreement** = verbal agreement between two parties who trust each other; **outline agreement** = general draft of an agreement, without giving any details

aim [eɪm] **1** *noun* something which you try to do; *one of our aims is to increase the quality of our products;* **the company has achieved all its aims** = the company has done all the things it had hoped to do **2** *verb* to try to do something; *we aim to be No. 1 in the market within two years; each salesman must aim to double his previous year's sales*

air [eə] *verb* **to air a grievance** = to talk about or to discuss a grievance; *the management committee is valuable as a place where workers' representatives can air their grievances*

alarm [ə'lɑːm] *noun* device which gives a loud warning; **fire alarm** = bell with rings if there is a fire

alcoholism ['ælkəhɒlɪzm] *noun* excessive drinking of alcohol which becomes addictive

alien ['eɪlɪən] *noun* person who is not a citizen of a country; *(in the UK)* person who is not a citizen of the United Kingdom, not a citizen of a Commonwealth country, and not a citizen of the Irish Republic; **illegal aliens** or **illegal immigrants** = persons who live or work in a country, but have no right to do so; *the farmers employed illegal aliens who were not in a position to complain about their low wages*

◊ **alienation** [eɪlɪə'neɪʃn] *noun* lack of a sense of fulfilment when a worker cannot see the result of his work; *the monotony of the job created a sense of alienation; the management wanted to combat any sense of alienation by involving the workers in company decisions*

alignment [ə'laɪnmənt] *noun* **internal alignment** = relationship between positions in an organization in terms of rank and pay

allege [ə'ledʒ] *verb* to suggest something, without being able to prove it; *the management alleged that the union had broken the agreement*

◊ **allegation** [ælɪ'geɪʃn] *noun* suggestion that something has happened, without being able to prove it

all-in **1** ['ɔːlɪn] *adjective* including everything; **all-in price** or **all-in rate** = price which covers all items in a purchase (goods, delivery, tax, insurance); **all-in rate** or **all-in wage** = wage which includes all extra payments, bonuses, merit pay, etc. **2** [ɔːl 'ɪn] *adverb* including everything; *the fee payable is £150.00 all-in*

all-out ['ɔːlaʊt] *adjective* complete or very serious; *the personnel manager has launched an all-out campaign to improve productivity on Friday afternoons;* **all-out strike** = strike by all the workers; *the union called for an all-out strike; the solidarity of the workers in the factory led to an all-out strike*

allow [ə'laʊ] *verb* **(a)** to say that someone can do something; *junior members of staff are not allowed to use the chairman's lift; the company allows all members of staff to take six days' holiday at Christmas* **(b)** to give; *to allow someone a discount; to allow 5% discount to members of staff; to allow 10% interest on large investments* **(c)** to agree or to accept legally; *to allow a claim or an appeal*

◊ **allow for** [ə'laʊ fɔː] *verb* to give a discount for or to add an extra sum to cover something; *to allow for money paid in advance; to allow 10% for packing;* **delivery is not allowed for** = delivery charges are not included; **allow 28 days for delivery** = calculate that delivery will take at least 28 days

◊ **allowable** [ə'lauəbl] *adjective* legally accepted; **allowable expenses** = expenses which can be claimed against tax

◊ **allowance** [ə'lauəns] *noun* **(a)** money which is given for a special reason; **clothing allowance** = addition to normal salary to cover the cost of buying special clothing to wear when on duty; **cost-of-living allowance** = addition to normal salary to cover increases in the cost of living; **entertainment allowance** = money which a manager is allowed to spend each month on meals with visitors; **mobility allowance** = addition to normal salary paid to a worker who is willing to travel to different places of work; **relocation allowance** = special payment given to a worker who agrees to move to another town to work; **travel allowance** = special payment made to a worker who has to travel in order to carry out his work **(b)** part of an income which is not taxed; *allowances against tax or tax allowances; personal allowances* **(c)** money removed in the form of a discount; *allowance for depreciation; allowance for exchange loss*

◊ **allowed time** [ə'laud 'taim] *noun* paid time, agreed with the management, which a worker spends on rest *or* cleaning *or* meals, not working; *the worker's allowed time is for recreation as well as for the maintenance of the machinery; the unions hope to increase members' allowed time, so as to lighten their daily workload*

all-risks policy ['ɔ:lrisks 'pɒlisi] *noun* insurance policy which covers risks of any kind, with no exclusions

alphabet ['ælfəbet] *noun* the 26 letters used to make words

◊ **alphabetical order** [ælfə'betikəl 'ɔ:də] *noun* arrangement of records (such as files, index cards) in the order of the letters of the alphabet (A,B,C,D, etc.)

alter ['ɒltə] *verb* to change; *to alter the terms of a contract*

◊ **alteration** [ɒltə'reiʃən] *noun* change which has been made; *he made some alterations to the terms of a contract; the agreement was signed without any alterations*

alternate ['ɒltəneit] *verb* to do something by turns *or* in rotation; *two workers alternate on the machine; alternating shift*

system = system where two groups of workers work day or night shifts, and after a certain period, change round

◊ **alternation ranking** [ɒltə'neiʃn 'ræŋkiŋ] *noun* method of ranking, beginning with the highest and lowest, then the second highest and lowest, and so on

◊ **alternative** [ɒl'tɜ:nətiv] **1** *noun* thing which can be done instead of another; *what is the alternative to firing half the staff?*; **we have no alternative** = there is nothing else we can do **2** *adjective* other *or* which can take the place of something; **to find someone alternative employment** = to find someone another job

amalgamation [əmælgə'meiʃn] *noun* joining together of several trade unions to increase their strength

◊ **amalgamate** [ə'mælgəmeit] *verb* to join together with another group; *the amalgamated union has a total membership of 250,000*

ambition [æm'biʃn] *noun* what a person wants to do *or* achieve in his or her life; *we insist that our salesmen have plenty of ambition; her ambition is to become the senior partner in the firm*

◊ **ambitious** [æm'biʃəs] *adjective* full of ambition; wanting to do *or* achieve something; *he is ambitious, but not very competent*

amend [ə'mend] *verb* to change and make more correct *or* acceptable; *please amend your copy of the contract accordingly*

◊ **amendment** [ə'men(d)mənt] *noun* change to a document; *to propose an amendment to the constitution; to make amendments to a contract*

amenities [ə'mi:mətiz] *noun* services provided by an organization for the people who work in it; *the staff amenities included a subsidized canteen and sports facilities*

amount [ə'maunt] **1** *noun* quantity of money; *amount paid; amount deducted; amount owing; amount written off; what is the amount outstanding? a small amount invested in gilt-edged stock* **2** *verb* **to amount to** = to make a total of; *their debts amount to over £1m*

analogue ['ænəlɒg] *noun* a person's

opposite in another organization; *the conference of production managers gave those attending the opportunity to meet their analogues in other industries*

analyse *or* **analyze** ['ænəlaɪz] *verb* to examine someone *or* something in detail by separating it into parts; *to analyse a statement of account; to analyse the market potential*

◊ **analysis** [ə'næləsɪs] *noun* detailed examination of someone *or* something by separating into parts; *market analysis; sales analysis; an analysis of the manpower requirements was carried out before the recruitment drive; to carry out an analysis of the staffing position;* **character analysis** = analysis of a job applicant's general nature and qualities; *all candidates for the job underwent a character analysis;* **cost analysis** = examination in advance of the costs of a new product; **factor analysis** = method of analysing the results of an attitude survey by identifying what factors or criteria produced these results; **job analysis** = detailed examination and report on a job to establish what it consists of and what skills are needed for it; **systems analysis** = using a computer to suggest how a company can work more efficiently by analysing the way in which it works at present; *see also* TRANSACTIONAL ANALYSIS (NOTE: plural is **analyses**)

◊ **analyst** ['ænəlɪst] *noun* person who analyses; *market analyst; systems analyst*

◊ **analytical** [ænə'lɪtɪkl] *adjective* using analysis; **analytical estimating** = work measurement technique where the time taken to perform a job is estimated on the basis of prior experience; *analytical estimating was used on those jobs that hadn't changed since the original work measurement; analytical estimating was not considered a satisfactory work measurement technique because the union complained that previously established time periods for doing the job were too short;* **analytical job evaluation** = method of evaluating a job using a points system to compare one job with another (as opposed to non-analytical evaluation)

ancillary staff [æn'sɪləri 'stɑːf] *noun* staff who are not administrators, production staff or sales staff (such as cleaners, porters, canteen staff, etc.)

andragogy ['ændrægədʒi] *noun* science of adult learning, that is of teaching adults in an adult way, as opposed to teaching them as if they were children; *andragogy has developed in response to the increasing number of adults with the time and money to spend on further education; the training officer was aware of the latest theories in andragogy of importance in the training of machinists*

anniversary [ænɪ'vɜːsəri] *noun* date in a following year, which is the same as a particular occasion, such as the date of joining a pension scheme

announce [ə'naʊns] *verb* to tell something to the public; *to announce the results for 1984; to announce a programme of investment*

◊ **announcement** [ə'naʊnsmənt] *noun* telling something in public; *announcement of a cutback in expenditure; announcement of the appointment of a new managing director; the managing director made an announcement to the staff*

annual ['ænjuəl] *adjective* for one year; *we get an annual bonus; he has six weeks' annual leave; the employees were required to undergo an annual medical check-up;* **annual hours** = total of all the hours worked in a year (say, 1720 hours per annum), laid out in a contract of employment, so allowing a worker more flexibility than a weekly hour system; **annual report** = report of a company's financial situation at the end of a year, sent to all the shareholders; **on an annual basis** = each year; *the figures are revised on an annual basis*

◊ **annual general meeting (AGM)** ['ænjuəl 'dʒenərəl 'miːtɪŋ] *noun* meeting of all the shareholders, when the company's financial situation is discussed with the directors (NOTE: the US term is **annual meeting** or **annual stockholders' meeting**)

◊ **annualized** ['ænjuəlaɪzd] *adjective* shown on an annual basis; **annualized percentage rate** = yearly percentage rate, calculated by multiplying the monthly rate by twelve (not as accurate as the APR, which includes fees and other charges)

◊ **annually** ['ænjuəli] *adverb* each year; *the figures are updated annually*

◊ **Annual Percentage Rate (APR)** ['ænjuəl pə'sentɪdʒ reɪt] *noun* rate of interest (such as on a hire-purchase agreement) shown on an annual compound basis, including fees and charges

annuity [ə'njuːəti] *noun* money paid each year to a retired person, usually in return for a lump-sum payment; *he has a government annuity or an annuity from the government; to buy or to take out an annuity;* **contingent annuity** *or* **reversionary annuity** = annuity paid to someone on the death of another person; **annuity for life** *or* **life annuity** = annual payments made to someone as long as he is alive; **retirement annuity** = annuity bought when someone retires, using part of the sum put into a personal pension plan (NOTE: plural is **annuities)**

◊ **annuitant** [ə'njuːitənt] *noun* person who receives an annuity

annul [ə'nʌl] *verb* to cancel *or* to stop something being legal; *the contract was annulled by the court* (NOTE: **annulling - annulled)**

◊ **annullable** [ə'nʌləbl] *adjective* which can be cancelled

◊ **annulling** [ə'nʌlɪŋ] **1** *adjective* which cancels; *an annulling clause in a contract* **2** *noun* act of cancelling; *the annulling of a contract*

◊ **annulment** [ə'nʌlmənt] *noun* act of cancelling; *annulment of a contract*

answer ['ɑːnsə] **1** *noun* reply *or* letter or conversation coming after someone has written or spoken; *I am writing in answer to your letter of October 6th; my letter got no answer or there was no answer to my letter; I tried to phone his office but there was no answer* **2** *verb* to speak or write after someone has spoken or written to you; **to answer a letter** = to write a letter in reply to a letter which you have received; **to answer the telephone** = to lift the receiver when the telephone rings and listen to what the caller is saying

◊ **answering** ['ɑːnsərɪŋ] *noun* **answering machine** = ANSWERPHONE **answering service** = office which answers the telephone and takes messages for someone *or* for a company

◊ **answerphone** ['ɑːnsə'fəʊn] *noun* machine which answers the telephone automatically when a person is not in the office and allows messages to be recorded; *he wasn't in when I called so I left a message on his answerphone*

antedate ['ænti'deit] *verb* to put an earlier date on a document; *the contract was antedated to January 1st*

anticipation [æntisi'peiʃn] *noun* doing something before it is due to be done

◊ **anticipatory** [æntisi'peitri] *adjective* done before it is due; **anticipatory breach** = refusal by a party to a contract to perform his or her obligations under the contract at a time before they were due to be performed

appeal [ə'piːl] **1** *noun* **(a)** being attractive; **customer appeal** = being attractive to customers; **sales appeal** = quality which makes customers want to buy (NOTE: no plural in this meaning) **(b)** asking a court *or* a government department to change its decision; *the appeal against the planning decision will be heard next month; he lost his appeal for damages against the company;* **she won her case on appeal** = her case was lost in the first court, but the appeal court said that she was right **2** *verb* **(a)** to attract; *this record appeals to the under-25 market; the idea of working in Australia for six months appealed to her* **(b)** to ask a government department *or* a law court to alter its decision; *the company appealed against the decision of the planning officers; the union appealed against the decision of the tribunal; she appealed on behalf of the workers who had been made redundant* (NOTE: you appeal **to** a court or a person **against** a decision)

appendix [ə'pendiks] *noun* additional sheets at the back of a contract

apply [ə'plai] *verb* **(a)** to ask for something, usually in writing; *to apply for a job; to apply for promotion; to apply in writing; to apply in person; the more ambitious of the office workers will apply for the management trainee programme; about fifty people have applied for the job, but there is only one vacancy* **(b)** to affect *or* to touch; *this clause applies only to deals outside the EU*

◊ **applicant** ['æplikənt] *noun* person who applies for something; *applicant for a job or job applicant; applicant to an industrial tribunal*

◊ **application** [æplɪ'keɪʃən] *noun* **(a)** asking for something, usually in writing; *application for a job or job application;* **job application form** = form to be filled in when applying for a job; *to fill in an application (form) for a job or a job application (form);* **letter of application** = letter in which someone applies for a job; *US* **application blank** = form for recording an applicant's qualifications for a job **(b)** effort *or* diligence; *she has shown great application in her work on the project*

appoint [ə'pɔɪnt] *verb* to choose someone for a job; *they've appointed James Smith (to the post of) manager; we have appointed a new distribution manager* (NOTE: you appoint a person **to** a job)

◊ **appointee** [əpɔɪn'tiː] *noun* person who is appointed to a job

◊ **appointment** [ə'pɔɪntmənt] *noun* **(a)** arrangement to meet; *to make or to fix an appointment for two o'clock; to make an appointment with the boss for two o'clock; he was late for his appointment; she had to cancel her appointment;* **appointments book** = desk diary in which appointments are noted **(b)** being appointed to a job; *the appointment of one of the workers as supervisor;* **on his appointment as manager** = when he was made manager; **letter of appointment** = letter in which someone is appointed to a job **(c)** job; **staff appointment** = job on the staff; **appointments vacant** = list (in a newspaper) of jobs which are available

apportion [ə'pɔːʃən] *verb* to share out (costs, blame, etc.); *costs are apportioned according to projected revenue*

◊ **apportionment** [ə'pɔːʃənmənt] *noun* sharing out of (costs); **apportionment of wages** = decision as to what payment is made to an employee who leaves before pay day; *the union objected to the company's apportionment of wages, claiming that employees were not receiving amounts corresponding to days worked; a generous apportionment of wages was favoured by the personnel department so that workers would not leave resentful of their treatment by management*

appraise [ə'preɪz] *verb* to assess *or* to calculate the value of something

◊ **appraisal** [ə'preɪzəl] *noun* calculation of the value of someone *or* something; *the employee was disappointed by the result of his performance appraisal;* **appraisal interview** = interview where the manager (the appraiser) discusses with the worker (the appraisee) his or her performance; **group appraisal** = appraisal of an employee by a group of other employees; **performance appraisal** = assessment of the quality of person's work in a job; **staff appraisals** = reports on how well each member of staff is working

◊ **appraiser** [ə'preɪzə] *noun* person who appraises another worker

QUOTE we are now reaching a stage in industry and commerce where appraisals are becoming part of the management culture. Most managers now take it for granted that they will appraise and be appraised

Personnel Management

appreciate [ə'priːʃɪeɪt] *verb* **(a)** to notice how good something is; *the customer always appreciates efficient service; callers do not appreciate long delays in answering the telephone* **(b)** to increase in value; *the dollar has appreciated in terms of the yen; these shares have appreciated by 5%*

◊ **appreciation** [əpriːʃɪ'eɪʃən] *noun* **(a)** increase in value; *these shares show an appreciation of 10%; the appreciation of the dollar against the peseta* **(b)** valuing something highly; *he was given a rise in appreciation of his excellent work* (NOTE: no plural)

apprentice [ə'prentɪs] **1** *noun* young person who works under contract with a skilled workman in order to learn from him **2** *verb* **to be apprenticed to someone** = to work with a skilled workman in order to learn from him

◊ **apprenticeship** [ə'prentɪsʃɪp] *noun* time spent learning a skilled trade; *he served a six-year apprenticeship in the steel works;* **student apprenticeship** = scheme where a student at a college is sponsored by a commercial company and is apprenticed to that company

approach [ə'prəʊtʃ] **1** *noun* getting in touch with someone with a proposal; *the company made an approach to the supermarket chain; the board turned down all approaches on the subject of mergers; he* *has had an approach from a firm of headhunters* **2** *verb* to get in touch with someone with a proposal; *he approached the bank with a request for a loan; she was approached by a headhunter with the offer of a job; the company was approached by an American publisher with the suggestion of a merger; we have been approached several times but have turned down all offers*

appropriate [ə'prəuprɪeɪt] *verb* to put a sum of money aside for a special purpose; *to appropriate a sum of money for a capital project*

◊ **appropriation** [əprəuprɪ'eɪʃən] *noun* act of putting money aside for a special purpose; *appropriation of funds to the reserve;* **appropriation account** = part of a profit and loss account which shows how the profit has been dealt with (i.e. how much has been given to the shareholders as dividends, how much is being put into the reserves, etc.) (NOTE: no plural)

approve [ə'pruːv] *verb* **(a) to approve of** = to think something is good; *the chairman approves of the new company letter heading; the sales staff do not approve of interference from the accounts division* **(b)** to agree to something officially; *to approve the terms of a contract; the proposal was approved by the board*

◊ **approval** [ə'pruːvəl] *noun* **(a)** agreement; *to submit a budget for approval;* **to give something your approval** = to approve something; **certificate of approval** = document showing that an item has been approved officially **(b) on approval** = sale where the buyer only pays for goods if they are satisfactory; *to buy a photocopier on approval* (NOTE: no plural)

approximate [ə'prɒksɪmət] *adjective* not exact, but almost correct; *the sales division has made an approximate forecast of expenditure*

◊ **approximately** [ə'prɒksɪmətli] *adverb* almost correctly; *expenditure is approximately 10% down on the previous quarter*

◊ **approximation** [əprɒksɪ'meɪʃən] *noun* rough calculation; *approximation of expenditure; the final figure is only an approximation*

APR = ANNUAL PERCENTAGE RATE

aptitude ['æptɪtjuːd] *noun* ability (to do a task); *he has great aptitude for administrative work; personality is sometimes considered more important than aptitude in selling; he had an aptitude for the work, but never developed it by training;* **aptitude test** = test designed to measure someone's ability to use his or her skills in the future (as opposed to an attainment test, which measures the skills a person is currently using); *the assessment was based on aptitude tests and personality tests; we were all given an aptitude test after the interview to test our mathematical ability*

arbitrate ['ɑːbɪtreɪt] *verb (of an outside party)* to be chosen by both sides to try to settle an industrial dispute (both sides agree in advance to abide by the arbitrator's decision); *he was chosen to arbitrate in a dispute*

◊ **arbitration** [ɑːbɪ'treɪʃən] *noun* settling of a dispute by specially appointed officials outside a court of law; *arbitration in an industrial dispute; to submit a dispute to arbitration; to refer a question to arbitration; to take a dispute to arbitration; to go to arbitration; the two parties wished to avoid the legal process and resorted to arbitration;* **advisory arbitration** = arbitration which recommends a solution to a dispute, but is not binding on either party; **arbitration agreement** = agreement between two parties that any differences between them shall be settled by arbitration; **arbitration award** = decision by an arbitration tribunal; **arbitration board** *or* **arbitration tribunal** = group which arbitrates; **arbitration clause** = clause in a contract stating how differences between the parties can be settled by arbitration; **industrial arbitration tribunal** = court which decides in industrial disputes; *to accept the ruling of the arbitration board*

◊ **arbitrator** ['ɑːbɪtreɪtə] *noun* person not concerned with a dispute who is chosen by both sides to try to settle it; *industrial arbitrator; to accept or to reject the arbitrator's ruling*

area ['eərɪə] *noun* **(a)** measurement of the space taken up by something (calculated by multiplying the length by the width); *the area of this office is 3,400 square feet; we are looking for a shop with a sales area of about 100 square metres* **(b)** region of the world; **free trade area** = group of countries practising free trade; **dollar area** or **sterling area** = areas of the world where the dollar or the pound is the main trading currency **(c)** district or part of a town; *the office is in the commercial area of the town; their factory is in a very good area as regards getting to motorways and airports* **(d)** part of a country, a division for commercial purposes; *his sales area is the North-West; he finds it difficult to cover all his area in a week* **(e)** part of a room, factory, restaurant, etc.; *a no-smoking area* **(f)** subject; *a problem area* or *an area for concern*

◊ **area code** ['eərɪə 'kəud] *noun* special telephone number which is given to a particular area; *the area code for central London is 0171*

◊ **area manager** ['eərɪə 'mænɪdʒə] *noun* manager who is responsible for a part of the country

argue ['ɑːgjuː] *verb* to discuss something about which you do not agree; *they argued over* or *about the price; we spent hours arguing with the managing director about the site for the new factory; the union officials argued amongst themselves over the best way to deal with the management's ultimatum;* **to argue against something** = to give reasons why you think something should not be done (NOTE: you argue **with** someone **about** or **over** something)

◊ **argument** ['ɑːgjumənt] *noun* **(a)** discussing something without agreeing; *they got into an argument with the customs officials over the documents; he was sacked after an argument with the managing director* **(b)** reason for supporting or rejecting something; *the document gives the management's arguments in favour of flexible working hours*

arising [ə'raɪzɪŋ] *adjective* which comes from; *differences arising from the contract;* **matters arising** = business of a meeting which refers back to items discussed at a previous meeting

around [ə'raund] *preposition* approximately; *the office costs around £2,000 a year to heat; his salary is around $85,000*

arrange [ə'reɪndʒ] *verb* **(a)** to put into a correct or pleasing order; *the office is arranged as an open-plan area with small separate rooms for meetings; the files are arranged in alphabetical order; arrange the invoices in order of date* **(b)** to organize; *we arranged to have the meeting in their offices; she arranged for a car to meet him at the airport* (NOTE: you arrange **for** someone to do something; you arrange **for** something to be done; or you arrange **to** do something)

◊ **arrangement** [ə'reɪndʒmənt] *noun* **(a)** way in which something is organized; *the company secretary is making all the arrangements for the AGM* **(b)** settling of a financial dispute; **to come to an arrangement with the creditors; deed of arrangement** = agreement made between a debtor and his creditors whereby the creditors accept an agreed sum in settlement of their claim rather than make the debtor bankrupt

arrears [ə'rɪəz] *plural noun* money which is owed, but which has not been paid at the right time; *arrears of interest; to allow the payments to fall into arrears; salary with arrears effective from January 1st;* **wage arrears** or **arrears of wages** = unpaid wages which are owed; **in arrears** = owing money which should have been paid earlier; *the payments are six months in arrears; he is six weeks in arrears with his rent*

article ['ɑːtɪkl] *noun* **(a)** product or thing for sale; *a black market in imported articles of clothing* **(b)** section of a legal agreement (such as a contract, treaty, etc.); *see article 8 of the contract;* **Article 117 of the Treaty of Rome** = article which requires member states to improve working conditions and workers' living conditions; **Article 118(a) of the Treaty of Rome** = article which requires member states to improve health and safety in the working environment; **Article 119 of the Treaty of Rome** = article which requires all member states to apply equal pay to men and women doing equal jobs **(c)** **articles of association** = document which lays down the rules for a company regarding the issue of shares, the conduct of meetings, the appointment of directors, etc. (NOTE: in the US, called **bylaws)** *director appointed under the articles of the company; this procedure is not allowed under the articles of association of the company* US **articles of incorporation** = document which sets up a company and lays down the relationship between the shareholders and the company (NOTE: in the UK called **Memorandum of**

Association) **articles of partnership** = document which sets up the legal conditions of a partnership; *he is a director appointed under the articles of the company; this procedure is not allowed under the articles of association of the company* **(d) articles** = time when a clerk is working in a solicitor's office learning the law; **articles of indenture** = contract by which a trainee craftsman works for a master for some years to learn a trade; **to serve articles** = to work in a solicitor's office to learn the law

◊ **articled clerk** ['ɑːtɪkld'klɑːk] *noun* clerk who is bound by contract to work in a solicitor's office for some years to learn the law

artisan ['ɑːtɪzæn] *noun* worker who has special training in a manual skill

ASAP = AS SOON AS POSSIBLE

ascribed status [ə'skraɪbd 'steɪtəs] *noun* status which someone has in an organization by right (as opposed to status achieved by merit)

aspire [ə'spaɪə] *verb* **to aspire to** = to have a strong ambition to

◊ **aspiration** [æspɪ'reɪʃn] *noun* **aspirations** = ambitions *or* hopes of advancement in one's job

assembly line [ə'semblɪ'laɪn] *noun* production system where the product (such as a car) moves slowly through the factory with new sections added to it as it goes along; *he works on an assembly line or he is an assembly line worker*

assert [ə'sɜːt] *verb* **to assert yourself** = to show that you have control *or* can make decisions; *he doesn't assert himself much in public meetings, but his sales figures are impressive*

◊ **assertiveness** [ə'sɜːtɪvnəs] *noun* stating opinions *or* showing that you can make decisions; **assertiveness training** = training employees to have more confidence in themselves

assess [ə'ses] *verb* to judge the quality *or* quantity of something; *to assess damages at £1,000; to assess a property for the purposes of insurance*

◊ **assessment** [ə'sesmənt] *noun* judging

the value of a person *or* thing; *they made a complete assessment of each employee's contribution to the organization;* **character assessment** = judging the personality of an employee; **performance assessment** = assessment of the quality of person's work in a job; **performance-based assessment** = assessment of a worker's knowledge and skills as shown in his work (as opposed to 'knowledge-based assessment'); **staff assessments** = reports on how well members of staff are working; **assessment centre** = special place which assesses the abilities of a group of employees sent by their organizations; *the three days at the assessment centre consisted of in-basket tests and personal interviews; the assessment centre aims to spot those individuals with management potential*

◊ **assessor** [ə'sesə] *noun* person who assesses someone; person who advises a tribunal

assign [ə'saɪn] *verb* **(a)** to give legally; *to assign a right to someone; to assign shares to someone* **(b)** to give someone something to use *or* a job of work to do, and be responsible for; *to assign a job to a worker; he was assigned the job of checking the sales figures*

◊ **assignee** [æsaɪ'niː] *noun* person who receives something which has been assigned

◊ **assignment** [ə'saɪnmənt] *noun* **(a)** legal transfer of a property *or* of a right; *assignment of a patent or of a copyright; to sign a deed of assignment;* **deed of assignment** = document which legally transfers a property from a debtor to a creditor; **assignment of wages** = procedure when a deduction is made from an employee's wages and is paid to a third party; *an assignment of wages was arranged to pay a worker who had filled in while the regular worker was ill* **(b)** particular job of work given to someone; *her assignment as managing director was to improve the company's profits; the oil team is on an assignment in the North Sea*

◊ **assignor** [æsaɪ'nɔː] *noun* person who assigns something to someone

assist [ə'sɪst] *verb* to help; *can you assist the stock controller in counting the stock? he assists me with my income tax returns* (NOTE: you assist someone **in** doing something or **with** something)

◊ **assistance** [ə'sıstəns] *noun* help; *some candidates need assistance in filling in the form;* financial assistance = help in the form of money (NOTE: no plural)

◊ **assistant** [ə'sıstənt] *noun* person who helps *or* a clerical employee; **personal assistant (PA)** = secretary who also helps the boss in various ways; **shop assistant** = person who serves the customers in a shop; **assistant manager** = person who helps a manager

associate [ə'səusıət] **1** *adjective* linked; **associate company** = ASSOCIATED COMPANY **associate director** = director who attends board meetings, but has not been elected by the shareholders **2** *noun* person who works in the same business as someone; *she is a business associate of mine*

◊ **associated** [ə'səusıeıtıd] *adjective* linked; **associated company** = company which is partly owned by another (though less than 50%), and where the share-owning company exerts some management control or has a close trading relationship with the associate; *Smith Ltd and its associated company, Jones Brothers*

◊ **association** [əsəusı'eıʃən] *noun* **(a)** group of people *or* of companies with the same interest; **trade association; employers' association; manufacturers' association; freedom of association** = being able to join together in a group with other people without being afraid of prosecution; **right of association** = right of workers to join a union (as opposed to the right to dissociate, i.e. the right to refuse to join a union) **(b)** **articles of association** = document which lays down the rules for a company regarding the issue of shares, the conduct of meetings, the appointment of directors, etc.; **Memorandum of Association** = document drawn up at the same time as the articles of association of a company, in which the company's objects are defined, the details of the share capital, directors, registered office, etc. are set out (NOTE: in the USA, called **articles of incorporation**)

assume [ə'sjuːm] *verb* to take for oneself; *the company will assume all risks; he has assumed responsibility for marketing*

◊ **assumption** [ə'sʌm(p)ʃən] *noun* taking for oneself; *assumption of risks*

assure [ə'ʃuə] *verb* **(a)** to insure *or* to have a contract with a company where if regular payments are made, the company will pay compensation if you die; *to assure someone's life; he has paid the premiums to have his wife's life assured;* **the life assured** = the person whose life has been covered by the life assurance **(b)** **to assure someone that** = to state something firmly so that someone is sure that it is true

◊ **assurance** [ə'ʃuərəns] *noun* **(a)** firm statement that something will happen; *he received an assurance from the personnel director that he would not be demoted* **(b)** insurance, agreement that in return for regular payments, a company will pay compensation for loss of life; *assurance company; assurance policy;* **life assurance** = insurance which pays a sum of money when someone dies

◊ **assurer** *or* **assuror** [ə'ʃuərə] *noun* insurer *or* company which insures (NOTE: **assure** and **assurance** are used in Britain for insurance policies relating to something which will certainly happen (such as death); for other types of policy use **insure** and **insurance**)

attach [ə'tætʃ] *verb* to fasten *or* to link; *I am attaching a copy of my previous letter; please find attached a copy of my letter of June 24th; the machine is attached to the floor so it cannot be moved; the company attaches great importance to good timekeeping*

◊ **attachment** [ə'tætʃmənt] *noun* holding a debtor's property to prevent it being sold until debts are paid; **attachment of earnings** = legal power to take money from a person's salary to pay money, which is owed, to the courts; **attachment of earnings order** = court order to make an employer pay part of an employee's salary to the court to pay off debts

attainment [ə'teınmənt] *noun* reaching a certain standard *or* goal; **attainment test** = test designed to measure the skills which someone is currently using (as opposed to an aptitude test, which measures the skills a person could use in the future)

attend [ə'tend] *verb* to be present at; *the chairman has asked all managers to attend the meeting; none of the shareholders attended the AGM*

◊ **attendance** [ə'tendəns] *noun* being

present at a meeting *or* at work; *some of the workers were reprimanded for poor attendance; the supervisor kept a strict record of the workers' attendance; promotion to the post of supervisor depends to a certain extent on a person's attendance record; attendance at the staff meeting is not compulsory; the attendance at the union meeting was very poor;* **attendance allowance (AA)** = benefit paid to a disabled person over 65 to cover the costs of having someone to care for them; **attendance bonus** = bonus given to employees for good attendance; *you may find that payment of an attendance bonus will motivate workers; an attendance bonus is awarded for a 95% attendance record;* **attendance money** = payment made to workers who turn up even when there is no work for them to do; **attendance time** = hours spent at work that are paid for

◊ **attendant** [ə'tendənt] *noun* lower-level employee who is given a measure of responsibility

◊ **attend to** [ə'tend 'tuː] *verb* to give careful thought to (something) and deal with it; *the managing director will attend to your complaint personally; we have brought in experts to attend to the problem of installing the new computer*

◊ **attention** [ə'tenʃən] *noun* careful thought *or* consideration; *for the attention of the Managing Director; your orders will have our best attention;* **to pay attention to** = to study carefully and follow (instructions, rules, etc.)

attitude ['ætɪtjuːd] *noun* way in which a person behaves *or* thinks; *he has a very negative attitude towards the company; management is trying to change the workers' attitudes to profit-sharing*

attract [ə'trækt] *verb* to make something or someone join *or* come in; *the company is offering free holidays in Spain to attract buyers; we have difficulty in attracting skilled staff to this part of the country*

◊ **attractive** [ə'træktɪv] *adjective* which attracts; **attractive prices** = prices which are cheap enough to make buyers want to buy; **attractive salary** = good salary to make high-quality applicants apply for the job

attrition [ə'trɪʃn] *noun* loss of labour through natural wastage; **attrition of salary**

costs = reduction of a company's total salary costs when staff are made redundant, retiring staff are not replaced, etc.

at will ['æt 'wɪl] *adverb* *see* EMPLOYMENT-AT-WILL

audio-typing ['ɔːdɪəʊ'taɪpɪŋ] *noun* typing to dictation from a recording (NOTE: no plural)

◊ **audio-typist** ['ɔːdɪəʊ'taɪpɪst] *noun* typist who types to dictation from a recording on a dictating machine

audit ['ɔːdɪt] **1** *noun* **(a)** examination of the books and accounts of a company; *to carry out the annual audit;* **external audit** *or* **independent audit** = audit carried out by an independent auditor; **internal audit** = audit carried out by a department inside the company; *he is the manager of the internal audit department* **(b)** detailed examination of something in order to assess it; *a thorough job audit was needed for job evaluation; a manpower audit showed up a desperate lack of talent* **2** *verb* to examine the books and accounts of a company; *to audit the accounts; the books have not yet been audited*

◊ **auditing** ['ɔːdɪtɪŋ] *noun* action of examining the books and accounts

◊ **auditor** ['ɔːdɪtə] *noun* person who audits; *the AGM appoints the company's auditors;* **external auditor** = independent person who audits the company's accounts; **internal auditor** = member of staff who audits a company's accounts

QUOTE other plans include the development of a training needs audit and a checklist for training evaluation
Personnel Today

Aufsichtsrat ['aʊfsɪχtsræt] *German noun* supervisory board

authority [ɔː'θɒrəti] *noun* **(a)** power to do something; *a manager with authority to sign cheques; he has no authority to act on our behalf; without the necessary authority, the manager could not command respect; only senior managers have the authority to initiate these changes* (NOTE: no plural for this meaning) **(b)** **local authority** = elected section of government which runs a small area of a country; **the authorities** = the government *or* the people in control

◊ **authoritarian** [ɔːθɒrɪ'teərɪən] *adjective* demanding a high level of discipline *or* obedience; *the workers disliked the authoritarian management style; the managing director is very authoritarian and expects immediate obedience*

authorize ['ɔːθəraɪz] *verb* **(a)** to give permission for something to be done; *to authorize payment of £10,000* **(b)** to give someone the authority to do something; *to authorize someone to act on the company's behalf*

◊ **authorization** [ɔːθəraɪ'zeɪʃən] *noun* permission *or* power to do something; *do you have authorization for this expenditure? he has no authorization to act on our behalf*

autocratic [ɔːtəʊ'krætɪk] *adjective* **autocratic management style** = style of management where the managers tell the workers what to do, without involving them in the decision-making processes (NOTE: the opposite is **democratic management style**)

automated ['ɔːtəmeɪtɪd] *adjective* worked automatically by machines; *fully automated car assembly plant*

automatic [ɔːtə'mætɪk] *adjective* which works *or* takes place without any person making it happen; *there is an automatic increase in salaries on January 1st;* **automatic data processing** = data processing done by a computer; **automatic sanction** = penalty which is applied automatically, outside the legal process, to an employee taking part in industrial action; *the fear of automatic sanction stopped the workers going on strike for better working conditions;* **automatic telling machine** *or US* **automatic teller machine** = machine which gives out money when a special card is inserted and special instructions given; **automatic vending machine** = machine which provides drinks, cigarettes, etc. when a coin is put in; **automatic wage adjustment** = automatic increase in wages in line with the cost of living; *one of the attractions of the job in a time of rapid inflation, was the automatic wage adjustment attached to it;* **automatic wage progression** = automatic increase in wages according to the time a person has worked in the organization; *automatic wage progression was seen as a way of motivating workers to stay in the company*

◊ **automatically** [ɔːtə'mætɪkəli] *adverb* working without a person giving instructions; *the invoices are sent out automatically; addresses are typed in automatically; a demand note is sent automatically when the invoice is overdue;* **automatically unfair dismissals** = dismissals which are always unfair, whatever the circumstances (such as when a woman employee is dismissed for being pregnant, someone is dismissed for belonging to a trade union, etc.)

automation [ɔːtə'meɪʃən] *noun* use of machines to do work with very little supervision by people; **fixed automation** = using machines in a way which does not allow any change in their operation; **flexible automation** = using machines in a way which allows the operator to change the operation of the machine and so improve productivity (NOTE: no plural)

autonomy [ɔː'tɒnəmi] *noun* working by oneself, without being managed

◊ **autonomous** [ɔː'tɒnəməs] *adjective* which rules itself; *the workforce in the factory is made up of several autonomous work groups;* **autonomous bargaining** = direct bargaining between management and workers, without involving unions; **autonomous learning** = learning by oneself, without teachers; **autonomous teamworking** *or* **autonomous working group** = group of workers who can work independently, taking decisions together as a group (also called 'self-managing team')

available [ə'veɪləbl] *adjective* **(a)** (thing) which can be obtained *or* bought; *available in all branches; item no longer available; items available to order only; funds which are made available for investment in small businesses;* **available capital** = capital which is ready to be used **(b)** (person) who is free to do something; *the headhunter approached her about the job but she was not available until December;* **to make yourself available** = to arrange things so that you are free to do something; *the MD was due to leave on a tour of the Far East, but cancelled it to make himself available to attend the negotiations*

◊ **availability** [əveɪlə'bɪləti] *noun* being easily obtained; **offer subject to availability** = the offer is valid only if the goods are available (NOTE: no plural)

AVCs = ADDITIONAL VOLUNTARY CONTRIBUTIONS

average ['ævərɪdʒ] **1** *noun* **(a)** number calculated by adding together several figures and dividing by the number of figures added; *the average for the last three months or the last three months' average; sales average or average of sales;* **weighted average** = average which is calculated taking several factors into account, giving some more value than others; **on an average** = in general; *on an average, £15 worth of goods are stolen every day* **(b)** sharing of the cost of damage or loss of a ship between the insurers and the owners; **average adjuster** = person who calculates how much of an insurance is to be paid **2** *adjective* **(a)** middle (figure); *average cost per unit; average price; average sales per representative; the average figures for the last three months; the average increase in prices;* **average age** = age of a group of people, calculated by adding all the ages and dividing by the number of people in the group; *the average age of our managers is 32;* **average earnings scheme** = pension scheme where the benefit is calculated annually on the earnings in each year **(b)** not very good; *the company's performance has been only average; he is an average worker* **3** *verb* to produce as an average figure; *price increases have averaged 10% per annum; days lost through sickness have averaged twenty-two over the last four years*

◊ **average out** ['ævərɪdʒ 'aʊt] *verb* to come to a figure as an average; *it averages out at 10% per annum; sales increases have averaged out at 15%*

◊ **average-sized** ['ævərɪdʒ'saɪzd] *adjective* not large or small; *they are an average-sized company; he has an average-sized office*

avert [ə'vɜːt] *verb* to stop something happening; *the management made an increased offer in the hope of averting the strike*

avoid [ə'vɔɪd] *verb* to try not to do something; *the company is struggling to avoid bankruptcy; my aim is to avoid paying too much tax; we want to avoid direct competition with Smith Ltd* (NOTE: you avoid something or avoid **doing** something)

◊ **avoidance** [ə'vɔɪdəns] *noun* trying not to do something; *avoidance of an agreement or of a contract;* **tax avoidance** = trying (legally) to pay as little tax as possible (NOTE: no plural)

await [ə'weɪt] *verb* to wait for; *we are awaiting the decision of the planning department; they are awaiting a decision of the court; the agent is awaiting our instructions*

award [ə'wɔːd] **1** *noun* money which an industrial tribunal decides should be paid by an employer to an employee in settling a dispute (such as a dismissal); *an award by an industrial tribunal; the arbitrator's award was set aside on appeal;* **arbitration award** = decision by an arbitration tribunal; **basic award** = award based on the employee's age, length of service and current salary; **compensatory award** = award based on what the tribunal considers is just compensation for the employee's loss; **special award** = award in cases of unfair dismissal, where the worker was sacked either for joining or for refusing to join a trade union; *see also* ADDITIONAL AWARD **2** *verb* to decide the amount of money to be paid to someone; *to award someone a salary increase; to award damages; the judge awarded costs to the defendant;* **to award a contract to someone** = to decide that someone will have the contract to do work

axe [æks] **1** *noun* **the project got the axe** = the project was stopped **2** *verb* to cut or to stop; *to axe expenditure; several thousand jobs are to be axed*

Bb

back [bæk] **1** *noun* opposite side to the front; *write your address on the back of the envelope; the conditions of sale are printed on the back of the invoice; please endorse the cheque on the back* **2** *adjective* referring to the past; **back interest** = interest not yet paid; **back orders** = orders received in the past and not fulfilled (usually because the item is out of stock); *after the strike it took the factory six weeks to clear all the accumulated back orders;* **back pay** *or* **back wages** = salary which has not been paid; *I am owed £500 in back pay;* **back payment** = paying money which is owed; *the salesmen are claiming for back payment of unpaid commission;* **back payments** = payments which are due; **back rent** = rent owed; *the company owes £100,000 in back rent* **3** *adverb* as things were before; *he will pay back the money in monthly instalments; the store sent back the cheque because the date was wrong; the company went back on its agreement to supply at £1.50 a unit;* **back to work** = returning to work after being unemployed **4** *verb* **(a) to back someone** = to help someone financially; *the bank is backing him to the tune of £10,000; he is looking for someone to back his project* **(b) to back a bill** = to sign a bill promising to pay it if the person it is addressed to is not able to do so

◊ **backdate** ['bækdeɪt] *verb* to put an earlier date on a cheque *or* an invoice; *backdate your invoice to April 1st; the pay increase is backdated to January 1st*

◊ **back down** ['bæk 'daʊn] *verb* to give up something which you claimed

◊ **background** ['bækgraʊnd] *noun* **(a)** past work *or* experience; *his background is in the steel industry; the company is looking for someone with a background of success in the electronics industry; she has a publishing background; what is his background or do you know anything about his background?* **(b)** past details; *he explained the background of the claim; I know the contractual situation as it stands now, but can you fill in the background details?*

◊ **backhander** ['bækhændə] *noun (informal)* bribe *or* money given to someone to get him or her to help you

◊ **backing** ['bækɪŋ] *noun* **(a)** support; *he gave his backing to the proposal; the proposal has the backing of the board* **(b)** financial support; *he has the backing of an Australian bank; the company will succeed only if it has sufficient backing; who is providing the backing for the project or where does the backing for the project come from?*

◊ **backlog** ['bæklɒg] *noun* work (such as orders *or* letters) which has piled up waiting to be done; *the warehouse is trying to cope with a backlog of orders; my secretary can't cope with the backlog of paperwork*

◊ **back out** ['bæk 'aʊt] *verb* to stop being part of a deal *or* an agreement; *the bank backed out of the contract; we had to cancel the project when our German partners backed out*

◊ **backpedal** ['bækpedl] *verb* to go back on something which was stated earlier; *when questioned by reporters about the redundancies, the MD backpedalled fast*

◊ **backshift** ['bækʃɪft] *noun* the afternoon shift in a three-shift system, working from late afternoon until late evening (after the morning shift and before the night shift)

◊ **backtrack** ['bæktræk] *verb* to go back on what had been said before

◊ **back up** ['bæk 'ʌp] *verb* to support *or* to help; *he brought along a file of documents to back up his claim; the employee said his union had refused to back him up in his argument with management*

◊ **backup** ['bækʌp] *adjective* supporting *or* helping; *we offer a free backup service to customers; after a series of sales tours by representatives, the sales director sends backup letters to all the contacts;* **backup copy** = copy of a computer disk to be kept in case the original disk is damaged

bad [bæd] *adjective* not good; **bad bargain**

= item which is not worth the price asked; **bad buy** = thing bought which was not worth the money paid for it; **bad debt** = debt which will not be paid; *the company has written off £30,000 in bad debts*

badge [bædʒ] *noun* piece of plastic or card, which can be clipped to a person's shirt or coat, and on which a name can be written; *all the staff at the exhibition must wear badges; visitors have to sign in at reception, and will be given visitors' badges*

balance ['bæləns] 1 *noun* (a) amount in an account which makes the total debits and credits equal; **credit balance** = balance in an account showing that more money has been received than is owed; **debit balance** = balance in an account showing that more money is owed than has been received; *the account has a credit balance of £100; because of large payments to suppliers, the account has a debit balance of £1,000;* **balance in hand** = cash held to pay small debts; **balance brought down** *or* **forward** = the closing balance of the previous period used as the opening balance of the current period; **balance carried down** *or* **forward** = the closing balance of the current period (b) rest of an amount owed; *you can pay £100 deposit and the balance within 60 days;* **balance due to us** = amount owed to us which is due to be paid (c) **balance of payments** = the international financial position of a country, including invisible as well as visible trade; **balance of trade** *or* **trade balance** = international trading position of a country, excluding invisible trade; **adverse** *or* **unfavourable balance of trade** = situation where a country imports more than it exports; **favourable trade balance** = situation where a country exports more than it imports; *the country has had an adverse balance of trade for the second month running* (d) **bank balance** = state of an account at a bank at a particular time 2 *verb* (a) to calculate the amount needed to make the two sides of an account equal; *I have finished balancing the accounts for March; the February accounts do not balance* = the two sides are not equal (b) to plan a budget so that expenditure and income are equal; *the president is planning for a balanced budget*

◊ **balance sheet** ['bæləns 'ʃiːt] *noun* statement of the financial position of a company at a particular time, such as the end of the financial year or the end of a

quarter; *the company balance sheet for 1984 shows a substantial loss; the accountant has prepared the balance sheet for the first half-year*

ball [bɔːl] *noun* **the ball is in the management's court** = the management has to make the next move

ballot ['bælət] 1 *noun* (a) (i) election where people vote for someone by marking a cross on a paper with a list of names; (ii) vote where voters decide on an issue by marking a piece of paper; **ballot box** = sealed box into which ballot papers are put; **ballot paper** = paper on which the voter marks a cross to show who he wants to vote for; **postal ballot** = election where the voters send their ballot papers by post; **secret ballot** = election where the voters vote in secret; **strike ballot** = vote by workers to decide on a strike (b) selecting by taking papers at random out of a box; *six names were put forward for three vacancies on the committee so a ballot was held* 2 *verb* to take a vote by ballot; *the union is balloting for the post of president*

◊ **ballot-rigging** ['bælət'rɪgɪŋ] *noun* illegal arranging of the votes in a ballot, so that a particular candidate or party wins (NOTE: no plural)

ban [bæn] 1 *noun* official order which forbids someone from doing something; *a government ban on the import of weapons; a ban on the export of computer software;* **overtime ban** = order by a trade union which forbids overtime work by its members; **to impose a ban on smoking** = to make an order which forbids smoking; **to lift the ban on smoking** = to allow people to smoke; **to beat the ban on something** = to do something which is forbidden - usually by doing it rapidly before a ban is imposed, or by finding a legal way to avoid a ban 2 *verb* to forbid something *or* to make something illegal; *the company has banned drinking on company premises*

band [bænd] 1 *noun* grade *or* level; **salary bands** = all salaries at certain levels; *the pay structure is made up of five salary bands* 2 *verb* to divide into bands

◊ **bandwidth** ['bændwɪdθ] *noun* limits to a band, such as upper and lower performance levels or work hours

bank [bæŋk] *noun* (a) business which holds

money for its clients, lends money at interest, and trades generally in money; *Lloyds Bank; The First National Bank; The Royal Bank of Scotland; he put all his earnings into his bank; I have had a letter from my bank telling me my account is overdrawn;* bank loan *or* bank advance = loan from a bank; *he asked for a bank loan to start his business* (b) data bank = store of information in a computer

◊ **bank account** ['bæŋk ə'kaʊnt] *noun* account which a customer has with a bank, where the customer can deposit and withdraw money; *to open a bank account; to close a bank account; how much money do you have in your bank account? she has £100 in her savings bank account; if you let the balance in your bank account fall below £100, you have to pay bank charges*

◊ **bank balance** ['bæŋk 'bæləns] *noun* state of a bank account at any particular time; *our bank balance went into the red last month*

◊ **bank book** ['bæŋk 'bʊk] *noun* book, given by a bank, which shows money which you deposit or withdraw from your savings account

◊ **bank charges** ['bæŋk 'tʃɑːdʒɪz] *plural noun* charges which a bank makes for carrying out work for a customer (NOTE: in US English this is **a service charge)**

◊ **bank giro** ['bæŋk 'dʒaɪrəʊ] *noun GB* method used by clearing banks to transfer money rapidly from one account to another

◊ **bank holiday** ['bæŋk 'hɒlədi] *noun* a weekday which is a public holiday, when the banks are closed; *New Year's Day is a bank holiday; are we paid for bank holidays in this job?*

◊ **banking** ['bæŋkɪŋ] *noun* the business of banks; *he is studying banking; she has gone into banking; US* banking account = account which a customer has with a bank; a banking crisis = crisis affecting the banks; banking hours = hours when a bank is open for its customers; *you cannot get money out of the bank after banking hours*

◊ **bank manager** ['bæŋk 'mænɪdʒə] *noun* person in charge of a branch of a bank; *he asked his bank manager for a loan*

◊ **bank statement** ['bæŋk 'steɪtmənt] *noun* written statement from a bank showing the balance of an account

bankrupt ['bæŋkrʌpt] **1** *adjective & noun* (person) who has been declared by a court not to be capable of paying his debts and whose affairs are put into the hands of a receiver; *he was adjudicated or declared bankrupt; a bankrupt property developer; he went bankrupt after two years in business;* certificated bankrupt = bankrupt who has been discharged from bankruptcy with a certificate to show he was not at fault; discharged bankrupt = person who has been released from being bankrupt because he has paid his debts; undischarged bankrupt = person who has been declared bankrupt and has not been released from that state **2** *verb* to make someone become bankrupt; *the recession bankrupted my father*

◊ **bankruptcy** ['bæŋkrəp(t)si] *noun* state of being bankrupt; *the recession has caused thousands of bankruptcies;* adjudication of bankruptcy *or* declaration of bankruptcy = legal order making someone bankrupt; discharge in bankruptcy = being released from bankruptcy after paying debts; to file a petition in bankruptcy = to apply officially to be made bankrupt *or* to ask officially for someone else to be made bankrupt

COMMENT: in the UK, 'bankruptcy' is applied only to individual persons, but in the USA the term is also applied to corporations. In the UK, a bankrupt cannot hold public office (for example, he cannot be elected an MP) and cannot be the director of a company. He also cannot borrow money. In the USA, there are two types of bankruptcy: 'involuntary', where the creditors ask for a person or corporation to be made bankrupt; and 'voluntary', where a person or corporation applies to be made bankrupt (in the UK, this is called 'voluntary liquidation')

bar chart ['bɑːtʃɑːt] *noun* chart where values *or* quantities are shown as thick columns of different heights set on a base line, the different lengths expressing the quantity of the item *or* unit; *a bar chart comparing the salaries of workers in different grades*

◊ **bar code** ['bɑːkəʊd] *noun* system of lines printed on a product which, when read by a computer, give a reference number or price

bargain ['bɑːgɪn] **1** *noun* **(a)** agreement on the price of something; *to make a bargain;* to drive a hard bargain = to be a difficult negotiator; to strike a hard bargain = to agree a deal which is favourable to you; **it is a bad bargain** = it is not worth the price **(b)** thing which is cheaper than usual; *that car is a (real) bargain at £500;* **bargain hunter** = person who looks for cheap deals **2** *verb* to discuss a price for something; *you will have to bargain with the dealer if you want a discount; they spent two hours bargaining about* or *over the price* (NOTE: you bargain **with** someone **over** or **about** or **for** something)

◊ **bargain offer** ['bɑːgɪn 'ɒfə] *noun* sale of a particular type of goods at a cheap price; *this week's bargain offer - 30% off all carpet prices*

◊ **bargain price** ['bɑːgɪn 'praɪs] *noun* cheap price; *these carpets are for sale at a bargain price*

◊ **bargain sale** ['bɑːgɪn 'seɪl] *noun* sale of all goods in a store at cheap prices

◊ **bargaining** ['bɑːgɪnɪŋ] *noun* act of discussing between two persons or groups, to achieve a settlement, usually wage increases for workers; *in spite of a week of hard bargaining the union and employers could not reach a wage settlement; the number of strikes shows that collective bargaining is not working;* **to come to** or **to sit round the bargaining table** = to meet for negotiations; **(free) collective bargaining** = negotiations between employers and workers' representatives over wage increases and conditions; **bargaining level** = level at which bargaining takes place (i.e. at department level, whole company level, industry level, etc.); **bargaining power** = strength of one person or group when discussing prices or wage settlements; **bargaining position** = statement of position by one group during negotiations; **bargaining structure** = structure of collective bargaining negotiations, comprising the subjects dealt with, the number of employees covered, whether the negotiations apply to a single factory or to the whole industry, etc.; **bargaining theory of wages** = theory which states that the relative bargaining power of the employers and employees will decide wage levels; **bargaining unit** = group of employees who negotiate with their employer to reach a collective agreement; *the bargaining unit had a meeting with top management in order to thrash out their differences; the bargaining unit was supported by the union in its attempt to improve conditions*

BARS = BEHAVIOURALLY ANCHORED RATING SCALES method of appraising performance based on typical performance criteria set for each individual member of staff

base [beɪs] **1** *noun* **(a)** lowest or first position; **base period** = (i) period against which comparisons are made; (ii) *US* time that an employee must work before becoming eligible for state unemployment insurance benefits; *because he had not worked for the base period, he had to rely on the support of his family when he lost his job; the new government shortened the base period, in order to increase social service spending US* **base pay** = pay for a job which does not include extras such as overtime pay or bonuses; **base year** = first year of an index, against which changes in later years are measured **(b)** place where a company has its main office or factory or place where a businessman has his office; *the company has its base in London and branches in all European countries; he has an office in Madrid which he uses as a base while he is travelling in Southern Europe;* **to touch base** = to get in touch with someone to see how things are going **2** *verb* **(a)** to start to calculate or to negotiate from a position; *we based our calculations on last year's turnover;* **based on** = calculating from; *based on last year's figures; based on population forecasts* **(b)** to set up a company or a person in a place; *the European manager is based in our London office; our foreign branch is based in the Bahamas; a London-based sales executive*

basic ['beɪsɪk] **1** *adjective* **(a)** normal; **basic award** = award by an industrial tribunal based on the employee's age, length of service and current salary and equal to what the employee would have received if he had been made redundant (used in cases of unfair dismissal); **basic pay** or **basic salary** or **basic wage** = normal part of an employee's salary to which extra payments may be added; *a basic salary* or *wage plus bonus; salesmen are paid a small basic salary to which commissions are added; the waitress is paid a small basic wage because tips are high; the basic salary, though small, does give a degree of security;* **basic rate tax** = lowest rate of income tax; **basic time** = normal time taken to do a job, established by work study; *the basic time for the job was not accepted by the workers who found it too* *demanding* **(b)** most important; **basic commodities** = ordinary farm produce, produced in large quantities (such as corn, rice, sugar) **(c)** simple *or* from which everything starts; *he has a basic knowledge of the market; to work at the cash desk, you need a basic qualification in maths*

◊ **basics** ['beɪsɪks] *plural noun* simple and important facts; **to get back to basics** = to start discussing the basic facts again

◊ **basically** ['beɪsɪkəli] *adverb* seen from the point from which everything starts

◊ **BASIC** ['beɪsɪk] *noun* = BEGINNER'S ALL-PURPOSE SYMBOLIC INSTRUCTION CODE simple language for writing computer programs

basis ['beɪsɪs] *noun* **(a)** point *or* number from which calculations are made; *we have calculated the turnover on the basis of a 6% price increase* **(b)** general terms of agreement *or* general principles on which something is decided; **on a short-term** *or* **long-term basis** = for a short *or* long period; *he has been appointed on a short-term basis; we have three people working on a freelance basis* (NOTE: the plural is **bases**)

batch [bætʃ] **1** *noun* **(a)** group of items which are made at one time; *this batch of shoes has the serial number 25-02;* **batch production** = production of goods in small groups **(b)** group of documents which are processed at the same time; *a batch of invoices; today's batch of orders; the accountant signed a batch of cheques; we deal with the orders in batches of fifty;* **batch processing** = system of data processing where information is collected into batches before being loaded into the computer **2** *verb* to put items together in groups; *to batch invoices or cheques*

◊ **batch number** ['bætʃ 'nʌmbə] *noun* number attached to a batch; *when making a complaint always quote the batch number on the packet*

battery ['bætəri] *noun* series (of difficulties); *candidates have to pass a battery of tests*

beat [biːt] *verb* **(a)** to win in a fight against someone; *they have beaten their rivals into second place in the computer market* **(b)** to **beat a ban** = to do something which is forbidden by doing it rapidly before the ban is enforced

beginner [bɪ'gɪnə] *noun* person who is starting in a job

behalf [bɪ'hɑːf] *noun* **on behalf of** = acting for (someone *or* a company); *I am writing on behalf of the minority shareholders; she is acting on my behalf; solicitors acting on behalf of the American company*

behaviour [bɪ'heɪvjə] *noun* way in which someone behaves; *the manager had to talk to him about his disruptive behaviour;* **behaviour expectation rate** *or* **scale** = BEHAVIOURALLY ANCHORED RATING SCALES

◊ **behavioural** [bɪ'heɪvjərəl] *adjective* referring to behaviour; **behavioural sciences** = sciences which study human behaviour, such as sociology, psychology, etc.

◊ **behaviourally** [bɪ'heɪvjərəli] *adverb* **behaviourally anchored rating scales (BARS)** = method of appraising performance based on typical performance criteria set for each individual member of staff

behind [bɪ'haɪnd] **1** *preposition* at the back *or* after; *the company is No. 2 in the market, about £4m behind their rivals;* **behind schedule** = late, not following the expected schedule; *the unit's work is three days behind schedule* **2** *adverb* after; *we have fallen behind our rivals* = we have fewer sales *or* make less profit than our rivals; *he has fallen behind with his loan repayments* = he is late with his payments

belong [bɪ'lɒŋ] *verb* **(a)** **to belong to** = to be the property of; *the company belongs to an old American banking family; the patent belongs to the inventor's son* **(b)** **to belong with** = to be in the correct place with; *those documents belong with the sales reports*

◊ **belongings** [bɪ'lɒŋɪŋz] *plural noun* things which belong to someone; *the company is not responsible for personal belongings left in the cloakrooms; when he was sacked he had five minutes to collect his personal belongings*

below [bɪ'ləʊ] *preposition* lower down than *or* less than; *the company has a policy of paying staff below the market rates; salaries in the area are below the industry norm; the company pays below-average salaries*

benchmark ['ben(t)ʃmɑːk] *noun* point *or*

level which is important, and can be used as a reference when making evaluations *or* assessments; *what rate shall we use as a benchmark when measuring workers' performances?;* **benchmark jobs** = jobs used as a measure of performance

◊ **benchmarking** ['ben(t)ʃmɑːkɪŋ] *noun* measuring the performance of a company against the performance of other companies in the same sector

beneficiary [benɪ'fɪʃəri] *noun* person who gains money from something; *the beneficiaries of a will*

benefit ['benɪfɪt] **1** *noun* **(a)** payments which are made to someone under a national or private insurance scheme; **death benefit** = money paid to the family of someone who dies in an accident at work; **housing benefit** = local government benefit paid to people who cannot pay their rent; **national insurance benefits** = various benefits which are dependent on having paid NI contributions (such as retirement pension); **unemployment benefit** = government payment made to an unemployed person; *she receives £20 a week as unemployment benefit; the sickness benefit is paid monthly; the insurance office sends out benefit cheques each week* **(b)** advantage attached to a job apart from the basic salary *or* wage; **employment benefits** *or* **fringe benefits** = extra items given by a company to workers in addition to their salaries (such as company cars, private health insurance) **2** *verb* **(a)** to make better *or* to improve; *a fall in inflation benefits the exchange rate* **(b)** **to benefit from** *or* **by something** = to be improved by something *or* to gain more money because of something; *exports have benefited from the fall in the exchange rate; the employees have benefited from the profit-sharing scheme*

benevolent [bɪ'nevələnt] *adjective* which does good to other people; **benevolent fund** = fund contributed to by employers and employees to provide employees and their families with financial help in case of sickness, injury or death; *benevolent funds are set up to provide employees with more security; the employer's contribution to the staff benevolent fund was the most attractive of the fringe benefits offered with the job*

bi- [baɪ] *prefix* twice; **bi-monthly** = twice a month; **bi-annually** = twice a year

bias ['baɪəs] *noun* favouring one group *or* person rather than another; *management has shown bias in favour of graduates in its recent appointments;* **leniency bias** = unjustifiably high rating of an employee's job performance

◊ **biased** ['baɪəst] *adjective* (person) who favours one group rather than another; *she is biased towards younger staff*

bid [bɪd] **1** *noun* **(a)** offer to buy something at a certain price; **to make a bid for something** = to offer to buy something; *he made a bid for the house; the company made a bid for its rival;* **to make a cash bid** = to offer to pay cash for something; **to put in a bid for something** *or* **to enter a bid for something** = to offer (usually in writing) to buy something; *(at an auction)* **opening bid** = first bid; **closing bid** = last bid at an auction *or* the bid which is successful **(b)** offer to do some work at a certain price; *he made the lowest bid for the job* **(c)** *US* offer to sell something at a certain price; *they asked for bids for the supply of spare parts* **(d)** **takeover bid** = offer to buy all or a majority of shares in a company so as to control it; **to make a takeover bid for a company; to withdraw a takeover bid;** the company rejected the takeover bid = the directors recommended the shareholders not to accept it **2** *verb* *(at an auction)* **to bid for something** = to offer to buy something; *he bid £1,000 for the jewels* = he offered to pay £1,000 for the jewels

◊ **bidding** ['bɪdɪŋ] *noun* **(a)** attempt by an employee to be considered for a vacant post in the same organization; *when the vacancy was pinned up on the notice board there was much bidding for the job among the staff in the department* **(b)** action of making offers to buy (usually at an auction); **the bidding started at £1,000** = the first and lowest bid was £1,000; **the bidding stopped at £250,000** = the last (successful) bid was for £250,000 (NOTE: no plural)

bilateral [baɪ'lætərəl] *adjective* between two parties *or* countries; *the minister signed a bilateral trade agreement*

bilingual [baɪ'lɪŋgwəl] *adjective* (person) who is able to speak and write two languages fluently; *a bilingual secretary; secretaries working overseas are required to be bilingual; having worked for a French company for some years, he is now* *completely bilingual* (NOTE: in the USA, the word **bilingual** normally means speaking English and Spanish)

bind [baɪnd] *verb* to tie *or* to attach; *the company is bound by its articles of association; he does not consider himself bound by the agreement signed by his predecessor*

◊ **binder** ['baɪndə] *noun* **(a)** stiff cardboard cover for papers; **ring binder** = cover with rings in it which fit into special holes made in sheets of paper **(b)** *US* temporary agreement for insurance sent before the insurance policy is issued (NOTE: the GB English for this is **cover note)**

◊ **binding** ['baɪndɪŋ] *adjective* which legally forces someone to do something; *a binding contract; this document is not legally binding;* **the agreement is binding on all parties** = all parties signing it must do what is agreed

biodata [baɪəʊ'deɪtə] *noun* biographical information about an employee and his or her employment history

◊ **biological clock** [baɪə'lɒdʒɪkl 'klɒk] *noun* system inside a person's body which regulates cyclical activities, such as biorhythms and has an effect on night-shift working

◊ **biorhythms** ['baɪəʊrɪðəmz] *plural noun* recurring cycles of different lengths which some people believe affect a person's behaviour, sensitivity and intelligence; *see also* CIRCADIAN RHYTHMS

black [blæk] **1** *adjective* **(a)** **black market** = buying and selling goods in a way which is not allowed by law (as in a time of rationing); *there is a flourishing black market in spare parts for cars; you can buy gold coins on the black market;* **to pay black market prices** = to pay high prices to get items which are not easily available **(b)** **black economy** = work which is paid for in cash, and therefore not declared to the tax authorities **(c)** **in the black** = in credit; *the company has moved into the black; my bank account is still in the black* **2** *verb* to forbid trading in certain goods or with certain suppliers; *three firms were blacked by the government; the union has blacked a trucking firm*

◊ **black-coated workers** ['blækkəʊtɪd] *noun* white-collar workers, workers in administrative jobs, not manual workers

◊ **blacking** ['blækɪŋ] *noun* refusal by employees to work with materials normally supplied by employees of another organization who are engaged in industrial action; *blacking of the rubber already delivered to the factory held up tyre production for days; blacking of materials was carried out by workers in another factory who were sympathetic to the strikers' cause*

◊ **blackleg** ['blækleg] *noun* strikebreaker *or* worker who goes on working when there is a strike; *blacklegs were threatened by the strike leaders; most of the blacklegs couldn't face the insecurity of not working*

◊ **black list** [blæk 'lɪst] *noun* list of goods *or* people *or* companies which have been blacked; list of persons considered by an employer to be too dangerous *or* disruptive to employ

◊ **blacklist** ['blæklɪst] *verb* to put goods *or* people *or* a company on a black list; *his firm was blacklisted by the government*

blame [bleɪm] **1** *noun* saying that someone has done something wrong *or* that someone is responsible; *the sales staff got the blame for the poor sales figures* **2** *verb* to say that someone has done something wrong *or* is responsible for a mistake; *the managing director blamed the chief accountant for not warning him of the loss; the union is blaming the management for poor industrial relations*

blank [blæŋk] **1** *adjective* with nothing written; **a blank cheque** = a cheque with no amount of money or name written on it, but signed by the drawer; **blank vote** = voting paper which has not been marked **2** *noun* space on a form which has to be completed; *fill in the blanks and return the form to your local office*

blanket ['blæŋkɪt] *noun* **blanket agreement** = (i) any agreement which covers many items; (ii) agreement between management and union which covers all employees; **blanket dismissal** = dismissal of a group of workers because one unidentified worker is suspected of having committed an offence, and the others refuse to reveal the identity of the culprit

block [blɒk] **1** *noun* **(a)** series of items grouped together; *he bought a block of 6,000 shares;* **block booking** = booking of several seats *or* rooms at the same time; *the* *company has a block booking for twenty seats on the plane or for ten rooms at the hotel;* **block vote** = casting of a large number of votes in the same way and at the same time (such as those of a trade union delegation at a conference) **(b)** series of buildings forming a square with streets on all sides; *they want to redevelop a block in the centre of the town;* **a block of offices** *or* **an office block** = a large building which only contains offices **(c) block capitals** *or* **block letters** = capital letters (as A,B,C); *write your name and address in block letters* **2** *verb* to stop something taking place; *he used his casting vote to block the motion; the planning committee blocked the redevelopment plan;* **blocked currency** = currency which cannot be taken out of a country because of exchange controls; *the company has a large account in blocked roubles;* **blocked mobility** = limited potential for promotion that is not dependent on educational background of the employee

◊ **block-release** ['blɒk rɪ'liːs] *noun* permission for an employee to attend a series of courses outside his place of work

blood [blʌd] *noun* **fresh blood** *or* **new blood** = new younger staff, employed because the company feels it needs to have new ideas

blue [bluː] *adjective* **blue-collar worker** = manual worker in a factory; *the most ambitious of the blue-collar workers can be considered for supervisory posts;* **blue-collar union** = trade union formed mainly of blue-collar workers; *US* **blue circle rate** = pay rate which is below the minimum rate of an employee's evaluated pay level; *US* **Blue Laws** = regulations governing business activities on Sundays

◊ **blueprint** ['bluːprɪnt] *noun* plan *or* model of something; *the agreement will be the blueprint for other agreements in the industry*

board [bɔːd] *noun* **(a)** official group of people; **board interview** = interview in which a candidate is asked questions by several representatives of an organization **(b)** official body; **arbitration board** *or* **arbitration tribunal** = group which arbitrates in industrial disputes; **the Pay Review Board** = official body which examines pay scales in a nationalized industry or public service and recommends

changes; **training board** = government organization set up for each industry to provide training for the workers in the industry **(c)** group of people who run a trust *or* a society; **advisory board** = group of advisors; **editorial board** = group of editors **(d)** *GB* **board of directors** = group of directors elected by the shareholders to run a company; *the bank has two representatives on the board; he sits on the board as a representative of the bank; two directors were removed from the board at the AGM;* **she was asked to join the board** = she was asked to become a director; **board meeting** = meeting of the directors of a company; **board member** = one of the directors of a company; **executive board** = board of directors which deals with the day-to-day running of the company (as opposed to a supervisory board, which deals with policy and planning); **supervisory board** = board of directors which deals with general policy and planning (as opposed to the executive board, which deals with day-to-day running of the company in a two-tier system) **(e)** *US* **board of directors** = group of people elected by the shareholders to draw up company policy and to appoint the president and other executive officers who are responsible for managing the company (NOTE: the board of an American company may be made up of a large number of non-executive directors and only one or two executive officers; a British board has more executive directors) **(f)** large flat piece of wood or card; **bulletin board** *or* **notice board** = board fixed to a wall where notices can be put up; **clipboard** = stiff board with a clip at the top so that a piece of paper can be clipped to the board to allow you to write on it easily

◊ **boardroom** ['bɔːdrʊm] *noun* room where the directors of a company meet

body language ['bɒdi 'læŋgwɪdʒ] *noun* gestures, movements, etc. which a person makes which show what he or she is actually thinking

bona fide ['bəʊnə 'faɪdi] *adjective* trustworthy *or* which can be trusted; **a bona fide offer** = an offer which is made honestly; **bona fide union** = union which is freely chosen by employees without any influence from the employer; *most of the workers in the industry are members of bona fide unions*

bonus ['bəʊnəs] *noun* extra payment; **attendance bonus** = bonus given to employees for good attendance; **capital bonus** = extra payment by an insurance company which is produced by capital gain; **cost-of-living bonus** = money paid to meet the increase in the cost of living; **Christmas bonus** = extra payment made to staff at Christmas; **efficiency bonus** = extra payment for efficiency in a job; **incentive bonus** = extra pay offered to a worker to encourage him to work harder; **no-claims bonus** = reduction of premiums on an insurance because no claims have been made; **productivity bonus** = extra payment made because of increased productivity; **bonus share** = extra share given to an existing shareholder; **bonus system** *or* **bonus schemes** = schemes by which workers can earn bonuses (such as for exceeding targets, completing a task within the deadline, etc.) (NOTE: plural is **bonuses)**

book [bʊk] **1** *noun* **(a)** set of sheets of paper attached together; **a company's books** = the financial records of a company; **account book** = book which records sales and purchases; **cash book** = record of cash; **order book** = record of orders; **the company has a full order book** = it has sufficient orders to keep the workforce occupied; **purchase book** = records of purchases; **sales book** = records of sales; **book sales** = sales as recorded in the sales book; **book value** = value as recorded in the company's books **(b) bank book** = book which shows money which you have deposited or withdrawn from a bank account; **cheque book** = book of new cheques; **phone book** *or* **telephone book** = book which lists names of people or companies with their addresses and telephone numbers **2** *verb* to order *or* to reserve something; *to book a room in a hotel or a table at a restaurant or a ticket on a plane; I booked a table for 7.45; he booked a ticket through to Cairo;* **to book someone into a hotel** *or* **onto a flight** = to order a room *or* a plane ticket for someone; *he was booked on the 09.00 flight to Zurich;* **the hotel** *or* **the flight is fully booked** *or* **is booked up** = all the rooms *or* seats are reserved; *the restaurant is booked up over the Christmas period*

◊ **booking** ['bʊkɪŋ] *noun* act of ordering a room *or* a seat; *hotel bookings have fallen since the end of the tourist season;* **booking clerk** = person who sells tickets in a booking office; **booking office** = office where you can book seats at a theatre *or*

tickets for the railway; **block booking** = booking of several seats *or* rooms at the same time; **to confirm a booking** = to say that a booking is certain; **double booking** = booking by mistake of two people into the same hotel room *or* the same seat on a plane

◊ **bookkeeper** ['bʊkiːpə] *noun* person who keeps the financial records of a company

◊ **bookkeeping** ['bʊkiːpɪŋ] *noun* keeping of the financial records of a company *or* an organization; **single-entry bookkeeping** = noting a deal with only one entry; **double-entry bookkeeping** = noting of both credit and debit sides of an account (NOTE: no plural)

◊ **booklet** ['bʊklət] *noun* small book with a paper cover

◊ **bookwork** ['bʊkwɜːk] *noun* keeping of financial records

boost [buːst] **1** *noun* help to increase; *this publicity will give sales a boost; the government hopes to give a boost to industrial development* **2** *verb* to make something increase; *we expect our publicity campaign to boost sales by 25%; the company hopes to boost its market share; incentive schemes are boosting production*

boot [buːt] *noun (informal)* **to get the boot** = to be sacked

borderline case ['bɔːdəlaɪn 'keɪs] *noun* situation which is not easy to resolve, being either one way or the other; worker who may *or* may not be recommended for promotion, for dismissal, etc.

borrow ['bɒrəʊ] *verb* to take money from someone for a time, possibly paying interest for it, and repaying it at the end of the period; *he borrowed £1,000 from the bank; the company had to borrow heavily to repay its debts; they borrowed £25,000 against the security of the factory;* **to borrow short** *or* **long** = to borrow for a short *or* long period

◊ **borrower** ['bɒrəʊə] *noun* person who borrows; *borrowers from the bank pay 12% interest*

◊ **borrowing** ['bɒrəʊɪŋ] *noun* **(a)** action of borrowing money; *the new factory was financed by bank borrowing;* **borrowing power** = amount of money which a company can borrow **(b) borrowings** = money borrowed; *the company's borrowings have doubled;* **bank borrowings** = loans made by banks

boss [bɒs] *noun (informal)* employer *or* person in charge of a company *or* an office; *if you want a pay rise, go and talk to your boss; he became a director when he married the boss's daughter*

bottleneck ['bɒtlnek] *noun* position when business activity is slowed down because one section of the operation cannot cope with the amount of work; *a bottleneck in the supply system; there are serious bottlenecks in the production line*

bottom ['bɒtəm] **1** *noun* lowest part *or* point; **sales have reached rock bottom** = the very lowest point of all; **the bottom has fallen out of the market** = sales have fallen below what previously seemed to be the lowest point; **bottom price** = lowest price; **rock-bottom price** = lowest price of all **2** *verb* **to bottom (out)** = to reach the lowest point; **the market has bottomed out** = has reached the lowest point and does not seem likely to fall further

◊ **bottom line** ['bɒtəm 'laɪn] *noun* **(a)** last line on a balance sheet indicating profit or loss; **the boss is interested only in the bottom line** = he is only interested in the final profit **(b)** final decision on a matter; *the bottom line was that any workers showing dissatisfaction with conditions would be fired*

box [bɒks] *noun* **(a)** cardboard *or* wood *or* plastic container; *the goods were sent in thin cardboard boxes; the watches are prepacked in plastic display boxes;* **paperclips come in boxes of two hundred** = packed two hundred to a box; **box file** = file (for papers) made like a box; **suggestions box** = box into which members of staff can put papers with their ideas for improving profitability, safety, etc. **(b) box number** = reference number used in a post office or an advertisement to avoid giving an address; *please reply to Box No. 209; our address is: P.O. Box 74209, Edinburgh* **(c) cash box** = metal box for keeping cash; **letter box** *or* **mail box** = place where incoming mail is put; **call box** = outdoor telephone kiosk **(d)** *(on a form)* small square in which something must be written; *if you want a receipt, tick the box marked "R"*

◊ **boxed** [bɒkst] *adjective* put in a box *or* sold in a box; **boxed set** = set of items sold together in a box

boycott ['bɔɪkɒt] **1** *noun* refusal to buy *or* to deal in certain products; *the union organized a boycott against or of imported cars* **2** *verb* to refuse to buy *or* to deal in a certain product; *we are boycotting all imports from that country;* **the management has boycotted the meeting** = has refused to attend the meeting

BR tax code [biː'ɑː 'tæks 'kəʊd] *noun* number given to an employee and sent to the employer, which allows the employer to deduct tax from the employee's pay at the correct rate

bracket ['brækɪt] **1** *noun* group of items *or* people taken together; **age bracket** = group of people of about the same age; **income bracket** = group of people earning roughly the same income; **lower** *or* **upper income bracket** = groups of people who earn low or high salaries considered for tax purposes; **he comes into the higher income bracket** = he is in a group of people earning high incomes and therefore paying more tax; **people in the middle-income bracket** = people with average incomes, not high or low; **tax bracket** = percentage level of tax; **he is in the top tax bracket** = he pays the highest level of tax **2** *verb* **to bracket together** = to treat several items together in the same way; *in the sales reports, all the European countries are bracketed together*

brain *noun* part of the body in which decisions are taken; **he is the brains behind the organization** = he is the clever person who is running the organization; **brain drain** = movement of clever people away from a country to find better jobs in other countries

◊ **brainstorming** ['breɪnstɔːmɪŋ] *noun* intensive discussion by a small group of people as a method of producing new ideas or solving problems; **brainstorming session** = meeting to thrash out problems, where everyone puts forward different ideas

branch [brɑːn(t)ʃ] *noun* **(a)** local office of a bank or large business; local shop of a large chain of shops; *the bank or the store has branches in most towns in the south of the country; the insurance company has closed its branches in South America; he is the manager of our local branch of Lloyds bank;*

we have decided to open a branch office in Chicago; the manager of our branch in Lagos or of our Lagos branch; **branch manager** = manager of a branch **(b)** local office of a union, based in a factory; **branch committee** = elected committee of union members which deals with general day-to-day problems

breach [briːtʃ] *noun* failure to carry out the terms of an agreement; **breach of contract** = failing to do something which is in a contract; **the company is in breach of contract** = it has failed to carry out the duties of the contract; **breach of discipline** = action which goes against the company rules or against instructions; **breach of trust** = legal term for the failure of an employee to carry out duties properly and honestly; **breach of warranty** = supplying goods which do not meet the standards of the warranty applied to them

breadwinner [ˈbredwɪnə] *noun* person who earns the main income in a family, and so provides food for the others

break [breɪk] **1** *noun* **(a)** short space of time, when you can rest; *she typed for two hours without a break; you can take a break now, and come back to the office in ten minutes' time;* **coffee break** or **tea break** = rest time during work when the workers can drink coffee or tea **(b)** **break point** = dividing point between one job or element and the next, or between one level established on a job evaluation and the next; *a break point was established between unskilled and semi-skilled jobs, separating the two categories, with different rates of pay* **2** *verb* **(a)** to fail to carry out the duties (of a contract, etc.); *the company has broken the contract or the agreement;* **to break an engagement to do something** = not to do what has been agreed; **to break the law** = to do something which is against the law **(b)** to cancel (a contract); *the company is hoping to be able to break the contract*

◊ **break down** [ˈbreɪk ˈdaun] *verb* **(a)** to stop working because of mechanical failure; *the fax machine has broken down; what do you do when your photocopier breaks down?* **(b)** to stop; *negotiations broke down after six hours* **(c)** to show all the items in a total list of costs or expenditure; *we broke the expenditure down into fixed and variable costs; can you break down this invoice into spare parts and labour?*

◊ **breakdown** [ˈbreɪkdaun] *noun* **(a)** stopping work because of mechanical failure; *we cannot communicate with our Nigerian office because of a breakdown of the telex lines* **(b)** stopping talking; *a breakdown in wage negotiations* **(c)** showing details item by item; *give me a breakdown of investment costs*

◊ **break off** [ˈbreɪk ˈɒf] *verb* to stop; *we broke off the discussion at midnight; management broke off negotiations with the union*

◊ **break up** [ˈbreɪk ˈʌp] *verb* **(a)** to split something large into small sections; *the company was broken up and separate divisions sold off* **(b)** to come to an end; *the meeting broke up at 12.30*

bribe [braɪb] **1** *noun* money given to someone in authority to get him or her to help; *the minister was dismissed for taking bribes* **2** *verb* to pay someone money to get him or her to do something for you; *we had to bribe the minister's secretary to let us see her boss*

bridge job [ˈbrɪdʒ ˈdʒɒb] *noun* position designed to help the movement of employees from one job category to another; *he was given a bridge job while being considered for real promotion; the bridge job between machinist and supervisor consisted of some tasks from each of these posts*

bridging loan [ˈbrɪdʒɪŋ ˈləun] or *US* **bridge loan** [ˈbrɪdʒ ˈləun] *noun* interest-free loan given to an employee who has transferred his job to a new locality; *the company had to be generous with its bridging loans to persuade employees to move to areas where they were most needed; he requested a bridging loan to pay all expenses involved in moving his family to a new town*

brief [briːf] **1** *noun* instructions given to an employee **2** *verb* to explain to someone in detail; *the salesmen were briefed on the new product; the managing director briefed the board on the progress of the negotiations*

◊ **briefing** [ˈbriːfɪŋ] *noun* telling someone details; *all salesmen have to attend a sales briefing on the new product;* **briefing session** = meeting between managers and staff where the staff are informed of decisions, plans, etc.

bring [brɪŋ] *verb* to come to a place with

someone or something; *he brought his documents with him; the finance director brought her secretary to take notes of the meeting;* **to bring a lawsuit against someone** = to tell someone to appear in court to settle an argument

◊ **bring down** [brɪŋ 'daʊn] *verb* **(a)** to reduce; *petrol companies have brought down the price of oil* **(b)** to add a figure to an account at the end of a period to balance expenditure and income; *balance brought down: £365.15*

◊ **bring forward** [brɪŋ 'fɔːwəd] *verb* **(a)** to make earlier; *to bring forward the date of repayment; the date of the next meeting has been brought forward to March* **(b)** to take a balance brought down as the starting point for the next period in a balance sheet; *balance brought forward: £365.15*

◊ **bring in** [brɪŋ 'ɪn] *verb* to earn (an interest); *the shares bring in a small amount*

◊ **bring out** [brɪŋ 'aʊt] *verb* to produce something new; *they are bringing out a new model of the car for the Motor Show*

◊ **bring up** [brɪŋ 'ʌp] *verb* to refer to something for the first time; *the chairman brought up the question of redundancy payments*

broke [brəʊk] *adjective informal* having no money; *the company is broke; he is to broke to pay for a new car;* **to go broke** = to become bankrupt; *the company went broke last month*

broom [bruːm] *noun* **new broom** = manager *or* director brought into a company to change existing practices and possibly remove old-established staff

BS ['biː 'es] = BRITISH STANDARDS quality standards which apply to various products or services

buddy system ['bʌdi 'sɪstəm] *noun US* on-the-job training system, where a trainee works with an experienced employee; *the buddy system teaches the trainee the practical realities of the job; the company operates both a buddy system and some off-the-job classroom instruction for its trainees*

budget ['bʌdʒɪt] **1** *noun* plan of expected spending and income; *to draw up a budget for salaries for the coming year; the unexpected rise in wages has resulted in overspending on our budget* **2** *verb* to plan probable income and expenditure; *we are budgeting for £10,000 of sales next year*

◊ **budgetary** ['bʌdʒɪtəri] *adjective* referring to a budget; keeping check on spending; **budgetary control** = keeping check on spending; **budgetary policy** = policy of planning income and expenditure

build [bɪld] *verb* to make by putting pieces together; *to build a sales structure;* **to build on past experience** = to use experience as a base on which to act in the future (NOTE: **building - built**)

◊ **building** ['bɪldɪŋ] *noun* house *or* factory *or* office block, etc.; *they have redeveloped the site of the old office building;* **the Shell Building** = the office block where the head office of Shell is

◊ **building and loan association** ['bɪldɪŋ ənd 'ləʊn əsəʊsɪ'eɪʃən] *noun US* = SAVINGS AND LOAN ASSOCIATION

◊ **building society** ['bɪldɪŋ sə'saɪəti] *noun GB* financial institution which accepts and pays interest on deposits and lends money to people who are buying property; *he put his savings into a building society or into a building society account; I have an account with the Halifax Building Society; I saw the building society manager to ask for a mortgage*

◊ **build into** ['bɪld 'ɪntʊ] *verb* to add something to something being set up; *you must build all the forecasts into the budget;* **we have built 10% for contingencies into our cost forecast** = we have added 10% to our basic forecast to allow for unexpected items

◊ **build up** ['bɪld 'ʌp] *verb* **(a)** to create something by adding pieces together; *he bought several shoe shops and gradually built up a chain* **(b)** to expand something gradually; *to build up a profitable business; to build up a team of salesmen*

◊ **buildup** ['bɪldʌp] *noun* gradual increase; *a buildup in sales or a sales buildup; there will be a big publicity buildup before the launch of the new model; there has been a buildup of complaints about customer service*

◊ **built-in** ['bɪlt'ɪn] *adjective* forming part of the system *or* of a machine; *the micro has a built-in clock; the accounting system has a series of built-in checks*

bully ['bʊli] **1** *noun* person who is in a

powerful position and continually harasses others **2** *verb* to threaten and intimidate other members of staff; *she complained that she was being bullied by the assistant manager*

◊ **bullying** ['bʊlɪŋ] *noun* intimidation and harassment of someone by another member of staff in a more powerful position

bumping ['bʌmpɪŋ] *noun US* (i) lay-off procedure that allows an employee with greater seniority to displace a more junior employee; (ii) situation where a senior employee takes the place of a junior (in a restaurant); *the economic recession led to extensive bumping in companies where only the most qualified were retained for certain jobs; the trade unions strongly objected to bumping practices since they considered that many employees were being laid off unfairly*

burden ['bɜːdən] *noun* heavy load which you have to carry; **tax burden** = heavy tax charge (as a percentage of a company's profits); *the burden of business taxes on small companies*

bureau ['bjʊərəʊ] *noun* office which specializes; **computer bureau** = office which offers to do work on its computers for companies which do not own their own computers; **employment bureau** = office which finds jobs for people; **information bureau** = office which gives information; **trade bureau** = office which specializes in commercial enquiries; **visitors' bureau** = office which deals with visitors' questions; **word-processing bureau** = office which specializes in word-processing; *we farm out the office typing to a local bureau* (NOTE: the plural is **bureaux**)

◊ **bureaucracy** [bjʊ'rɒkrəsi] *noun* system of administration where an individual person's responsibilities and powers are strictly defined and processes are strictly followed

◊ **bureaucratic** [bjʊərəʊ'krætɪk] *adjective* following strict administrative principle

burn out ['bɜːn 'aʊt] *verb* to become tired and incapable for further work because of stress; *he's a burnt-out case and had to give up his job*

◊ **burnout** *or* **burnt out case** ['bɜːnaʊt *or* bɜːnt aʊt 'keɪs] *noun* case where an employee is tired and incapable of doing any more work as a result of overwork

business ['bɪznəs] *noun* **(a)** work in buying or selling; *business is expanding; business is slow; he does a thriving business in repairing cars; what's your line of business?;* **business call** = telephone call *or* visit to talk to someone on business; **business centre** = part of a town where the main banks, shops and offices are located; **business class** = type of airline travel which is less expensive than first class and more comfortable than tourist class; **business college** *or* **business school** = place where commercial studies are taught; **business correspondent** = journalist who writes articles on business news for newspapers; **business cycle** *or* **trade cycle** = period during which trade expands, then slows down and then expands again; **business efficiency exhibition** = exhibition which shows products (computers, word-processors) which help a business to be efficient; **business games** = problem-solving projects which are used in training managers; *business school students played a business game on the computer which demanded quick decisions on marketing strategy; business games are considered by the college to provide practical training to complement the more theoretical lectures;* **business hours** = time (usually 9 a.m. to 5 p.m.) when a business is open; **business letter** = letter about commercial matters; **business lunch** = lunch to discuss business matters; **business plan** = document drawn up to show how a business is planned to work, with cash flow forecasts, sales forecasts, etc. (often used when trying to raise a loan, or when setting up a new business); **business trip** = trip to discuss business matters with clients; **to be in business** = to be in a commercial firm; **to go into business** = to start a commercial firm; *he went into business as a car dealer;* **to go out of business** = to stop trading; *the firm went out of business during the recession;* **on business** = on commercial work; *he had to go abroad on business; the chairman is in Holland on business* **(b)** commercial company; *he owns a small car repair business; she runs a business from her home; he set up in business as an insurance broker;* **business address** = details of number, street and town where a company is located; **business card** = card showing a businessman's name and the name and address of the company he works for;

business correspondence = letters concerned with a business; **business equipment** = machines used in an office; **business expenses** = money spent on running a business, not on stock or assets; **business hours** = time (usually 9 a.m. to 5 p.m.) when a business is open; **big business** = very large commercial firms **(c)** affairs discussed; *the main business of the meeting was finished by 3 p.m.;* **any other business** = item at the end of an agenda, where any matter can be raised (NOTE: no plural for meanings (a) and (c); (b) has the plural **businesses)**

◊ **business agent** ['bɪznəs 'eɪdʒənt] *noun* US chief local official of a trade union

◊ **businessman** *or* **businesswoman** ['bɪznɪsmæn *or* 'bɪznɪswʊmən] *noun* man *or* woman engaged in business; **she's a good businesswoman** = she's good at commercial deals; **a small businessman** = man who owns a small business

busy ['bɪzi] *adjective* occupied in doing something/in working; *he is busy preparing the annual accounts; the manager is busy at the moment, but he will be free in about* *fifteen minutes; the busiest time of year for stores is the week before Christmas; summer is the busy season for hotels;* **the line is busy** = the telephone line is being used

buyin ['baɪɪn] *noun* **management buyin** = purchase of a company by a group of outside directors

buyout ['baɪaʊt] *noun* **management buyout (MBO)** = takeover of a company by a group of employees (usually managers and directors); **leveraged buyout (LBO)** = buying all the shares in a company by borrowing money against the security of the shares to be bought

QUOTE we also invest in companies whose growth and profitability could be improved by a management buyout
Times

QUOTE in a normal leveraged buyout, the acquirer raises money by borrowing against the assets or cash flow of the target company
Fortune

Cc

CAC = CENTRAL ARBITRATION COMMITTEE

cafeteria [kæfɪ'tɪərɪə] *noun* self-service restaurant which belongs to a factory or office, where the staff can eat; *most people have lunch in the staff cafeteria;* **cafeteria style benefits plan** = scheme for benefits for employees, where the employee can choose from a range of benefits on offer, depending on different levels of contribution

calculate ['kælkjʊleɪt] *verb* **(a)** to find the answer to a problem using numbers; *the bank clerk calculated the rate of exchange for the dollar* **(b)** to estimate; *I calculate that we have six months' stock left*

◊ **calculating machine** ['kælkjʊleɪtɪŋ mə'ʃiːn] *noun* machine which calculates

◊ **calculation** [kælkjʊ'leɪʃən] *noun* answer to a problem in mathematics; **rough calculation** = approximate answer; *I made some rough calculations on the back of an envelope; according to my calculations, we have six months' stock left;* **we are £20,000 out in our calculations** = we have £20,000 too much or too little

◊ **calculator** ['kælkjʊleɪtə] *noun* electronic machine which adds, subtracts, etc.; *my pocket calculator needs a new battery; he worked out the discount on his calculator*

calendar ['kæləndə] *noun* book *or* set of sheets of paper showing the days and months in a year, often attached to pictures; *for the New Year the garage sent me a calendar with photographs of old cars;* **calendar month** = a whole month as on a calendar, from the 1st to the 30th or 31st; **calendar year** = year from the 1st January to 31st December

call [kɔːl] **1** *noun* **(a)** conversation on the telephone; **local call** = call to a number on the same exchange; **trunk call** *or* **long-distance call** = call to a number in a different zone *or* area; **overseas call** *or* **international call** = call to another country; **person-to-person call** = call where you ask the operator to connect you with a named person; **reverse charge call** *or* **transferred charge call** *or* US **collect call** = call where the person receiving the call agrees to pay for it; **to make a call** = to dial and speak to someone on the telephone; **to take a call** = to answer the telephone; **to log calls** = to note all details of telephone calls made **(b)** official request for something; **roll call** = calling out the names of employees to see if their are present (as during a fire in an office or factory); **strike call** = request by a trade union asking its members to strike **(c)** demand for repayment of a loan by a lender; **money at call** *or* **money on call** *or* **call money** = money loaned for which repayment can be demanded without notice **(d)** visit; *the salesmen make six calls a day;* **business call** = visit to talk to someone on business; **cold call** = sales visit where the salesman has no appointment and the client is not an established customer; **call rate** = number of calls (per day or per week) made by a salesman **2** *verb* **(a)** to telephone to someone; *I'll call you at your office tomorrow* **(b)** to call on someone = to visit; *our salesmen call on their best accounts twice a month* **(c)** to ask someone to do something; **the union called a strike** = the union told its members to go on strike

◊ **call-back pay** ['kɔːlbæk 'peɪ] *noun* pay given to a worker who has been called back to work after his normal working hours; *the union did not consider the call-back pay rate high enough to make up for the inconvenience of being called back to work*

◊ **caller** ['kɔːlə] *noun* **(a)** person who telephones **(b)** person who visits

◊ **call in** ['kɔːl 'ɪn] *verb* **(a)** to visit; *the sales representative called in twice last week* **(b)** to telephone to make contact; *we ask the reps to call in every Friday to report on the weeks' sales* **(c)** to ask for a debt to be paid

◊ **call-in pay** ['kɔːlɪn 'peɪ] *noun* payment

guaranteed to workers who report for work even if there is no work for them to do; *call-in pay is often necessary to ensure the attendance of workers where there is at least the possibility of work needing to be done; the personnel manager found call-in pay to be uneconomical because too many men were being paid for doing nothing*

◊ **call off** ['kɔːl 'ɒf] *verb* to ask for something not to take place; *the union has called off the strike; the deal was called off at the last moment*

cancel ['kænsəl] *verb* (a) to stop something which has been agreed *or* planned; *the manager is still ill, so the interviews planned for this week have been cancelled* (b) **to cancel a cheque** = to stop payment of a cheque which you have signed (NOTE: GB English: **cancelling - cancelled** but US English: **canceling - canceled**)

◊ **cancellation** [kænsə'leɪʃən] *noun* stopping something which has been agreed *or* planned; *cancellation of an appointment; cancellation of an agreement;* **cancellation clause** = clause in a contract which states the terms on which the contract may be cancelled

◊ **cancel out** ['kænsəl 'aut] *verb* to balance and so make invalid *or* even; *the two clauses cancel each other out; costs have cancelled out the sales revenue*

candidate ['kændɪdət] *noun* person who applies or is considered suitable for a job *or* for a training course; *there are six candidates for the post of assistant manager; the candidates were each given a personality test and an intelligence test; for every fifty candidates about ten may be shortlisted, but only one will be selected*

can-do ['kænduː] *adjective* go-ahead, liking to cope with new challenges; *he's a can-do individual*

canteen [kæn'tiːn] *noun* restaurant which belongs to a factory or office, where the staff can eat; *most people have lunch in the canteen*

cap [kæp] **1** *noun* upper level for something (such as a maximum rate of interest) **2** *verb* to place an upper limit on something; *to cap a department's budget* (NOTE: **capping - capped**)

capable ['keɪpəbl] *adjective* (a) capable of = able *or* clever enough to do something; *she is capable of very fast typing speeds; the sales force must be capable of selling all the stock in the warehouse* (b) efficient; *she is a very capable departmental manager* (NOTE: you are capable **of** something or **of doing** something)

◊ **capability** [keɪpə'bɪlɪti] *noun* skill which an employee has learnt and which can be applied to his work

capacity [kə'pæsəti] *noun* (a) amount which can be produced *or* amount of work which can be done; *industrial or manufacturing or production capacity;* **to work at full capacity** = to do as much work as possible; **to use up spare** *or* **excess capacity** = to make use of time *or* space which is not fully used; **capacity planning** = forward planning to relate production needs to anticipated demand (b) amount of space; **storage capacity** = space available for storage; **warehouse capacity** = space available in a warehouse (c) ability; *he has a particular capacity for business;* **earning capacity** = amount of money someone is able to earn (d) **in a capacity** = acting as; *he signed the document in his capacity as chairman;* **speaking in an official capacity** = speaking officially

captain ['kæptɪn] *noun* person in command of a ship *or* aircraft; **captains of industry** = the heads of major industrial companies

car [kɑː] *noun* small motor vehicle for carrying people; **company car** = car owned by a company and lent to a member of staff to use as if it were his or her own

◊ **car-hire** ['kɑːhaɪə] *noun* business of lending cars to people for money; *he runs a car-hire business*

carbon ['kɑːbən] *noun* (a) carbon paper; *you forgot to put a carbon in the typewriter* (b) carbon copy; *make a top copy and two carbons*

◊ **carbon copy** ['kɑːbən 'kɒpi] *noun* copy made with carbon paper; *give me the original, and file the carbon copy*

◊ **carbonless** ['kɑːbənləs] *adjective* which makes a copy without using carbon paper; *our reps use carbonless order pads*

◊ **carbon paper** ['kɑːbən 'peɪpə] *noun* sheet of paper with a black material on one side, used in a typewriter to make a copy; *you put the carbon paper in the wrong way round*

card [kɑːd] *noun* **(a)** stiff paper; *we have printed the instructions on thick white card* (NOTE: no plural) **(b)** small piece of stiff paper or plastic; *he showed his staff card to get a discount in the store;* **business card** = card showing a businessman's name and the address of the company he works for; **cash card** = plastic card used to obtain money from a cash dispenser; **charge card** = plastic card which allows you to buy goods and pay for them later; **cheque (guarantee) card** = plastic card from a bank which guarantees payment of a cheque; **credit card** = plastic card which allows you to borrow money or to buy goods without paying for them immediately; **filing card** = card with information written on it, used to classify information in correct order; **ID card** *or* **identity card** = a plastic card which carries details of the person it belongs to; **index card** = card used to make a card index; **punched card** = card with holes punched in it which a computer can read; **union card** = card showing that the holder is a member of a trade union; **card vote** = vote at a Trades Union Congress where the representatives of unions vote according to the numbers of union members; *see also* GREEN CARD, TIME CARD **(c) to get one's cards** = to be dismissed

◊ **cardboard** ['kɑːdbɔːd] *noun* thick stiff brown paper; **cardboard box** = box made of cardboard

◊ **card-carrying** ['kɑːdkærɪɪŋ] *adjective* (person) who has a membership card of an organization, such as a union; *the union had many sympathisers, but few actual card-carrying members; only card-carrying union members will be allowed to vote on whether there should be a strike*

◊ **card index** ['kɑːd 'ɪndeks] *noun* series of cards with information written on them, kept in special order so that the information can be found easily; *we use an alphabetical card-index system for staff records;* **card-index file** = information kept on filing cards

◊ **card-index** [kɑːd'ɪndeks] *verb* to put information onto a card index

◊ **card-indexing** [kɑːd'ɪndeksɪŋ] *noun*

putting information onto a card index; *no one can understand her card-indexing system*

career [kə'rɪə] *noun* job which you are trained for, and which you expect to do all your life; *he made his career in electronics; she has had a varied career, having worked in education and industry; the company offered its employees no advice on their future careers;* **to embark on a career** = to start a career; **to pursue a career as** = to follow a career as; **career break** = period when a worker leaves a career job for several years, as to study for a degree, or to have a baby, and then returns at the same level; **career development** = planning of an employee's future career in an organization; *a career development programme; if the company does not spend more time on career development, many employees will leave; career development involves a very comprehensive training programme;* **career expectations** = hopes which an employee has of how his or her career will develop (promotion, salary, etc.); **careers guidance** = professional help to people in choosing their career; *many employees are in the wrong jobs due to poor careers guidance at school;* **careers officer** = person who gives advice to students or new employees on their career prospects; **career opportunities** *or* **career prospects** = possibilities of advancement in a career; **career pattern** = way in which a person has spent his or her employed life (years employed in each firm, promotions, salary, etc.); **career planning** = examining the way in which career opportunities are available, leading to advice on which careers to pursue or how to further an employee's existing career; **career structure** = way in which jobs in a company are planned to lead on to other posts at a higher level; *he left the company because of its poor career structure;* **career woman** *or* **girl** = woman who is working in business and does not plan to stop working to look after the house or children

caretaker ['keəteɪkə] *noun* person who looks after a building, making sure it is clean and that the rubbish is cleared away (a caretaker often lives on the premises); *go and ask the caretaker to replace the light bulb* (NOTE: US English is **janitor**)

carousel training [kæruː'sel 'treɪnɪŋ] *noun* training which involves moving from job to job or from department to department in an organization; *carousel training was instituted in order to provide trainees with a wide range of practical experience; during their carousel training, trainee managers spend time in the marketing, personnel and finance departments*

carry ['kæri] *verb* (a) to take from one place to another; *to carry goods; a tanker carrying oil from the Gulf; the train was carrying a consignment of cars for export* (b) to vote to approve; **the motion was carried** = the motion was accepted after a vote (c) to produce; *the bonds carry interest at 10%* (d) to keep in stock; *to carry a line of goods; we do not carry pens*

◊ **carry down** *or* **carry forward** ['kæri 'daʊn *or* 'kæri 'fɔːwəd] *verb* to take an account balance at the end of the current period as the starting point for the next period; **balance carried forward** *or* **balance c/f** = amount entered in an account at the end of a period or page of an account book to balance the debit and credit entries; it is then taken forward to start the next period or page

◊ **carrying** ['kæriɪŋ] *noun* transporting from one place to another; *carrying charges; carrying cost*

◊ **carry on** ['kæri 'ɒn] *verb* to continue *or* to go on doing something; *the staff carried on working in spite of the fire;* **to carry on a business** = to be active in running a business

◊ **carry out** ['kæri 'aʊt] *verb* **to carry out one's duties** = to do what one has to do in one's job

◊ **carry over** ['kæri 'əʊvə] *verb* to take over to another period; *to carry over a holiday entitlement until the next year;* **to carry over a balance** = to take a balance from the end of one page or period to the beginning of the next

case [keɪs] *noun* (a) typical example of something; *the company has had several cases of petty theft in the post room;* **case study** = study of a particular situation to illustrate general principles; *case studies were handed out to students who were expected to make suggestions on what strategies the companies described should develop* (b) reasons for doing something; *the negotiations put the union's case for a pay rise;* **to state one's case** = to put forward

arguments which support your position (c) **court case** = legal action or trial; **the case is being heard next week** = the case is coming to court; **case law** = law as established by precedents, that is by decisions of courts in earlier cases

casual ['kæʒjʊəl] *adjective* (a) informal *or* not serious; *he was reprimanded for his casual attitude to working hours;* **the attitude of the company to poor timekeeping was fairly easy-going and casual** (b) not permanent *or* not regular; **casual labour** *or* **casual workers** = workers who are hired for short periods from time to time; **casual leave** = paid time off from work given to an employee to deal with personal affairs; *he was granted casual leave to settle his family affairs;* **casual vacancy** = job which has become vacant because the previous employee left unexpectedly; **casual work** = work where the workers are hired for a short period; *he lives on various types of casual work all year round; the only work available is casual work during the summer months;* **casual labourer** *or* **casual worker** = worker who can be hired for a short period

QUOTE casual workers however were less qualified than permanent workers
Employment Gazette

catastrophe [kə'tæstrəfiː] *noun* sudden disaster

◊ **catastrophic** [kætə'strɒfɪk] *adjective* disastrous; **catastrophic health insurance** = health insurance which provides for the high cost of treating severe or lengthy illnesses; *miners are advised to take out catastrophic health insurance since lung diseases are expensive to treat*

category ['kætəgəri] *noun* type *or* sort of item; *the company has vacancies for most categories of office staff; we deal only in the most expensive categories of watches*

◊ **categorical** [kætɪ'gɒrɪkl] *adjective* straightforward *or* definite

caution ['kɔːʃn] **1** *noun* (a) warning from someone in authority, telling someone not to repeat a minor crime; *the boys were let off with a caution* (b) warning by a police officer, that someone will be charged with a crime, and that what he says will be used in evidence **2** *verb* (a) to warn (someone) that what he has done is wrong and should not be repeated; *the manager cautioned the clerks after the he caught them drinking beer in the office* (b) to warn (someone) that he will be charged with a crime, and that what he says will be used as evidence at his trial; *the accused was arrested by the detectives and cautioned*

COMMENT: the person who is cautioned has the right not to answer any question put to him

CBI = CONFEDERATION OF BRITISH INDUSTRY

CCTV = CLOSED CIRCUIT TELEVISION

ceiling ['si:lɪŋ] *noun* high point; upper limit placed on wages *or* prices *or* output; *what ceiling has the government put on wage increases this year? output has reached a ceiling; to fix a ceiling to a budget;* **ceiling price** *or* **price ceiling** = highest price that can be reached; **wage ceiling** = highest wage which can be legally paid

cell [sel] *noun* **cell work system** = system of working where an item is produced within a separate production unit, and does not move round an assembly line

central ['sentrəl] *adjective* organized by one main point; **Central Arbitration Committee (CAC)** = independent arbitration body dealing mainly with union claims for disclosure of information by management; **central bank** = main government-controlled bank in a country, which controls the financial affairs of the country by fixing main interest rates, issuing currency and controlling the foreign exchange rate; **central office** = main office which controls all smaller offices; **central purchasing** = purchasing organized by a central office for all branches of a company

◊ **centralization** [sentrəlaɪ'zeɪʃən] *noun* organization of everything from a central point

◊ **centralize** ['sentrəlaɪz] *verb* to organize from a central point; *all purchasing has been centralized in our main office; the group benefits from a highly centralized organizational structure; the company has become very centralized, and far more staff work at headquarters*

centre *or* US **center** ['sentə] *noun* (a) **business centre** = part of a town where the main banks, shops and offices are; **centre of excellence** = organization which is recognised as being successful and having a world-wide reputation in its field, and so receives special funding (b) important town; *industrial centre; manufacturing centre; the centre for the shoe industry* (c) *GB* **job centre** = government office which lists jobs which are vacant; **shopping centre** = group of shops linked together with car parks and restaurants; **training centre** = government-run organization which trains adults in job skills; *several of our workers are at a training centre to learn how to operate the new machinery* (d) group of items in an account; **cost centre** = person or group whose costs can be itemized and to which fixed costs can be allocated; **profit centre** = person or department which is considered separately for the purposes of calculating a profit

CEO = CHIEF EXECUTIVE OFFICER

certificate [sə'tɪfɪkət] *noun* official document carrying an official declaration by someone, and signed by that person; *it was a condition of employment that he had to produce a medical certificate; when he claimed he had passed his diploma course, he was asked to prove it by showing the certificate;* **birth certificate** = paper giving details of a person's parents, date and place of birth; **death certificate** = paper signed by a doctor, stating that a person has died and giving details of the person; **doctor's certificate** *or* **medical certificate** = paper signed by a doctor, giving a patient permission to be away from work *or* not to do certain types of work

◊ **certificated** [sə'tɪfɪkeɪtɪd] *adjective* **certificated bankrupt** = bankrupt who has been discharged from bankruptcy with a certificate to show that he was not at fault

◊ **certification** [sɜːtɪfɪ'keɪʃn] *noun* giving an official certificate of approval; **certification officer** = official responsible for trade unions, seeing that they are properly registered, well conducted and that trade union legislation is adhered to

certify ['sɜːtɪfaɪ] *verb* to make an official declaration in writing; *I certify that this is a true copy; the document is certified as a true copy;* **certified accountant** = accountant who has passed the professional examinations and is a member of the Association of Certified Accountants; **certified cheque** or US **certified check** = cheque which a bank says is good and will be paid out of money put aside from the bank account; **certified copy** = copy which has been declared officially to be correct

chain [tʃeɪn] *noun* series of things linked together; **chain of command** = series of links between directors, management and employees, by which instructions, information, etc. are passed up or down

chair [tʃeə] **1** *noun* position of the chairman, presiding over a meeting; *to be in the chair; she was voted into the chair;* **Mr Jones took the chair** = Mr Jones presided over the meeting; **to address the chair** = in a meeting, to speak to the chairman and not to the rest of the people at the meeting; *please address your remarks to the chair* **2** *verb* to preside over a meeting; *the meeting was chaired by Mrs Smith*

◊ **chairman** ['tʃeəmən] *noun* **(a)** person who is in charge of a meeting; *Mr Howard was chairman* or *acted as chairman;* **Mr Chairman** or **Madam Chairman** = way of speaking to the chairman **(b)** person who presides over the board meetings of a company; *the chairman of the board* or *the company chairman;* **the chairman's report** = annual report from the chairman of a company to the shareholders

◊ **chairmanship** ['tʃeəmənʃɪp] *noun* being a chairman; *the committee met under the chairmanship of Mr Jones*

◊ **chairperson** ['tʃeə'pɜːsn] *noun* person who is in charge of a meeting

◊ **chairwoman** ['tʃeəwʊmən] *noun* woman who is in charge of a meeting (NOTE: the plurals are **chairmen, chairpersons, chairwomen.** Note also that in a US company the president is less important than the chairman of the board)

chance [tʃɑːns] *noun* **(a)** being possible; *the company has a good chance of winning the contract; his promotion chances are small* **(b)** opportunity to do something; *she is waiting for a chance to see the managing director; he had his chance of promotion when the finance director's assistant resigned* (NOTE: you have a chance **of doing** something or **to do** something)

change [tʃeɪndʒ] **1** *noun* **(a)** alteration in the way something is done or in the way work is carried out; **management of change** or **managing change** = managing the way changes in the working environment are implemented and how they affect the workforce; **personnel changes** or **staff changes** = when members of staff leave or new members arrive; **change of management** = situation when the person running a shop is replaced by someone else; **change of ownership** = situation when the owner of a business sells it to someone else; **change of use** = permission given by a local authority for premises to be used for a different purpose (such as house to become a shop, a shop to become a restaurant) **(b)** money in coins or small notes; **small change** = coins; **to give someone change for £10** = to give someone coins or notes in exchange for a ten pound note; **change machine** = machine which gives small change for a larger coin **(c)** money given back by the seller, when the buyer can pay only with a larger note or coin than the amount asked; *he gave me the wrong change; you paid the £5.75 bill with a £10 note, so you should have £4.25 change;* **keep the change** = keep it as a tip (said to waiters, etc.) **2** *verb* **(a)** **to change a £10 note** = to give change in smaller notes or coins for a £10 note **(b)** to give one type of currency for another; *to change £1,000 into dollars; we want to change some traveller's cheques* **(c)** **to change hands** = to be sold to a new owner; *the shop changed hands for £100,000*

channel ['tʃænl] **1** *noun* way in which information or goods are passed from one place to another; **to go through the official channels** = to deal with government officials (especially when making a request); **channels of communication** or **channels of information** = ways in which information can be passed (post, telephone, fax, the Internet, newspapers, TV, etc.); **to open up new channels of communication** = to find new ways of communicating with someone; **distribution channels** or **channels of distribution** = ways of sending goods from the manufacturer for sale by retailers **2** *verb* to send in a certain direction; *they are channelling their research funds into developing European communication systems*

character ['kærəktə] *noun* **(a)** general nature or qualities of a person, which make that person different from others; *the* secretary needs an easy-going character to work in this office; **to give someone a character reference** = to say that someone has good personal qualities **(b)** strong will or decisiveness; a post needing character and a willingness to work hard

charge [tʃɑːdʒ] **1** noun **(a)** money which must be paid or price of a service; to make no charge for delivery; to make a small charge for rental; there is no charge for service or no charge is made for service; **admission charge** or **entry charge** = price to be paid before going into an exhibition, etc.; **bank charges** or US **service charge** = charges made by a bank for carrying out work for a customer; **handling charge** = money to be paid for packing or invoicing or dealing with goods which are being shipped; **solicitors' charges** = payments to be made to solicitors for work done on behalf of clients; **scale of charges** = list showing various prices; **free of charge** = free or with no payment to be made **(b) charge on land** or **charge over property** = mortgage or liability on a property which has been used as security for a loan; **fixed charge** = charge over a particular asset or property; **floating charge** = charge over changing assets of a business; **charge by way of legal mortgage** = way of borrowing money on the security of a property, where the mortgagor signs a deed which gives the mortgagee an interest in the property **(c)** management or control; **to take charge of something** = to start to deal with something or to become responsible for something; when the manager was ill, his deputy took charge of the department; **to be in charge of something** = to be the manager or to deal with something; she is in charge of all our personnel documentation **(d)** official statement in a court accusing someone of having committed a crime; he appeared in court on a charge of embezzling or on an embezzlement charge; the clerk of the court read out the charges; the charges against him were **withdrawn** or **dropped** = the prosecution decided not to continue with the trial; **to press charges against someone** = to say formally that someone has committed a crime; he was furious when his neighbour's son set fire to his car, but decided not to press charges **2** verb **(a)** to ask someone to pay for services; to ask for money to be paid; to charge £5 for delivery; how much does he charge?; **he charges £6 an hour** = he asks to be paid £6 for an hour's work **(b)** (in a court) to accuse someone

formally of having committed a crime; he was charged with embezzling his clients' money; they were charged with murder (NOTE: you charge someone **with** a crime) **(c)** to pay for something by putting it on an account; reps charge their hotel expenses to the company's account

◊ **chargeable** ['tʃɑːdʒəbl] adjective which can be charged

◊ **chargehand** ['tʃɑːdʒhænd] noun senior operator in a group of workers under a foreman who has responsibility for seeing that day-to-day problems are solved

chart [tʃɑːt] noun diagram showing information as a series of lines or blocks, etc.; this chart shows annual salary increases over five years; the personnel department has a chart recording workers' absences; **bar chart** = diagram where quantities and values are shown as thick columns of different heights or lengths; **flip chart** = way of showing information to a group of people by writing on large sheets of paper which can then be turned over to show the next sheet; **flow chart** = diagram showing the arrangement of various work processes in a series; **organization chart** = diagram showing how a company or an office is organized; **pie chart** = diagram where information is shown as a circle cut up into sections of different sizes; **sales chart** = diagram showing how sales vary from month to month

charter ['tʃɑːtə] noun document giving special legal rights to a group; a shoppers' charter or a customers' charter

◊ **chartered** ['tʃɑːtəd] adjective **chartered accountant** = accountant who has passed the professional examinations and is a member of the Institute of Chartered Accountants

cheap [tʃiːp] adjective & adverb not costing a lot of money or not expensive; **cheap labour** = workforce which does not earn much money; cheap labour is being recruited to reduce costs; cheap labour proved unprofitable in the long run, since the workers did not have the right skills; we have opened a factory in the Far East to take advantage of the cheap labour or because labour is cheap; **cheap money** = money which can be borrowed at low interest

◊ **cheaply** ['tʃiːpli] adverb without paying

much money; *the salesman was living cheaply at home and claiming an enormous hotel bill on expenses*

◊ **cheapness** ['tʃiːpnəs] *noun* being cheap; *the cheapness of the pound means that many more tourists will come to London*

check [tʃek] **1** *noun* **(a)** sudden stop; **to put a check on imports** = to stop some imports **(b)** examination *or* act of verifying if something is correct; *the auditors carried out checks on the petty cash book; a routine check of the fire equipment;* **check sample** = sample to be used to see if a consignment is acceptable; **check time** = time recorded between the start of a work study and the start of the first element observed, plus the time recorded between the last element observed and the end of the study **(c)** *US* = CHEQUE **2** *verb* **(a)** to stop *or* to delay; *to check the entry of contraband into the country* **(b)** to examine *or* to investigate; *to check that an invoice is correct; to check and sign for goods;* **he checked the computer printout against the invoices** = he examined the printout and the invoices to see if the figures were the same

◊ **checking** ['tʃekɪŋ] *noun* **(a)** examination *or* investigation; *the inspectors found some defects during their checking of the building* **(b)** *US* **checking account** = bank account which allows the customer to write cheques (NOTE: no plural)

◊ **checklist** ['tʃeklɪst] *noun* list of points which have to be checked before something can be done (such as a list of points to be discussed with a new employee, practical matters such as the fire regulations, or financial matters, such as the company pension plan)

◊ **checkoff** ['tʃekɒf] *noun* system where union dues are automatically deducted by the employer from a worker's paycheck; *checkoffs are seen by most employees as worthwhile as long as their interests are well represented by the union; after checkoffs and tax deductions the workers' pay had been reduced by one third*

◊ **checkup** ['tʃekʌp] *noun* medical examination; *all staff have to have regular checkups*

cheque *or US* **check** [tʃek] *noun* note to a bank asking them to pay money from your account to the account of the person whose name is written on the note; *a cheque for £10 or a £10 cheque;* **cheque account** = bank account which allows the customer to write cheques; **cheque to bearer** = cheque with no name written on it, so that the person who holds it can cash it; **crossed cheque** = cheque with two lines across it showing that it can only be deposited at a bank and not exchanged for cash; **open** *or* **uncrossed cheque** = cheque which can be cashed anywhere; **blank cheque** = cheque with the amount of money and the payee left blank, but signed by the drawer; **pay cheque** *or* **salary cheque** = monthly cheque by which an employee is paid; **traveller's cheques** = cheques taken by a traveller, which can be cashed in a foreign country; **dud cheque** *or* **bouncing cheque** *or* **cheque which bounces** *or* *US* **rubber check** = cheque which cannot be cashed because the person writing it has not enough money in the account to pay it **(b) to cash a cheque** = to exchange a cheque for cash; **to endorse a cheque** = to sign a cheque on the back to show that you accept it; **to make out a cheque to someone** = to write someone's name on a cheque; *who shall I make the cheque out to?;* **to pay by cheque** = to pay by writing a cheque, and not using cash or a credit card; **to pay a cheque into your account** = to deposit a cheque; **the bank referred the cheque to drawer** = returned the cheque to the person who wrote it because there was not enough money in the account to pay it; **to sign a cheque** = to sign on the front of a cheque to show that you authorize the bank to pay the money from your account; **to stop a cheque** = to ask a bank not to pay a cheque which you have written

◊ **cheque book** *or US* **checkbook** ['tʃekbʊk] *noun* booklet with new cheques

chief [tʃiːf] *adjective* most important; *he is the chief accountant of an industrial group;* **chief executive** *or US* **chief executive officer (CEO)** = most important director in charge of a company

chilling effect ['tʃɪlɪŋ ɪ'fekt] *noun* negative effect on workers of regulations *or* practices that limit their freedom and opportunities; *the chilling effect of punctuality checks; too many restrictions have a chilling effect which is counterproductive*

Chinese walls ['tʃaɪniːz 'wɔːlz] *noun*

imaginary barriers between departments in the same organization, set up to avoid insider dealing or conflict of interest (as when a merchant bank is advising on a planned takeover bid, its investment department should not know that the bid is taking place, or they would advise their clients to invest in the company being taken over)

choice [tʃɔɪs] 1 *noun* (a) thing which is chosen; *you must give the customer time to make his choice* (b) range of items to choose from; *we have only a limited choice of suppliers;* the shop carries a good choice of paper = the shop carries many types of paper to choose from 2 *adjective* specially selected (food); *choice meat; choice wines; choice foodstuffs*

choose [tʃuːz] *verb* to decide to do a particular thing *or* to buy a particular item (as opposed to something else); *there were several good candidates to choose from; they chose the only woman applicant as sales director; you must give the customers plenty of time to choose* (NOTE: **choosing - chose - chosen**)

chose in action ['tʃəʊz ɪn 'ækʃn] *noun* legal term for a personal right which can be enforced or claimed as if it were property (such as a patent *or* copyright *or* debt)

Christmas ['krɪsməs] *noun* Christian holiday celebrated on 25th December; *the office closes for ten days at Christmas; we have allocated £50 for organizing the office Christmas party;* **Christmas bonus** = extra payment paid to staff at Christmas

chronological order [krɒnə'lɒdʒɪkəl 'ɔːdə] *noun* arrangement of records (files, invoices, etc.) in order of their date

circadian rhythms [sɜː'keɪdiən 'rɪðəmz] *noun* (a) rhythm of daily activities and bodily processes (eating *or* defecating *or* sleeping, etc.) frequently controlled by hormones, which repeats every twenty-four hours (b) biorhythms, recurring cycles of different lengths which some people believe affect a person's behaviour, sensitivity and intelligence

circular ['sɜːkjʊlə] 1 *adjective* sent to many people; **circular letter of credit** = letter of credit sent to all branches of the

bank which issues it 2 *noun* leaflet *or* letter sent to many people; *senior management sent out a circular to all the employees explaining the changes in the payment scheme*

◊ **circularize** ['sɜːkjʊləraɪz] *verb* to send a circular to; *the committee has agreed to circularize the members; they circularized all their customers with a new list of prices*

◊ **circulate** ['sɜːkjʊleɪt] *verb* to send information to; *they circulated information about job vacancies to all colleges in the area*

◊ **circulation** [sɜːkjʊ'leɪʃən] *noun* (a) movement; *the company is trying to improve the circulation of information amongst departments* (b) *(of newspapers)* number of copies sold; *the audited circulation of a newspaper; the new editor of the house journal hopes to improve the circulation*

CIRO = CONTEXT, INPUT, REACTION, OUTCOME **Ciro method** = method of assessing the value of a training programme under these four headings

civil ['sɪvl] *adjective* referring to ordinary people; **civil action** = court case brought by a person *or* a company against someone who has done them wrong; **civil law** = laws relating to people's rights and duties, and agreements between individuals; **civil rights** = rights and privileges of each individual person according to the law

◊ **civil servant** ['sɪvl 'sɜːvənt] *noun* person who works in the civil service

◊ **civil service** ['sɪvl 'sɜːvɪs] *noun* organization and personnel which administer a country; *you have to pass an examination to get a job in the civil service or to get a civil service job*

claim [kleɪm] 1 *noun* (a) asking for money; **wage claim** = asking for an increase in wages; **the union put in a 6% wage claim** = the union asked for a 6% increase in wages for its members (b) **legal claim** = statement that you think you own something legally; *he has no legal claim to the property;* **to file a claim** *or* **to lodge a claim against someone** = to make an official claim against someone (c) **insurance claim** = asking an insurance company to pay for damages *or* for loss; **claims department** = department of an insurance company which deals with claims; **claim form** = form to be filled in when making an insurance claim; **claims**

manager = manager of a claims department; **no claims bonus** = lower premium paid because no claims have been made against the insurance policy; **to put in a claim** = to ask the insurance company officially to pay damages; *to put in a claim for repairs to the car; she put in a claim for £250,000 damages against the driver of the other car;* **to settle a claim** = to agree to pay what is asked for; *the insurance company refused to settle his claim for storm damage* (d) **small claims court** = court which deals with claims for small amounts of money **2** *verb* (a) to ask for money; *he claimed £100,000 damages against the cleaning firm; she claimed for repairs to the car against her insurance policy* (b) to say that something is your property; *he is claiming possession of the house; no one claimed the umbrella found in my office* (c) to state that something is a fact; *he claims he never received the goods; she claims that the shares are her property*

◊ **claimant** ['kleɪmənt] *noun* person who claims; **rightful claimant** = person who has a legal claim to something

◊ **claim back** ['kleɪm 'bæk] *verb* to ask for money to be paid back

◊ **claimer** ['kleɪmə] *noun* = CLAIMANT

◊ **claiming** ['kleɪmɪŋ] *noun* act of making a claim

class [klɑːs] *noun* (a) category *or* group into which things are classified; *(National Insurance contributions)* **Class 1 NI contributions** = contributions paid by an employee; **Class 2 NI contributions** = contributions paid by a self-employed person at a flat rate; **Class 3 NI contributions** = voluntary contributions paid by someone who is not earning enough to pay Class 1 contributions and is not self-employed; **Class 4 NI contributions** = contributions paid by a self-employed person whose earnings are higher than for Class 2 contributions (Class 4 contributions are a percentage of profits, not a flat fee) (b) category *or* group into which things are classified according to quality or price; **first-class** = top quality *or* most expensive; *he is a first-class accountant;* **economy class** *or* **tourist class** = lower quality *or* less expensive way of travelling; *I travel economy class because it is cheaper; tourist class travel is less comfortable than first class; he always travels first class because tourist class is too*

uncomfortable GB **first-class mail** = more expensive mail service, designed to be faster; *a first-class letter should get to Scotland in a day;* **second-class mail** = less expensive, slower mail service; *the letter took three days to arrive because he sent it second class* (c) *US* **class action** *or* **class suit** = legal action brought on behalf of a group of people (d) group of students; **evening classes** = courses of study, usually for adults, organized in the evenings

classify ['klæsɪfaɪ] *verb* to put into classes *or* categories according to certain characteristics; *the employees are classified into five groups according to their qualifications;* **classified advertisements** = advertisements listed in a newspaper under special headings (such as 'property for sale' *or* 'jobs wanted'); **classified directory** = book which lists businesses grouped under various headings (such as computer shops *or* newsagents)

◊ **classification** [klæsɪfɪ'keɪʃən] *noun* arrangement into groups; *the classification of employees by ages or skills; jobs in this organization fall into several classifications;* **job classification** = describing jobs listed in various groups

clause [klɔːz] *noun* section of a contract; *there are ten clauses in the contract of employment; according to clause six, payment will not be due until next year; there is a clause in this contract concerning the employer's right to dismiss an employee;* **exclusion clause** = clause in an insurance policy *or* contract which says which items are not covered by the policy *or* gives details of circumstances where the insurance company will refuse to pay; **no-strike clause** = clause in a contract where the workers promise never to strike; **penalty clause** = clause which lists the penalties which will be imposed if the terms of the contract are not fulfilled; **termination clause** = clause which explains how and when a contract can be terminated

clear [klɪə] *verb* **to clear one's desk** = to remove personal belongings from one's desk when leaving a job; *he was given five minutes to clear his desk*

clerical ['klerɪkəl] *adjective* (work) done in an office *or* done by a clerk; *we have several clerical posts vacant; some of our clerical workers were originally typists; experience* *of bookkeeping is required for this clerical post;* **clerical error** = mistake made in an office; **clerical staff** = staff of an office; **clerical work** = paperwork done in an office; **clerical worker** = person who works in an office

clerk [klɑːk *US* klɜːk] **1** *noun* **(a)** person who does routine work in an office; *two of the clerks are studying accountancy at evening classes in order to move into management;* **articled clerk** = clerk who is bound by a contract to work in a lawyer's office for some years to learn the profession; **chief clerk** *or* **head clerk** = most important clerk; **filing clerk** = clerk who files documents; **invoice clerk** = clerk who deals with invoices; **payroll clerk** *or* **wages clerk** = person who administers the payment of wages and salaries to employees **(b) bank clerk** = person who works in a bank; **booking clerk** = person who works in a booking office; *US* **sales clerk** = person who sells in a store **2** *verb US* to work as a clerk

◊ **clerkess** [klɑːˈkes] *noun (in Scotland)* woman clerk

clock [klɒk] *noun* machine which shows the time; *the office clock is fast; the micro has a built-in clock;* **digital clock** = clock which shows the time using numbers (as 12:05)

◊ **clock card** [ˈklɒk ˈkɑːd] *noun* special card which a worker puts into the time clock when clocking on or off

◊ **clock in** *or* **clock on** [ˈklɒk ˈɪn *or* ˈklɒk ˈɒn] *verb (of worker)* to record the time of arriving for work by putting a card into a special timing machine; *if workers do not clock in on arrival at the factory, they may be sent a written warning*

◊ **clock out** *or* **clock off** [ˈklɒk ˈaʊt *or* ˈklɒk ˈɒf] *verb (of worker)* to record the time of leaving work by putting a card into a special timing machine

◊ **clocking in** *or* **clocking on** [ˈklɒkɪŋ ˈɪn *or* ˈklɒkɪŋ ˈɒn] *noun* arriving for work and recording the time on a time-card

◊ **clocking out** *or* **clocking off** [ˈklɒkɪŋ ˈaʊt *or* ˈklɒkɪŋ ˈɒf] *noun* leaving work and recording the time on a time-card

close 1 [kləʊz] *noun* end; *at the close of the day's trading the shares had fallen 20%*

(NOTE: no plural) **2** [kləʊs] *adjective* **close to** = very near *or* almost; *the company was close to bankruptcy; we are close to meeting our sales targets* **3** [kləʊz] *verb* to end **(a)** to stop doing business for the day; *the office closes at 5.30; we close early on Saturdays (of a chairman)* **to close a meeting** = to end a meeting formally **(b) to close the accounts** = to come to the end of an accounting period and make up the profit and loss account **(c) to close an account** = (i) to stop supplying a customer on credit; (ii) to take all the money out of a bank account and stop the account; *he closed his building society account* = he took all the money out and stopped using the account **(d) the shares closed at $15** = at the end of the day's trading the price of the shares was $15

◊ **close company** *or* ◊ *US* **close(d) corporation** [ˈkləʊs ˈkʌmpənɪ *or* ˈkləʊs kɔːpəˈreɪʃən *or* ˈkləʊzd kɔːpəˈreɪʃən] *noun* privately owned company where the public may own a small number of shares

◊ **closed** [kləʊzd] *adjective* **(a)** shut *or* not open *or* not doing business; *the office is closed on Mondays; all the banks are closed on Christmas Day* **(b)** restricted; **closed circuit television (CCTV)** = television system, where images are sent by cable to a limited series of screens only; **closed interview** = interview where the interviewer asks only fixed questions with 'yes' or 'no' answers; **closed system** = work system which is inflexible and does not allow the workers much freedom to work in their own way (NOTE: the opposite is **open system**) **closed shop** = system where an organization agrees to employ only union members in certain occupations *or* at certain places of work; *a closed shop agreement; the union is asking the management to agree to a closed shop; some of the staff consider a closed shop will make the union too powerful*

| COMMENT: closed shops are illegal in many countries

◊ **close down** [ˈkləʊz ˈdaʊn] *verb* to shut a shop *or* factory for a long period or for ever; *the company is closing down its London office; the strike closed down the railway system*

◊ **closing** [ˈkləʊzɪŋ] **1** *adjective* **(a)** final *or* coming at the end; **closing bid** = last bid at an auction *or* the bid which is successful; **closing date** = last date; *the closing date for* *tenders to be received is May 1st;* **closing price** = price of a share at the end of a day's trading **(b)** at the end of an accounting period; *closing balance; closing stock* **2** *noun* **(a)** shutting of a shop *or* being shut; **Sunday closing** = not opening a shop on Sundays; **closing time** = time when a shop or office stops work; **early closing day** = weekday (usually Wednesday or Thursday) when many shops close in the afternoon **(b) closing of an account** = act of stopping supply to a customer on credit

◊ **closing down sale** ['kləʊzɪŋ daʊn 'seɪl] *noun* sale of goods when a shop is closing for ever

◊ **closing out** ['kləʊzɪŋ 'aʊt] *noun US* selling goods cheaply to try to get rid of them

◊ **closure** ['kləʊʒə] *noun* act of closing

clothing ['kləʊðɪŋ] *noun* clothes which a person wears; *the company provides special clothing for its employees;* **clothing allowance** = money paid to an employee to buy special clothes to wear at work; **protective clothing** = clothes which protect the worker from heat, radiation, etc.

club [klʌb] **1** *noun* group of people who have the same interest; place where these people meet; *if you want the managing director, you can phone him at his club; he has applied to join the sports club;* **club membership** = all the members of a club; **club subscription** = money paid to belong to a club; **staff club** = club for the staff of a company, which organizes staff parties, sports and meetings **2** *verb* **to club together** = to give money each for a special purpose; *they clubbed together to buy the manager a wedding present*

cluster ['klʌstə] *noun* group of things or people taken together

co- [kəʊ] *prefix* working *or* acting together

◊ **co-creditor** [kəʊ'kredɪtə] *noun* person who is a creditor of the same company as you are

◊ **co-director** [kəʊdɪ'rektə] *noun* person who is a director of the same company as you

◊ **co-insurance** [kəʊɪn'ʃʊərəns] *noun* insurance policy where the risk is shared among several insurers

coaching ['kəʊtʃɪŋ] *noun* face-to-face instruction where a subordinate is shown how to change his or her behaviour; *the personnel manager found coaching useful in dealing with workers needing a more tactful approach when attempting to change their attitude; in our company coaching has made management more aware of workers' attitudes*

code [kəʊd] *noun* **(a)** system of signs *or* numbers *or* letters which mean something; **area code** = numbers which indicate an area for telephoning; *what is the code for Edinburgh?;* **bar code** = system of lines printed on a product which can be read by a computer to give a reference number or price; **international dialling code** = numbers used for dialling to another country; **machine-readable codes** = sets of signs or letters (such as bar codes *or* post codes) which can be read by computers; **post code** *or US* **zip code** = letters and numbers used to indicate a town or street in an address on an envelope; **stock code** = numbers and letters which refer to an item of stock **(b)** set of rules; **code of conduct** = guideline showing how someone (such as shop assistants, railway station staff, etc.) should behave towards customers; **code of practice** *or* **code of ethics** = guidelines on correct behaviour drawn up by a group *or* profession for its members; *the Institute of Personnel Management's code of ethics gives some guidance on how to deal with redundancy*

◊ **coding** ['kəʊdɪŋ] *noun* act of putting a code on something; *the coding of invoices*

co-determination [kəʊdɪtɜːmɪ'neɪʃn] *noun* system where a certain percentage of representatives of the workers must be part of the supervisory board of a company (used in Germany and some other countries)

coercion [kəʊ'ɜːʃn] *noun* forcing someone to do something

coffee break ['kɒfi 'breɪk] *noun* rest time during work when workers can have a cup of coffee

cognition [kɒg'nɪʃn] *noun* thinking processes

◊ **cognitive** ['kɒgnɪtɪv] *adjective* relating to thinking processes; **cognitive dissonance** = conflicts and contradictions and feelings of dissatisfaction experienced by a person who cannot reconcile apparently contradictory information; *clear signs of cognitive dissonance emerged from the applicant's personality test*

cohort ['kəʊhɔːt] *noun* group of people who do the same thing at the same time (such as a group of managers who joined a company as trainees together)

cold [kəʊld] *adjective* (a) not hot; *the machines work badly in cold weather; the office was so cold that the staff started complaining; the coffee machine also sells cold drinks* (b) without being prepared; **cold call** = sales call where the salesman has no appointment and the client is not an established customer; **cold start** = starting a new business *or* opening a new shop where there was none before

◊ **cold storage training** [kəʊld 'stɔːrɪdʒ 'treɪnɪŋ] *noun* training of employees for jobs that will be created in the future; *cold storage training was set up in the company based on forecasts of future increases in productivity; start your cold storage training in good time so that you have the skilled manpower available when you need it*

collaborate [kə'læbəreɪt] *verb* to work together; *to collaborate with a French firm on a building project; they collaborated on the new aircraft* (NOTE: you collaborate **with** someone **on** something)

◊ **collaboration** [kəlæbə'reɪʃən] *noun* working together; *their collaboration on the project was very profitable*

◊ **collaborator** [kə'læbəreɪtə] *noun* person who works together with someone on a project

collapse [kə'læps] **1** *noun* (a) sudden failure; *the collapse of the pay negotiations* (b) sudden failure of a company; *investors lost thousands of pounds in the collapse of the company* **2** *verb* to fail suddenly; *talks between management and unions collapsed last night*

collar ['kɒlə] *noun* part of a coat *or* shirt which goes round the neck; **blue-collar worker** = manual worker in a factory; **white-collar worker** = office worker; **he has a white-collar job** = he works in an office

colleague ['kɒliːg] *noun* person who does

the same type of work as another; person who works in the same organization as another; *she was unpopular with her colleagues in the machine room; he asked his colleagues for advice*

collect [kə'lekt] **1** *verb* (a) to make someone pay money which is owed; **to collect a debt** = to go and make someone pay a debt (b) to take things away from a place; *we have to collect the stock from the warehouse; can you collect my letters from the typing pool?*; **letters are collected twice a day** = the post office workers take them from the letter box to the post office for dispatch **2** *adverb & adjective US* (phone call) where the person receiving the call agrees to pay for it; *to make a collect call; he called his office collect*

◊ **collecting agency** [kə'lektɪŋ 'eɪdʒənsi] *noun* agency which collects money owed to other companies for a commission

◊ **collection** [kə'lekʃən] *noun* (a) getting money together *or* making someone pay money which is owed; *tax collection or collection of tax;* **debt collection** = collecting money which is owed; **debt collection agency** = company which collects debts for other companies for a commission; **bills for collection** = bills where payment is due (b) fetching of goods; *the stock is in the warehouse awaiting collection;* **collection charges** *or* **collection rates** = charge for collecting something; **to hand something in for collection** = to leave something for someone to come and collect (c) **collections** = money which has been collected (d) taking of letter from a letter box or mail room to the post office for dispatch; *there are six collections a day from the letter box*

◊ **collective** [kə'lektɪv] *adjective* referring to a group of people together; **collective agreement** = agreement on salaries, working conditions, etc., negotiated through collective bargaining; **they signed a collective wage agreement** = an agreement was signed between management and the trade union about wages; **(free) collective bargaining** = negotiations about wage increases and working conditions between management and representatives of the workers; **collective ownership** = ownership of a business by the workers who work in it; **collective relations** = relations between employers associations and trade unions; *the sudden wave of strikes shows that collective bargaining is not working; the* *government has put through legislation to make collective bargaining easier*

collectivism [kə'lektıvızm] *noun* system where the individual has to give up some rights to the group of which he is a member, in return for support and protection from the group

college ['kɒlıdʒ] *noun* place where people can study after they have left full-time school; **business college** *or* **commercial college** = college which teaches general business methods; **secretarial college** = college which teaches shorthand, typing and word-processing

command [kə'mɑːnd] *noun* **she has a good command of German** = she speaks and writes German well

commission [kə'mıʃən] *noun* **(a)** money paid to a salesman *or* an agent, usually a percentage of the sales made; *he is paid on a commission basis; she gets 10% commission on everything she sells;* **he charges 10% commission** = he asks for 10% of sales as his payment; **commission agent** = agent who is paid a percentage of sales; **commission rep** = representative who is not paid a salary, but receives a commission on sales; **commission sale** *or* **sale on commission** = sale where the salesman is paid a commission **(b)** group of people officially appointed to examine some problem; *the government has appointed a commission of inquiry to look into the problems of small exporters; he is the chairman of the government commission on export subsidies;* **fact-finding commission** = committee set up by a third party to carry out an impartial review of issues in a labour dispute; *a fact-finding commission was set up to look into the reasons for the pay dispute;* **joint commission** = group with equal numbers of members from two or more groups; *they set up a joint management/union commission;* **the Commission for Racial Equality (CRE)** = statutory body set up to monitor racial matters in companies, and to issue guidelines on best practice

◊ **commissioner** [kə'mıʃənə] *noun* ombudsman; **the Parliamentary Commissioner for Administration** = the Ombudsman, the official who investigates complaints by the public against government departments; **the Local Commissioners** = the Local Government Ombudsmen, officials who investigate complaints against local authorities

commit [kə'mıt] *verb* **(a)** to carry out (a crime) **(b)** to agree to do something; *management is committed to improving working conditions;* **to commit funds to a project** = to agree to spend money on a project; **to commit yourself** = to state publicly that you will do something; *the MD refused to commit himself on the question of redundancies* (NOTE: **committing - committed**)

◊ **commitment** [kə'mıtmənt] *noun* **(a)** thing which you have agreed to do; *to make a commitment or to enter into a commitment to do something* **(b)** **commitments** = things which you have agreed to do, especially money which you have agreed to spend; **to meet one's commitments** = to pay money which you had agreed to pay

committee [kə'mıti] *noun* official group of people formally appointed to assume a particular responsibility on behalf of a larger group; *a committee of workers' representatives or a workers' committee; to be a member of a committee or to sit on a committee; he is chairman of the shop stewards committee; she was elected to the committee of the staff club; the new plans have to be approved by the committee members; the workers' committee meets management every week to air the views of the shop floor; a committee was formed to see the new payment system through;* **to chair a committee** = to be the chairman of a committee; *he is the chairman of the planning committee; she is the secretary of the finance committee;* **ad hoc committee** = temporary committee set up to study a particular problem; **management committee** = committee which manages a club *or* a pension fund, etc.; **standing committee** = permanent committee which deals with matters not given to other committees; **works committee** = committee of workers and management which discusses the organization of work in a factory

common ['kɒmən] *adjective* **(a)** which happens very often; *putting the carbon paper in the wrong way round is a common mistake; being caught by the customs is very common these days* **(b)** belonging to several different people or to everyone; **common carrier** = firm which carries goods or passengers, and which anyone can use; **common ownership** = ownership of a company *or* a property by a group of people; **common pricing** = illegal fixing of prices by several businesses so that they all charge the same price; *US* **common stock** = ordinary shares in a company, giving shareholders a right to vote at meetings and to receive dividends; *(in the EU)* **Common Agricultural Policy** = agreement between members of the EU to protect farmers by paying subsidies to fix prices of farm produce

◊ **common law** ['kɒmən 'lɔː] *noun* **(a)** law as laid down in decisions of courts, rather than by statute **(b)** general system of laws which were developed from custom and precedent, and which formerly were the only laws existing in England

communicate [kə'mjuːnɪkeɪt] *verb* to exchange views *or* information with someone; *he finds it impossible to communicate with his staff; communicating with head office has been quicker since we installed the telex*

◊ **communication** [kəmjuːnɪ'keɪʃən] *noun* **(a)** passing of views *or* information; *lack of communication between management and workers; communication with the head office has been made easier by the telex; communication between management and workforce is at an all-time low; a house journal was started to improve communication;* a **breakdown** of **communications** = time when people do not communicate with each other; *there has been a breakdown of communications between management and shopfloor workers;* **channels of communication** = ways in which information can be passed (post, telephone, fax, the Internet, newspapers, TV, etc.); **to open up new channels of communication** = to find new ways of communicating with someone; **to enter into communication with someone** = to start discussing something with someone, usually in writing; *we have entered into communication with the relevant government department;* **employee communication(s)** *or* **communication with employees** = passing information to employees and receiving information from employees **(b)** official message; *we have had a communication from the local tax inspector* **(c)** **communications** = being able to contact people *or* to pass messages; *after*

the flood all communications with the outside world were broken

◊ **communicative** [kə'mjuːnɪkətɪv] *adjective* (person) who can communicate easily with others

QUOTE that kind of approach will require a new style of communication, both upwards and downwards, throughout the organization

QUOTE it has a forward-looking and communicative management team
Personnel Management

commute [kə'mjuːt] *verb* **(a)** to travel to work from home each day; *he commutes from the country to his office in the centre of town; she spends two hours a day commuting to and from work; he has bought a house within commuting distance of London* **(b)** to exchange one form of payment for another; *he decided to commute part of his pension rights into a lump sum payment*

◊ **commutation** [kɒmjʊ'teɪʃn] *noun* exchanging something for money in another form; **commutation of pension rights** = taking a lump sum instead of a pension

◊ **commuter** [kə'mjuːtə] *noun* person who commutes to work; **he lives in the commuter belt** = area of country where the commuters live round a town; **commuter train** = train which commuters take in the morning and evening

company ['kʌmpəni] *noun* **(a)** legal organization of people for business purposes, to buy, sell or provide a service; **to put a company into liquidation** = to close a company by selling its assets for cash; **to set up a company** = to start a company legally; **associate company** = company which is partly owned by another company; **family company** = company where most of the shares are owned by members of a family; **holding company** = company which exists only to own shares in subsidiary companies; **joint-stock company** = company whose shares are held by many people; **limited (liability) company** = company where a shareholder is responsible for repaying the company's debts only to the face value of the shares he owns; **listed company** = company whose shares can be bought or sold on the Stock Exchange; **parent company** = company which owns more than half of another company's shares; **private (limited) company** = company with a small number of shareholders, whose shares are not traded on the Stock Exchange; **public limited company (plc)** = company whose shares can be bought on the Stock Exchange; **subsidiary company** = company which is owned by a parent company **(b) finance company** = company which provides money for hire-purchase; **insurance company** = company whose business is insurance; **shipping company** = company whose business is transporting goods; **a tractor** *or* **aircraft** *or* **chocolate company** = company which makes tractors *or* aircraft *or* chocolate **(c) company car** = car which belongs to a company and is lent to an employee to make use of as if it were his or her own; **company doctor** = (i) doctor who works for a company and looks after sick workers; (ii) specialist businessman who rescues companies which are in difficulties; **company director** = person appointed by the shareholders to help run a company; **company flat** = flat belonging to a company and used by executives or visiting guests; **company handbook** = booklet containing information about the company's structure, employees' rights, grievance procedure, etc.; **company law** = laws which refer to the way companies may work; **company newspaper** = regular new bulletin, published by a company, to keep the workforce informed about recent developments within the company; **company secretary** = person responsible for the company's legal and financial affairs; **company town** = town in which most of the property and shops are owned by a large company which employs most of the population; **company union** = association of workers in a single business company; *GB* **the Companies Acts** = Acts of Parliament which regulate the workings of companies, stating the legal limits within which companies may do their business; **Companies Registration Office (CRO)** *or* **Companies House** = official organization where the records of companies must be deposited, so that they can be inspected by the public

COMMENT: a company can be incorporated (with memorandum and articles of association) as a private limited company, and adds the initials 'Ltd' after its name, or as a public limited company, when its name must end in 'Plc'. Unincorporated companies are partnerships such as firms of solicitors, architects, accountants, etc. and they add the initials Co. after their name

◊ **company-wide** ['kʌmpni 'waɪd] *adjective* affecting all the employees in a company; *we are introducing a company-wide bonus system*

compare [kəm'peə] *verb* to look at several things to see how they differ; *the finance director compared the figures for the first and second quarters*

◊ **compare with** [kəm'peə 'wɪð] *verb* to put two things together to see how they differ; *how do the sales this year compare with last year's? compared with 1982, last year was a boom year*

◊ **comparable** ['kɒmpərəbl] *adjective* which can be compared; *the two sets of figures are not comparable;* **which is the nearest company comparable to this one in size?** = which company is of a similar size and can be compared with this one?; **comparable worth** = principle of paying the same rate for jobs which are worth the same; *comparable worth is difficult to apply to jobs of very diverse character; the salary scale is drawn up on the principle of comparable worth*

◊ **comparability** [kəmpærə'bɪləti] *noun* being able to be compared; **comparability claim** = claim by workers to bring their wages and fringe benefits into line with those in other industries; **pay comparability** = similar pay system in two different companies

◊ **comparison** [kəm'pærɪsn] *noun* way of comparing; *sales are down in comparison with last year;* **there is no comparison between overseas and home sales** = overseas and home sales are so different they cannot be compared

compassionate leave [kəm'pæʃənət] *noun* time off work granted to an employee to deal with personal *or* family problems; *the staff have been told that compassionate leave will only be granted in extreme cases, such as a death in the family; I have been granted compassionate leave to visit a sick relative*

compatible [kəm'pætɪbl] *adjective* which can exist *or* function together; *it soon* *became clear that the new member of staff was not compatible with his colleagues; are the objectives of senior management and the interests of the workers compatible?*

◊ **compatibility** [kəmpærə'bılıti] *noun* ability of persons to work together; *the compatibility of employees sharing an office*

compensate ['kɒmpenseıt] *verb* to give someone something to make up for a loss *or* damage done; *to compensate a manager for loss of commission; the company will compensate the worker for the burns he suffered in the accident* (NOTE: you compensate someone **for** something)

◊ **compensation** [kɒmpen'seıʃən] *noun* (a) **compensation for damage** = payment for damage done; **compensation for loss of office** = payment to a director who is asked to leave a company before his contract ends; **compensation for loss of earnings** = payment to someone who has stopped earning money *or* who is not able to earn money (b) *US* salary; **indirect compensation** = non-financial benefit given by a company to employees (such as sports facilities, a company car, health insurance, etc.); **compensation package** = salary, pension and other benefits offered with a job

◊ **compensatory** [kɒmpən'seıtəri] *adjective* which compensates for something; **compensatory award** = award by an industrial tribunal based on what the tribunal considers is just compensation for the employee's loss of pension rights, etc., when dismissed

QUOTE compensation can also be via the magistrates courts for relatively minor injuries
Personnel Management

QUOTE golden parachutes are liberal compensation packages given to executives leaving a company
Publishers Weekly

compete [kəm'piːt] *verb* **to compete with someone** *or* **with a company** = to try to do better than another person *or* another company; *we have to compete with cheap imports from the Far East; they were competing unsuccessfully with local companies on their home territory;* **the two companies are competing for a market share** *or* **for a contract** = each company is trying to win a larger part of the market *or* to win the contract

◊ **competing** [kəm'piːtıŋ] *adjective* which competes; **competing firms** = firms which compete with each other; **competing products** = products from different companies which have the same use and are sold in the same markets at similar prices

competence ['kɒmpətəns] *noun* (a) being efficient; *the training sessions are intended to increase staff competence* (b) **the case falls within the competence of the court** = the court is legally able to deal with the case

◊ **competency** ['kɒmpıtənsi] *noun* ability to do tasks required in a job; **competency statement** = list of qualities which a worker needs to do his work

◊ **competent** ['kɒmpətənt] *adjective* (a) able to do something *or* efficient; *she is a competent secretary or a competent manager; though he is a competent engineer he has no ambition; she is competent enough to do the work of two secretaries* (b) **the court is not competent to deal with this case** = the court is not legally able to deal with the case

QUOTE the area of competence of an occupation is defined as the field of competence required to conduct the associated tasks
Employment Gazette

competition [kɒmpə'tıʃən] *noun* (a) trying to do better than another supplier; **free competition** = being free to compete without government interference; **keen competition** = strong competition; *we are facing keen competition from European manufacturers;* **unfair competition** = trying to do better than another company by using techniques such as importing foreign goods at very low prices or by wrongly criticizing a competitor's products (b) **the competition** = companies which are trying to compete with your product; *we have lowered our prices to beat the competition; the competition have brought out a new range of products* (NOTE: singular, but can take a plural verb)

◊ **competitive** [kəm'petıtıv] *adjective* which competes fairly; **competitive edge** = advantage over a rival; *the fully-computerized factory gives us a competitive edge over our rivals;* **competitive exam** = examination (such as for entry to the civil service) where only the best candidates are offered jobs; **competitive price** = low price intended to compete with a rival product; **competitive pricing** = putting low prices on goods so as to compete with other products; **competitive products** = products made to compete with existing products

◊ **competitively** [kəm'petɪtɪvli] *adverb* **competitively priced** = sold at a low price which competes with the price of similar products from other companies

◊ **competitiveness** [kəm'petɪtɪvnəs] *noun* being competitive

◊ **competitor** [kəm'petɪtə] *noun* person *or* company which competes; *two German firms are our main competitors*

> QUOTE sterling labour costs continue to rise between 3% and 5% a year faster than in most of our competitor countries
> **Sunday Times**

complain [kəm'pleɪn] *verb* to say that something is no good *or* does not work properly; *the office is so cold the staff have started complaining; she complained about the service; they are complaining that our prices are too high; if you want to complain, write to the manager*

◊ **complaint** [kəm'pleɪnt] *noun* statement showing dissatisfaction; *complaints from the workforce about conditions in the factory; when making a complaint, always quote the reference number; she sent her letter of complaint to the managing director;* **to make** *or* **lodge a complaint against someone** = to write and send an official complaint to someone's superior; **to uphold a complaint** = to agree that a complaint is well founded; **complaints department** = department which deals with complaints from customers; **complaints procedure** = agreed way for workers to make complaints to the management about working conditions

complete [kəm'pliːt] **1** *adjective* whole *or* with nothing missing **2** *verb* to finish; *he has completed his probationary period; how long will it take you to complete the job?*

◊ **completion** [kəm'pliːʃən] *noun* act of finishing something; **completion date** = date when something will be finished

comply [kəm'plaɪ] *verb* **to comply with the law** = to obey the law; **to comply with a court order** = to obey an order given by a court

◊ **compliance** [kəm'plaɪəns] *noun*

agreement to do what is ordered; **in compliance with** = doing what has been ordered; *in compliance with EU directives on workers' pension rights;* **compliance with company rules** = obeying the rules set out by the company for good behaviour of employees (NOTE: no plural)

comprehensive [kɒmprɪ'hensɪv] *adjective* which includes everything; **comprehensive insurance** = insurance policy which covers you against all possible risks

compressed [kəm'prest] *adjective* **compressed (working) time** = normal number of hours of work spread over fewer days (such as four 10-hour days instead of five 8-hour days); *compressed time is popular because it enables more workers to enjoy long weekend breaks; compressed time will become more common when flexible work hours are accepted by more organizations*

◊ **compression** [kəm'preʃn] *noun* **wage compression** = narrowing the difference between the highest and lowest paid jobs

compromise ['kɒmprəmaɪz] **1** *noun* agreement between two sides, where each side gives way a little; *management offered £5 an hour, the union asked for £9, and a compromise of £7.50 was reached* **2** *verb* to reach an agreement by giving way a little; *he offered £5 per hour, I asked for £10 and we compromised on £7*

compulsory [kəm'pʌlsəri] *adjective* which is forced *or* ordered; **compulsory liquidation** = liquidation which is ordered by a court; **compulsory redundancy** = situation where a worker is made redundant (as opposed to a voluntary redundancy)

computer [kəm'pjuːtə] *noun* electronic machine which calculates *or* stores information and processes it automatically; **computer bureau** = office which offers to do work on its computers for companies which do not have their own computers; **computer department** = department in a company which manages the company's computers; **computer error** = mistake made by a computer; **computer file** = section of information on a computer (such as the payroll, list of addresses, customer accounts); **computer language** = system of signs, letters and words used to instruct a computer; **computer listing** = printout of a list of items taken from data stored in a computer; **computer manager** = person in charge of a computer department; **computer program** = instructions to a computer, telling it to do a particular piece of work; **computer programmer** = person who writes computer programs; **computer services** = work using a computer, done by a computer bureau; **computer time** = time when a computer is being used (paid for at an hourly rate); *running all those sales reports costs a lot in computer time;* **business computer** = powerful small computer which is programmed for special business uses; **personal computer** *or* **home computer** = small computer which can be used in the home

◊ **computerize** [kəm'pjuːtəraɪz] *verb* to install computers to do a certain type of work; *our stock control has been completely computerized; we should computerize the personnel records to save time; we want to computerize the data on company personnel, including each worker's pay and conditions of service*

◊ **computerized** [kəm'pjuːtəraɪzd] *adjective* worked by computers; *a computerized personnel filing system*

◊ **computer-literate** [kəm'pjuːtə 'lɪtrət] *adjective* (person) who knows how to use more or less any type of computer

◊ **computer-readable** [kəm'pjuːtə 'riːdəbl] *adjective* which can be read and understood by a computer; *computer-readable codes*

comrade ['kɒmreɪd] *noun* friend *or* fellow worker *or* fellow member of a union

◊ **comradeship** ['kɒmreɪdʃɪp] *noun* feeling of friendship and solidarity with other workers

concentration [kɒnsən'treɪʃn] *noun* situation when members of a certain social group are overrepresented; *the high percentage of receptionists who are women is an example of concentration*

concern [kən'sɜːn] **1** *noun* **(a)** business *or* company; **his business is a going concern** = the company is working (and making a profit); **sold as a going concern** = sold as an actively trading company **(b)** being worried about a problem; *the management showed no concern at all for the workers' safety* **2**

verb to deal with *or* to be connected with; *the sales staff are not concerned with the cleaning of the store; he filled in a questionnaire concerning computer utilization;* **'to whom it may concern'** = words used at the heading of a letter of recommendation, etc., addressed to anyone who may be interested (such as a potential employer)

concession [kən'seʃn] *noun* (i) agreement to something; (ii) allowance, such as a reduction of tax or price; *the union obtained some important concessions from management during negotiations;* **concession bargaining** = situation where a union sees that it cannot negotiate large pay increases for its members, and so negotiates improvements in working conditions, etc. instead; **tax concession** = allowing less tax to be paid

conciliation [kənsɪlɪ'eɪʃən] *noun* bringing together the parties in a dispute with a third party, so that the dispute can be settled through a series of negotiations; *conciliation in an industrial dispute;* **conciliation officer** = official of ACAS who tries to get the parties in an industrial dispute to settle their differences; **the Conciliation Service** = ADVISORY, CONCILIATION AND ARBITRATION SERVICE

condition [kən'dɪʃən] *noun* **(a)** term of a contract *or* duties which have to be carried out as part of a contract *or* which if not fulfilled by the relevant party, allows the other to consider the contract as ended; *one of the conditions of the contract of employment was that each salesman should secure a minimum amount of business for the company;* **conditions of employment** *or* **conditions of service** = terms of a contract of employment; **conditions of sale** = agreed ways in which a sale takes place (such as discounts *or* credit terms); **on condition that** = provided that; *they were granted the lease on condition that they paid the legal costs* **(b)** general state *or* general way of life in a certain place; *the union has complained of the bad working conditions in the factory; working in unhealthy conditions is responsible for various illnesses after retirement; working conditions were so bad that the high salaries soon lost their incentive value*

◊ **conditional** [kən'dɪʃənl] *adjective*

depending on certain conditions; provided that certain things take place; *he has had the conditional offer of a job provided he passes a medical examination; the offer of the job is conditional on excellent references;* **to give a conditional acceptance** = to accept, provided that certain things happen *or* certain terms apply; **the offer is conditional on the board's acceptance** = provided the board accepts; **he made a conditional offer** = he offered to buy, provided that certain terms applied

conduct 1 [kɒndʌkt] *noun* way of behaving; *he was sacked for bad conduct at the staff Christmas party* **2** [kən'dʌkt] *verb* to carry on; *to conduct negotiations; the chairman conducted the negotiations very negligently; he conducted the training session very efficiently*

Confederation of British Industry (CBI) [kɒnfedə'reɪʃn əv 'brɪtɪʃ 'ɪndəstrɪ] organization formed in 1965 which represents British employers in commerce and industry

confer [kən'fɜː] *verb* to discuss a problem with another person *or* within a group; *the interview board conferred in the next room before announcing the names of the successful candidates*

◊ **conference** ['kɒnfərəns] *noun* **(a)** meeting of people to discuss problems; *many useful tips can be picked up at a sales conference; the conference of personnel managers included talks on payment and recruitment policies;* **to be in conference** = to be in a meeting; **conference method** = method of teaching using discussion *or* exchange of ideas amongst students; **conference phone** = telephone so arranged that several people can speak into it from around a table; **conference room** = room where small meetings can take place; **press conference** = meeting where newspaper and TV reporters are invited to hear news of a new product *or* a takeover bid, etc.; **sales conference** = meeting of sales managers, representatives, publicity staff, etc., to discuss future sales plans **(b)** meeting of an association *or* a society *or* a union; *the annual conference of the Electricians' Union; the conference of the Booksellers' Association; the conference agenda or the agenda of the conference was drawn up by*

the secretary; **Trades Union Conference (TUC)** = association of British trade unions

confidence ['kɒnfɪdəns] *noun* **(a)** feeling sure *or* being certain; *the sales teams do not have much confidence in their manager; the board has total confidence in the managing director* **(b) in confidence** = in secret; *I will show you the report in confidence*

◊ **confidence trick** ['kɒnfɪdəns 'trɪk] *noun* business deal where someone gains another person's confidence and then tricks him

◊ **confidence trickster** ['kɒnfɪdəns 'trɪkstə] *noun* person who carries out a confidence trick on someone

◊ **confident** ['kɒnfɪdənt] *adjective* certain *or* sure; *I am confident the turnover will increase rapidly; are you confident the sales team can handle this product?*

◊ **confidential** [kɒnfɪ'denʃəl] *adjective* secret *or* not to be told or shown to other people; *the references sent by the applicant's last employer were in an envelope marked 'confidential'; whatever a worker tells his boss in an interview should be treated as confidential; he sent a confidential report to the chairman; please mark the letter 'Private and Confidential';* **confidential information** = information which has to be kept secret

◊ **confidentiality** [kɒnfɪdenʃɪ'ælətɪ] *noun* being secret; *confidentiality of personnel data is guaranteed by the Data Protection Act 1984;* **he broke the confidentiality of the discussions** = he told someone about the secret discussions

confirm [kən'fɜːm] *verb* to say that something is certain; *to confirm a hotel reservation or a ticket or an agreement or a booking;* **to confirm someone in a job** = to say that someone is now permanently in the job

◊ **confirmation** [kɒnfə'meɪʃən] *noun* **(a)** being certain; **confirmation of a booking** = checking that a booking is certain **(b)** document which confirms something; *he received confirmation from the bank that the deeds had been deposited*

conflict ['kɒnflɪkt] *noun* antagonism between people, such as between management and workers; *there was conflict between the two groups of workers;*

conflict of rights = situation where it is claimed that the terms of the workers' contracts of employment or a negotiated agreement have not been met

◊ **conflict of interest** ['kɒnflɪkt əv 'ɪntrest] *noun* (i) situation where a person may profit personally from decisions which he takes in his official capacity; (ii) situation where a firm may be recommending a course of action to clients which is not in their best interest, but may well profit the firm, or where different departments of the same firm are acting for rival clients

conformance [kən'fɔːməns] *noun* acting in accordance with a rule; *the machine used is not in conformance with safety regulations;* **conformance quality** = in total quality management, the way in which the product is made to fit the desired specifications

congratulate [kən'grætjʊleɪt] *verb* to give someone your good wishes for having done something well; *the sales director congratulated the salesmen on doubling sales; I want to congratulate you on your promotion*

◊ **congratulations** [kəngrætjʊ'leɪʃənz] *plural noun* good wishes; *the staff sent him their congratulations on his promotion*

conjunctive bargaining [kən'dʒʌŋktɪv 'baːgənɪŋ] *noun* collective bargaining where the union has to settle on the management's terms

conscientious [kɒnʃi'ənʃəs] *adjective* (person) who works carefully and well; *she's a very conscientious worker*

consensus [kən'sensəs] *noun* agreement *or* approval by a group collectively; *management by consensus*

◊ **consensus ad idem** [kən'sensəs æd 'ɪdem] *Latin phrase meaning* 'agreement to this same thing': real agreement to a contract by both parties

◊ **consensual** [kən'sensjuːəl] *adjective* by means of a consensus; **consensual validation** = validating an action by agreeing with other people's attitudes

consent [kən'sent] **1** *noun* agreement that something should be done; *change of use requires the consent of the local planning authorities;* **by mutual consent** = by agreement between the parties concerned **2** *verb* to agree that something should be done; *the management consented to the union's proposals*

consider [kən'sɪdə] *verb* to think seriously about something; **to consider the terms of a contract** = to examine and discuss if the terms are acceptable

◊ **consideration** [kənsɪdə'reɪʃən] *noun* **(a)** serious thought; *we are giving consideration to moving the head office to Scotland;* **the proposal under consideration** = the proposal which is being considered at the moment **(b)** something valuable exchanged as part of a contract; **for a small consideration** = for a small fee *or* payment

consist of [kən'sɪst 'ɒv] *verb* to be formed of; *the trade mission consists of the sales directors of ten major companies; the package tour consists of air travel, six nights in a luxury hotel, all meals and visits to places of interest*

conspiracy [kən'spɪrəsi] *noun* legal term used to describe the intention of workers to break the law when resorting to industrial action; *sanctions were laid down to discourage conspiracy; the dockers resorted to conspiracy since they felt they could only oppose the bad working conditions through an illegal strike*

construct [kən'strʌkt] *verb* to build; *the company has tendered for the contract to construct the new bridge*

◊ **constructive** [kən'strʌktɪv] *adjective* which helps in the making of something; *she made some constructive suggestions for improving management-worker relations; we had a constructive proposal from a distribution company in Italy;* **constructive dismissal** = legal right of an employee to resign owing to improper behaviour on the part of the employer and still claim payment for wrongful dismissal

consult [kən'sʌlt] *verb* to ask an expert for advice; *he consulted his accountant about his tax*

◊ **consultancy** [kən'sʌltənsi] *noun* act of giving specialist advice; *a consultancy firm; he offers a consultancy service*

◊ **consultant** [kən'sʌltənt] *noun* specialist

who gives advice; *engineering consultant; management consultant; tax consultant; recruitment consultant* = agency which recruits staff for a company (usually interviewing and drawing up a shortlist of candidates for a final decision by the management)

◊ **consultation** [kɒnsʌl'teɪʃn] *noun* asking other people for advice before coming to a decision; **consultation agreement** = agreement which lays down the areas where management commits itself to consult the opinion of the employees; **joint consultation** = discussions between management and workers on subjects of common interest and concern

◊ **consultative** [kən'sʌltətɪv] *adjective* which advises; **consultative committee** = committee of representatives of the employees which meets regularly with top management; *the consultative committee was able to keep senior management in touch with feelings in the organization; two workers and a foreman form the workers' part of the consultative committee;* **to play a consultative role in** = to act as consultant in

◊ **consulting** [kən'sʌltɪŋ] *adjective* person who gives specialist advice; *consulting engineer*

QUOTE consultants are part of the services industry, and last year produced invisible earnings of over £1.2 billion

QUOTE management consultancy is a growth industry in which accountants have been much involved
British Business

consumer [kən'sjuːmə] *noun* person *or* company which buys and uses goods and services; *gas consumers are protesting at the increase in prices; the factory is a heavy consumer of water;* **consumer council** = group representing the interests of consumers; **consumer credit** = credit given by shops, banks and other financial institutions to consumers so that they can buy goods; **Consumer Credit Act, 1974** = Act of Parliament which licenses lenders, and requires them to state clearly the full terms of loans which they make (including the APR); **consumer panel** = group of consumers who report on products they have used so that the manufacturers can improve them or use what the panel says about them in advertising

contact 1 ['kɒntækt] *noun* **(a)** person you know *or* person you can ask for help or advice; *he has many contacts in the city; who is your contact in the ministry?* **(b)** act of getting in touch with someone; **I have lost contact with them** = I do not communicate with them any longer; **he put me in contact with a good lawyer** = he told me how to get in touch with a good lawyer; **contact effect** = impression received when comparing the various performances of candidates in interviews **2** ['kɒntækt *or* kən'tækt] *verb* to get in touch with someone *or* to communicate with someone; *he tried to contact his office by phone; can you contact the managing director at his club?*

contention [kən'tenʃn] *noun* **(a)** opinion *or* belief; *it is our contention that the decision of the tribunal is wrong* **(b)** dispute; *an area of contention between management and workers*

◊ **contentious** [kən'tenʃəs] *adjective* which is a source of dispute; *management made a series of contentious proposals*

contingency [kən'tɪn(d)ʒənsi] *noun* possible state of emergency when decisions will have to be taken quickly; **contingency allowance** = time added to the basic time established for a job to allow for irregularities in the job content; *a contingency allowance was necessary since the machinery used was not wholly reliable; the unions protested that no contingency allowances were established in those jobs where delays were not the fault of the workers;* **contingency fund** *or* **contingency reserve** = money set aside in case it is needed urgently; **contingency plans** = plans which will be put into action if something unexpected happens; **add on 10% to provide for contingencies** = to provide for further expenditure which may be incurred; *we have built 10% into our cost forecast for contingencies*

◊ **contingent** [kən'tɪn(d)ʒənt] *adjective* **(a) contingent expenses** = expenses which will be incurred only if something happens **(b) contingent policy** = insurance policy which pays out only if something happens (as if the person named in the policy dies before the person due to benefit)

continue [kən'tɪnjʊ] *verb* to go on doing something *or* to do something which you were doing earlier; *the chairman continued* *speaking in spite of the noise from the shareholders; the meeting started at 10 a.m. and continued until 6 p.m.; negotiations will continue next Monday*

◊ **continual** [kən'tɪnjuəl] *adjective* which happens again and again; *production was slow because of continual breakdowns*

◊ **continually** [kən'tɪnjuəli] *adverb* again and again; *the photocopier is continually breaking down*

◊ **continuation** [kəntɪnju'eɪʃən] *noun* act of continuing

◊ **continuous** [kən'tɪnjuəs] *adjective* with no end *or* with no breaks; **continuous assessment** = assessment of a trainee's work carried out through the course (as opposed to terminal assessment at the end of the course); **continuous development** = system of continuous training for employees; **in continuous employment** = employed for a period of time, without more than a week's gap (holidays, sickness, etc. are not counted as gaps); *she was in continuous employment for the period 1993 to 1996;* **continuous feed** = device which feeds continuous stationery into a printer; **continuous process production** = system of automated production for a series of identical products; **continuous shift system** = system where groups of workers work shifts throughout the week, including weekends; **continuous stationery** = paper made as one long sheet, used in computer printers

contract 1 ['kɒntrækt] *noun* (a) legally binding agreement between two parties (persons *or* groups *or* organizations); *to draw up a contract; to draft a contract; to sign a contract; the contract can be ended by three months' notice on either side; he was offered an attractive two year contract in the Middle East;* **the contract is binding on both parties** = both parties signing the contract must do what is agreed; **under contract** = bound by the terms of a contract; *the firm is under contract to deliver the goods by November;* **to void a contract** = to make a contract invalid; **contract of employment** = contract between management and employee showing all conditions of work; **contract of service** = legal agreement between an employer and an employee whereby the employee will work for the employer and be directed by him or her, in return for payment; **contract for services** =

agreement between employer and employee where the employee is hired as an independent party for a limited time and is not under the control of the employer; **fixed-term contract** = contract of employment for a stated period only (e.g. for one year); **personal contract** = contract negotiated between an employer and a single employee (as opposed to a collective contract, negotiated with a group of employees); **service contract** = contract between a company and a director listing his conditions of work; **exchange of contracts** = point in the sale of a property when the buyer and seller both sign the contract of sale which then becomes binding (b) **contract law** *or* **law of contract** = laws relating to agreements; **by private contract** = by private legal agreement; **contract note** = note showing that shares have been bought or sold but not yet paid for (c) agreement for supply of a service or goods; *contract for the supply of spare parts; to enter into a contract to supply spare parts; to sign a contract for £10,000 worth of spare parts;* **to put work out to contract** = to decide that work should be done by another company on a contract, rather than employing members of staff to do it; **to award a contract to a company** *or* **to place a contract with a company** = to decide that a company shall have the contract to do work for you; **to tender for a contract** = to put forward an estimate of cost for work under contract; **breach of contract** = breaking the terms of a contract; **the company is in breach of contract** = the company has failed to do what was agreed in the contract; **contract work** = work done according to a written agreement **2** ['kɒntrækt *or* kən'trækt] *verb* to agree to do some work by contract; *to contract to supply spare parts or to contract for the supply of spare parts*

◊ **contracting** [kən'træktɪŋ] *adjective* **contracting party** = person or company which signs a contract

◊ **contractor** [kən'træktə] *noun* person *or* company which does work according to a written agreement; **haulage contractor** = company which transports goods by contract; **government contractor** = company which supplies the government with goods by contract

◊ **contract out** ['kɒntrækt 'aʊt] *verb* (a) to hire another organization *or* person to carry out part *or* all of a certain piece of work; *the* *catering firm has contracted out the distribution of its products to a delivery firm; we shall contract out any work we are not specialized in; the supply of spare parts was contracted out to Smith Ltd* **(b) to contract out of an agreement** = to withdraw from an agreement with the written permission of the other party; *some of the employees have contracted out of the state pension scheme;* **contracted-out pension scheme** = private pension scheme which gives benefits at least as high as the state scheme

◊ **contractual** [kən'træktjuəl] *adjective* according to a contract; **contractual liability** = legal responsibility for something as stated in a contract; **to fulfil your contractual obligations** = to do what you have agreed to do in a contract; **he is under no contractual obligation to buy** = he has signed no agreement to buy

◊ **contractually** [kən'træktjuəli] *adverb* according to a contract; *the company is contractually bound to pay his expenses*

contribute [kən'trɪbjuːt] *verb* to give money *or* to add to money; *to contribute 10% of the profits; he contributed to the pension fund for 10 years*

◊ **contribution** [kɒntrɪ'bjuːʃən] *noun* money paid to add to a sum; **contribution of capital** = money paid to a company as additional capital; **employer's contribution** = money paid by an employer towards a worker's pension; **National Insurance contributions** = money paid each month by a worker and the company to the National Insurance; **pension contributions** = money paid by a company or worker into a pension fund

◊ **contributor** [kən'trɪbjutə] *noun* **contributor of capital** = person who contributes capital

◊ **contributory** [kən'trɪbjutəri] *adjective* **(a) contributory pension plan** *or* **scheme** = pension plan where the employee has to contribute a percentage of salary; *the contributory pensions scheme is one of the attractive fringe benefits of the job; how much does the employer contribute to the contributory pension scheme? see also* NON-CONTRIBUTORY **(b)** which helps to cause; *falling exchange rates have been a contributory factor in the company's loss of profits;* **contributory fault** = situation in an unfair dismissal where the employee was to a certain extent at fault; **contributory**

negligence = negligence partly caused by the plaintiff and partly by the defendant, resulting in harm done to the plaintiff

control [kən'trəul] **1** *noun* **(a)** power *or* being able to direct people *or* an organization; *top management exercises tight control over spending; the company is under the control of three shareholders; the family lost control of its business;* **to gain control of a business** = to buy more than 50% of the shares so that you can direct the business; **to lose control of a business** = to find that you have less than 50% of the shares in a company, and so are not longer able to direct it **(b)** restricting *or* checking something *or* making sure that something is kept in check; **under control** = kept in check; *expenses are kept under tight control; the company is trying to bring its overheads back under control;* **out of control** = not kept in check; *costs have got out of control;* **budgetary control** = keeping check on spending; **credit control** = checking that customers pay on time and do not exceed their credit limits; **quality control** = making sure that the quality of a product is good; **stock control** = making sure that movements of stock are noted **(c) control group** = small group which is used to check a sample group; **control systems** = systems used to check that a computer system *or* production process is working correctly **2** *verb* **(a) to control a business** = to direct a business; *the business is controlled by a company based in Luxembourg; the company is controlled by the majority shareholder* **(b)** to make sure that something is kept in check *or* is not allowed to develop; *the government is fighting to control inflation or to control the rise in the cost of living* (NOTE: **controlling - controlled**)

◊ **controlled** [kən'trəuld] *adjective* ruled *or* kept in check; **government-controlled** = ruled by a government; **controlled economy** = economy where most business activity is directed by orders from the government

◊ **controller** [kən'trəulə] *noun* **(a)** person who controls (especially the finances of a company); **stock controller** = person who notes movements of stock **(b)** *US* chief accountant in a company

◊ **controlling** [kən'trəulɪŋ] *adjective* **to have a controlling interest in a company** = to own more than 50% of the shares so that you can direct how the company is run

convene [kən'vi:n] *verb* to ask people to come together; *to convene a meeting of union members*

◊ **convenor** [kən'vi:nə] *noun* trade unionist who organizes union meetings

convention [kən'venʃn] *noun* international agreement; *the Geneva Convention on Human Rights*

convict [kən'vɪkt] *verb* **to convict someone of a crime** = to find that someone is guilty of a crime

◊ **conviction** [kən'vɪkʃn] *noun* finding that a person accused of a crime is guilty; *he has had ten convictions for burglary*

cooling off period ['ku:lɪŋ 'ɒf 'pɪːrɪəd] *noun* (i) during an industrial dispute, a period when negotiations have to be carried on and no action can be taken by either side; (ii) period when a person is allowed to think about something which he has agreed to buy on hire-purchase but may possibly change his mind

co-op ['kəʊɒp] *noun* = CO-OPERATIVE 2

◊ **co-operate** [kəʊ'ɒpəreɪt] *verb* to work together; *the governments are co-operating in the fight against piracy; the two firms have co-operated on the computer project*

◊ **co-operation** [kəʊɒpə'reɪʃən] *noun* working together; *the project was completed ahead of schedule with the co-operation of the workforce*

◊ **co-operative** [kəʊ'ɒpərətɪv] **1** *adjective* willing to work together; *the staff have not been co-operative over the management's productivity plan;* **co-operative society** = society where the customers and workers are partners and share the profits **2** *noun* business run by a group of workers who are the owners and who share the profits; *an industrial co-operative; to set up a workers' co-operative*

co-opt [kəʊ'ɒpt] *verb* **to co-opt someone onto a committee** = to ask someone to join a committee without being elected

co-owner [kəʊ'əʊnə] *noun* person who owns something with another person; *the two sisters are co-owners of the property*

◊ **co-ownership** ['kəʊ'əʊnəʃɪp] *noun* ownership by employees of a share in the business which employs them; *co-ownership will make the employees feel more important in the enterprise; with co-ownership, everyone in the organization has a stake in it*

copartner [kəʊ'pɑːtnə] *noun* person who is a partner in a business with another person

◊ **copartnership** [kəʊ'pɑːtnəʃɪp] *noun* arrangement where partners *or* workers have shares in the company

cope [kəʊp] *verb* to manage to do something; *the new assistant manager coped very well when the manager was on holiday; the warehouse is trying to cope with the backlog of orders*

core [kɔː] *noun* central part; **core skills** = basic skills, which are needed by everyone; **core time** = period when people working under a flexitime system must be present at work; **core workers** = workers who are in full-time employment (as opposed to part-timers or casual workers who are called 'peripheral workers')

corporate ['kɔːpərət] *adjective* referring to a large organization; **corporate culture** = way of managing a corporation, by increasing the importance of the corporation itself, and therefore the loyalty of the workforce to the corporation; **corporate image** = idea which a company would like the public to have of it; **corporate planning** = planning the future work of a whole company; *planning manpower requirements fitted into the wider area of corporate planning;* **corporate strategy** = plans for future action by a corporation

corporation [kɔːpə'reɪʃən] *noun* large company; **finance corporation** = company which provides money for hire purchase; **multinational corporation** = company which has branches or subsidiary companies in several countries

correct [kə'rekt] **1** *adjective* accurate *or* right; *the published accounts do not give a correct picture of the company's financial position* **2** *verb* to remove mistakes from something; *the accounts department have corrected the invoice; you will have to correct all these typing errors before you send the letter*

◊ **correction** [kə'rekʃən] *noun* making something correct; change which makes something correct; *he made some corrections to the text of the speech*

correspondence [kɒrɪs'pɒndəns] *noun* letters *or* messages sent; **correspondence course** = course done by mail; *she learnt accountancy through a correspondence course; he is taking a correspondence course in company law*

cost [kɒst] **1** *noun* **(a)** amount of money which has to be paid for something; *what is the cost of a first class ticket to New York? computer costs are falling each year; we cannot afford the cost of two telephones;* **cover costs** = to produce enough money in sales to pay for the costs of production; *the sales revenue barely covers the costs of advertising or the manufacturing costs;* **to sell at cost** = to sell at a price which is the same as the cost of manufacture or the wholesale cost; **direct cost** = cost directly related to the production cost of a product; **fixed costs** = business costs which do not rise with the quantity of the product made; **indirect costs** = costs which are not directly related to the making of a product (such as cleaning, rent, administration); **labour costs** = cost of hourly-paid workers employed to make a product; **manufacturing costs** *or* **production costs** = costs of making a product; **operating costs** *or* **running costs** = cost of the day-to-day organization of a company; **variable costs** = production costs which increase with the quantity of the product made (such as wages, raw materials); **cost accountant** = accountant who gives managers information about their business costs; **cost accounting** = specially prepared accounts of manufacturing and sales costs; **cost analysis** = calculating in advance what a new product will cost; **cost centre** = person *or* group *or* machine whose costs can be itemized and to which fixed costs can be allocated; **cost, insurance and freight** = estimate of a price, which includes the cost of the goods, the insurance and the transport charges; **cost price** = selling price which is the same as the price which the seller paid for the item (i.e. either the manufacturing cost or the wholesale price); **cost of sales** = all the costs of a product sold, including manufacturing costs and the staff costs of the production department **(b)** **costs** = expenses involved in a court case; **to**

pay costs = to pay the expenses of a court case; *the judge awarded costs to the defendant; costs of the case will be borne by the prosecution* **2** *verb* **(a)** to have a price; *how much does the machine cost? this cloth costs £10 a metre* **(b)** **to cost a product** = to calculate how much money will be needed to make a product, and so work out its selling price

◊ **cost-benefit analysis** ['kɒst 'benɪfɪt ə'næləsɪs] *noun* comparing the costs and benefits of different possible ways of using available resources

◊ **cost-cutting** ['kɒst 'kʌtɪŋ] *noun* reducing costs; *we have taken out the telex as a cost-cutting exercise*

◊ **cost-effective** ['kɒstɪ'fektɪv] *adjective* which gives value, especially when compared with something else; *we find advertising in the Sunday newspapers very cost-effective*

◊ **cost-effectiveness** [kɒstɪ'fektɪvnəs] *noun* being cost-effective; *can we calculate the cost-effectiveness of air freight against shipping by sea?*

◊ **costing** ['kɒstɪŋ] *noun* calculation of the manufacturing costs, and so the selling price of a product; *the costings give us a retail price of $2.95; we cannot do the costing until we have details of all the production expenditure*

◊ **costly** ['kɒstli] *adjective* expensive *or* costing a lot of money

◊ **cost of living** ['kɒst əv 'lɪvɪŋ] *noun* money which has to be paid for food, heating, rent, etc.; *to allow for the cost of living in the salaries;* **cost-of-living allowance** = addition to normal salary to cover increases in the cost of living; **cost-of-living bonus** = extra money paid to meet the increase in the cost of living; **cost-of-living increase** = increase in salary to allow it to keep up with the increased cost of living; **cost-of-living index** = way of measuring the cost of living which is shown as a percentage increase on the figure for the previous year

cottage ['kɒtɪdʒ] *noun* little house in the country; **cottage industry** = production of goods, or other type of work, carried out by workers in their homes; **the electronic cottage** = the home where someone works for a company on a computer, usually linked to the office via a modem

council ['kaʊnsl] *noun* official group chosen to make decisions on certain matters *or* to advise on problems; **consumer council** = group representing the interests of consumers; **town council** = representatives elected to run a town; **wages councils** = organizations made up of employers and employees' representatives which fix basic employment conditions in industries where places of work are too small or too scattered for trade unions to be established; **works council** = committee of workers and management which discusses the organization of work in a factory

counselling ['kaʊnsəlɪŋ] *noun* giving professional advice to others on personal matters; *an office is being set up for counselling workers who have professional or social problems; counselling helps workers get accustomed to their new environment, by offering advice and guidance*

◊ **counsellor** ['kaʊnsələ] *noun* person who gives professional advice to others on personal matters

counter- ['kaʊntə] *prefix* against

◊ **counterbid** ['kaʊntəbɪd] *noun* higher bid in reply to a previous bid; *when I bid £20 he put in a counterbid of £25*

◊ **counter-claim** ['kaʊntəkleɪm] **1** *noun* claim for damages made in reply to a previous claim; *the union negotiators entered a counter-claim for a reduction in work hours* **2** *verb* to put in a counter-claim; *Jones claimed £25,000 in damages and Smith counter-claimed £50,000 for loss of office*

◊ **countermand** ['kaʊntə'mɑːnd] *verb* to **countermand an order** = to say that an order must not be carried out

◊ **counter-offer** ['kaʊntər 'ɒfə] *noun* higher offer made in reply to another offer; *Smith Ltd made an offer of £1m for the property, and Blacks replied with a counter-offer of £1.4m*

◊ **counterpart** ['kaʊntəpɑːt] *noun* person who has a similar job in another company; **John is my counterpart in Smith's** = he has the same post as I have here

◊ **counterproductive**
[kaʊntəprə'dʌktɪv] *adjective* which does not produce the right effect; *the MD's talk about profitability was quite*
counterproductive, as it encouraged the employees to ask for higher wages

◊ **countersign** ['kaʊntəsaɪn] *verb* to sign a document which has already been signed by someone else; *all cheques have to be countersigned by the finance director; the sales director countersigns all my orders*

couple ['kʌpl] *noun* two things or people taken together; **married couple** = husband and wife

course [kɔːs] *noun* **(a) in the course of** = during *or* while something is happening; *in the course of the discussion, the managing director explained the company's expansion plans; sales have risen sharply in the course of the last few months* **(b)** series of lessons *or* programme of instruction; *she has finished her secretarial course; the company has paid for her to attend a course for trainee sales managers; management trainees all took a six-month course in business studies; the training officer was constantly on the lookout for new courses in management studies; the company sent her on a management course;* **she went on a course** = she attended a course of study; **advanced course** = course for students who are not beginners; **beginners' course** = course for students who know nothing about the subject; **induction course** = course intended to help a person entering an organization *or* starting a new job; *the company is organizing a two-day induction course for new employees; the induction course spells out the main objectives of the organization and its procedures see also* REFRESHER, SANDWICH

court [kɔːt] *noun* place where a judge listens to a case and decides legally which of the parties in the argument is right; **court case** = legal action *or* trial; **court order** = legal order made by a court, telling someone to do *or* not to do something; **to take someone to court** = to tell someone to appear in court to settle an argument; **a settlement was reached out of court** *or* **the two parties reached an out-of-court settlement** = the dispute was settled between the two parties privately without continuing the court case

covenant ['kʌvənənt] **1** *noun* legal contract; **deed of covenant** = official signed agreement to pay someone a sum of money each year **2** *verb* to agree to pay a sum of money each year by contract; *to covenant to pay £10 per annum*

Coventry ['kɒvəntri] *noun* British industrial town; **to send someone to Coventry** = to ostracize someone *or* to reject and refuse to have anything to do with a member or members of a group; *workers who carried on working were sent to Coventry after the strike ended*

cover ['kʌvə] **1** *noun* **(a)** thing put over a machine, etc. to keep it clean; *put the cover over your micro when you leave the office; always keep a cover over the typewriter* **(b)** **to provide cover for someone** = to work in place of someone who is ill, on holiday, etc. **(c)** protection against something; **insurance cover** = protection guaranteed by an insurance policy; *do you have cover against theft?;* **to operate without adequate cover** = without being protected by insurance; **to ask for additional cover** = to ask the insurance company to increase the amount for which you are insured; **full cover** = insurance against all risks; **cover note** = letter from an insurance company giving details of an insurance policy and confirming that the policy exists (NOTE: the US English for this is **binder**) **(c) to send something under separate cover** = in a separate envelope; **to send a magazine under plain cover** = in an ordinary envelope with no company name printed on it **2** *verb* **(a)** to put something over a machine, etc. to keep it clean; *don't forget to cover your micro before you go home* **(b)** to protect; *an insurance policy covering workers doing dangerous work; the insurance covers fire, theft and loss of work;* **to be fully covered** = to have insurance against all risks

◊ **coverage** ['kʌvərɪdʒ] *noun* **(a)** **press coverage** *or* **media coverage** = reports about something in the newspapers *or* on TV, etc.; *the company had good media coverage for the launch of its new model* **(b)** *US* protection guaranteed by insurance; *do you have coverage against fire damage?*

◊ **covering letter** *or* **covering note** ['kʌvərɪŋ 'letə *or* 'kʌvərɪŋ 'nəʊt] *noun* letter or note sent with documents to say why you are sending them; *he sent a covering letter with his curriculum vitae, explaining why he wanted the job; the job advertisement asked for a CV and a covering letter see also above* COVER NOTE

CPM = CRITICAL PATH ANALYSIS

craft [krɑːft] *noun* traditional manufacture done by hand; **craft worker** = skilled manual worker, especially one who has been through an apprenticeship; **craft union** = oldest type of trade union, for skilled workers in a particular craft or trade

◊ **craftsman** ['krɑːftsmən] *noun* person who works in a craft

◊ **craftsmanship** ['krɑːftsmənʃɪp] *noun* skill in doing craft work

CRE = COMMISSION FOR RACIAL EQUALITY

create [krɪ'eɪt] *verb* to make something new; *by acquiring small unprofitable companies he soon created a large manufacturing group; the government scheme aims at creating new jobs for young people*

◊ **creation** [krɪ'eɪʃən] *noun* making; **job creation scheme** = government-backed scheme to make jobs for the unemployed

◊ **creativity** [kriːeɪ'tɪvɪti] *noun* ability to use the imagination to produce new ideas or things; **creativity test** = test designed to assess the originality *or* imagination which a person can apply to solving problems; *creativity tests will be given to those applying for jobs in our company where new approaches are needed to solve old problems; the personnel manager favours creativity tests instead of the more traditional IQ tests*

> QUOTE he insisted that the tax advantages he directed towards small businesses will help create jobs and reduce the unemployment rate
> *Toronto Star*

crèche [kreɪʃ] *noun* special room or building where babies and small children can be looked after (on a company's premises); *the company provides crèche facilities for its staff compare* NURSERY

credentials [krɪ'denʃlz] *noun* letters *or* documents which describe a person's qualities and skills; *the new production manager has very impressive credentials*

credit ['kredɪt] **1** *noun* **(a)** period of time a customer is allowed before he has to pay a debt incurred for goods or services; **consumer credit** = credit given by shops, banks and other financial institutions to consumers so that they can buy goods **(b)** amount entered in accounts to show a decrease in assets; **tax credit** = part of a dividend on which the company has already paid advance corporation tax which is deducted from the shareholder's income tax charge **(c)** certificate showing that one has completed a course of study at a recognised teaching establishment

◊ **creditworthy** ['kredɪtwɜːði] *adjective* able to buy goods on credit

◊ **creditworthiness** ['kredɪt'wɜːðɪnəs] *noun* ability of a customer to pay for goods bought on credit

crème de la crème [krem də læ 'krem] *noun* the elite *or* the very best of a profession; *it is a very exclusive recruitment agency and only looks for the crème de la crème*

crisis ['kraɪsɪs] *noun* serious economic situation where decisions have to be taken rapidly; *international crisis; banking crisis; financial crisis;* **to take crisis measures** = to take severe measures rapidly to stop a crisis developing; **crisis bargaining** = collective bargaining under the threat of a strike deadline; *if crisis bargaining doesn't produce agreement on the 12% pay increase, a strike will be called;* **crisis management** = measures taken to control a business during time of crisis (NOTE: plural is **crises**)

critical path analysis (CPM) ['krɪtɪkəl 'pɑːθ ə'næləsɪs] *noun* analysis of the way a project is organized in terms of the minimum time it will take to complete, calculating which parts can be delayed without holding up the rest of the project

criterion [kraɪ'tiːərɪən] *noun* standard by which something can be judged; *using the criterion of the ratio of cases solved to cases reported, the police force is becoming more efficient* (NOTE: plural is **criteria**)

criticize ['krɪtɪsaɪz] *verb* to say that something *or* someone is wrong *or* is working badly, etc.; *the MD criticized the sales manager for not improving the volume of sales; the design of the new catalogue has been criticized*

◊ **criticism** ['krɪtɪsɪzm] *noun* words showing that you consider that someone *or* something is wrong; *the tribunal made some*

criticisms of the way in which the company had presented its case

cross [krɒs] *verb* **(a)** to go across; *Concorde only takes three hours to cross the Atlantic; to get to the bank, you turn left and cross the street at the post office* **(b)** to cross a cheque = to write two lines across a cheque to show that it has to be paid into a bank; **crossed cheque** = cheque which has to be paid into a bank

◊ **cross-functional** [krɒs'fʌŋkʃnəl] *adjective* (worker) who can work at different and varied tasks

◊ **cross holding** ['krɒs 'həʊldɪŋ] *noun* situation where two companies hold shares in each other

◊ **cross off** ['krɒs 'ɒf] *verb* to remove something from a list; *he crossed my name off his list; you can cross him off our mailing list*

◊ **cross out** ['krɒs 'aʊt] *verb* to put a line through something which has been written; *she crossed out £250 and put in £500*

◊ **cross-picketing** ['krɒs 'pɪkɪtɪŋ] *noun* picketing by more than one union, when each claims to represent the workforce; *cross-picketing damaged the workers' case by showing up the divisions in their ranks; cross-picketing was due to the rivalry between the two unions rather than any real attempt to represent the workers' interests*

culture ['kʌltʃə] *noun* way of living in a society; civilization of a country; **corporate culture** = way of managing a corporation, by increasing the importance of the corporation itself, and therefore the loyalty of the workforce to the corporation; **culture shock** = shock when a person moves from type of society to another (as for emigrants from European countries to the USA); **enterprise culture** = general feeling that the commercial system works better with free enterprise, increased share ownership, property ownership, etc.

current ['kʌrənt] *adjective* referring to the present time; *the current round of wage negotiations;* **current account** = account in an bank from which the customer can withdraw money when he wants; *to pay money into a current account;* **current cost accounting** = method of accounting which notes the cost of replacing assets at current prices, rather than valuing assets at their original cost; **current price** = today's price; **current rate of exchange** = today's rate of exchange

◊ **currently** ['kʌrəntli] *adverb* at the present time; *we are currently negotiating with the bank for a loan*

curriculum vitae (CV) [kə'rɪkjuləm 'viːtaɪ] *noun* summary of a person's work experience and qualifications sent to a prospective employer by someone applying for a job; *candidates should send a letter of application with a curriculum vitae to the personnel officer; the curriculum vitae listed the candidate's previous jobs and his reasons for leaving them; just a glance at her CV showed that she wasn't right for the job* (NOTE: the plural is **curriculums** *or* **curricula vitae**. Note also that the US English is **résumé**)

cushy [kʊʃi] *adjective (informal)* which does not involve any effort; **cushy number** = work that offers the same money for less effort than another similar job; *he spends all his time looking for a cushy number* (NOTE: US English is **gravy job**)

cut [kʌt] **1** *noun* **(a)** sudden lowering of a price *or* salary *or* numbers of jobs; *price cuts or cuts in prices; salary cuts or cuts in salaries;* **job cuts** = reductions in the number of jobs; **he took a cut in salary** = he accepted a lower salary **(b)** share in a payment; *he introduces new customers and gets a cut of the salesman's commission* **2** *verb* **(a)** to lower suddenly; *we are cutting prices on all our models;* **to cut (back) production** = to reduce the quantity of products made; *the company has cut back its sales force; we have taken out the telex in order to try to cut costs* **(b)** to stop *or* to reduce the number of something; **to cut jobs** = to reduce the number of jobs by making people redundant; **he cut his losses** = he stopped doing something which was causing him to lose money

◊ **cutback** ['kʌtbæk] *noun* reduction; *cutbacks in government spending*

◊ **cut down (on)** ['kʌt 'daʊn (ɒn)] *verb* to reduce suddenly the amount of something used; *the government is cutting down on welfare expenditure; the office is trying to cut down on electricity consumption; we have installed a word-processor to cut down on paperwork*

◊ **cut out for** ['kʌt 'aʊt 'fɔː] *verb* **to be cut out for** = to be very suitable for; *she was not cut out for a post as a personal secretary*

◊ **cutting** ['kʌtɪŋ] *noun* **(a) cost cutting** = reducing costs; *we have made three secretaries redundant as part of our cost-cutting programme;* **price cutting** = sudden lowering of prices; **price-cutting war** = competition between companies to get a larger market share by cutting prices **(b) press cutting agency** = company which cuts out references to a client from newspapers and magazines and sends them on to him; **press cuttings** = references to a client *or* person *or* product cut out of newspapers or magazines; *we have a file of press cuttings on our rivals' products*

CV ['siː'viː] *noun* = CURRICULUM VITAE *please apply in writing, enclosing a current CV*

cybernetics [saɪbə'netɪks] *noun* the study of information communication systems and how they can be improved

cycle ['saɪkl] *noun* period of time in which certain events are regularly repeated; **economic cycle** *or* **trade cycle** *or* **business cycle** = period during which trade expands, then slows down and then expands again; **product life cycle** = course of a product's life in terms of sales and profitability from its launch to its decline; **cycle time** = time taken to complete a job; *the cycle time for the job will decrease with the introduction of new machinery*

◊ **cyclical** *adjective* which happens in cycles; **cyclical demand** = demand which varies in response to social, economic or political factors; **cyclical factors** = way in which a trade cycle affects businesses

Dd

damage ['dæmɪdʒ] **1** *noun* **(a)** harm done to things; **fire damage** = damage caused by a fire; **storm damage** = damage caused by a storm; **to suffer damage** = to be harmed; *we are trying to assess the damage which the shipment suffered in transit;* **to cause damage** = to harm something; *the fire caused damage estimated at £100,000;* **damage survey** = survey of damage done (NOTE: no plural) **(b) damages** = money claimed as compensation for harm done; *to claim £1,000 in damages; to be liable for damages; to pay £25,000 in damages;* **to bring an action for damages against someone** = to take someone to court and claim damages; **punitive damages** = damages which punish the defendant for the loss *or* harm caused to the plaintiff; *heavy damages awarded to show that the court feels the defendant has behaved badly towards the plaintiff* **2** *verb* to harm; *the storm damaged the cargo; stock which has been damaged by water*

◊ **damaged** ['dæmɪdʒd] *adjective* which has suffered damage *or* which has been harmed; *goods damaged in transit;* **fire-damaged goods** = goods harmed in a fire

danger ['deɪn(d)ʒə] *noun* possibility of being harmed or killed; *the red light means danger; the old machinery is a danger to the workforce;* **there is no danger of the sales force leaving** = it is not likely that the sales force will leave; **in danger of** = which may easily happen; *the company is in danger of being taken over; she is in danger of being made redundant*

◊ **danger money** ['deɪn(d)ʒə 'mʌni] *noun* extra money paid to workers in dangerous jobs; *the workforce has stopped work and asked for danger money; he decided to go to work on an oil rig because of the danger money offered as an incentive*

◊ **dangerous** ['deɪn(d)ʒərəs] *adjective* which can be harmful; **dangerous job** = job where the workers may be killed or hurt

◊ **danger zone bonus** ['deɪn(d)ʒə 'zəʊn 'bəʊnəs] *noun* bonus for working in a particularly dangerous area; *danger-zone bonuses are awarded to workers employed in countries experiencing civil unrest or war*

data ['deɪtə] *noun* information (letters or figures) available on computer; *all important data on employees was fed into the computer; to calculate the weekly wages, you need data on hours worked and rates of pay;* **to key in data** = to enter information into a computer; **data acquisition** = getting information; **data bank** *or* **bank of data** = store of information in a computer; **data processing** = selecting and examining data in a computer to produce special information; **Data Protection Act (1984)** = Act of parliament which regulates the ways in which information about individuals is held by organizations such as employers, banks, credit houses, etc., and its confidentiality; *confidentiality of personnel data is guaranteed by the Data Protection Act 1984* (NOTE: **data** is usually singular: **the data is easily available**)

◊ **database** ['deɪtəbeɪs] *noun* store of information in a large computer; *we can extract the lists of potential customers from our database*

date [deɪt] **1** *noun* **(a)** number of day, month and year; *I have received your letter of yesterday's date;* **date of birth** = day, month and year when someone was born; **anniversary date** = date in a following year, which is the same as a particular occasion, such as the date of joining a pension scheme; **date of departure** *or* **departure date** = date on which an employee leaves the company; **expiry date** = date when something will end; **retirement date** = date on which someone retires and takes a pension; **starting date** = date on which something starts; **date stamp** = rubber stamp for marking the date on letters received; **date of receipt** = date when something is received **(b)** **up to date** = current *or* recent *or* modern; *an up-to-date computer system;* **to bring something up to**

date = to add the latest information to something; **to keep something up to date** = to keep adding information to something so that it is always up to date; *we spend a lot of time keeping our mailing list up to date* (c) **to date** = up to now; **interest to date** = interest up to the present time (d) **out of date** = old-fashioned; *their computer system is years out of date they are still using out-of-date machinery* (e) *(financial)* **maturity date** = date when a government stock will mature; **date of bill** = date when a bill will mature **2** *verb* to put a date on a document; *the cheque was dated March 24th; you forgot to date the cheque;* **to date a cheque forward** = to put a later date than the present one on a cheque

◊ **dated** ['deɪtɪd] *adjective* (a) with a date written on it; *thank you for your letter dated June 15th* (b) out-of-date; *the unions have criticized management for its dated ideas*

day [deɪ] *noun* (a) period of 24 hours; *there are thirty days in June; the first day of the month is a public holiday;* **settlement day** = day when accounts have to be settled; **three clear days** = three whole working days; *to give ten clear days' notice; allow four clear days for the cheque to be paid into the bank* (b) period of work from morning to night; **working day** = day when workers work (as opposed to a public holiday); **full day** *or* **full working day** *or* **a full day's work** = period when a worker works all the hours stipulated; **she took two days off** = she did not come to work for two days; **he works three days on, two days off** = he works for three days, then has two days' holiday; **to work an eight-hour day** = to spend eight hours at work each day; **day of action** = day when workers do not work, but take part in strikes or protests; **day care** = provision of care for small children while their mothers are at work; *one of the fringe benefits of the job was a free day care centre; the excellent day care facilities in the area have increased the availability of staff;* **day rate** = payment system, where workers are paid per day worked; *temporary workers are paid on a day rate; they receive a flat day rate of £100;* **day release** = arrangement where a company gives a worker permission to go to college to study for one or two days each week during working hours; *the junior sales manager is attending a day release course; temporary staff had to be hired while some of the employees were on day release;* **day shift** = shift which works during the daylight

hours such as from 8 a.m. to 5.30 p.m.; *there are 150 men on the day shift; he works the day shift* (c) one of the days of the week; **pay day** = the day when weekly-paid workers always receive their money

◊ **day-to-day** ['deɪtə'deɪ] *adjective* ordinary *or* which goes on all the time; *he organizes the day-to-day running of the company; sales only just cover the day-to-day expenses*

◊ **day work** ['deɪ 'wɜːk] *noun* work done on the day shift; work done during a day; **measured day work** = payment scheme where payment for a day's work depends on a specified level of output being achieved

◊ **day worker** ['deɪ 'wɜːkə] *noun* person who works the day shift

dead [ded] *adjective* (a) not alive; *six people were dead as a result of the accident; the founders of the company are all dead* (b) not working; **dead account** = account which is no longer used; **the line went dead** = the telephone line suddenly stopped working; **dead loss** = total loss; *the car was written off as a dead loss;* **dead money** = money which is not invested to make a profit; **dead season** = time of year when there are few tourists about; **dead wood** = employees who are old *or* who do not work well; *the new management team is weeding out the dead wood from the sales department*

◊ **dead end** ['ded 'end] *noun* point where you cannot go any further forward; *negotiations have reached a dead end;* **dead end job** = job where there are no chances of promotion

◊ **deadline** ['dedlaɪn] *noun* date by which something has to be done; **to meet a deadline** = to finish something in time; *we've missed our October 1st deadline*

◊ **deadlock** ['dedlɒk] **1** *noun* point where two sides in a dispute cannot agree; *the negotiations have reached deadlock;* **to break a deadlock** = to find a way to start discussions again **2** *verb* to be unable to agree to continue discussing; **talks have been deadlocked for ten days** = after ten days the talks have not produced any agreement

deafness ['defnəs] *noun* not being able to hear; **occupational deafness** = deafness caused by noise at work (as in someone using a pneumatic drill)

deal [di:l] **1** *noun* business agreement; **to reach a deal** *or* **to strike a deal** = to come to an agreement; **to call off a deal** = to stop an agreement; *when the chairman heard about the deal he called it off;* **raw deal** = bad arrangement *or* bad treatment; *she got a raw deal from management;* **package deal** = agreement where several different items are agreed at the same time; *they agreed a package deal, which involves the shorter working hours, increased productivity payments and longer holidays* **2** *verb* **to deal with** = to organize; *leave it to the personnel department - they'll deal with it;* **to deal with a problem** = to decide how to solve a problem

death [deθ] *noun* act of dying; **death benefit** = state insurance benefit paid to the family of someone who dies in an accident at work; **death in service** = insurance benefit or pension paid when someone dies while employed by a company; *US* **death duty** *or* **death tax** = tax paid on the property left by a dead person

deauthorization [di:ɔ:θəraɪ'zeɪʃn] *noun* *US* way in which unionized employees can vote to determine whether or not they want an open shop

debenture [dɪ'bentʃə] *noun* agreement to repay a debt with fixed interest using the company's assets as security

debt [det] *noun* money owed for goods or services; **to be in debt** = to owe money; **he is in debt to the tune of £250** = he owes £250; **to get into debt** = to start to borrow more money than you can pay back; **to be out of debt** = not to owe money any more; **to pay back a debt** = to pay all the money owed; **to pay off a debt** = to finish paying money owed; **secured debts** *or* **unsecured debts** = debts which are guaranteed or not guaranteed by assets; **debt collecting** *or* **collection** = collecting money which is owed; **debt collection agency** = company which collects debts for a commission; **debt collector** = person who collects debts; **debt counselling** = advising someone who owes money how to arrange his affairs to get out of debt

decentralize [di:'sentrəlaɪz] *verb* to organize from various points, with little power concentrated at the centre; *the bank was decentralized, with many decisions*

being taken by branch managers; the group has a policy of decentralized purchasing where each division has its own buying department; since the union was decentralized, its headquarters has moved to a tiny office;* **decentralized bargaining** = separate bargaining between management and unions in different areas, not at national or industry-wide level

◊ **decentralization** [di:sentrəlaɪ'zeɪʃn] *noun* organization from various points, away from the centre; *the decentralization of the buying departments*

decertification [di:sɜ:tɪfɪ'keɪʃn] *noun* *US* vote by a group of unionized employees to take away a union's right to represent them in bargaining

decide [dɪ'saɪd] *verb* to make up your mind to do something; *to decide on a course of action; to decide to appoint a new managing director*

◊ **deciding** [dɪ'saɪdɪŋ] *adjective* **deciding factor** = most important factor which influences a decision

decision [dɪ'sɪʒən] *noun* making up one's mind to do something; *to come to a decision* *or* *to reach a decision;* **to put off a decision** = to delay deciding something; **decision making** = act of coming to a decision; **the decision-making processes** = ways in which decisions are reached; **decision maker** = person who has to decide; **decision tree** = chart showing the way in which one decision follows from another

◊ **decisive** [dɪ'saɪsɪv] *adjective* (person) who makes up his mind *or* who comes to a decision

◊ **decisiveness** [dɪ'saɪsɪvnəs] *noun* ability to come to a decision quickly (NOTE: opposites are **indecision, indecisive, indecisiveness**)

declaration [deklə'reɪʃən] *noun* official statement; **declaration of bankruptcy** = official statement that someone is bankrupt; **declaration of income** = statement declaring income to the tax office; **customs declaration** = statement declaring goods brought into a country on which customs duty should be paid; **tax declaration** = statement made to the tax authorities about money earned, expenses and allowances claimed, etc.; **VAT**

declaration = statement declaring VAT income to the VAT office

◊ **declare** [dɪ'kleə] *verb* to make an official statement *or* to announce to the public; *to declare someone bankrupt; to declare a dividend of 10%;* **to declare goods to the customs** = to state that you are importing goods which are liable to duty; *the customs officials asked him if he had anything to declare;* **to declare an interest** = to state in public that you own shares in a company being investigated *or* that you are related to someone who can benefit from your contacts, etc.

◊ **declared** [dɪ'kleəd] *adjective* which has been made public or officially stated; **declared value** = value of goods entered on a customs declaration

decline [di'klaɪn] **1** *noun* gradual fall; *a decline in real wages over a period of time* **2** *verb* to fall slowly; *the purchasing power of the pound declined over the decade*

decrease 1 ['diːkriːs] *noun* fall *or* reduction; *decrease in price; decrease in value; decrease in imports; exports have registered a decrease; sales show a 10% decrease on last year* **2** [dɪ'kriːs] *verb* to fall *or* to become less; *imports are decreasing; the value of the pound has decreased by 5%*

decruiting [diː'kruːtɪŋ] *noun* policy of replacing permanent workers with temporary ones; *decruiting is an important factor in running a young industry*

deduct [dɪ'dʌkt] *verb* to take money away from a total; *to deduct tax from wages; to deduct £3 from the price; to deduct a sum for expenses;* **tax deducted at source** = tax which is removed from a salary, interest payment *or* dividend payment on shares before the money is paid

◊ **deductible** [dɪ'dʌktəbl] *adjective* which can be deducted; **deductible expenses** = expenses which can be deducted against tax; **tax-deductible** = which can be deducted from an income before tax is paid; **these expenses are not tax-deductible** = tax has to be paid on these expenses

◊ **deduction** [dɪ'dʌkʃən] *noun* removing of money from a total *or* money removed from a total; *net salary is salary after deduction of tax and social security; the deduction from his wages represented the*

cost of repairing the damage he had caused to the machinery; **deductions from salary** *or* **salary deductions** *or* **deductions at source** = money which a company removes from salaries to give to the government as tax, national insurance contributions, etc.; **tax deductions** = (i) money removed from a salary to pay tax; (ii); *US* business expenses which can be claimed against tax

deed [diːd] *noun* legal document *or* written agreement; **deed of arrangement** = agreement made between a debtor and his creditors whereby the creditors accept an agreed sum in settlement of their claim rather than make the debtor bankrupt; **deed of assignment** = document which legally transfers a property from a debtor to a creditor; **deed of covenant** = signed legal agreement to pay someone a sum of money every year

default [dɪ'fɔːlt] **1** *noun* failure to carry out the terms of a contract, especially failure to pay back a debt; **he is in default** = he has failed to carry out the terms of the contract **2** *verb* to fail to carry out the terms of a contract, especially to fail to pay back a debt; **to default on payments** = not to make payments which are due under the terms of a contract

◊ **defaulter** [dɪ'fɔːltə] *noun* person who defaults

defence *or US* **defense** [dɪ'fens] *noun* **(a)** protecting someone *or* something against attack; *the merchant bank is organizing the company's defence against the takeover bid* **(b)** fighting a lawsuit on behalf of a defendant; arguing the case for a client before a tribunal; **defence counsel** = lawyer who represents the defendant in a lawsuit **(c)** explanation of actions; *his defence was that the expenditure had been authorized verbally by his manager*

◊ **defend** [dɪ'fend] *verb* to fight to protect someone *or* something which is being attacked; *the company is defending itself against the takeover bid; he hired the best lawyers to defend him against the tax authorities;* **to defend a lawsuit** = to appear in court to state your case when accused of something

◊ **defendant** [dɪ'fendənt] *noun* person who is sued *or* person against whom a legal action is taken

defer [dɪ'fɜː] *verb* to put back to a later date *or* to postpone; *to defer payment; the decision has been deferred until the next meeting* (NOTE: **deferring - deferred**)

◊ **deferred** [dɪ'fɜːd] *adjective* put back to a later date; **deferred payment** = (i) money paid later than the agreed date; (ii) payment for goods by instalments over a long period; **deferred pension** = pension plan where the pension is taken late, so as to allow benefits to accrue; **deferred retirement** = retirement which starts later than the statutory age

degree [dɪ'griː] *noun* (a) qualification awarded to someone who has passed a course of study at a university or polytechnic; *he has a degree in Business Studies; she has a degree in social work* (b) amount *or* level; *being promoted to a management position means a greater degree of responsibility; the personnel director is trying to assess the degree of discontent among the workforce*

delay [dɪ'leɪ] **1** *noun* time when someone *or* something is later than planned; *there was a delay of thirty minutes before the AGM started or the AGM started after a thirty minute delay; we are sorry for the delay in supplying your order or in replying to your letter* **2** *verb* to be late; to make someone late; *he was delayed because his taxi was involved in an accident; the company has delayed payment of all invoices*

delegate ['delɪgət] **1** *noun* person who represents others at a meeting; *the management refused to meet the trade union delegates;* **conference delegate** = person who attends a conference as the representative of a group; **delegate conference** = meeting of representatives from each of the main branches of a trade union **2** *verb* to pass authority or responsibility to someone else; *to delegate authority;* **he cannot delegate** = he wants to control everything himself and refuses to give up any of his responsibilities to his subordinates

◊ **delegation** [delɪ'geɪʃən] *noun* (a) group of delegates; *a Chinese trade delegation; the management met a union delegation* (b) act of passing authority or responsibility to someone else (NOTE: no plural for this meaning)

demand [dɪ'mɑːnd] **1** *noun* (a) asking for something and insisting on getting it; *the union's list of demands; the management refused to give in to union demands for a meeting;* **to meet the union's demands** = to agree to what the union is asking for (b) asking for payment; **payable on demand** = which must be paid when payment is asked for; *US* **demand deposit** = money in a bank account which can be taken out when you want it by writing a cheque; **final demand** = last reminder from a supplier, after which he will sue for payment (c) need for person *or* goods *or* services at a certain price; *there is a growing demand for manpower in the service sector; there is an acute demand for experienced salesmen in the insurance industry; the factory had to cut production when demand slackened; the office cleaning company cannot keep up with the demand for its services;* **to meet a demand** *or* **to fill a demand** = to supply what is needed; *to meet the demand for manpower in the service industries; the factory had to increase production to meet the extra demand for its products;* **there is not much demand for this item** = not many people want to buy it; **this book is in great demand** *or* **there is a great demand for this book** = many people want to buy it; **effective demand** = actual demand for a product which can be paid for; **demand price** = price at which a certain quantity of goods will be bought; **supply and demand** = amount of a product which is available and the amount which is wanted by customers; **law of supply and demand** = general rule that the amount of a product which is available is related to the needs of potential customers **2** *verb* to ask for something and expect to get it; *she demanded a refund; the suppliers are demanding immediate payment of their outstanding invoices; the shop stewards demanded an urgent meeting with the managing director*

demarcation [diːmɑː'keɪʃən] *noun* clear definition of the responsibilities of each employee or category of employment; *the union insisted on clear demarcation when tasks were assigned to different workers; demarcation ensures that no one does work which is not defined in his job description;* **demarcation dispute** = disagreement between different trade unions as to how work shall be divided between various classes of workers; *production of the new car was held up by demarcation disputes*

demerge [diː'mɜːdʒ] *verb* to separate a company into various separate parts

◊ **demerger** [diː'mɜːdʒə] *noun* separation of a company into several separate parts (especially used of a companies which have grown by acquisition)

democracy [dɪ'mɒkrəsi] *noun* system of government by freely elected representatives; **industrial democracy** = concept where power is shared by workers in an organization *or* industry; *industrial democracy was part of the political party's manifesto; the union claimed that industrial democracy required all workers to vote on important issues*

◊ **democratic** [demə'krætɪk] *adjective* **democratic style of management** = management style where the managers involve the workers in decision-making processes (NOTE: the opposite is **autocratic style**)

demography [dɪ'mɒgrəfi] *noun* study of populations, trends in birth rates, life expectancy, death rates, etc.

◊ **demographic** [demə'græfɪk] *adjective* referring to demography; **demographic time-bomb** = catastrophic population trends, such as a sharp increase in the number of people of pensionable age and a decrease in the number of younger people of working age; **demographic change** = changes in the population which may affect the working population in the future (a fall in the birth rate means fewer potential workers, a rise in life expectancy means more people drawing pensions, etc.)

demote [dɪ'məʊt] *verb* to give someone a less important job *or* to reduce an employee to a lower rank *or* grade; *he was demoted from manager to salesman; she lost a lot of salary when she was demoted; as he cannot cope with the responsibilities of the post the MD will be forced to demote him*

◊ **demotion** [dɪ'məʊʃən] *noun* reducing an employee to a lower rank *or* giving someone a less important job; *he was very angry at his demotion; demotion ended his dreams of becoming managing director; demotion means a considerable drop in income*

department [dɪ'pɑːtmənt] *noun* **(a)** specialized section of a large organization; *complaints department; design department;*

dispatch department; export department; legal department; trainee managers are put to work in each department to get an idea of the organization as a whole; **accounts department** = section which deals with money paid *or* received; **personnel department** = section of a company dealing with the staff; *working in the personnel department gives trainees a view of the human problems of management;* **head of department** *or* **department head** *or* **department manager** = person in charge of a department **(b)** section of the British government containing several ministries; **the Department of Trade and Industry (DTI)** = government department dealing with commerce, exports, industrial relations, etc.; **the Department for Education and Employment (DFEE)** = British government department responsible for education, training and unemployment benefit and unemployment statistics

◊ **departmental** [diːpɑːt'mentl] *adjective* referring to a department; **departmental manager** = manager of a department

departure [dɪ'pɑːtʃə] *noun* **(a)** leaving a company; **date of departure** *or* **departure date** = date on which an employee leaves the company **(b)** **departure from normal practice** = doing something in a different way from the usual one

depend [dɪ'pend] *verb* **(a)** **to depend on** = to need someone *or* something to exist; *the company depends on efficient service from its suppliers; we depend on government grants to pay the salary bill* **(b)** to happen because of something; *the success of the anti-drug campaign will depend on the attitude of the public;* **depending on** = happening as a result of something; *depending on the circumstances, she may be reprimanded or have the money docked from her pay*

◊ **dependant** [dɪ'pendənt] *noun* person who depends financially on someone else; *he has to provide for his family and dependants out of a very small salary*

◊ **dependence** *or* **dependency** [dɪ'pendəns *or* dɪpendənsi] *noun* being dependent on someone or something; **dependence on drugs**

◊ **dependent** [dɪ'pendənt] *adjective* (person) who is supported financially by someone else; *tax relief is allowed for dependent relatives*

QUOTE not only has the use of early retirement to downsize firms increased the burden of dependency on the remaining workforce but, in an ageing population, older workers will be better attuned to future markets, according to a study carried out by the University of Westminster

People Management

deploy [dɪ'plɔɪ] *verb* to send staff to a certain place to carry out a certain job

◊ **deployment** [dɪ'plɔɪmənt] *noun* **deployment of personnel** = sending staff to certain places to carry out certain jobs

deposit administration scheme [dɪ'pɒzɪt ædmɪnɪ'streɪʃn 'skiːm] *noun* pension scheme by which the worker's pension contributions are paid into a deposit account with an insurance company and are not used immediately to buy benefits

depreciation [dɪpriːʃɪ'eɪʃən] *noun* reduction in value of an asset; **depreciation rate** = rate at which an asset is depreciated each year in the accounts; **accelerated depreciation** = system of depreciation which reduces the value of assets at a high rate in the early years to encourage companies, as a result of tax advantages, to invest in new equipment; **annual depreciation** = reduction in the book value of an asset at a certain rate per year

COMMENT: various methods of depreciating assets are used, such as the 'straight line method', where the asset is depreciated at a constant percentage of its cost each year and the 'reducing balance method', where the asset is depreciated at a constant percentage which is applied to the cost of the asset after each of the previous years' depreciation has been deducted

depressed [dɪ'prest] *adjective* feeling miserable and worried; *she was depressed when she was not promoted*

◊ **depression** [dɪ'preʃən] *noun* mental state where someone feels miserable and hopeless; *he suffers from bouts of depression*

dept [dɪ'pɑːtmənt] = DEPARTMENT

deputy ['depjʊti] *noun* person who takes the place of another; *to act as deputy for someone or to act as someone's deputy;*

deputy chairman; deputy manager; deputy managing director

◊ **deputize** ['depjʊtaɪz] *verb* **to deputize for someone** = to take the place of someone who is absent; *he deputized for the chairman who was ill*

derecognise [diː'rekəgnaɪz] *verb* to cease to recognise a union as the representative of the workers

◊ **derecognition** [diːrekəg'nɪʃn] *noun* action of ceasing to recognise a union as able to represent the workers (typical reasons are: few of the workforce actually belong to the union, or the company has changed owner)

describe [dɪ'skraɪb] *verb* to say what someone *or* something is like; *the leaflet describes the services the company can offer; the managing director described the company's cash flow difficulties*

◊ **description** [dɪ'skrɪpʃən] *noun* detailed account of what something is like; **job description** = official document from the management which says what a job involves; **trade description** = description of a product to attract customers

designate ['dezɪgnət] *adjective* person who has been appointed to a job but who has not yet started work; *the chairman designate* (NOTE: always follows a noun)

desk [desk] *noun* writing table in an office, usually with drawers for stationery; **desk pad** = pad of paper kept on a desk for writing notes; **desk research** = looking for information which is in printed sources, such as directories

deskilling [diː'skɪlɪŋ] *noun* reducing the number of skilled jobs and replacing them with unskilled jobs

detail ['diːteɪl] **1** *noun* **(a)** small part of a description; *the catalogue gives all the details of our product range; we are worried by some of the details in the contract;* **in detail** = giving many particulars; *the catalogue lists all the products in detail* **(b)** temporary assignment of an employee to a different position for a specified time; *the union is complaining that employees are being given details that were never mentioned at the time of their recruitment; the secretary was sent to another branch on a* *two-week detail* **2** *verb* **(a)** to list in detail; *the catalogue details the payment arrangements for overseas buyers; the terms of the licence are detailed in the contract* **(b)** to give someone a temporary assignment; *two men were detailed to deal with the urgent order*

◊ **detailed** ['di:teɪld] *adjective* in detail; **detailed account** = account which lists every item

determine [dɪ'tɜ:mɪn] *verb* to fix *or* to arrange *or* to decide; *to determine prices or quantities; conditions of work are still to be determined*

◊ **determination** [dɪtɜ:mɪ'neɪʃn] *noun* **determination of salaries** = fixing the amount of salaries to be paid to different categories of workers

develop [dɪ'veləp] *verb* **(a)** to plan and produce; *to develop a new product* **(b)** to plan and build an area; *to develop an industrial estate*

◊ **development** [dɪ'veləpmənt] *noun* **(a)** growth; **career development** = planning of an employee's future career in an organization **(b)** planning the production of a new product; *research and development* **(c) industrial development** = planning and building of new industries in special areas; **development area** *or* **development zone** = area which has been given special help from a government to encourage the setting up of businesses and factories there

DFEE = DEPARTMENT FOR EDUCATION AND EMPLOYMENT

DHSS [di:'eɪtʃes'es] = DEPARTMENT OF HEALTH AND SOCIAL SECURITY

diagram ['daɪəgræm] *noun* design *or* drawing which shows information as a plan or a map; *diagram showing sales locations; he drew a diagram to show how the decision-making processes work; a diagram showing the company's organizational structure;* **flow diagram** = diagram showing the arrangement of work processes in a series

◊ **diagrammatic** [daɪəgrə'mætɪk] *adjective* **in diagrammatic form** = in the form of a diagram; *the chart showed the work flow in diagrammatic form*

◊ **diagrammatically** [daɪəgrə'mætɪkəli] *adverb* using a diagram; *the chart shows the sales pattern diagrammatically*

dialogue ['daɪəlɒg] *noun* discussion between two people or groups, in which views are exchanged; *the management refused to enter into a dialogue with the strikers*

differ ['dɪfə] *verb* not to be the same as something else; *the two managerial vacancies differ considerably - one deals with product design and the other with customer services*

◊ **difference** ['dɪfrəns] *noun* way in which two things are not the same; *what is the difference between a junior manager and a managerial assistant?*

◊ **different** ['dɪfrənt] *adjective* not the same; *our product range is quite different in design from that of our rivals; we offer ten models each in six different colours*

◊ **differential** [dɪfə'renʃəl] **1** *adjective* which shows a difference; **differential piecework** = payment for each piece of work completed, determined by the total number of pieces produced over a period, with extra bonus payments for work completed more quickly; *the management decided that differential piecework provided the best balance between incentives and wage security* **2** *noun* difference in pay for different ranks *or* grades in an organization; **pay differentials** *or* **salary differentials** *or* **wage differentials** = differences between one worker's wage and another's in similar types of jobs; **to erode wage differentials** = to reduce differences in salary gradually; *wage differentials cause resentment in the department; the new pay structure will try to do away with unjustified pay differentials*

dilution [daɪ'lu:ʃən] *noun* **dilution of labour** = deskilling, reducing the number of skilled jobs and replacing them with unskilled jobs; **dilution agreement** = agreement by which unskilled labour can be employed when skilled workers are not available; *the dilution agreement allowed for untrained administrative workers until more qualified manpower came to the area* (NOTE: no plural)

◊ **dilutee** [daɪlu:'ti:] *noun* *(informal)* unskilled or semi-skilled worker who has taken a short training course, instead of a longer full course, and is seen as someone who is diluting the pool of skilled labour

diploma [dɪ'pləumə] *noun* document

which shows that a person has reached a certain level of skill in a subject; *she has a diploma in personnel management; he is studying for a diploma in engineering; the new assistant personnel manager has a diploma in human resources management; a diploma is awarded at the end of the two-year course in accountancy*

direct [daɪ'rekt] **1** *verb* to manage *or* to organize; *he directs our South-East Asian operations; she was directing the development unit until last year;* **directed interview** = DIRECTIVE INTERVIEW *directed interviews are easier to conduct, but may fail to extract as much as less formal methods of interviewing* **2** *adjective* straight *or* with no interference; **direct action** = action (strike *or* go-slow, etc.) taken by workers to secure better conditions when talks with employers have broken down; *management was aware that if they did not give in to the union's demands, direct action would result;* **direct cost** = cost directly related to the production costs of a product; **direct labour** = (i) cost of labour directly related to the quantity of items produced; (ii) workers employed to do a specific job for an organization under the organization's direct control; **direct taxation** = tax, such as income tax, which is paid direct to the government; *the government raises more money by direct than by indirect taxation* **3** *adverb* straight *or* with no third party involved; *we pay income tax direct to the government;* **to dial direct** = to contact a phone number yourself without asking the operator to do it for you; *you can dial New York direct from London if you want*

◊ **direction** [daɪ'rekʃən] *noun* **(a)** organizing *or* managing; *he took over the direction of a multinational group* (NOTE: no plural for this meaning) **(b) directions for use** = instructions showing how to use something

directive [dɪ'rektɪv] *noun* order *or* command to someone to do something (especially order from the Council of Ministers *or* Commission of the European Community referring to a particular problem in certain countries); *the Commission issued a directive on food prices*

◊ **directive interview** *noun* interview built round specific questions instead of an open discussion; *candidates often find directive interviews inhibiting*

QUOTE employees will have the right to see almost all records held on them by their employers when a new EU directive is introduced into Britain. Whereas staff are already entitled to view and correct most of their computerized company records, the directive on data protection will allow them to view paper-based records as well

People Management

directly [daɪ'rektli] *adverb* **(a)** immediately; *he left for the airport directly after receiving the telephone message* **(b)** straight *or* with no third party involved; *we deal directly with the manufacturer, without using a wholesaler*

director [daɪ'rektə] *noun* **(a) company director** = person appointed by the shareholders to help run a company; *when he became a director his whole future was tied to that of the company;* **managing director** = director who is in charge of the whole company; **chairman and managing director** = managing director who is also chairman of the board of directors; **board of directors** = all the directors of a company; **directors' report** = annual report from the board of directors to the shareholders; **associate director** = director who attends board meetings but has not been elected by the shareholders; **executive director** = director who actually works full-time in the company; **non-executive director** = director who attends board meetings only to give advice; **outside director** = director who is not employed by the company **(b)** person who is in charge of a project, an official institute, etc.; *the director of the government research institute; she was appointed director of the organization*

◊ **directorate** [daɪ'rektərət] *noun* group of directors

◊ **directorship** [daɪ'rektəʃɪp] *noun* post of director; *he was offered a directorship with Smith Ltd*

disability [dɪsə'bɪlɪti] *noun* being unable to use one's body properly (as because you are blind *or* cannot walk, etc.); *disability is not considered a disadvantage in workers applying for certain types of jobs; the government awards special disability allowances for handicapped people who cannot find work;* **long-term disability** = disability which lasts or is likely to last a very long time; **partial disability** = situation where a worker is partly disabled, as so is eligible for less benefit; **total disability** = situation where a worker is completely disabled, and so can receive maximum benefit; **disability working allowance (DWA)** = benefit paid to people working more than 16 hours a week who have an illness or disability

◊ **disabled** [dɪs'eɪbld] *adjective* having a physical handicap; *each company is required by law to employ a certain percentage of disabled staff; there are special facilities for disabled employees; one of our managers is disabled and cannot travel far;* **disabled person** = person who is physically handicapped in some way (such as being blind or not able to walk)

◊ **disablement** [dɪs'eɪblmənt] *noun* condition where a person has a physical *or* mental handicap; **partial disablement** = being disabled to such an extent that you can only do part of your normal work; **temporary disablement** = being unable to work for a period because of illness or an accident; **disablement benefit** = disability allowance *or* government payment to a person who is disabled *or* handicapped; **industrial injuries disablement benefit** = benefit paid to a worker who has been injured or disabled at work

QUOTE the British Computer Society is launching a campaign to help disabled people find jobs
Personnel Today

disadvantage [dɪsəd'vɑːntɪdʒ] *noun* something which makes you less successful; *it is a disadvantage for a personnel manager to have had no experience of industry;* **to be at a disadvantage** = to be in a more awkward position (than another person); *not having taken a management course puts him at a disadvantage*

disbursement [dɪs'bɜːsmənt] *noun* payment of money

discharge [dɪs'tʃɑːdʒ] **1** *noun* **(a)** carrying out of a job; **in discharge of his duties as director** = carrying out his duties as director **(b) discharge in bankruptcy** = being released from bankruptcy after paying one's debts; **in full discharge of a debt** = paying a debt completely; **final discharge** = final payment of what is left of a debt **(c)**

dismissal from a job **2** *verb* **(a)** to carry out a job; *he has always discharged his duties with considerable expertise* **(b)** **to discharge a bankrupt** = to release someone from bankruptcy because he has paid his debts; **to discharge a debt** *or* **to discharge one's liabilities** = to pay a debt *or* one's liabilities in full **(c)** to dismiss *or* to sack; *to discharge an employee for negligence*

discipline ['dɪsɪplɪn] **1** *noun* self-control needed to do a job; *working his way up the company ladder gave him the discipline to take on further management responsibilities; lack of discipline is responsible for poor attendance figures;* **to keep discipline** = to make sure that everyone obeys the rules **2** *verb* to punish a worker for misconduct; *three members of staff were disciplined by the manager*

◊ **disciplinary** [dɪsɪ'plɪnəri] *adjective* referring to punishment; **disciplinary action** *or* **disciplinary measures** = action taken to control or punish bad behaviour by employees; *disciplinary action had to be taken to prevent further disputes between workers and managers; the union complained that the disciplinary action was too harsh;* **disciplinary board** = group of people who conduct a disciplinary interview; **disciplinary interview** = interview between management and worker to discuss a breach of discipline (the worker may be accompanied by a union representative); **disciplinary lay-off** = temporary dismissal of an employee as a punishment; **disciplinary procedure** = way of warning a worker officially that he is breaking rules

QUOTE disciplinary action is often regarded as synonymous with dismissal, but the new ACAS handbook takes a more positive view
Employment Gazette

disclosure [dɪs'kləʊʒə] *noun* act of telling details; **disclosure of information** = giving information to someone, such as the union representatives in collective bargaining, so that they know all the relevant facts about a case before presenting the defence

discretion [dɪs'kreʃən] *noun* being able to decide correctly what should be done; **I leave it to your discretion** = I leave it for you to decide what to do; **at the discretion of someone** = if someone decides; *membership* *is at the discretion of the committee* (NOTE: no plural)

◇ **discretionary** [dɪs'kreʃənəri] *adjective* which can be done if someone wants; **the minister's discretionary powers** = powers which the minister could use if he or she thought it necessary

discriminate [dɪs'krɪmɪneɪt] *verb* to treat people in different ways because of class, religion, sex, language or colour; *the management appeared to discriminate against handicapped applicants*

◇ **discrimination** [dɪskrɪmɪ'neɪʃən] *noun* treating people in different ways because of class, religion, race, language, colour or sex; **racial discrimination** = treating a person differently (usually worse) because of his or her race; **sexual discrimination** *or* **sex discrimination** *or* **discrimination on grounds of sex** = treating men and women in different ways; **positive discrimination** = giving more favourable treatment to a racial or sexual minority to help them be more equal (NOTE: no plural)

◇ **discriminatory** [dɪs'krɪmɪnətri] *adjective* which shows discrimination; *the appointment of only males to the three posts was clearly discriminatory*

QUOTE EEC legislation should formally recognize that sexual harassment is discrimination on grounds of sex
Personnel Management

QUOTE she claimed she was a victim of sex discrimination but this was rejected by the industrial tribunal and the Court of Appeal
Personnel Today

QUOTE discrimination in pensions is set to continue
Personnel Management

discuss [dɪs'kʌs] *verb* to talk about a problem; *they spent two hours discussing the details of the contract; the committee discussed the question of import duties on cars; the board will discuss wage rises at its next meeting; we discussed delivery schedules with our suppliers*

◇ **discussion** [dɪs'kʌʃən] *noun* talking about a problem; *after ten minutes' discussion the board agreed the salary increases; we spent the whole day in*

discussions with our suppliers; to hold discussions = to discuss formally; *management is holding discussions with representatives of the union*

disease [dɪ'ziːz] *noun* illness (of people *or* animals *or* plants, etc.) where the body functions abnormally; **industrial disease** *or* **occupational disease** = disease which is caused by the type of work *or* the conditions in which someone works (such as disease caused by dust *or* chemicals in a factory)

diseconomies of scale [dɪsiː'kɒnəmiːz əv 'skeɪl] *noun* situation where increased production actually increases unit cost

COMMENT: after having increased production using the existing workforce and machinery, giving economies of scale, the company finds that in order to increase production further it has to employ more workers and buy more machinery, leading to an increase in unit cost

disincentive [dɪsɪn'sentɪv] *noun* something which discourages, especially something which discourages people from working; *the low salary offered was a disincentive to work*

disk [dɪsk] *noun* round flat object, used to store information in computers; **floppy disk** = small disk for storing information through a computer; **hard disk** = computer disk in a sealed case, which will store a large amount of information; **disk drive** = part of a computer which makes a disk spin round in order to read it or store information on it

◇ **diskette** [dɪs'ket] *noun* small floppy disk

dismiss *verb* [dɪs'mɪs] **(a) to dismiss an employee** = to remove an employee from a job; *he was dismissed for being late* **(b)** to refuse to accept; *the court dismissed the claim*

◇ **dismissal** [dɪs'mɪsəl] *noun* ending an employee's job, either by sacking or by not renewing a contract; **blanket dismissal** = dismissal of a group of workers because one unidentified worker is suspected of having committed an offence, and the others refuse to reveal the identity of the culprit; **constructive dismissal** = legal right of an employee to resign owing to improper behaviour on the part of the employer and still claim payment for wrongful dismissal; **fair dismissal** = dismissal of a worker for reasons which are fair, such as the worker's bad conduct (theft, drunkenness, etc.), failure of the worker to work capably, real redundancy, etc.; **unfair dismissal** = removing someone from a job for reasons which are not fair; **summary dismissal** = dismissal without giving the worker any notice (usually because of a crime committed by the worker, drunkenness or violent behaviour towards other workers); **wrongful dismissal** = removing someone from a job for a reason which does not justify dismissal and which is in breach of the contract of employment; **dismissal procedures** = correct way of dismissing someone according to the contract of employment

QUOTE failure to follow a procedure may make a dismissal both wrongful and unfair
Personnel Management

QUOTE he did not consult them, just calling the five in and dismissing them one by one
Personnel Management

QUOTE the commission noted that in the early 1960s there was an average of 203 stoppages each year arising out of dismissals
Employment Gazette

QUOTE when deciding whether to dismiss an employee, any alternatives, such as part-time working, lighter duties or early retirement should be considered
Personnel Today

disobey [dɪsə'beɪ] *verb* not to do what someone tells you to do; *the workers disobeyed their union's instructions and held a 24-hour strike*

◊ **disobedience** [dɪsə'biːdiəns] *noun* not doing what you are told to do; **wilful disobedience** = not obeying lawful instructions issued by the management (as a means of antagonizing them)

disparity [dɪs'pærɪti] *noun* difference, not being the same; **disparities between salary levels** = differences between salaries paid to different workers at the same level of responsibility

dispose [dɪs'pəʊz] *verb* **(a) to dispose of** = to get rid of *or* to sell cheaply; *to dispose of excess equipment; to dispose of one's business* **(b) to dispose of day-to-day matters** = to deal with routine matters

◊ **disposable** [dɪs'pəʊzəbl] *adjective* **(a)** which can be used and then thrown away **(b) disposable income** = income left after tax and national insurance have been deducted; *his disposable income was small because he had a high mortgage, and paid high rates of tax*

◊ **disposal** [dɪs'pəʊzəl] *noun* sale; *disposal of securities or of property;* **lease** *or* **business for disposal** = lease *or* business for sale

dispute [dɪs'pjuːt] *noun* disagreement; *dispute between two departments in an organization;* **industrial disputes** *or* **labour disputes** = arguments between management and workers; **to adjudicate** *or* **to mediate in a dispute** = to try to settle a dispute between other parties; **disputes procedures** = correct way to deal with disputes, following the rules agreed between management and unions

disregard [dɪsri'gɑːd] **1** *noun* not paying any attention to something; **in complete disregard of regulations** = without paying any attention to the regulations **2** *verb* to take no notice of *or* not to obey; *the workers disregarded the instructions of the shop stewards*

dissatisfaction [dɪssætɪs'fækʃn] *noun* being discontented *or* not being satisfied; *dissatisfaction with bad working conditions; although the work itself was interesting, there was a lot of dissatisfaction with the organization and its rules;* **job dissatisfaction** = a worker's feeling of not being satisfied with his job

dissociate *verb* **to dissociate oneself from a statement** = not to agree with what someone has said; **right to dissociate** = right of workers to refuse to join a union (as opposed to the right of association, i.e. the right to join a union)

dissonance ['dɪsənəns] *see* COGNITIVE

distance learning ['dɪstəns 'lɜːnɪŋ] *noun* learning in one's own time away from the centre producing the course, by mail, radio, television or by occasional visits to centres; *the training department is organizing distance learning courses for employees to follow in their spare time*

distribute [dɪ'strɪbjuːt] *verb* **(a)** to share out dividends; *profits were distributed among the shareholders* **(b)** to send out goods from a manufacturer's warehouse to retail shops; *Smith Ltd distributes for several smaller companies*

◊ **distribution** [dɪstrɪ'bjuːʃən] *noun* **(a)** act of sending goods from the manufacturer to the wholesaler and then to retailers; *distribution costs; distribution manager;* **channels of distribution** *or* **distribution channels** = ways of sending goods from the manufacturer to the retailer **(b)** sharing something among several people; **distribution slip** = paper attached to a document *or* a magazine showing all the people in an office who should read it; **distribution of profits** = sharing of profits between shareholders, staff, etc.; **distribution of the workload** = sharing in a fair way the work which has to be done

◊ **distributive bargaining** [dɪ'strɪbjʊtɪv 'bɑːgənɪŋ] *noun* collective bargaining where the workers try to obtain as good a share of limited resources as possible

division [dɪ'vɪʒən] *noun* **(a)** main section of a large organization, with a certain degree of independence; *marketing division; production division; retail division; the paints division of ICI; the hotel division of the group; he is in charge of one of the company's major divisions* **(b)** company which is part of a large group; *Smith's is now a division of the Brown group of companies* **(c)** action of separating a whole into parts; *the division of responsibility between managers;* **division of labour** = production system where work is split up into clearly defined tasks and areas of responsibility

◊ **divisional** [dɪ'vɪʒənl] *adjective* referring to a division; *a divisional director; the divisional headquarters*

dock [dɒk] *verb* to remove money from someone's wages; *we will have to dock his pay if he is late for work again; he had £20 docked from his pay for being late*

doctor ['dɒktə] *noun* specialist who examines people when they are sick to see how they can be made well; *the staff are all sent to see the company doctor once a year;* **doctor's certificate** = document written by a doctor to say that a worker is ill and cannot work; *he has been off sick for ten days and still has not sent in a doctor's certificate;* **company doctor** = (i) doctor who works for a company and looks after sick workers; (ii) specialist businessman who rescues businesses which are in difficulties

dogsbody ['dɒgzbɒdi] *noun (informal)* person who does all types of work in an office for very low wages (NOTE: US English is **gofer**)

dole [dəʊl] *noun* money given by the government to unemployed people; **he is receiving dole payments** *or* **he is on the dole** = he is receiving unemployment benefits; **to sign on for the dole** = to register as unemployed; **dole queues** = lines of people waiting to collect the dole

domicile ['dɒmɪsaɪl] **1** *noun* place where someone lives *or* where a company's office is registered **2** *verb* **he is domiciled in Denmark** = he lives in Denmark officially; **bills domiciled in France** = bills of exchange which have to be paid in France

double ['dʌbl] **1** *adjective* **(a)** twice as large *or* two times the size; *their turnover is double ours; she has been promoted to manager at double her present salary;* **to work double shifts** = to work with two shifts of workers on duty; **they work double shifts** = two groups of workers are working shifts together; **double time** = time for which work is paid at twice the normal rate; **to be on double time** = to earn twice the usual wages for working on Sundays or other holidays; **double taxation** = taxing the same income twice; **double taxation agreement** = agreement between two countries that a person living in one country shall not be taxed in both countries on the income earned in the other country **(b)** **in double figures** = with two figures *or* 10 to 99; *inflation is in double figures; we have had double-figure inflation for some years* **2** *verb* to become twice as big; to make something twice as big; *we have doubled our profits this year* *or* *our profits have doubled this year; his mortgage repayments have doubled since he moved to the south of the country*

◊ **double-jobbing** ['dʌbl 'dʒɒbɪŋ] *noun* doing a second job, usually without paying tax; *double-jobbing has become more important since inflation made it difficult for workers to make ends meet; he makes thousands a year from double-jobbing; double-jobbing meant that he spent almost no time with his family see also* MOONLIGHTING

down [daʊn] **1** *adverb & preposition* in a lower position *or* to a lower position; *the inflation rate is gradually coming down; shares are slightly down on the day; the price of petrol has gone down;* to pay money down *or* to make a down payment = to make a deposit; *he paid £50 down and the rest in monthly instalments* **2** *verb* to down tools = to stop working

◊ **downgrade** [daʊn'greɪd] *verb* to reduce the importance of someone *or* of a job; *the post was downgraded in the company reorganization; he is to be downgraded because he has not kept up-to-date with new developments*

◊ **downgrading** [daʊn'greɪdɪŋ] *noun* moving an employee to a lower grade of job; *the reassessment of staff has led to some downgrading, which is never popular; we never resort to downgrading because it causes too much resentment*

◊ **downloading** [daʊn'ləʊdɪŋ] *noun* reducing the amount of work done in a department, factory, etc.

◊ **down payment** ['daʊn'peɪmənt] *noun* part of a total payment made in advance; *he made a down payment of $100*

◊ **downsize** ['daʊnsaɪz] *verb* to reduce the number of people employed, to make a company more profitable

◊ **downsizing** ['daʊnsaɪzɪŋ] *noun* reducing the size of something, especially reducing the number of people employed in a company to make it more profitable

◊ **down time** ['daʊn 'taɪm] *noun* time when a machine is not working because it is broken *or* being mended, etc.; time when a worker cannot work because machines have broken down, because components are not available, etc.; *too much down time is uneconomical for the company; better logistics will cut down on our down time*

◊ **downturn** ['daʊntɜːn] *noun* movement towards lower prices *or* sales *or* profits; *the last quarter saw a downturn in the economy*

◊ **downward** ['daʊnwəd] *adjective* towards a lower position; **downward communication** = communication from the top management to the lower levels of employee in an organization; *more effective downward communication will be helped by starting a house journal and by more informal talks between directors and employees*

◊ **downwards** ['daʊnwədz] *adverb* towards a lower position; *the company's profits have moved downwards over the last few years*

drag on ['dræg 'ɒn] *verb* to continue slowly without ending; *negotiations dragged on into the night*

draw up ['drɔː 'ʌp] *verb* to write a legal document; *to draw up a contract or an agreement*

drift [drɪft] **1** *noun* gradual movement without any control; **salary drift** *or* **earnings drift** = situation where an increase in pay is greater than that of officially negotiated rates **2** *verb* to move slowly and aimlessly; *workers are drifting back to work after the strike*

drill [drɪl] *noun* **fire drill** = procedure to be carried out to help people to escape from a burning building

drive [draɪv] **1** *noun* **(a)** energy *or* energetic way of working *or* ambition; *he is a young manager with drive; young men with enthusiasm and drive are sought by headhunters; the sales staff had the necessary drive to launch the new product successfully;* he has a lot of drive = he is very energetic in business; **economy drive** = vigorous effort to save money or materials; **sales drive** = vigorous effort to increase sales **(b)** part of a machine which makes other parts work; **disk drive** = part of a computer which makes the disk spin round in order to read or store information on it **2** *verb* **(a)** to make a car *or* lorry, etc. go in a certain direction; *he heard the news on the car radio when he was driving to work; she drives a company car* **(b)** he drives a hard bargain = he is a difficult negotiator

DTI [diːtiː'aɪ] = DEPARTMENT OF TRADE AND INDUSTRY

dual [djʊəl] *adjective* referring to two;

operated by two people; **dual career couple** = married couple where both husband and wife have different careers; **dual ladder** = two career paths in an organization leading to positions of equal importance and open to the same type of employee; *dual ladders attract employees who want to keep their career options open;* **dual unionism** = being a member of two trade unions; *dual unionism is common in industries where the workers want to be as well represented as possible; dual unionism is discouraged by unions who want to keep the loyalty of their members*

due [djuː] *adjective* **(a)** owed; *sum due from a debtor; bond due for repayment;* **to fall due** *or* **to become due** = to be ready for payment; **bill due on May 1st** = bill which has to be paid on May 1st; **balance due to us** = amount owed to us which should be paid **(b)** expected to arrive; *she is due to come for interview at 10.30* **(c)** **in due form** = written in the correct legal form; *receipt in due form; contract drawn up in due form;* **after due consideration of the problem** = after thinking seriously about the problem **(d)** caused by; *supplies have been delayed due to a strike at the manufacturers; the company pays the wages of staff who are absent due to illness*

◊ **dues** [djuːz] *plural noun* regular payments made by members to an organization; **union dues** = regular

payments paid by unions members to their union; *he was thrown out of the union for not paying his dues*

duly ['djuːli] *adverb* **(a)** properly; *duly authorized representative* **(b)** as was expected; *we duly met the union representatives to discuss the takeover*

duration [djʊəˈreɪʃn] *noun* length of time that something lasts; *the duration of a contract of employment; the clause is binding during the duration of the contract*

duty ['djuːti] *noun* **(a)** work which has to be done; **night duty** = period of work during the night; **on duty** = working as arranged; *he is on duty from 6 p.m. to midnight;* **the duty receptionist** = the receptionist who is working at the time; **duty roster** = list of times showing when each person is on duty at those times **(b)** moral *or* legal obligation; *the employee's duty to his employer; he felt he had a duty to show his successor how the job was done*

◊ **duties** ['djuːtiz] *noun* specified tasks which have to be done; *the job description lists the duties of a director's secretary; his duties are onerous but he's very well-paid*

DWA = DISABILITY WORKING ALLOWANCE

Ee

e.& o.e. = ERRORS AND OMISSIONS EXCEPTED

early ['ɜːli] *adjective & adverb* **(a)** before the usual time; *the mail arrived early;* **early closing day** = weekday (usually Wednesday or Thursday) when most shops in a town close in the afternoon; **at your earliest convenience** = as soon as possible; **at an early date** = very soon; **early retirement** = scheme where a company encourages employees to retire earlier than usual, and receive financial compensation for this; *early retirement at fifty-five; he took early retirement; the management offered some of the senior staff early retirement* **(b)** at the beginning of a period of time; *he took an early flight to Paris;* **we hope for an early resumption of negotiations** = we hope negotiations will start again soon

earn [ɜːn] *verb* **(a)** to be paid money for working; *to earn £50 a week; our agent in Paris certainly does not earn his commission; how much do you earn in your new job? her new job is more of a transfer than a promotion, since she doesn't earn any more;* **earned income** = money received as salary or wages **(b)** to produce interest or dividends; *what level of dividend do these shares earn? a building society account which earns interest at 10%*

◊ **earning** ['ɜːnɪŋ] *noun* **earning capacity** or **earning power** = amount of money someone should be able to earn; *his earning capacity has dramatically increased now that he has a university degree; he did not bother to look for jobs even though his earning capacity was considerable;* **earning potential** = (i) amount of money a person should be able to earn; (ii) amount of dividend a share should produce

◊ **earnings** ['ɜːnɪŋz] *plural noun* salary or wages or money received in return for work; *high earnings in top management reflect the heavy responsibilities involved; her earnings have increased since she has moved into a managerial position;* **attachment of earnings**

= legal power to take money from a person's salary to pay money, which is owed, to the courts; **attachment of earnings order** = court order to make an employer pay part of an employee's salary to the court to pay off debts; **compensation for loss of earnings** = payment to someone who has stopped earning money or who is not able to earn money; **gross earnings** = earnings before tax and other deductions; *how much is deducted from your gross earnings?;* **real earnings** = income which is available for spending after tax, etc. has been deducted, corrected for inflation; **earnings drift** = situation where an increase in pay is greater than that of officially negotiated rates; *the earnings drift is caused by a sudden increased demand for a certain class of employee;* **state earnings-related pension scheme (SERPS)** = state pension which is additional to the basic retirement pension and is based on average earnings over a worker's career; **earnings rule** = system where retirement pensions are reduced for those who earn more than a specified amount when working; *the earnings rule can be considered as a way of compensating for salary differentials*

QUOTE average hourly earnings of all full-time adult manual employees rose by 6.5 per cent between October 1986 and October 1987

Employment Gazette

EAT = EMPLOYMENT APPEAL TRIBUNAL

echelon ['eʃəlɒn] *noun* group of people of a certain grade in an organization; *the upper echelons of industry; communications have improved between the higher and lower echelons in the company*

econometrics [iːkənə'metrɪks] *plural noun* study of the statistics of economics, using computers to analyse statistics and make forecasts using mathematical models (NOTE: takes a singular verb)

economics [i:kə'nɒmɪks] *plural noun* **(a)** study of production, distribution, selling and use of goods and services **(b)** study of financial structures to show how a product or service is costed and what returns it produces (NOTE: takes a singular verb)

economy [ɪ'kɒnəmi] *noun* being careful not to waste money or materials; **an economy measure** = an action to save money or materials; **economies of scale** = making a product more profitable by manufacturing it in larger quantities

education [edjʊ'keɪʃn] *noun* training of the mind, especially through instruction at school, college, etc.; *jobs in management require a good basic education; people with no more than a basic education can be considered for manual positions;* **adult education** = education provided for adults; **basic education** = first level education, giving basic skills and information; **continuing education** = education which continues after school and university or college; **further education** = education after ending full-time education in school; **higher education** = education at university

effect [ɪ'fekt] *noun* **(a)** result; *the effect of the pay increase was to raise productivity levels* **(b)** terms of a contract which take effect *or* come into effect from January 1st = terms which start to operate on January 1st; **salaries are increased 10% with effect from January 1st** = a salary increase of 10% will apply from January 1st; **to remain in effect** = to continue to be applied **(c)** **personal effects** = personal belongings

effective [ɪ'fektɪv] *adjective* which works *or* which produces results; *she is an effective marketing manager;* **effective date** = date on which a rule *or* a contract starts to be applied; *the effective date of the employment contract is June 1st;* **effective date of termination** = the date at which an employee's employment ends (i.e., the date after notice, on which he leaves the company); **effective labour market** = labour market from which an employer actually draws applicants for posts, as opposed to the labour market from which the employer actually gets applicants; *see* COST-EFFECTIVE

◊ **effectiveness** [ɪ'fektɪvnəs] *noun* working *or* producing results; *his effectiveness as a manager was due to his*

quick grasp of detail; the effectiveness of any system depends on well-trained staff see COST-EFFECTIVENESS

efficiency [ɪ'fɪʃənsi] *noun* ability to work well *or* to produce the right work quickly and precisely; *with a high degree of efficiency; a business efficiency exhibition;* **an efficiency expert;** **efficiency bonus** = extra payment for efficiency in a job; **efficiency rating** = evaluation of an employee's efficiency in performing a job; *her efficiency rating is so high she will soon be promoted* (NOTE: no plural)

◊ **efficient** [ɪ'fɪʃənt] *adjective* able to work well *or* to produce the right work quickly and precisely; *an efficient secretary doesn't waste time; he needs an efficient secretary to look after his correspondence; really efficient secretaries become personal assistants*

◊ **efficiently** [ɪ'fɪʃəntli] *adverb* in an efficient way; *she organized the sales conference very efficiently*

effort [efət] *noun* using the mind or body to do something; *the salesmen made great efforts to increase sales; thanks to the efforts of the finance department, overheads have been reduced; if we make one more effort, we should clear the backlog of orders*

e.g. ['i:'dʒi:] for example *or* such as; *the contract is valid in some countries (e.g. France and Belgium) but not in others*

EGM = EXTRAORDINARY GENERAL MEETING

ego drive ['i:gəʊ 'draɪv] *noun* a person's ambition *or* motivation to succeed; *ego drive is highly valued in salesmen*

eighty/twenty rule ['eɪtɪ'twentɪ 'ru:l] *noun* rule that a small percentage of customers may account for a large percentage of sales; *see also* PARETO'S LAW

eighty per cent rule ['eɪtɪpə 'sent 'ru:l] *noun US* principle which states that if selection of a particular ethnic, age or sex group is less than 80% of another group, then the selection system is defective; *according to the eighty per cent rule our recruitment practices used to be highly discriminatory*

elasticity [elæs'tɪsəti] *noun* ability to change easily; **elasticity of supply and demand** = changes in supply and demand of an item depending on its market price

elect [ɪ'lekt] *verb* (a) to choose someone by a vote; *to elect the officers of an association; she was elected president of the staff club* (b) to choose to do something; *he elected to take early retirement*

◊ **-elect** [ɪ'lekt] *suffix* person who has been elected but has not yet started the term of office; *she is the president-elect* (NOTE: the plural is **presidents-elect)**

◊ **election** [ɪ'lekʃən] *noun* act of electing; *the election of directors by the shareholders;* **to stand for election** = to be a candidate in an election

element ['elɪmənt] *noun* basic part; smallest unit into which a job can be divided; *work study resulted in a standard time for each job element; each element of the job was timed during the work study*

eligible ['elɪdʒəbl] *adjective* person who can be chosen; *she is eligible for re-election;* **eligible list** = list of qualified applicants in an order based on the results of tests; *after marking the candidates' tests, they drew up an eligible list*

◊ **eligibility** [elɪdʒə'bɪləti] *noun* being eligible; *the chairman questioned her eligibility to stand for re-election*

eliminate [ɪ'lɪmɪneɪt] *verb* to remove; *we need to eliminate half the candidates if we want to draw up a short list; most of the candidates were eliminated after the first batch of tests*

embezzle [ɪm'bezl] *verb* to use illegally *or* to steal money which is not yours, or which you are looking after for someone; *he was sent to prison for six months for embezzling his clients' money*

◊ **embezzlement** [ɪm'bezlmənt] *noun* act of embezzling; *he was sent to prison for six months for embezzlement* (NOTE: no plural)

◊ **embezzler** [ɪm'bezlə] *noun* person who embezzles

emigrate ['emɪgreɪt] *verb* to go to another country to live permanently

◊ **emigration** [emɪ'greɪʃn] *noun* leaving a country to go to live permanently in another country

◊ **emigrant** ['emɪgrənt] *noun* person who emigrates

emoluments [ɪ'mɒljʊmənts] *plural noun* pay, salary or fees, or the earnings of directors who are not employees

empathy ['empəθi] *noun* ability to appreciate the feelings of a subordinate in a particular situation; *the need for empathy to understand the frustration of a worker in the wrong job; she had little empathy with less ambitious colleagues*

employ [ɪm'plɔɪ] *verb* to give someone regular paid work; **to employ twenty staff** = to have twenty people working for you; **to employ twenty new staff** = to give work to twenty new people

◊ **employed** [ɪm'plɔɪd] **1** *adjective* **to be employed** = to be in regular paid work; **he is not gainfully employed** = he has no regular paid work; **self-employed** = working for yourself; *he worked in a bank for ten years but is now self-employed; she is self-employed, running her own antiques business* **2** *plural noun* people who are in regularly paid work; *the employers and the employed; many of the employed are frightened of losing their jobs;* **the self-employed** = people who work for themselves

◊ **employee** [emplɔɪ'iː] *noun* worker *or* person employed by another; *the interests of employees are protected by trade unions; employees of the firm are eligible to join a profit-sharing scheme; relations between management and employees have improved; the company has decided to take on new employees;* **employee assistance programme** = programme set up to help employees with personal problems; **employee communication(s)** *or* **communication with employees** = passing information to employees and receiving information from employees; **employee participation** = sharing by employees in the company's planning and decision-making (as in quality circles, works councils, etc.); **employee profile** = person specification, form of job description which gives the ideal personal qualities needed for the job and a description of the ideal candidate for the job; **employee share ownership programme (ESOP)** = plan by which employees can acquire shares in the company they work for

◊ **employer** [ɪm'plɔɪə] *noun* person *or* company which has regular workers and pays them; **employers' organization** *or* **association** = organization of employers which represents them and protects their interests; *the employers' organization gave its members advice on legal matters when threatened with a national strike;* **employer's contribution** = money paid by an employer towards a worker's pension; **employer's liability** = legal responsibility of an employer when employees suffer accidents due to negligence on the part of the employer

employment [ɪm'plɔɪmənt] *noun* hiring employees *or* being hired as an employee; *employment is suffering in this area because of the recession; this is an area of high employment because it is near the airport;* **to be in continuous employment** = to be employed for a period of time, without more than a week's gap (holidays, sickness, etc. are not counted as gaps); *she was in continuous employment for the period 1993 to 1996;* **full employment** = situation where everyone in a country who can work has a job; **full-time employment** = work for all of a working day; *to be in full-time employment;* **part-time employment** = work for part of a working day; **temporary employment** = work which does not last for more than a few months; **to be without employment** = to have no work; **to find someone alternative employment** = to find another job for someone; **conditions of employment** = terms of a contract where someone is employed; **contract of employment** *or* **employment contract** = contract between management and an employee showing all the conditions of work; **security of employment** = feeling by a worker that he has the right to keep his job until he retires; **employment agency** *or* **bureau** *or* **office** = office which finds employees for organizations; **employment appeal tribunal (EAT)** = tribunal which deals with appeals against the decisions of industrial tribunals; **employment law** = the law as referring to workers, employers, and their rights

◊ **employment-at-will** [ɪm'plɔɪmənt ət 'wɪl] *noun* term in common law that a contract of employment with no specified period of service may be terminated by either side without notice or reason

COMMENT: this is a basic principle of US employment law, where an employer has the right to hire workers as he feels necessary and sack them for any reason and at any time, provided this is under the terms of the contract of employment agreed between him and the employee

QUOTE 70 per cent of Australia's labour force was employed in service activity
Australian Financial Review

QUOTE the blue-collar unions are the people who stand to lose most in terms of employment growth
Sydney Morning Herald

QUOTE companies introducing robotics think it important to involve individual employees in planning their introduction
Economist

empower [ɪm'pauə] *verb* to give someone the power to do something; *she was empowered by the company to sign the contract; her new position empowers her to hire and fire at will*

◊ **empowerment** [ɪm'pauəmənt] *noun* giving someone (such as an employee) the power to take decisions

QUOTE a district-level empowerment programme run in one of the government's executive agencies failed because middle managers blocked it. Empowerment was officially defined by the agency as involving delegation of responsibility and the encouragement of innovation
People Management

enc *or* **encl** = ENCLOSURE note put on a letter to show that a document is enclosed with it

enclose [ɪn'kləuz] *verb* to put something inside an envelope with a letter; *to enclose a recent photograph with your CV; I am enclosing a copy of the contract of employment; letter enclosing a cheque; please find the cheque enclosed herewith*

◊ **enclosure** [ɪn'kləuʒə] *noun* document enclosed with a letter; *letter with enclosures*

encounter group [en'kauntə 'gru:p] *noun* form of group psychotherapy which encourages people with personal problems to express their emotions; *encounter groups* *are used to accustom management trainees to criticism; the use of encounter groups to develop assertiveness in salesmen*

encourage [ɪn'kʌrɪdʒ] *verb* (a) to make it easier for something to happen; *the general rise in wages encourages consumer spending; leaving your credit cards on your desk encourages people to steal or encourages stealing; the company is trying to encourage sales by giving large discounts* (b) to help someone to do something by giving advice; *he encouraged me to apply for the job*

◊ **encouragement** [ɪn'kʌrɪdʒmənt] *noun* giving advice to someone to help him to succeed; *the designers produced a very marketable product, thanks to the encouragement of the sales director; his family has been a source of great encouragement to him*

energy ['enədʒi] *noun* force *or* strength; *he hasn't the energy to be a good salesman; they wasted their energies on trying to sell cars in the German market*

◊ **energetic** [enə'dʒetɪk] *adjective* with a lot of energy; *the salesmen have made energetic attempts to sell the product*

enforce [ɪn'fɔːs] *verb* to make sure something is done *or* is obeyed; *to enforce the terms of a contract*

◊ **enforcement** [ɪn'fɔːsmənt] *noun* making sure that something is obeyed; *enforcement of the terms of a contract*

engage [ɪn'geɪdʒ] *verb* to arrange to employ workers *or* advisors, etc.; *if we increase production we will need to engage more machinists; he was engaged as a temporary replacement for the marketing manager who was ill; the company has engaged twenty new salesmen*

◊ **engagement** [ɪn'geɪdʒmənt] *noun* arrangement to employ workers or to reemploy them in the same job, but not necessarily under the same conditions; *the engagement of two new secretaries will relieve management of some of the administrative duties*

enhance [en'hɑːns] *verb* to make better or more attractive; *working for a German company enhances the value of her work experience*

enlargement [ɪn'lɑːdʒmənt] *noun*

horizontal job enlargement = expanding a job to include new activities *or* responsibilities, but still at the same level in the organization; *we have implemented horizontal job enlargement to increase individual workloads while at the same time making the work more interesting*

enquire, enquiry [ɪn'kwaɪə *or* ɪn'kwaɪəri] = INQUIRE, INQUIRY

enrichment [ɪn'rɪtʃmənt] *noun* **job enrichment** = making a job more satisfying for the person doing it

enter ['entə] *verb* (a) to go in; *they all stood up when the chairman entered the room* (b) to write; *to enter a name on a list; she entered a competition for a holiday in Greece; they entered the sum in the ledger* (c) **to enter into** = to begin; *to enter into relations with someone; to enter into a partnership with a legal friend; to enter into an agreement or a contract*

enterprise ['entəpraɪz] *noun* (a) initiative *or* willingness to take risks *or* to take responsibility; *we are looking for enterprise and ambition in our top managers* (b) system of carrying on a business; **free enterprise** = system of business free from government interference; **private enterprise** = businesses which are owned privately, not nationalized; *the project is completely funded by private enterprise;* **enterprise culture** = general feeling that the commercial system works better with free enterprise, increased share ownership, property ownership, etc.; **enterprise zone** = area of the country where businesses are encouraged to develop by offering special conditions such as easy planning permission for buildings, reduction in the business rate, etc. (c) a business; **a small-scale enterprise** = a small business; **a state enterprise** = a state-controlled company; *bosses of state enterprises are appointed by the government;* **enterprise union** = single union which represents all the workers in a company

◊ **enterprising** ['entəpraɪzɪŋ] *adjective* having initiative; *an enterprising salesman can always find new sales outlets*

entertainment [entə'teɪnmənt] *noun* offering meals, etc., to business visitors; **entertainment allowance** = money which a manager is allowed by his company to spend on meals with visitors; **entertainment expenses** = money spent on giving meals to business visitors

entice [ɪn'taɪs] *verb* to try to persuade someone to do something; *the company was accused of enticing staff from other companies by offering them higher salaries*

◇ **enticement** [ɪn'taɪsmənt] *noun* attracting someone away from his job to another job which is better paid

entitle [ɪn'taɪtl] *verb* to give the right to someone to have something; *after one year's service the employee is entitled to four weeks' holiday; as senior manager he is entitled to one of the larger offices*

◇ **entitlement** [ɪn'taɪtlmənt] *noun* a person's right to something; **benefits entitlement** = the type of social security benefit to which someone has the right; **holiday entitlement** = number of days' paid holiday which a worker has the right to take; *she has not used up all her holiday entitlement;* **pension entitlement** = amount of pension which someone has the right to receive when he or she retires

entrance ['entrəns] *noun* going into a new job; **entrance rate** = rate of pay for employees when first hired; *though the entrance rate is very low, the salary goes up considerably after the first year; the entrance rate depends on whether the entrants are skilled or not*

◇ **entrant** ['entrənt] *noun* person who is going into a new job; *there are several highly qualified people in this month's batch of entrants*

entrepreneur [ɒntrəprə'nɜː] *noun* person who directs a company and takes commercial risks

◇ **entrepreneurial** [ɒntrəprə'nɜːrɪəl] *adjective* taking commercial risks; *an entrepreneurial decision*

entrust [ɪn'trʌst] *verb* **to entrust someone with something** *or* **to entrust something to someone** = to give someone the responsibility for something; *he was entrusted with the keys to the office safe*

entry ['entri] *noun* **(a)** act of going into a new job; *entry of recruits from school;* **graduate entry** = entry of graduates into

employment with a company; *the graduate entry into the civil service;* **entry level job** = job for which no previous experience is needed; *it is only an entry level job, but you can expect promotion within six months* **(b)** written information put in an accounts ledger; **credit entry** *or* **debit entry** = entry on the credit *or* debit side of an account; **to make an entry in a ledger** = to write in details of a transaction

environment [ɪn'vaɪrənmənt] *noun* surroundings; *trade unions demand a good working environment for employees*

◇ **environmental** [ɪnvaɪrən'mentl] *adjective* referring to the environment; **environmental audit** = assessment made by a company or organization of the financial benefits and disadvantages to be derived from adopting a more environmentally sound policy

EOC ['iː'əʊ'siː] = EQUAL OPPORTUNITIES COMMISSION

equal ['iːkwəl] *adjective* exactly the same; **equal pay** = system where both men and women are paid the same rate for the same job; *male and female workers have equal pay; equal pay for men and women doing the same job; the politician was in favour of equal pay for equal effort;* **equal opportunities** = avoiding discrimination in employment; *does the political party support equal opportunities for women?;* **Equal Opportunities Commission (EOC)** = government body set up to make sure that no sex discrimination exists in employment; **equal opportunities programme** = programme to avoid discrimination in employment (NOTE: the US equivalent is **affirmative action**)

◇ **equality** [ɪ'kwɒlɪti] *noun* being equal; **equality bargaining** = collective bargaining where the conditions and advantages agreed apply to both male and female workers equally; **equality of opportunity** = situation where everyone, regardless of sex, race, class, etc., has the same opportunity to get a job; *the women staff are demanding equality of pay and opportunities with the men;* **equality of treatment** = treating male and female workers equally

QUOTE essentially equal opportunity managers are concerned with the management of change
Personnel Management

> QUOTE managers' leadership qualities exclude the ability to understand the concept of equality of opportunity
> *Personnel Management*

> QUOTE the industrial tribunal found the jobs to be of equal worth
> *Personnel Today*

> QUOTE according to the EOC, this was the first equal opportunities case in this country to be decided on European law
> *Personnel Today*

equity ['ekwɪti] *noun* fairness, such as equality of pay for the same type of job; *equity was the most important factor taken into account in drawing up the new pay structure*

equivalence [ɪ'kwɪvələns] *noun* condition of having the same value *or* of being the same

◊ **equivalent** [ɪ'kwɪvələnt] **1** *adjective* **to be equivalent to** = to have the same value as *or* to be the same as; *our managing director's salary is equivalent to that of far less experienced employees in other organizations;* **equivalent pension benefit** = the right of an opted-out pensioner to receive the same pension as he would have done under the state graduated pension scheme **2** *noun* person who is the equal of someone else; **full-time equivalent** = notional employee earning the full-time wage, used as a comparison to part-time employees

> QUOTE many institutions in the public sector count their part-timers in terms of full-time equivalents: for example, if an individual contracts to work for 36 hours a week when the full-time equivalent is 40 hours, that individual's full-time equivalent is 0.9
> *Labour Market Trends*

ergonomics [ɜːɡə'nɒmɪks] *plural noun* study of the relationship between people at work and their working conditions, especially the machines they use; *ergonomics has improved the design of machinery to make it more manageable; by making tasks easier to perform, ergonomics has contributed to increased productivity and job satisfaction* (NOTE: takes a singular verb)

◊ **ergonometrics** [ɜːɡɒnə'metrɪks] *noun* measurement of the quantity of work done

◊ **ergonomist** [ɜː'ɡɒnəmɪst] *noun* scientist who studies people at work and tries to improve their working conditions

erode [ɪ'rəʊd] *verb* to wear away gradually; **to erode wage differentials** = to reduce gradually differences in salary between different grades

◊ **erosion** [ɪ'rəʊʒn] *noun* gradual wearing away; *erosion of differentials*

error ['erə] *noun* mistake; *he made an error in calculating the tax deductions; the secretary must have made a typing error;* **clerical error** = mistake made in an office; **computer error** = mistake made by a computer; **human error** = mistake made by a person, not by a machine; **in error** *or* **by error** = by mistake; *the letter was sent to the London office in error*

escalate ['eskəleɪt] *verb* to increase steadily

◊ **escalation** [eskə'leɪʃən] *noun* steady increase; *an escalation of wage demands; the union has threatened an escalation in strike action;* **escalation clause** = ESCALATOR CLAUSE

◊ **escalator clause** ['eskəleɪtə 'klɔːz] *noun* clause in a contract of employment allowing for periodic wage increases in accordance with the cost of living

escape [ɪs'keɪp] *noun* getting away from a difficult situation; **fire escape** = stairs which allow people to get out of a buring building; **escape clause** = clause in a contract of employment which allows a period of time in which a member may withdraw from a union without affecting his or her employment

escrow ['eskrəʊ] *noun* **in escrow** = held in safe keeping by a third party; **document held in escrow** = document given to a third party to keep and to pass on to someone when money has been paid; *US* **escrow account** = account where money is held in escrow until a contract is signed *or* until goods are delivered, etc.

ESOP = EMPLOYEE SHARE OWNERSHIP PROGRAMME

essay method ['eseɪ 'meθəd] *noun*

evaluation method in performance appraisal where the evaluator writes a short description of the worker's performance

establish [ɪs'tæblɪʃ] *verb* to set up *or* to make *or* to open; *the company has established a branch in Australia; the business was established in Scotland in 1823; it is still a young company, having been established for only four years;* **to establish oneself in business** = to become successful in a new business

◊ **establishment** [ɪs'tæblɪʃmənt] *noun* number of people working in a company; **to be on the establishment** = to be a full-time employee; **office with an establishment of fifteen** = office with a budgeted staff of fifteen; **establishment charges** = cost of people and property in a company's accounts

ethic ['eθɪk] *noun* **(a)** general rules of conduct in society; **the Anglo-Saxon work ethic** = feeling in Britain and the USA that work is the most important task for an adult **(b)** **code of ethics** = code of working which shows how a professional group should work, and in particular what type of relationship they should have with their clients

ethnic ['eθnɪk] *adjective* belonging to a certain racial group; **ethnic minority** = section of the population from a certain racial group, which does not make up the majority of the population

COMMENT: in a recent British survey, the main ethnic groups were defined as: White, Black-Caribbean, Black-African, Black-Other, Indian, Pakistani, Bangladeshi, Chinese and Other

ethos ['i:θɒs] *noun* characteristic way of working and thinking; **corporate ethos** = a company's special way of working and thinking

EU ['i:'ju:] = EUROPEAN UNION *EU ministers met today in Brussels; the USA is increasing its trade with the EU*

European Commission [juərə'pi:ən kə'mɪʃn] *noun* main executive body of the EU, made up of members nominated by each member state

European Social Charter [juərə'pi:ən səʊʃl 'tʃɑːtə] charter for workers, drawn up by the EU in 1989, by which workers have the right to a fair wage, to equal treatment for men and women, a safe work environment, training, freedom of association and collective bargaining, provision for disabled workers, freedom of movement from country to country, guaranteed standards of living both for the working population as well as for retired people, etc. (there is no machinery for enforcing the Social Charter) (NOTE: the **Social Charter** is not the same as the **Social Chapter**)

European Union (EU) [juərə'pi:ən 'junɪən] (formerly, the European Economic Community (EEC), the Common Market) a group of European countries linked together by the Treaty of Rome in such a way that trade is more free, people can move from one country to another more freely, and people can work more freely in other countries of the group

evacuate [ɪ'vækjueɪt] *verb* to get people to leave (a dangerous building *or* an aircraft on fire, etc.); *they evacuated the premises when fire broke out in the basement*

◊ **evacuation** [ɪvækju'eɪʃn] *noun* action of getting people out of a dangerous building *or* aircraft, etc.

evaluate [ɪ'væljueɪt] *verb* to calculate a value; *we will evaluate jobs on the basis of their contribution to the organization as a whole; we need to evaluate the experience and qualifications of all the candidates*

◊ **evaluation** [ɪvælju'eɪʃən] *noun* calculation of value; **job evaluation** = examining different jobs within a company to see what skills and qualifications are needed to carry them out; *after job evaluation a more rational pay scale was introduced see also* ANALYTICAL, NON-ANALYTICAL

◊ **evaluator** [ɪ'væljueɪtə] *noun* person who carries out an evaluation

evasion [ɪ'veɪʒən] *noun* **tax evasion** = trying illegally not to pay tax

evict [ɪ'vɪkt] *verb* to force someone to leave premises which they are occupying; *they had to call in the police to evict the squatters; the company obtained an injunction to evict the striking workers from the factory*

◊ **eviction** [ɪ'vɪkʃn] *noun* forcing someone to leave premises

evidence ['evɪdəns] *noun* written or spoken report produced in a court of law to prove a fact; *what evidence is there that the new employee is causing all the trouble?;* **documentary evidence** = evidence in the form of documents; **the secretary gave evidence for** *or* **against her former employer** = the secretary was a witness, and her report suggested that her former employer was not guilty *or* guilty (NOTE: no plural)

ex- [eks] *preposition* (a) formerly; *Mr Smith, the ex-chairman of the company* (b) **ex-directory** = telephone number which is not printed in the telephone book; *he has an ex-directory number see also* EX OFFICIO

examine [ɪg'zæmɪn] *verb* to look at someone *or* something very carefully to see if it can be accepted; *the customs officials asked to examine the inside of the car; the police are examining the papers from the managing director's safe*

◊ **examination** [ɪgzæmɪ'neɪʃən] *noun* (a) looking at something very carefully to see if it is acceptable; **medical examination** = examination of a person by a doctor to find out his or her state of health; *all members of staff have to have an annual medical examination* (b) written or oral test to see if someone has passed a course; *he passed his accountancy examinations; she came first in the final examination for the course; he failed his proficiency examination and so had to leave his job; examinations are given to candidates for jobs in insurance to test their mathematical ability;* **to sit** *or* **to take an examination** = to write the answers to an examination test

example [ɪg'zɑːmpl] *noun* something chosen to show how things should be done; *his sales success in Europe is an example of what can be achieved by determination;* **to follow someone's example** = to do what someone else has done earlier; **to set a good** *or* **bad example to someone** = to work well *or* badly, and show others how the work should *or* should not be done; *the foreman worked hard to set a good example to the others*

exceed [ɪk'siːd] *verb* to be more than; **he exceeded his target** = he did more than he aimed to do; **he exceeded his powers** = he acted in a way which was not allowed

excellent ['eksələnt] *adjective* very good; *the quality of the firm's products is excellent, but its sales force is not large enough*

except [ɪk'sept] *preposition & conjunction* not including; *VAT is levied on all goods and services except books, newspapers and children's clothes; sales are rising in all markets except the Far East*

◊ **excepted** [ɪk'septɪd] *adverb* not including; **errors and omissions excepted (e. & o.e.)** = note on an invoice to show that the company has no responsibility for mistakes in the invoice

excess 1 [ɪk'ses] *noun* amount which is more than what is allowed; *an excess of expenditure over revenue;* **in excess of** = above *or* more than; *salaries in excess of £100,000 per annum* 2 ['ekses] *adjective noun* more than what is allowed; *excess costs have caused us considerable problems;* **excess plan** = pension plan providing higher pensions for higher wages

exclude [ɪks'kluːd] *verb* to keep out *or* not to include; *the interest charges have been excluded from the document; damage by fire is excluded from the policy*

◊ **excluding** [ɪks'kluːdɪŋ] *preposition* not including; *all salesmen, excluding those living in London, can claim expenses for attending the sales conference*

◊ **exclusion** [ɪks'kluːʒən] *noun* (a) act of not including; **exclusion clause** = clause in an insurance policy *or* in a contract, which says which items are not covered by the policy *or* which gives details of circumstances where the insurance company will refuse to pay (b) cutting people off from being full members of society, because of lack of education, alcoholism or drug abuse, unemployment, etc.

◊ **exclusive** [ɪks'kluːsɪv] *adjective* (a) **exclusive agreement** = agreement where a person is made sole agent for a product in a market (b) **exclusive of** = not including; *all payments are exclusive of tax; the invoice is exclusive of VAT*

excuse 1 [ɪks'kjuːs] *noun* reason for doing something wrong; *his excuse for not coming to the meeting was that he had been told about it only the day before; every day she is late for work, and every day she has a new* *excuse;* the managing director refused to accept the sales manager's excuses for the poor sales = he refused to believe that there was a good reason for the poor sales **2** [ɪksˈkjuːz] *verb* to forgive a small mistake; *she can be excused for not knowing the French for 'photocopier'*

execute [ˈeksɪkjuːt] *verb* to carry out (an order); *failure to execute orders may lead to dismissal; there were many practical difficulties in executing the managing director's instructions*

◊ **execution** [eksɪˈkjuːʃən] *noun* carrying out of an order; **stay of execution** = temporary stopping of a legal order; *the court granted the company a two-week stay of execution* (NOTE: no plural)

◊ **executive** [ɪgˈzekjutɪv] **1** *adjective* which puts decisions into action; **executive board** = board of directors which deals with the day-to-day running of the company (as opposed to a supervisory board, which deals with policy and planning); **executive committee** = committee which runs a society *or* a club; **executive director** = director who actually works full-time in the company; **executive powers** = right to put decisions into actions; *he was made managing director with full executive powers over the European operation* **2** *noun* **company executive** = person in a business who takes decisions *or* top or senior manager *or* director; *sales executive; senior or junior executive; account executive* = employee who is the link between his company and certain customers; **chief executive** = executive director in charge of a company; **executive pension plan** = special pension plan for managers and directors of a company; **executive search** = looking for new managers for organizations, usually by approaching managers in their existing jobs and asking them if they want to work for different companies; **executive share option scheme** = special scheme for senior managers, by which they can buy shares in the company they work for, at a fixed price at a later date

exemplary [ɪgˈzempləri] *adjective* excellent, so good it can be used as an example; *her behaviour has been exemplary*

exempt [ɪgˈzem(p)t] **1** *adjective* not covered by a law; not forced to obey a law; *he was exempt from military service in his country;* **exempt from tax** *or* **tax-exempt** = not required to pay tax; *as a non-profit-making organization we are exempt from tax;* **exempt personnel** = personnel who do not receive payment for overtime or whose wages are not affected by minimum wage legislation **2** *verb* to free someone from having to do a task; *I hope to be exempted from taking these tests; he was exempted from fire duty*

◊ **exemption** [ɪgˈzem(p)ʃən] *noun* act of exempting something from a contract *or* from a tax; **exemption from tax** *or* **tax exemption** = being free from having to pay tax; *as a non-profit-making organization you can claim tax exemption*

exercise [ˈeksəsaɪz] **1** *noun* use of something; **exercise of a right** = using a right **2** *verb* to use; **to exercise a right** = to put a right into action; *he exercised his right to refuse to do tasks not listed on his employment contract*

ex gratia [ˈeks ˈgreɪʃə] *adjective* **an ex gratia payment** = payment made as a gift, with no other obligations

exhaust [ɪgˈzɔːst] *verb* to use up totally; *we will go on negotiating until all possible solutions have been exhausted*

exit [ˈeksɪt] *noun* **(a)** leaving a job; **exit interview** = interview with an employee when he or she is leaving an organization to find out his or her views on how the organization is run and reasons for leaving; *only at his exit interview did he admit how much he had disliked working for the company* **(b)** way out of a building; *the customers all rushed towards the exits;* **emergency exit** = special way out of a building, used if there is a fire or other emergency; **fire exit** = door which leads to a way out of a building if there is a fire

ex officio ['eks ə'fɪʃɪəu] *adjective & adverb* because of an office held; *the treasurer is ex officio a member or an ex officio member of the finance committee*

ex parte ['eks 'pɑːteɪ] *Latin phrase* meaning 'on behalf of'; **an ex parte application** = application made to a court where only one side is represented and no notice is given to the other side (often where tne application is for an injunction); *see also* INTER PARTES

expatriate [eks'pætrɪət] *noun & adjective* person who lives and works in a country which is not his own; *expatriate staff are paid higher rates than locally recruited staff; all expatriates in the organization have two months' leave a year*

expect [ɪk'spekt] *verb* to hope that something is going to happen; *we are expecting him to arrive at 10.45; they are expecting a cheque from their agent next week; the house was sold for more than the expected price*

◊ **expectancy** [ɪk'spektənsɪ] *noun* **expectancy theory** = theory that employees will only be motivated to produce if they expect that higher performance will lead to greater personal satisfaction; **life expectancy** = number of years a person is likely to live

◊ **expectations** [ekspek'teɪʃnz] *noun* hopes of what is to come; *she has great expectations of her new job, and I hope she won't be disappointed;* **salary expectations** = how the employee hopes his salary will increase

expel [ɪk'spel] *verb* to throw someone out of an organization; *the worker was expelled from the union for embezzlement*

expense account [ɪk'spens ə'kaunt] *noun* account of expenses incurred on a job which are later repaid by the employer; money which a businessman is allowed to his company to spend on travelling and entertaining clients in connection with his business; *I'll put this lunch on my expense account; expense account lunches form a large part of our current expenditure; a generous expense account is one of the main fringe benefits of the job*

◊ **expenses** [ɪk'spensɪz] *plural noun* costs incurred by the employee in doing a job; *the*

salary offered is £10,000 plus expenses; he has a high salary and all his travel expenses are paid by the company; **all expenses paid** = with all costs paid by the company; *the company sent him to San Francisco all expenses paid;* **allowable expenses** = business expenses which are allowed against tax; **business expenses** = money spent on running a business, not on stock or assets; **car expenses** = money spent on a private car used during work for a company; **entertainment expenses** = money spent on giving meals to business visitors; **living expenses** = money spent on rent, food, etc., which may be paid by the company if the worker has been asked to live away from home; **relocation expenses** = payment of expenses involved when a worker has to move house because his place of work has changed, or when a new employee has to move house to join the company; **travel** *or* **travelling expenses** = money spent on travelling and hotels for business purposes

experience [ɪk'spɪərɪəns] *noun* process of learning through activity or observation, having lived through various situations and therefore knowing how to make decisions; *he is a man of considerable experience; she has a lot of experience of dealing with German companies; he gained most of his experience in the Far East; some experience is required for this job; the applicant was pleasant, but did not have any relevant experience;* **proven experience** = experience showing that someone has been successful; *(for a student)* **work experience** = working for a company to gain experience of how businesses work; **experience curve** = becoming more experienced as you work, and so becoming more efficient and cost-effective; **experience rating** = evaluation of a person to decide on his or her eligibility for insurance coverage

◊ **experienced** [ɪk'spɪərɪənst] *adjective* (person) who has learnt through activity or observation; *he is the most experienced negotiator I know; we have appointed a very experienced woman as sales director; our more experienced staff have dealt with a crisis like this before*

◊ **experiential learning** [ɪkspərɪ'enʃl 'lɜːnɪŋ] *noun* learning skills through practice

expert ['eksp3:t] *noun* person who knows a lot about something; *an expert in the field of electronics or an electronics expert; the company asked a financial expert for advice or asked for expert financial advice;* **expert's report** = report written by an expert; **expert system** = software that applies the knowledge, advice and rules defined by experts in a particular field to a user's data to help solve a problem

◊ **expertise** [eksp3:'ti:z] *noun* specialist knowledge *or* skill in a particular field; *we hired Mr Smith because of his financial expertise or because of his expertise in the African market; with years of experience in the industry, we have plenty of expertise to draw on; lack of marketing expertise led to low sales figures* (NOTE: no plural)

expiration [ekspɪ'reɪʃən] *noun* coming to an end; *expiration of an insurance policy; to repay before the expiration of the stated period;* **on expiration of the lease** = when the lease comes to an end

◊ **expire** [ɪk'spaɪə] *verb* to come to an end

◊ **expiry** [ɪk'spaɪəri] *noun* coming to an end; *expiry of an insurance policy;* **expiry date** = date when something will end

explain [ɪk'spleɪn] *verb* to give reasons for something; *he explained to the customs officials that the two computers were presents from friends; can you explain why sales in the first quarter are so high? he was asked to explain why he had been late for work three days in a row*

◊ **explanation** [eksplə'neɪʃən] *noun* reason for something; *the personnel department did not accept her explanation for being late; the VAT inspector asked for an explanation of the invoices*

exploit [ɪk'splɔɪt] *verb* to make unfair use of someone (usually by paying very low wages); *the directors exploit their employees, who have to work hard for very little pay*

◊ **exploitation** [eksplɔɪ'teɪʃn] *noun* unfair use of cheap labour to get work done; *the exploitation of migrant farm workers was only stopped when they became unionized*

expulsion [ɪks'pʌlʃn] *noun* being thrown out of an organization; *what is the chance of expulsion for breaking house rules?*

extend [ɪk'stend] *verb* to make longer; *his contract of employment was extended for two years; we have extended the deadline for making the appointment be two weeks*

◊ **extension** [ɪk'stenʃən] *noun* **(a)** allowing longer time for something; **extension of a contract of employment** = continuing the contract for a further period **(b)** *(in an office)* individual telephone linked to the main switchboard; *can you get me extension 21? extension 21 is engaged; the sales manager is on extension 53* (NOTE: often written **x: phone x23**)

◊ **extensive** [ɪk'stensɪv] *adjective* very large *or* covering a wide area; *an extensive recruitment drive*

external [ɪk'stɜ:nl] *adjective* outside a company; **external audit** = audit carried out by an independent auditor from outside the company; **external auditor** = independent person who audits the company's accounts; **external growth** = development of a company by acquiring other businesses, as opposed to growing its existing business with its own finances (called 'internal growth'); **external recruitment** = recruitment of workers from outside an organization; *internal recruitment is normally attempted before resorting to external recruitment;* **external workers** = workers who are outside the company (casual workers, freelancers, contract workers, etc.)

◊ **externally** [ɪk'stɜ:nəli] *adverb* from outside an organization; *the new sales director was recruited externally* (NOTE: opposite is **internal, internally**)

extra ['ekstrə] *adjective* which is added *or* which is more than usual; *there is no extra charge for heating; he had £25 extra pay for working on Sunday; all these orders have given us a lot of extra work; she had to work extra hours to catch up with the backlog of orders*

extraordinary [ekstrə'ɔ:dɪnəri] *adjective* very unusual; **Extraordinary General Meeting (EGM)** = special meeting of shareholders to discuss an important matter

extremely [ɪk'striːmli] *adverb* very much; *it is extremely difficult to break into the US market; their management team is extremely efficient*

extrinsic reward [ɪks'trɪnzɪk rɪ'wɔːd] *noun* financial or material reward for work; *extrinsic rewards can be measured, whereas intrinsic rewards cannot*

Ff

face value ['feɪs 'vælju:] *noun* value written on a coin *or* banknote *or* share certificate; **to take something at face value** = to believe something to be true or genuine

◊ **face validity** ['feɪs və'lɪdɪti] *noun* degree to which a test seems to be valid; *though the personality test had a high face validity for some years, it was later considered ineffective and was dropped as a recruitment tool*

facilitator [fə'sɪlɪteɪtə] *noun* person who actively encourages discussion, new initiatives, etc.

facilities [fə'sɪlətɪz] *noun* services *or* equipment *or* buildings which make it easy to do something; *there are very good sports facilities on the company premises; with such poor staff facilities, it is not surprising we have so much difficulty in recruiting the right type of employee; the company offers child-care facilities for all staff; there are no facilities for handicapped visitors*

fact [fækt] *noun* something which is true and real; *the chairman asked to see all the facts on the income tax claim; the sales director can give you the facts and figures about the African operation;* **the fact of the matter is** = what is true is that; *the fact of the matter is that the product does not fit the market;* **in fact** = really; *the chairman blamed the finance director for the loss when in fact he was responsible for it himself*

◊ **fact-finding** ['fæktfaɪndɪŋ] *noun* looking for information; **fact-finding commission** = committee set up by a third party to carry out an impartial review of issues in a labour dispute; *a fact-finding commission was set up to look into the reasons for the pay dispute;* **fact-finding mission** = visit, usually by a group of people, to search for information about a problem; *the minister went on a fact-finding tour of the region*

factor ['fæktə] *noun* thing which is important *or* which is taken into account when making a decision; *the drop in sales is an important factor in the company's lower profits; some of the factors considered during job evaluation are effort, danger and experience; motivation was an important factor in drawing up the new pay scheme;* **cost factor** = problem of cost; **cyclical factors** = way in which a trade cycle affects businesses; **deciding factor** = most important factor which influences a decision; **factors of production** = things needed to produce a product (land, labour and capital); **factor analysis** = method of analysing the results of an attitude survey by identifying what factors or criteria produced these results; **factor comparison** = method of comparing jobs in relation to factors such as 'training' or 'effort'; **factor evaluation** = method of evaluating *or* assessing jobs in relation to factors such as 'training' or 'effort'; **factor ranking** = method of grading jobs in relation to factors such as 'training' or 'effort'

factory ['fæktri] *noun* building where products are manufactured; *car factory; shoe factory;* **factory hand** *or* **factory worker** = person who works in a factory; **factory inspector** *or* **inspector of factories** = government official who inspects factories to see if they are safely run; *the factory inspector found that many health and safety regulations were being ignored;* **the factory inspectorate** = all factory inspectors; **Factories Act** = act which governs the conditions in which workers work (heating, lighting, toilet facilities, etc.)

fail [feɪl] *verb* not to do something which you were trying to do; *they failed to agree on agenda for the meeting; negotiations continued until midnight but the two side failed to come to an agreement*

◊ **failure** ['feɪljə] *noun* **(a)** breaking down *or* stopping; *the failure of the negotiations* **(b)** not to do something which you were trying to do; **(minute of) failure to agree** = official record of a meeting which states that the two sides did not reach an agreement

fair [feə] **1** *noun* **recruitment fair** = exhibition where employers try to recruit college graduates as new members of staff; **trade fair** = large exhibition and meeting for advertising and selling a certain type of product **2** *adjective* honest *or* reasonable; *we expect fair pay for a fair day's work; the supervisor is strict but fair in her dealing with subordinates;* **fair deal** = arrangement where both parties are treated equally; *the workers feel they did not get a fair deal from the management;* **fair dismissal** = dismissal of a worker for reasons which are fair, such as the worker's bad conduct (theft, drunkenness, etc.), failure of the worker to work capably, real redundancy, etc.; **fair employment** = employment where no racial *or* religious *or* sex discrimination takes place; *the company has a strong policy of fair employment; the recruitment of twice as many men as women was a denial of the principle of fair employment;* **fair representation** = representation of all members of a bargaining unit fairly and without discrimination; **fair share agreement** = arrangement where both management and unions agree that employees are not obliged to join a union, but that all employees pay the union a share of bargaining costs as a condition of employment; *a fair share agreement was reached, since even employees who were not union members benefited from bargains struck between union and management;* **fair trading** *or* **fair dealing** = way of doing business which is reasonable and does not harm the consumer; *GB* **Office of Fair Trading** = government department which protects consumers against unfair or illegal business; **fair wear and tear** = acceptable damage caused by normal use; *the insurance policy covers most damage, but not fair wear and tear to the machine*

◊ **fairly** ['feəli] *adverb* **(a)** in a fair way; *the union representatives put the employees' side of the case fairly and without argument* **(b)** quite; *the company is fairly close to breaking even; she is a fairly fast keyboarder*

faith [feɪθ] *noun* **to have faith in something** *or* **someone** = to believe that something *or* a person is good or will work well; *the salesmen have great faith in the product; the sales teams do not have much faith in their manager; the board has faith in the*

managing director's judgement; **faith validity** = face validity *or* degree to which a test seems to be valid; **to buy something in good faith** = to buy something thinking that is of good quality *or* that it has not been stolen *or* that it is not an imitation

false [fɔːls] *adjective* not true *or* not correct; *to make a false entry in the balance sheet;* **false negative** = exclusion of a suitable candidate by a screening process; **false positive** = inclusion of an unsuitable candidate by a screening process; *false positive results from recruitment tests can end in the selection of very unsuitable candidates*

◊ **falsification** [fɔːlsɪfɪ'keɪʃən] *noun* **falsification of accounts** = action of making false entries in a record *or* of destroying a record

◊ **falsify** ['fɔːlsɪfaɪ] *verb* to change something to make it wrong; **to falsify accounts** = to change *or* destroy a record

family allowance ['fæmɪli ə'lauəns] *noun* payment to a mother, in addition to regular wages, based on the number of dependent children in the family; *family allowances were increased since the government had put a limit on basic wage increases*

farm out ['fɑːm 'aut] *verb* **to farm out work** = to hand over work for another person *or* company to do it for you; *she farms out the office typing to various local bureaux*

fast track ['fɑːst 'træk] *noun* rapid promotion for able employees; *be entered the company at 21, and by 25 he was on the fast track*

◊ **fast-tracking** ['fɑːst 'trækɪŋ] *noun* rapid promotion given to certain able workers

fat work ['fæt 'wɜːk] *noun* (*in the printing industry*) job that offers the same money for less effort than another similar job; *workers were moving to more prosperous areas of the country in search of fat work*

fatigue [fə'tiːg] *noun* great tiredness; **fatigue curve** = curve on a chart showing how output varies depending on how long a worker has been working; *the fatigue curve helps to determine when rest periods should be allowed; the fatigue curve shows a sharp slump in output after three hours' work*

fault [fɔːlt] *noun* **(a)** being to blame for something which is wrong; *it is the stock controller's fault if the warehouse runs out of stock; the chairman said the lower sales figures were the fault of a badly motivated sales force* **(b)** wrong working; *the technicians are trying to correct a programming fault; we think there is a basic fault in the product design*

◊ **faulty** ['fɔːlti] *adjective* which does not work properly; *faulty equipment; they installed faulty computer programs*

favour *or US* **favor** ['feivə] **1** *noun* **(a) as a favour** = to help *or* to be kind to someone; *he gave the secretary a loan as a favour* **(b) in favour of** = in agreement with *or* feeling that something is right; *six members of the board are in favour of the proposal, and three are against it* **2** *verb* to agree that something is right *or* to vote for something; *the board members all favour Smith Ltd as partners in the project*

◊ **favourable** *or US* **favorable** ['feivərəbl] *adjective* which gives an advantage; **favourable balance of trade** = situation where a country's exports are more than the imports; **on favourable terms** = on specially good terms; *the shop is let on very favourable terms*

◊ **favourite** *or US* **favorite** ['feivərit] *adjective* which is liked best; *this brand of chocolate is a favourite with the children's market*

◊ **favouritism** *or US* **favoritism** ['feivəritizm] *noun* treating one subordinate better than the others; *the promotion of the inexperienced secretary to supervisor was seen as favouritism by the rest of the workforce*

feasibility [fiːzə'biləti] *noun* ability to be done; *to report on the feasibility of a project;* **feasibility report** = report saying if something can be done; **to carry out a feasibility study on a project** = to carry out an examination of costs and profits to see if the project should be started (NOTE: no plural)

feather-bedding ['feðə 'bedɪŋ] *noun* **(a)** heavy subsidizing of unprofitable industry by government **(b)** employing more staff than necessary, usually as a result of union pressure; *feather-bedding has raised the cost of labour; management complained that feather-bedding was holding up the introduction of new technology*

fee [fiː] *noun* **(a)** money paid for work carried out by a professional person (such as an accountant *or* a doctor *or* a lawyer); *we charge a small fee for our services;* **consultant's fee** = money paid to a consultant; **director's fees** = money paid to a director for attendance at board meetings **(b)** money paid for something; *entrance fee or admission fee; registration fee*

feedback ['fiːdbæk] *noun* information, especially about the result of an activity which allows the person carrying it out to make adjustments; *the management received a lot of feedback on how popular the new pay scheme was proving; weekly meetings with the workers' committee provided feedback on production policy; have you any feedback from the sales force about the customers' reaction to the new model?* (NOTE: no plural)

feeling ['fiːlɪŋ] *noun* way in which someone reacts to something; *the board's insensitive attitude has created bad feelings or ill-feeling between the managers and the junior staff;* **feelings are running high** = people are getting angry

fellow- ['feləu] *prefix* meaning 'person working with'; **fellow-director** = one of the other directors; **fellow-workers** = other workers; **fellow-servant doctrine** = common law concept that removes responsibility from an employee for an accident to another employee, if the accident was caused by negligence

fiddle ['fidl] **1** *noun* *(informal)* cheating; *it's all a fiddle;* **he's on the fiddle** = he is trying to cheat **2** *verb informal* to cheat on; *he tried to fiddle his tax returns; the salesman was caught fiddling his expense account*

field [fiːld] *noun* **(a) in the field** = outside the office *or* among the customers; *we have sixteen reps in the field;* **field review** = form of employee appraisal whereby the employee's work performance is assessed at the place of work (and not in the manager's office); **field sales manager** = manager in charge of a group of salesmen;

field staff = employees who work outside the organization's offices; **field research** *or* **field work** = examination of the situation among possible customers; *he was worried that his performance during field review would not be satisfactory; the manager laid down rules as to how often the field staff had to report to the central office; he had to do a lot of field work to find the right market for the product* (b) area of study or interest; *he's the top specialist in his field;* **field of research** = area of research interest; **field of work** = type of work a person does; *what's his field?*

FIFO ['faɪfəʊ] = FIRST IN FIRST OUT

fight [faɪt] *verb* **to fight against something** = to struggle to try to overcome something; *the unions are fighting (against) the proposed redundancies*

file [faɪl] **1** *noun* (a) cardboard holder for documents, which can fit in the drawer of a filing cabinet; *put these letters in the personnel file; look in the file marked 'temporary staff'* (b) documents kept for reference; **to place something on file** = to keep a record of something; **to keep someone's name on file** = to keep someone's name on a list for reference; **file copy** = copy of a document which is kept for reference in an office; **card-index file** = information kept on filing cards (c) section of data on a computer (such as payroll, address list, personnel); *how can we protect our computer files?* **2** *verb* to store information so that it can be found easily; *you will find the salary scales filed by department; the correspondence is filed under 'complaints'*

◊ **filing** ['faɪlɪŋ] *noun* documents which have to be put in order; *there is a lot of filing to do at the end of the week; the manager looked through the week's filing to see what letters had been sent;* **filing basket** *or* **filing tray** = container kept on a desk for documents which have to be filed; **filing cabinet** = metal box with several drawers for keeping files; **filing card** = card with information written on it, used to classify information into the correct order; **filing clerk** = clerk who files documents; **filing system** = way of putting documents in order for reference (NOTE: no plural)

fill [fɪl] **1** *verb* (a) to make something full; *we have filled our order book with orders for Africa; the production department has filled the warehouse with unsellable products* (b) **to fill a gap** = to provide a product *or* service which is needed, but which no one has provided before; *the new range of small cars fills a gap in the market* (c) **to fill a post** *or* **a vacancy** = to find someone to do a job; *your application arrived too late - the post has already been filled*

◊ **fill in** ['fɪl 'ɪn] *verb* (a) to write in the blank spaces on a form; *fill in your name and address in block capitals* (b) **to fill in for someone** = to do someone else's job temporarily; *I'll fill in for him while he is away at his brother's wedding*

◊ **fill out** ['fɪl 'aʊt] *verb* to write the required information in the blank spaces on a form; *to get customs clearance you must fill out three forms*

◊ **fill up** ['fɪl 'ʌp] *verb* to finish writing on a form; *he filled up the form and sent it to the bank*

final ['faɪnl] *adjective* last, coming at the end of a period; **final salary** = salary earned by an employee on the date of leaving or retiring

fine tune ['faɪn 'tjuːn] *verb* to make small adjustments to (a plan or the economy) so that it works better

◊ **fine-tuning** ['faɪn 'tjuːnɪŋ] *noun* making small adjustments so that something works better

fink [fɪŋk] *noun US (informal)* worker hired to replace a striking worker

fire ['faɪə] **1** *noun* thing which burns; **to catch fire** = to start to burn; **fire certificate** = document from the local fire brigade stating that a building meets official requirements as regards fire safety; **fire damage** = damage caused by fire; **fire door** = special door to prevent fire going from one part of a building to another; **fire drill** = procedure to be carried out to help people to escape from a burning building; **fire escape** = door *or* stairs which allow people to get out of a building which is on fire; **fire extinguisher** = can (usually painted red) containing chemical foam which can be sprayed onto a fire to put it out; **fire hazard** *or* **fire risk** = situation *or* goods which could start a fire; **fire insurance** = insurance against damage by fire; **fire precautions** = care taken to avoid damage or casualties by fire; **fire safety officer** = person in a company responsible for seeing that the workers are safe if a fire breaks out **2** *verb* **to fire someone** = to dismiss someone from a job; *the new managing director fired half the sales force; he was fired for poor performance;* **to hire and fire** = to employ new staff and dismiss existing staff very frequently

firm [fɜːm] *noun* company *or* business *or* partnership; *he is a partner in a law firm; a manufacturing firm; an important publishing firm*

◊ **firm up** ['fɜːm 'ʌp] *verb* to finalize *or* to agree final details; *we expect to firm up the deal at the next trade fair*

first [fɜːst] **1** *noun* person *or* thing which is there at the beginning *or* earlier than others; *our company was one of the first to sell into the European market* **2** *adjective* **first aid** = help given by an ordinary person to someone who is suddenly ill *or* injured, given until full-scale medical treatment can be given; **first aid kit** *or* **box** = box with bandages and dressings kept ready to be used in an emergency; **first aid post** = special place where injured people can be taken for immediate attention; **first quarter** = three months' period from January to the end of March; **first half** *or* **first half-year** = six months' period from January to the end of June; **first in first out (FIFO)** = (i) redundancy policy, where the people who have been working longest are the first to be made redundant; (ii) accounting policy where stock is valued at the price of the oldest purchases

◊ **first-class** ['fɜːs(t) 'klɑːs] *adjective & noun* **(a)** top quality *or* most expensive; *she's a first-class worker; he is a first-class accountant* **(b)** most expensive and comfortable type of travel *or* type of hotel; *to travel first-class; first-class travel provides the best service; a first-class ticket; to stay in first-class hotels*

◊ **first-line** ['fɜːst 'laɪn] *adjective* **first-line management** = level of managers who have immediate contact with the workers; **first-line supervisor** = supervisor who is in direct control of production workers; *the first-line managers play an important role in explaining company policy to the workers; the personnel department will liaise with first-line supervisors with regard to individual workers*

five-fold *or* **five-point system**

['faɪv'fəʊld *or* 'faɪv'pɔɪnt] *noun* system of grading an employee *or* a candidate for a job

fix [fɪks] *verb* **(a)** to arrange *or* to agree; *to fix a budget; to fix a meeting for 3 p.m.; the date has still to be fixed; the price of gold was fixed at $300; the mortgage rate has been fixed at 11%* **(b)** to mend; *the technicians are coming to fix the telephone switchboard; can you fix the photocopier?*

◊ **fixed** [fɪkst] *adjective* permanent *or* which cannot be changed *or* removed; **fixed assets** = property *or* machinery which a company owns and uses, but which the company does not buy or sell as part of its regular trade, including the company's investments in shares of other companies; **fixed benefit retirement plan** = pension plan where the benefits are not related to earnings; **fixed costs** = business costs which do not rise with the quantity of the product made; **fixed day rate** *or* **fixed day work** = pay scheme where pay for the day's work does not vary with the amount of output; **fixed-price agreement** = agreement where a company provides a service *or* a product at a price which stays the same for the whole period of the agreement; **fixed scale of charges** = rate of charging which cannot be altered; **fixed shifts** = hours of work assigned to a worker for an indefinite period; *some workers complain that fixed shifts make for monotony;* **fixed-term contract** = contract of employment valid for a fixed period of time; *I have a fixed-term contract with the company, and no guarantee of an extension when it ends in May;* **fixed(-term) contract worker** = worker who has a fixed-term contract for a period of time (e.g. one year)

flag [flæg] **1** *noun* **(a)** piece of cloth with a design on it which shows which country it belongs to; *a ship flying a British flag;* **ship sailing under a flag of convenience** = ship flying the flag of a country which may have no ships of its own, but allows ships of other countries to be registered in its ports **(b)** mark which is attached to information in a computer so that the information can be found easily **2** *verb* to insert marks on information in a computer so that the information can be found easily; **flagged rate** = special pay rates paid to employees whose positions warrant lower rates of pay; *flagged rates helped to reduce the pay differentials in the organization*

flat [flæt] *adjective* **(a) flat organization** = organization with few grades in the hierarchical structure; *a flat organization does not appeal to those who like traditional bureaucratic organizations* **(b)** fixed *or* not changing; **flat rate** = charge which always stays the same; *we pay a flat rate for electricity each quarter; he is paid a flat rate of £2 per thousand*

◊ **flat out** ['flæt 'aut] *adverb* working hard *or* at full speed; *the factory worked flat out to complete the order on time*

flexible ['fleksəbl] *adjective* which can be altered *or* changed; **flexible manufacturing system (FMS)** = way of manufacturing using computerized systems to allow certain quantities of the product to be made to a specific order; **flexible retirement scheme** = scheme where employees can choose the age at which they retire (between certain age limits, 55 and 65, for example); **flexible working hours** = system where workers can start or stop work at different hours of the morning or evening provided that they work a certain number of hours per day or week; *we work flexible hours*

◊ **flexibility** [fleksə'bɪləti] *noun* **(a)** being easily changed; *there is no flexibility in the company's pricing policy* **(b)** = FLEXIBLE WORKING (NOTE: no plural)

◊ **flexitime** ['fleksɪtaɪm] *noun* system where workers can start or stop work at different hours of the morning or evening, provided that they work a certain number of hours per day or week; *we work flexitime; the company introduced flexitime working two years ago; flexitime means that workers work when they feel most productive* (NOTE: no plural)

> QUOTE clearly a human resources strategy for new technology has to be a flexible strategy
> *Personnel Management*

flier *or* **flyer** ['flaɪə] *noun* **high flier** = person who is very successful *or* who is likely to rise to a very important position

flip chart ['flɪp 'tʃɑːt] *noun* way of showing information to a group of people by writing on large sheets of paper which can then be turned over to show the next sheet

floor [flɔː] *noun* **(a)** part of the room which you walk on; **floor space** = area of floor in an office *or* warehouse; *we have 3,500 square metres of floor space to let;* **the factory floor** = main works of a factory; **on the shop floor** = in the works *or* in the factory *or* among the ordinary workers; *the feeling on the shop floor is that the manager does not know his job* **(b)** bottom limit; *the government will impose a floor on wages to protect the poor* (NOTE: the opposite is **ceiling**)

◊ **floorwalker** ['flɔːwɔːlkə] *noun* employee of a department store who advises the customers, and supervises the shop assistants in a department

flow [fləu] **1** *noun* **(a)** movement; *the flow of capital into a country; the flow of investments into Japan* **(b) cash flow** = cash which comes into a company from sales and goes out in purchases *or* overhead expenditure; **discounted cash flow** = calculation of forecast sales of a product in current terms with reductions for current interest rates; *the company is suffering from cash flow problems* = cash income is not coming in fast enough to pay for the expenditure going out; **work flow** = sequence of jobs which results in a final product *or* service; *a flow chart on the wall showed the work flow for the coming month* **(c) flow chart** *or* **flow diagram** = chart which shows the arrangement of work processes as a series of stages **2** *verb* to move smoothly; *production is now flowing normally after the strike*

◊ **flowcharting** ['fləutʃɑːtɪŋ] *noun* setting out the arrangement of work processes in the form of a chart

fluidity [flu'ɪdɪti] *noun* moving about like a liquid; **fluidity of labour** = extent to which workers move from one place to another to find work *or* move from one type of work to another; *acute unemployment will dramatically increase the fluidity of labour*

flying pickets ['flaɪɪŋ 'pɪkɪts] *noun* pickets who travel round the country to try to stop workers going to work

FMS = FLEXIBLE MANUFACTURING SYSTEM

forbid [fə'bɪd] *verb* to tell someone not to do something *or* to say that something must not be done; *smoking is forbidden in our offices; the contract forbids resale of the* *goods to the USA; the staff are forbidden to use the front entrance* (NOTE: **forbidding - forbade - forbidden**)

force [fɔːs] 1 *noun* (a) strength; **to be in force** = to be operating *or* working; *the rules have been in force since 1946;* **to come into force** = to start to operate *or* work; *the new regulations will come into force on January 1st* (b) group of people; **labour force** *or* **workforce** = all the workers in a company *or* in an area; *the management has made an increased offer to the labour force; we are opening a new factory in the Far East because of the cheap local labour force;* **sales force** = group of salesmen 2 *verb* to make someone do something; *after the takeover several of the managers were forced to take early retirement; competition has forced the company to lower its prices*

◊ **forced** [fɔːst] *adjective* **forced distribution method** = performance appraisal technique where certain percentages of workers are put in various categories in advance

forecast ['fɔːkɑːst] 1 *noun* description *or* calculation of what will probably happen in the future; *the chairman did not believe the sales director's forecast of higher turnover; we based our calculations on the forecast turnover;* **cash flow forecast** = forecast of when cash will be received or paid out; **population forecast** = calculation of how many people will be living in a country *or* in a town at some point in the future; **sales forecast** = calculation of future sales 2 *verb* to calculate *or* to say what will probably happen in the future; *he is forecasting sales of £2m; economists have forecast a fall in the exchange rate* (NOTE: **forecasting - forecast)**

◊ **forecasting** ['fɔːkɑːstɪŋ] *noun* calculating what will probably happen in the future; *the forecasting of long-term manpower requirements;* **manpower planning will depend on forecasting the future levels of production;** **manpower** *or* **human resources forecasting** = calculating how many workers will be needed in the future, and how many will actually be available (NOTE: no plural)

foreman *or* **forewoman** ['fɔːmən *or* 'fɔːwʊmən] *noun* skilled worker in charge of several other workers (NOTE: plural is **foremen** *or* **forewomen)**

form [fɔːm] 1 *noun* (a) **form of words** = words correctly laid out for a legal document; **receipt in due form** = correctly written receipt (b) official printed paper with blank spaces which have to be filled in with information; *you have to fill in form A20; customs declaration form; a pad of order forms;* **application form** = form which has to be filled in to apply for something; **job application form** = form which has to be filled in when applying for a job; *candidates were asked to fill in a form with their name, address and telephone number;* **claim form** = form which has to be filled in when making an insurance claim; **tax form** = blank form to be filled in with details of income and allowances and sent to the tax office each year 2 *verb* to start *or* to organize; *the brothers have formed a new company*

formal ['fɔːməl] *adjective* clearly and legally written; *is this a formal job offer? the factory is prepared for the formal inspection by the government inspector; to make a formal application for promotion;* **formal procedures** = agreed written rules for dealing with grievances, dismissals, etc.; **formal warning** = warning to a worker according to formal procedures

◊ **formality** [fɔː'mæləti] *noun* something which has to be done to obey the law; **customs formalities** = declaration of goods by the shipper and examination of them by the customs

◊ **formally** ['fɔːməli] *adverb* in a formal way; *we have formally applied for planning permission for the new shopping precinct*

formation *or* **forming** [fɔː'meɪʃən *or* 'fɔːmɪŋ] *noun* act of organizing; *the formation of a new company* (NOTE: no plural)

◊ **formative assessment** ['fɔːmətɪv ə'sesmənt] *noun* appraisal of an employee, where the employee is given notes on what is wrong and what he should do to improve his performance

former ['fɔːmə] *adjective* before *or* at an earlier time; *she got a reference from her former employer*

◊ **formerly** ['fɔːməli] *adverb* at an earlier time; *he is currently managing director of Smith Ltd, but formerly he worked for Jones*

four-fifths rule [fɔː 'fɪfθs ruːl] *noun US* =

80/20 principle that states that if selection of a particular ethnic, age or sex group is less than four-fifths of another group, then the selection procedure is defective; *also called* EIGHTY PER CENT RULE

framework agreement ['freɪmwɜːk ə'griːmənt] *noun* draft of the main points of an agreement, with further details to be added later

fraud [frɔːd] *noun* harming someone by obtaining property or money after making him believe something which is not true; *he got possession of the property by fraud; he was accused of frauds relating to foreign currency;* **to obtain money by fraud** = to obtain money by saying or doing something to cheat someone; **computer fraud** = fraud committed by using computer files (as in a bank); **Fraud Squad** = special police department which investigates frauds

◊ **fraudulent** ['frɔːdjʊlənt] *adjective* not honest *or* aiming to cheat people; **fraudulent conversion** = using money which does not belong to you for a purpose for which it is not supposed to be used; **fraudulent misrepresentation** = false statement made to trick someone *or* to persuade someone to sign a contract; *a fraudulent transaction*

◊ **fraudulently** ['frɔːdjʊləntli] *adverb* not honestly; *goods imported fraudulently*

free [friː] **1** *adjective & adverb* **(a)** not costing any money; *to be given a free ticket to the exhibition; the price includes free delivery; goods are delivered free; catalogue sent free on request;* **carriage free** = the customer does not pay for the shipping; **free gift** = present given by a shop to a customer who buys a certain amount of goods; *there is a free gift worth £25 to any customer buying a washing machine;* **free sample** = sample given free to advertise a product; **free trial** = testing of a machine with no payment involved; *to send a piece of equipment for two weeks' free trial;* **free of charge** = with no payment to be made **(b)** with no restrictions; **free collective bargaining** = negotiations over wage increases and working conditions between the management and the trade unions; **free competition** = being free to compete without government interference; **free enterprise** = system of business with no interference from the government; **free market economy** = system where the government does not interfere in business activity in any way; **free trade** = system where goods can go from one country to another without any restrictions; *the government adopted a free trade policy;* **free trade area** = group of countries practising free trade; **interest-free credit** *or* **loan** = credit *or* loan where no interest is paid by the borrower; **free of duty** *or* **duty-free** = with no duty to be paid; *to import wine free of duty* *or* **duty-free (c)** not busy *or* not occupied; *are there any free tables in the restaurant? I shall be free in a few minutes; the chairman always keeps Friday afternoon free for a game of bridge* **2** *verb* to make something available *or* easy; *the government's decision has freed millions of pounds for investment*

◊ **freedom** ['friːdəm] *noun* being free to do anything; **freedom of association** = being able to join together in a group with other people without being afraid of prosecution; **freedom of movement** = ability of workers in the EU to move from country to country and obtain work without any restrictions

◊ **freelance** ['friːlɑːns] **1** *adjective & noun* independent worker who works for several different companies but is not employed by any of them; *we have about twenty freelances working for us or about twenty people working for us on a freelance basis; she is a freelance journalist* **2** *adverb* selling one's work to various firms, but not being employed by any of them; *he works freelance as a designer* **3** *verb* **(a)** to do work for several firms but not be employed by any of them; *she freelances for the local newspapers* **(b)** to send work out to be done by a freelancer; *we freelance work out to several specialists*

◊ **freelancer** ['friːlɑːnsə] *noun* freelance worker

◊ **freely** ['friːli] *adverb* with no restrictions; *money should circulate freely within the Common Market*

◊ **free-rider** [friː'raɪdə] *noun* person who receives benefits which have been negotiated by a union for its members, even if he has not joined the union; *many union members resent free-riders who benefit from the recent pay increase negotiated by the union*

freeze [friːz] **1** *noun* **wages and prices freeze** *or* **a freeze on wages and prices** =

period when wages and prices are not allowed to be increased **2** *verb* to keep money *or* costs, etc., at their present level and not allow them to rise; *we have frozen expenditure at last year's level; to freeze wages and prices; to freeze credits; to freeze company dividends* (NOTE: **freezing - froze - has frozen**)

◊ **freeze out** ['fri:z 'aut] *verb* **to freeze out competition** = to trade successfully and cheaply and so prevent competitors from operating

frequent ['fri:kwənt] *adjective* which comes *or* goes *or* takes place often; *there is a frequent ferry service to France; we send frequent telexes to New York; how frequent are flights to Birmingham?*

◊ **frequently** ['fri:kwəntli] *adverb* often; *the photocopier is frequently out of use; we telex our New York office frequently - at least four times a day*

friction ['frɪkʃn] *noun* small disagreements (between people in the same office); *there was a lot of friction between the sales and accounts staff; the personnel manager is trying to reduce friction in the typing pool*

◊ **frictional unemployment** ['frɪkʃnəl ʌnɪm'plɔɪmənt] *noun* unemployment due to unforeseen circumstances, such as changes in technology or lack of labour mobility or variations in the demand and supply of certain products

Friday ['fraɪdeɪ] *noun* fifth and last day of the normal working week in an office; *the hours of work are 9.30 to 5.30, Monday to Friday;* **Friday afternoon** = period after lunch on Fridays, when some companies stop work; **Friday afternoon car** = new car with numerous defects, presumably because it was made on a Friday afternoon; **Girl Friday** = female employee who does various tasks in an office; **Man Friday** = male employee who does a variety of tasks in an office (NOTE: sometimes **person Friday** is used in job advertisements to avoid sexism)

fringe benefits ['frɪn(d)ʒ 'benɪfɪts] *plural noun* extra items given by a company to workers in addition to a salary (such as company cars, private health insurance); *the fringe benefits make up for the poor pay; use of the company recreation facilities is one of the fringe benefits of the job*

front [frʌnt] *noun* **(a)** part of something which faces away from the back; *the front of the office building is on the High Street; the front page of the company report has a photograph of the managing director; our ad appeared on the front page of the newspaper* **(b)** **in front of** = before *or* on the front side of something; *they put up a 'for sale' sign in front of the factory; the chairman's name is in front of all the others on the staff list* **(c)** business or person used to hide an illegal trade; *his restaurant is a front for a drugs organization* **(d)** **money up front** = payment in advance; *they are asking for £10,000 up front before they will consider the deal; he had to put money up front before he could clinch the deal*

◊ **front-line management** ['frʌnt'laɪn 'mænɪdʒmənt] *noun* managers who have immediate contact with the workers

◊ **front man** ['frʌnt 'mæn] *noun* person who seems honest but is hiding an illegal trade

frozen ['frəuzn] *adjective* not allowed to be changed or used; *wages have been frozen at last year's rates*

fulfil *or* US **fulfill** [ful'fɪl] *verb* to complete something in a satisfactory way; *the clause regarding payments has not been fulfilled;* **to fulfil an order** = to supply the items which have been ordered; *we are so understaffed that we cannot fulfil any more orders before Christmas*

◊ **fulfilment** *or* US **fulfillment** [ful'fɪlmənt] *noun* carrying something out in a satisfactory way; **order fulfilment** = supplying items which have been ordered

full [ful] *adjective* **(a)** with as much inside it as possible; *the train was full of commuters; is the container full yet? we sent a lorry full of spare parts to our warehouse; when the disk is full, don't forget to make a backup copy* **(b)** complete *or* including everything; **we are working at full capacity** = we are doing as much work as possible; **full costs** = all the costs of manufacturing a product, including both fixed and variable costs; **full cover** = insurance cover against all risks; **in full discharge of a debt** = paying a debt completely; **full employment** = situation where all the people who can work have jobs **(c)** **in full** = completely; *give your full* *name and address or your name and address in full; he accepted all our conditions in full; full refund or refund paid in full; he got a full refund when he complained about the service;* **full payment** *or* **payment in full** = paying all money owed

◊ **full-scale** ['ful'skeɪl] *adjective* complete *or* very thorough; *the personnel department will start a full-scale review of the present pay structure*

◊ **fully** ['fuli] *adverb* completely; **fully insured pension scheme** = pension scheme where each contributor is insured to receive the full pension to which he or she is entitled

full-time ['ful 'taɪm] *adjective & adverb* working all the normal working time (i.e. about eight hours a day, five days a week); *she is in full-time work or she works full-time or she is in full-time employment; he is one of our full-time staff;* **full-time equivalents** = part-timers who work more than a certain number of weeks or hours per week, and so are entitled to the same privileges and benefits as full-time staff; **full-time employee** *or* **worker** = worker who works more than 16 hours per week for a company

◊ **full-timer** ['ful'taɪmə] *noun* person who works full-time

QUOTE as in previous quarters, respondents who described themselves as full-time self-employed worked more hours per week on average (42.4) than full-time employees
Labour Force Survey

function ['fʌŋ(k)ʃən] **1** *noun* duty *or* job; **management function** *or* **function of management** = the duties of being a manager **2** *verb* to work; *the advertising campaign is functioning smoothly; the new management structure does not seem to be functioning very well*

◊ **functional** ['fʌŋ(k)ʃnəl] *adjective* **(a)** referring to a job; **functional authority** = the authority which is associated with the job **(b)** which can function properly; *it will be some time before the new pay system is really*

functional; **functional job analysis** = assessment of the specific requirements of a job; *functional job analysis is used to identify what type of person should be appointed to fill the vacancy*

◊ **functionary** ['fʌŋ(k)ʃənri] *noun (slightly derogatory)* civil servant

fund [fʌnd] **1** *noun* money set aside for a special purpose; *a fund is being set up for the families of workers killed in the accident;* **contingency fund** = money set aside in case it is needed urgently; **pension fund** = money which provides pensions for retired members of staff; *the company contributes to the workers' pension fund;* **sinking fund** = fund built up out of amounts of money put aside regularly to meet a future need, such as the repayment of a loan; **slush fund** = money kept to one side to give to people to persuade them to do what you want; **strike fund** = money collected by a trade union from its members, used to pay strike pay **2** *plural noun* money which is available for spending; *the company has no funds to pay for the research programme;* **the company called for extra funds** = the company asked for more money; **to run out of funds** = to come to end of the money available; **public funds** = government money available for expenditure; *the cost was paid for out of public funds;* **conversion of funds** = using money which does not belong to you for a purpose for which it is not supposed to be used; **to convert funds to another purpose** = to use money for a wrong purpose; **to convert funds to one's own use** = to use someone else's money for yourself **3** *verb* to provide money for a purpose; **to fund a company** = to provide money for a company to operate; *the company does not have enough resources to fund its expansion programme*

◊ **funded** ['fʌndɪd] *adjective* backed by long-term loans; **funded pension plan** *or* **funded pension scheme** = pension plan where money is set aside annually to fund employees' pensions

◊ **funding** ['fʌndɪŋ] *noun* providing money for spending; **funding rate** = the employer's contributions to a pension fund shown as a percentage of the total pensionable salaries of the employees

◊ **fund-raising** ['fʌnd'reɪzɪŋ] *noun* trying to get money for a charity, etc.; *a fund-raising sale*

furlough ['fɜːləʊ] *noun* unpaid leave *or* period of absence from work, especially for military personnel or government workers, or for expatriates; *many employees resent being contacted by head office when on furlough*

Gg

gain [geɪn] **1** *noun* increase *or* becoming larger; **gain in experience** = getting more experience; **gain in profitability** = becoming more profitable **2** *verb* to get *or* to obtain; *he gained some useful experience working in a bank;* **to gain control of a business** = to buy more than 50% of the shares so that you can direct the business

◊ **gainful** ['geɪnf(ʊ)l] *adjective* **gainful employment** = employment which pays money

◊ **gainfully** ['geɪnfʊli] *adverb* **gainfully employed** = working and earning money

◊ **gainsharing** ['geɪn'ʃeərɪŋ] *noun* payment scheme where all members of a group of workers are paid extra for increased productivity; *gainsharing will be instituted to increase motivation; gainsharing has allowed workers to identify with the company's successful performance*

garden leave ['gɑːdən 'liːv] *noun (informal)* period of leave stipulated in a contract of employment, where an employee has a long period of notice when he or she leaves a company and cannot take up any other job and is not even allowed into the company offices during this period (this prevents an ex-employee taking industrial secrets or customer details to another employer)

garnishee [gɑːnɪ'ʃiː] *noun* person who owes money to a creditor and is ordered by a court to pay that money to a creditor of the creditor, and not to the creditor himself; **garnishee order** = court order, making a garnishee pay money to a judgment creditor

◊ **garnishment** ['gɑːnɪʃmənt] *noun* procedure by which wages *or* salary are withheld to pay off a debt; *the company had to resort to garnishment to ensure that the worker paid for the damage he caused to machinery*

gatekeeper ['geɪtkiːpə] *noun* person who acts as a screen between a group and people outside the group (such as an interviewer in the human resources department who screens job applicants)

gear [gɪə] *verb* to link to *or* to connect with; *bank interest rates are geared to American interest rates;* **salary geared to the cost of living** = salary which rises as the cost of living increases; **geared scheme** = system by which payment by results increases in stages rather than in direct proportion to increase in output

◊ **gearing** ['gɪərɪŋ] *noun* ratio of capital borrowed by a company at a fixed rate of interest to the company's total capital

◊ **gear up** ['gɪər 'ʌp] *verb* to get ready; **to gear up for a sales drive** = to make all the plans and get ready for a sales drive; *the company is gearing itself up for expansion into the African market*

general ['dʒenərəl] *adjective* **(a)** ordinary *or* not special; **general expenses** = all kinds of minor expenses *or* money spent on the day-to-day costs of running a business; **general manager** = manager in charge of the administration of a company; **General National Vocational Qualifications (GNVQs)** = system of examinations and qualifications in vocational subjects for young people who are in full-time education, giving a board-based training in vocational subjects (run alongside traditional academic studies and of equal value to them) **2 general office** = main administrative office of a company **(b)** dealing with everything *or* with everybody; **general audit** = examining all the books and accounts of a company; **general meeting** = meeting of all the shareholders of a company; **Annual General Meeting (AGM)** = meeting of all the shareholders, when the company's financial situation is discussed with the directors; **Extraordinary General Meeting (EGM)** = special meeting of shareholders to discuss an important matter; **general strike** = strike of all the workers in all industries in a country; *the General Strike of 1926 paralysed the country;* general **union** = union which recruits usually semi-skilled workers in all industries **(c)** general **trading** = dealing in all types of goods; general **store** = small country shop which sells a large range of goods

◊ **generally** ['dʒenərəli] *adverb* normally *or* usually; *the office is generally closed between Christmas and the New Year; we generally give a 25% discount for bulk purchases*

◊ **General Secretary** ['dʒenərəl 'sekrətri] *noun* head official of a trade union

generic [dʒə'nerik] *adjective* which is shared by a group, and does not refer to one individual; generic **skills** = skills which are applicable in various types of work and can be transferred from one job to another

generous ['dʒenərəs] *adjective* (person) who is glad to give money; *he received a generous redundancy payment; the staff contributed a generous sum for the manager's retirement present*

genuine ['dʒenjuin] *adjective* true *or* real; genuine **material factor** = acceptable reason for a difference in salary between a male and a female employee (such as longer experience); **genuine occupational qualifications (GOQs)** = situation where a person of a certain sex or racial background is needed for a job, and this can be stated in the job advertisement

get [get] *verb* **(a)** to receive; *we got a letter from the solicitor this morning; when do you expect to get more stock? he gets £250 a week for doing nothing; she got £5,000 for her car* **(b)** to arrive at a place; *the shipment got to Canada six weeks late; she finally got to the office at 10.30* (NOTE: **getting - got - has got** *or US* **gotten**)

◊ **get across** ['get ə'krɒs] *verb* to make someone understand something; *the manager tried to get across to the workforce why some people were being made redundant*

◊ **get ahead** ['get ə'hed] *verb* to advance in one's career

◊ **get along** ['get ə'lɒŋ] *verb* **(a)** to manage; *we are getting along quite well with only half the staff* **(b)** to be friendly *or* to work well with someone; *she does not get along very well with her new boss*

◊ **get back** ['get 'bæk] *verb* to receive something which you had before; *I got my money back after I had complained to the manager; he got his initial investment back in two months*

◊ **get on** ['get 'ɒn] *verb* **(a)** to work or to manage; *how is the new secretary getting on?* **(b)** to succeed; *my son is getting on well - he has just been promoted*

◊ **get on with** ['get 'ɒn wɪð] *verb* **(a)** to be friendly *or* to work well with someone; *she does not get on with her new boss* **(b)** to go on doing work; *the staff got on with the work and finished the order on time*

◊ **get out** ['get 'aut] *verb* to produce something (on time); *the accounts department got out the draft accounts in time for the meeting*

◊ **get through** ['get 'θruː] *verb* **(a)** to speak to someone on the phone; *I tried to get through to the complaints department* **(b)** to be successful; *he got through his exams, so he is now a qualified engineer* **(c)** to try to make someone understand; *I could not get through to her that I had to be at the airport by 2.15*

Girl Friday ['gɜːl 'fraideɪ] *noun* female employee who does various tasks in an office; *see also* DOGSBODY, GOFER

giro ['dʒairəu] *noun* the giro **system** = banking system in which money can be transferred from one account to another without writing a cheque; *a giro cheque; giro account; giro account number; she put £25 into her giro account; to pay by bank giro transfer*

◊ **Girobank** ['dʒairəubæŋk] *noun* bank in a giro system; *she has her salary paid into her National Girobank account*

give [gɪv] *verb* **(a)** to pass something to someone as a present; *the office gave him a clock when he retired* **(b)** to pass something to someone; *she gave the documents to the accountant; can you give me some information about the new computer system? do not give anybody personal details about staff members* **(c)** to organize; *the company gave a party on a boat to say goodbye to the retiring sales director*

◊ **give back** ['gɪv 'bæk] *verb* to hand something back to someone

◊ **give-back** ['gɪvbæk] *noun US* demand

by management that the employees accept less favourable terms of employment; *the give-back was insisted on by management because of the high costs of labour*

◊ **give in to** ['gɪv 'ɪn tu] *verb* to yield *or* to surrender; *to give in to pressure from the strikers*

◊ **give up** ['gɪv 'ʌp] *verb* to hand something over to someone; *workers refused to give up any of their rights*

◊ **give way to** ['gɪv 'weɪ tu] *verb* to make concessions *or* to agree to demands; *to give way to the union's wage demands*

glass ceiling ['glɑːs 'siːlɪŋ] *noun* mysteriously invisible barrier to promotion; *women managers complain that they find it difficult to break through the glass ceiling and become members of the board*

GMP = GUARANTEED MINIMUM PENSION

GNVQs = GENERAL NATIONAL VOCATIONAL QUALIFICATIONS

go [gəʊ] *verb* (a) to move from one place to another; *the cheque went to your bank yesterday; the plane goes to Frankfurt, then to Rome; he is going to our Lagos office; she went on a management course* (b) to be placed; *the date goes at the top of the letter* (NOTE: **going - went - has gone**)

◊ **go-ahead** ['gəʊəhed] **1** *noun* **to give something the go-ahead** = to approve something *or* to say that something can be done; *his project got a government go-ahead; the board refused to give the go-ahead to the expansion plan* **2** *adjective* energetic *or* keen to do well; *he is a very go-ahead type; she works for a go-ahead clothing company*

◊ **go back on** ['gəʊ 'bæk ɒn] *verb* not to do what has been promised; *two months later they went back on the agreement*

◊ **go-between** ['gəʊbɪtwiːn] *noun* person who acts as an intermediary in the negotiations between two others; *the head of the workers' committee was the effective go-between in the dispute*

◊ **go up** ['gəʊ 'ʌp] *verb* to rise; *NI contributions are going up 3% next month*

goal [gəʊl] *noun* aim *or* something which

you try to do; aim of an organization; **to achieve one's goal** = to do what one set out to do; **to set someone goals** = to give someone objectives to aim at; *bonus payments are motivating workers to achieve company goals; one of the personnel manager's goals was a fair payment scheme; our goal is to break even within twelve months; the company achieved all its goals*

gofer ['gəʊfə] *noun US* person who does all types of work in an office for low wages; *see also* DOGSBODY, GIRL FRIDAY, MAN FRIDAY

going ['gəʊɪŋ] *adjective* (a) active *or* busy; **to sell a business as a going concern** = to sell a business as an actively trading company; **it is a going concern** = the company is working (and making a profit) (b) **the going price** = the usual *or* current price *or* the price that is being charged now; *what is the going price for secondhand 1975 Volkswagens?;* **the going rate** = the usual *or* current rate of payment for a job, paid by other employers in the field; *we pay the going rate for typists; the going rate for machinists is rising since the demand for them is increasing*

gold [gəʊld] *noun* very valuable yellow metal; *to buy gold; to deal in gold; he collects gold coins*

◊ **gold-bricking** ['gəʊld 'brɪkɪŋ] *noun* regulating production by not claiming production achieved on some days so as to be able to carry it over and so allow workers to take time off work on other days; *gold-bricking has reduced production by half*

◊ **gold-circle rate** ['gəʊld 'sɜːkl 'reɪt] *noun US* pay that exceeds the maximum rate of employees evaluated pay level; *the gold-circle rate is resented by some workers who see it as an unmerited bonus*

golden ['gəʊldən] *adjective* made of gold *or* like gold; **golden formula** = rule that unions are immune from prosecution if their action is taken in pursuance of a trade dispute; **golden hallo** = cash inducement paid to someone to encourage him to change jobs and move to another company; **golden handcuffs** = contractual arrangement to make sure that a valued member of staff stays in his job, by which he is offered special financial advantages if he stays and heavy penalties if he leaves;

golden handshake = large, usually tax-free, sum of money given to a director who resigns from a company before the end of his service contract; *when the company was taken over, the sales director received a golden handshake of £25,000;* **golden parachute** = special contract for a director of a company, which gives him advantageous financial terms if he has to resign when the company is taken over

good [gʊd] *adjective* (a) not bad; **a good buy** = excellent item which has been bought cheaply; **to buy something in good faith** = to buy something thinking it is of good quality *or* that it has not been stolen *or* that it is not an imitation (b) **a good deal of** = a large quantity of; *we wasted a good deal of time discussing the arrangements for the AGM; the company had to pay a good deal for the building site;* **a good many** = very many; *a good many staff members have joined the union*

◊ **goods** [gʊdz] *plural noun* items which can be moved and are for sale; **capital goods** = machinery, buildings and raw materials which are used to make other goods; **consumer goods** *or* **consumable goods** = goods bought by the general public and not by businesses; **finished goods** = manufactured goods which are ready to be sold; **manufactured goods** = items which are made by machine

◊ **goodwill** [gʊdwɪl] *noun* (a) good reputation of a business; *he paid £10,000 for the goodwill of the shop and £4,000 for the stock* (b) good feeling towards someone; *to show goodwill, the management increased the terms of the offer* (NOTE: no plural)

goon [guːn] *noun US* person who deliberately provokes disputes between employers and employees

GOQs = GENUINE OCCUPATIONAL QUALIFICATIONS

go-slow [ˈgəʊ ˈsləʊ] *noun* slowing down of production by workers as a protest against the management; *a series of go-slows reduced production*

grade [greɪd] **1** *noun* (a) level *or* rank (in a structure); *top grade of civil servant; to reach the top grade in the civil service my salary will increase when I move into a higher grade;* **high-grade** = of very good quality; **a high-grade trade delegation** = a delegation made up of important people; **low-grade** =

not very important *or* not of very good quality; *a low-grade official from the Ministry of Commerce;* **top-grade** = most important *or* of the best quality (b) *US* mark given in a test; *he got good grades in college; what grade was he given in his performance appraisal?* **2** *verb* to make something rise in steps according to value *or* quantity; **graded advertising rates** = rates which become cheaper as you take more advertising space; **graded hourly rate** = pay scale where piece workers receive different rates per piece completed according to their appraisal ratings; **graded tax** = tax which rises according to income

◊ **grading** [ˈgreɪdɪŋ] *noun* assessment of an employee's performance by giving a certain grade *or* mark; *the company has adopted a new grading system for appraisals;* **job grading** = arranging jobs in a certain order of importance

gradual [ˈgrædʒʊəl] *adjective* slow *or* step by step; *1984 saw a gradual return to profits; his CV describes his gradual rise to the position of company chairman*

◊ **gradually** [ˈgrædʒʊəli] *adverb* slowly *or* step by step; *the company has gradually become more profitable; she gradually learnt the details of the import-export business*

graduate [ˈgrædʒʊət] *noun* person who has a degree from a university or polytechnic; **graduate entry** = entry of graduates into employment with a company; *the graduate entry into the civil service;* **graduate training scheme** = training scheme for graduates; **graduate trainee** = person in a graduate training scheme

◊ **graduated** [ˈgrædʒʊeɪtɪd] *adjective* rising in steps according to quantity; **graduated income tax** = tax which rises in steps (each level of income is taxed at a higher percentage); **graduated pension plan** *or* **graduated pension scheme** = pension scheme where the contributions are calculated on the salary of each person in the scheme; **graduated taxation** = tax system where the percentage of tax paid rises as the income rises; **graduated wages** = wages which increase in accordance with established pay levels

QUOTE as companies recognise that they rely more on people than capital, mistakes at graduate entry level can be costly
Sunday Times

grand [grænd] **1** *adjective* important; **grand plan** = major plan; *he explained his grand plan for redeveloping the factory site;* **grand total** = final total made by adding several subtotals **2** *noun (informal)* one thousand pounds *or* dollars; *he's earning fifty grand plus car and expenses* (NOTE: no plural)

◊ **grandfather** ['grændfɑːðə] *noun* **grandfather clause** = clause in an insurance policy that exempts a category of insured employee from meeting new standards; *the grandfather clause exempts the older workers from the retraining scheme;* **grandfather system** = appraisal system, where the manager's appraisals of employees are sent for review to the manager's superior

grant [grɑːnt] **1** *noun* money given by the government to help pay for something; *the laboratory has a government grant to cover the cost of the development programme; the government has allocated grants towards the costs of the scheme;* **grant-aided scheme** = scheme which is funded by a government grant **2** *verb* to agree to give someone something; *to grant someone a loan or a subsidy; the local authority granted the company an interest-free loan to start up the new factory; to grant someone three weeks' leave of absence*

grapevine ['greɪpvaɪn] *noun* unofficial communications network in an organization; *I heard on the grapevine that the managing director has been sacked*

graph [grɑːf] *noun* diagram *or* chart which shows statistics as a drawing; *a graph was used to show salary increases in relation to increases in output; according to the graph, as average salaries have risen so has absenteeism; the personnel manager asked her to set out the results of the questionnaire in a graph;* **graph paper** = special paper with many little squares, used for drawing graphs

graphology [grəˈfɒlədʒi] *noun* study of handwriting, which is believed to show the writer's characteristics

◊ **graphologist** [grəˈfɒlədʒɪst] *noun* person who studies handwriting, and can identify the writer's characteristics from it; *some companies ask for job applications to be handwritten, so that they can be shown to a consultant graphologist*

grassroots ['grɑːsˈruːts] *noun* basic ordinary members of a union, political party, of society in general

gratia ['greɪʃə] *see* EX GRATIA

gratuity [grəˈtjuːəti] *noun* **(a)** terminal gratuity = bonus given to someone at the end of a fixed term contract of employment **(b)** tip, money given to someone who has helped you; *the staff are instructed not to accept gratuities*

graveyard shift ['greɪvjɑːd ˈʃɪft] *noun (informal)* night shift in a continuous shift system, starting around midnight

gravy ['greɪvi] *noun (informal)* something which does not involve effort; **gravy job** = work that offers the same money for less effort than another similar job; *workers were moving to more prosperous areas of the country in search of gravy jobs* (NOTE: in British English also called **cushy number**) **gravy train** = means of getting money easily; **to be on the gravy train** = to have a good well-paid civil service job

green card ['griːn ˈkɑːd] *noun* **(a)** special British insurance certificate to prove that a car is insured for travel abroad **(b)** work permit for a foreigner in the USA

◊ **green circle rate** ['griːn ˈsɜːkl ˈreɪt] *noun* US rate of pay which is below the minimum rate

◊ **green hands** *or* **green labour** ['griːn ˈhændz *or* ˈleɪbə] *noun* inexperienced workers; *the induction week allowed green hands to familiarize themselves with the workplace; green labour will only be recruited if there is a shortage of experienced workers*

◊ **greenfield site** ['griːnfiːld ˈsaɪt] *noun* field which are chosen as the site for a new housing development *or* factory

grid [grɪd] *noun* system of numbered squares; **grid method** = two-dimensional method of job evaluation based on breadth and depth of responsibility; *some jobs score high on the grid method since they involve many different tasks and a lot of decision-making;* **grid structure** = structure based on a grid

grievance ['griːvəns] *noun* complaint *or* protest made by a trade union *or* worker to the management; **to air a grievance** = to talk about *or* to discuss a grievance; *the management committee is valuable as a place where workers' representatives can air their grievances;* **grievance interview** = meeting between management and a worker or group of workers where the managers listen to the worker's complaints and try to find a solution to the problem; **grievance procedure** = way of settling complaints from a trade union *or* worker to the management

QUOTE ACAS has a legal obligation to try and resolve industrial grievances before they reach industrial tribunals

Personnel Today

gross [grəus] **1** *adjective* **(a)** total *or* with no deductions; **gross earnings** = total earnings before tax and other deductions; **gross income** *or* **gross pay** *or* **gross salary** = salary before tax is deducted; **gross receipts** = total amount of money received before expenses are deducted; *his gross pay is £100 per week, but he takes home £70 net; the gross profit is high, but because of high overheads, the net profit is disappointing* (NOTE: the opposite is **net**) **(b)** very serious; **gross misconduct** = very bad behaviour by a worker, which is a fair reason for dismissal (such as drunkenness, theft, etc.); *he was dismissed for gross misconduct* **2** *adverb* with no deductions; *his salary is paid gross* **3** *verb* to earn as gross salary; *he grosses £500 a week*

ground [graund] *noun* **to gain ground** = to start to win against an enemy; **to give ground** = to give way against an enemy

◊ **grounds** [graundz] *noun* basic reasons; *does he have good grounds for complaint? there are no grounds on which he can be dismissed or there are no grounds for dismissal; what are the grounds for the pay demand?*

◊ **groundless** ['graundləs] *adjective* with no real reason; *the complaint was proved to be groundless*

group [gru:p] *noun* **(a)** several things or people together; *a group of staff has sent a memo to the chairman complaining about noise in the office;* **age group** = group of people of about the same age; *the 25-30 age group;* **pressure group** = group of people who try to influence the government *or* the local town council, etc.; **group appraisal** = appraisal of an employee by a group of other employees; **group incentive** = incentive payment made to a group, rather than to an individual worker; **group incentive scheme** *or* **group incentive plan** = scheme whereby payment by results is based on the output of all the employees in an organization; **group insurance** = insurance scheme where a group of employees are covered by one policy; **group interview** = type of interview in which several candidates are interviewed together by one or more representatives of an organization; **group pension plan** *or* **scheme** = life insurance plan which provides a number of employees with a retirement pension; **group selection methods** = methods of assessing the ability of individuals to work with others; *group selection methods are being introduced to complement individual intelligence and personality tests;* **group training** = training method, where a group trains together and so learn from each other **(b)** several companies linked together in the same organization; *the group chairman or the chairman of the group; group turnover or turnover for the group;* **group results** = results of a group of companies taken together

growth [grəuθ] *noun* increase in size; **population growth** = increase in the population; **growth rate** = speed at which something grows

guarantee [gærən'ti:] **1** *noun* legal document which promises that a machine will work properly *or* that an item is of good quality; *certificate of guarantee or guarantee certificate; the guarantee lasts for two years; it is sold with a twelve-month guarantee;* **the car is still under guarantee** = is still covered by the maker's guarantee **2** *verb* to give a promise that something will happen; **to guarantee a debt** = to promise that you will pay a debt made by someone else; **the product is guaranteed for twelve months** = the manufacturer says that the product will work well for twelve months, and will mend it free of charge if it breaks down; **guaranteed annuity** = arrangement in a pension scheme by which a final lump sum is used to purchase a fixed annuity; **guaranteed minimum pension (GMP)** = minimum pension which must be provided by an occupational pension scheme;

guaranteed wage = wage which is agreed between employers and employees which a company promises to pay whether there is work or not; **guaranteed minimum wage** = (i) wage which a company promises will not fall below a certain figure; (ii) legal established minimum wage which must be paid to all workers

◊ **guarantor** [gærən'tɔː] *noun* person who promises to pay someone's debts; *he stood guarantor for his brother*

guard [gɑːd] *noun* person who protects someone *or* a building; **security guard** = person who protects a building; **guard dog** = dog kept to protect a building

guidance ['gaɪdəns] *noun* **vocational guidance** = professional help for people in choosing a suitable career

guideline ['gaɪdlaɪn] *noun* unofficial suggestion from the government as to how something should be done; *the government has issued guidelines on increases in incomes and prices; the increase in retail price goes against the government guidelines;* **guideline method** = job evaluation technique which takes into account attitudes to the job in the industry as a whole; *the personnel manager justified the guideline method as adapting to the laws of supply and demand*

guild [gɪld] *noun* association of merchants *or* of shopkeepers; *trade guild; the guild of master bakers*

guilty ['gɪlti] *adjective* (person) who has done something wrong; *he was found guilty of libel; the company was guilty of not reporting the sales to the auditors*

Hh

hack [hæk] *noun* ordinary worker; *a hack copywriter*

haggle ['hægl] *verb* to discuss prices and terms and try to reduce them; *to haggle about or over the details of a contract; after two days' haggling the contract was signed*

halo effect ['heɪləʊ ɪ'fekt] *noun* crude and over-simple classification of employees into 'good' and 'bad' (i.e., just because a candidate does well in an interview, and seems a pleasant man, it must not be assumed that he will make an excellent manager, accountant, etc.)

◊ **halo error** ['heɪləʊ 'erə] *noun* mistake made by promoting the wrong person because of the halo effect

hand [hænd] *noun* **(a)** part of the body at the end of each arm; **to shake hands** = to hold someone's hand when meeting to show you are pleased to meet him or to show that an agreement has been reached; *the two negotiating teams shook hands and sat down at the conference table;* **to shake hands on a deal** = to shake hands to show that a deal has been agreed; **show of hands** = vote where people show how they vote by raising their hands; *the motion was carried on a show of hands;* **to change hands** = to be bought by a new owner or manager **(b) by hand** = using the hands, not a machine; *these shoes are made by hand;* **to send a letter by hand** = to ask someone to carry and deliver a letter personally, not sending it through the post **(c)** worker; *we are taking on ten more hands owing to the increased workload;* **factory hand** = worker in a factory

◊ **handbook** ['hænbʊk] *noun* **user's handbook** = book which gives instructions on how something is to be used; *the handbook does not say how you open the photocopier; look in the handbook to see if it tells you how to clean the typewriter;* **service handbook** = book which shows how to service a machine

◊ **handcuffs** ['hænkʌfs] *see* GOLDEN

◊ **hand in** ['hænd 'ɪn] *verb* to deliver (a letter) by hand; **he handed in his notice** *or* **he handed in his resignation** = he resigned

◊ **hand-operated** ['hænd 'ɒpəreɪtɪd] *adjective* worked by hand, not automatically; *a hand-operated machine*

◊ **hand over** ['hænd 'əʊvə] *verb* to pass something to someone; *she handed over the documents to the lawyer;* **he handed over to his deputy** = he passed his responsibilities to his deputy

◊ **handover** ['hændəʊvə] *noun* passing of responsibilities to someone else; *there was a smooth handover to the new management team; the handover from the old chairman to the new went very smoothly; when the ownership of a company changes, the handover period is always difficult*

◊ **hand-picked** ['hænd 'pɪkt] *adjective* carefully selected; *a hand-picked sales team*

◊ **hands-on** ['hændz 'ɒn] *adjective* involving direct contact with the working of a system *or* organization; *we need a hands-on manager who will supervise operations closely; more hands-on management means we will have to increase the technical input in our management training schemes;* **hands-on experience** = direct experience of a system

◊ **handshake** ['hænʃeɪk] *noun* **golden handshake** *see* GOLDEN

◊ **handwriting** ['hændraɪtɪŋ] *noun* writing done by hand; *I have difficulty in reading her handwriting;* **send a letter of application in your own handwriting** = written by you with a pen, and not typed (NOTE: no plural)

◊ **handwritten** ['hændrɪtn] *adjective* written by hand, not typed; *it is more professional to send in a typed rather than a handwritten letter of application*

handicap ['hændɪkæp] **1** *verb* **(a)** something which prevents a person from doing something; *she found that her lack of* *qualifications was a great handicap to getting her first job* (b) physical disability *or* condition which makes it difficult for someone to do a normal activity; *he is confined to a wheelchair, but holds down a normal office job in spite of his handicap* 2 *verb* to prevent someone from doing some normal activity; *she is handicapped by being blind in one eye*

◊ **handicapped** ['hændɪkæpd] *adjective* (a) without the advantage of something; *she is handicapped by not having a secretarial qualification* (b) **handicapped person** = person with a disability; **physically handicapped** = having a physical disability; **mentally handicapped** = having a mental disability; *the company has special facilities for handicapped workers*

handle ['hændl] *verb* to deal with something *or* to organize something; *the accounts department handles all the cash; we can handle orders for up to 15,000 units; they handle all our overseas orders*

◊ **handling** ['hændlɪŋ] *noun* moving something by hand *or* dealing with something; **handling charges** = money to be paid for packing and invoicing *or* for dealing with something in general *or* for moving goods from one place to another; *the bank adds on 5% handling charge for changing travellers' cheques*

happy ['hæpi] *adjective* very pleased; *the workforce seems quite happy with the new offer from the management; the personnel director was not at all happy to receive the unions new demands*

harass ['hærəs] *verb* to worry *or* to bother someone, especially by continually checking on him or her *or* making sexual approaches

◊ **harassment** ['hærəsmənt] *noun* action of harassing someone; **sexual harassment** = making unpleasant sexual gestures, comments, or approaches to someone; *she complained of sexual harassment by the manager;* **harassment procedure** = written and agreed rules as to how cases of harassment should be dealt with in a company (NOTE: no plural)

QUOTE EEC legislation should formally recognize that sexual harassment is discrimination on grounds of sex
Personnel Management

hard [hɑːd] **1** *adjective* **(a)** strong *or* not weak; **to take a hard line in trade union negotiations** = to refuse to accept any proposal from the other side **(b)** difficult; *these typewriters are hard to sell; it is hard to get good people to work for low salaries* **(c)** solid; **hard copy** = printout of a text which is on a computer *or* printed copy of a document which is on microfilm; *he made the presentation with diagrams and ten pages of hard copy;* **hard disk** = computer disk in a sealed case, which is capable of storing large quantities of information **(d) hard bargain** = bargain with difficult terms; **to drive a hard bargain** = to be a difficult negotiator; **to strike a hard bargain** = to agree a deal where the terms are favourable to you; **after weeks of hard bargaining** = after weeks of difficult discussions **2** *adverb* with a lot of effort; *the sales team sold the new product range hard into the supermarkets; if everyone in the workforce works hard, the order should be completed on time*

◊ **harden** ['hɑːdn] *verb* to become more fixed *or* more inflexible; *the union's attitude to the management has hardened since the lockout*

◊ **hardship** ['hɑːdʃɪp] *noun* bad conditions which make someone suffer; **hardship allowance** = additional pay for an employee who accepts an assignment in difficult conditions

◊ **hardware** ['hɑːdweə] *noun* **computer hardware** = machines used in data processing, including computers and printers, but not programs; *we are negotiating a new hardware maintenance contract; she is going to the exhibition to see the latest Japanese hardware; compare* SOFTWARE (NOTE: no plural)

◊ **hard-working** ['hɑːd 'wɜːkɪŋ] *adjective* (person) who works hard

hassle ['hæsəl] *noun* bother *or* trouble; *dealing with these people is too much of a hassle*

hatchet man ['hætʃɪt 'mæn] *noun* recently appointed manager, whose job is to make staff redundant and reduce expenditure

hazard ['hæzəd] *noun* **fire hazard** = situation *or* goods which could start a fire; *that warehouse full of wood and paper is a fire hazard;* **health hazard** = danger to the health of a person; **occupational hazards** = dangers which apply to certain jobs; *heart attacks are one of the occupational hazards of managers;* **hazard pay** = additional pay for dangerous work; *all the construction workers received hazard pay; hazard pay has to be pretty high to attract workers to this type of work*

◊ **hazardous** ['hæzədəs] *adjective* dangerous; *hazardous equipment; hazardous occupations;* **hazardous substance** = substance (such as an acid) which could harm anyone who handles it

head [hed] **1** *noun* **(a)** most important person; **head of department** *or* **department head** = person in charge of a department **(b)** top part *or* first part; *write the name of the company at the head of the list* **(c)** person; *representatives cost on average £25,000 per head per annum* **2** *adjective* most important *or* main; *head clerk; head porter; head salesman; head waiter;* **head buyer** = most important buyer in a department store; **head office** = main office, where the board of directors works and meets **3** *verb* to be the manager *or* to be the most important person; *to head a department; he is heading a buying mission to China*

◊ **headed paper** ['hedɪd 'peɪpə] *noun* notepaper with the name of the company and its address printed on it

◊ **headhunt** ['hedhʌnt] *verb* to look for managers and offer them jobs in other companies; **he was headhunted** = he was approached by a headhunter and offered a new job

◊ **headhunter** ['hedhʌntə] *noun* person *or* company whose job is to find suitable top managers to fill jobs in companies; *the headhunter is looking for marketing talent for one of the multinationals*

◊ **headhunting** ['hedhʌntɪŋ] *noun* = EXECUTIVE SEARCH

◊ **heading** ['hedɪŋ] *noun* **(a)** words at the top of a piece of text; *items are listed under several headings; look at the figure under the heading 'Costs 95-96'* **(b)** letter **heading** *or* **heading on notepaper** = name and address of a company printed at the top of a piece of notepaper

headquarters (HQ) [hed'kwɔːtəz] *plural noun* main office, where the board of directors meets and works; *the company's*

headquarters are in New York; **divisional headquarters** = main office of a division of a company; **to reduce headquarters staff** = to have fewer people working in the main office

◊ **head up** ['hed 'ʌp] *verb* to be in charge of; *he has been appointed to head up our European organization*

QUOTE reporting to the deputy managing director, the successful candidate will be responsible for heading up a team which provides a full personnel service

Times

headway ['hedweɪ] *noun* progress in a difficult situation; **to make headway** = to go forward *or* to make progress; *we are not making any headway in our negotiations*

health [helθ] *noun* being fit and well, not ill; *GB* **Health and Safety at Work Act (1974)** = Act of Parliament which rules how the health of workers should be protected by the companies they work for; **Health and Safety Commission (HSC)** = government body, set up to see that the provisions of the Health and Safety at Work Act are obeyed (employers must report fatal accidents, work-related diseases, etc.); **Health and Safety Executive** = executive committee of the Health and Safety Commission; **Environmental Health Officer (EHO)** *or* **Public Health Inspector** = official of a local authority who examines the environment and tests for air pollution *or* bad sanitation *or* noise pollution, etc.; **health insurance** = insurance which pays the cost of treatment for illnesses; *the company offers private health insurance as part of the pay package;* **a private health scheme** = insurance which will pay for the cost of treatment in a private hospital, not a state one; **Health Register** = list kept by a company, of medical examinations given to employees who handle hazardous substances (NOTE: no plural)

hearing ['hɪərɪŋ] *noun* case which is being heard by a committee *or* tribunal *or* court of law, or by an official body; **court hearing** = court case; **preliminary hearing** = court proceedings where the witnesses and the defendant are examined to see if there are sufficient grounds for the case to proceed; **public hearing** = hearing held in public (as opposed to a hearing held in camera)

help [help] **1** *noun* thing which makes it

easy to do something; *she finds the word-processor a great help in writing letters; the company was set up with financial help from the government; her assistant is not much help - he can't type or drive* (NOTE: no plural) **2** *verb* to make it easy for something to be done; *he helped the salesman carry his case of samples; the computer helps in the rapid processing of orders or helps us to process orders rapidly; the government helps exporting companies with easy credit;* **helping interview** = interview which uses a sympathetic approach to achieve its ends; *helping interviews are effective in getting nervous candidates to relax; the management finds regular helping interviews with workers improves relations* (NOTE: you help someone *or* something **to do** something)

hesitate ['hezɪteɪt] *verb* not to be sure what to do next; *the company is hesitating about starting up a new computer factory; she hesitated for some time before accepting the job*

hidden agenda ['hɪdn ə'dʒendə] *noun* secret plan which one party to discussions has, which the other side does not know about

hierarchy ['haɪrɑːki] *noun* organizational structure with several levels of responsibility *or* authority; *at the bottom of the hierarchy are the unskilled workers*

◇ **hierarchical** [haɪ'rɑːkɪkl] *adjective* (organization) which has several levels; *the company has a very traditional hierarchical structure*

high [haɪ] *adjective* **(a)** tall; *the shelves are 30 cm high; the door is not high enough to let us get the machines into the building; they are planning a 30-storey high office block* **(b)** large *or* not low; *high overhead costs increase the unit price; high prices put customers off; they are budgeting for a high level of expenditure; investments which bring in a high rate of return; high interest rates are killing small businesses;* **high day rate** = payment system where high rates of pay are paid to skilled workers for time worked; **high flier** = person who is very successful *or* who is likely to get a very important job; **high taxation** = taxation which imposes large taxes on incomes *or* profits; **highest tax bracket** = the group which pays the most tax

◇ **high-grade** ['haɪ'greɪd] *adjective* of very good quality; **a high-grade trade delegation** = a delegation made up of very important people

◇ **high-level** ['haɪ'levl] *adjective* very important; **a high-level meeting** *or* **delegation** = meeting *or* delegation of the most important people (such as ministers, managing directors); **a high-level decision** = decision taken by the most important person or group

◇ **highly** ['haɪli] *adverb* very well; **highly-paid** = earning a large salary; **highly-placed** = occupying an important post; *the delegation met a highly-placed official in the Trade Ministry;* **she is highly thought of by the managing director** = the managing director thinks she is very competent

◇ **high pressure** ['haɪ'preʃə] *noun* strong force by other people to do something; **working under high pressure** = working with a manager telling you what to do and to do it quickly *or* with customers asking for supplies urgently; **high-pressure salesman** = salesman who forces the customer to buy something he does not really need; **high-pressure sales techniques** *or* **high-pressure selling** = forcing a customer to buy something he does not really want

hike [haɪk] **1** *noun US* increase; **pay hike** = increase in salary **2** *verb US* to increase; *the union hiked its demand to $3 an hour*

hire ['haɪə] **1** *noun* **(a)** paying money to rent a car *or* boat *or* piece of equipment for a time; *car hire; truck hire;* **car hire firm** *or* **equipment hire firm** = company which owns cars *or* equipment and lends them to customers for a payment; **hire car** = car which has been rented; *he was driving a hire car when the accident happened* **(b)** *US* for **hire contract** = freelance contract; **to work for hire** = to work freelance **2** *verb* **(a)** to hire staff = to engage new staff to work for you; **to hire and fire** = to employ new staff and dismiss existing staff frequently; *we have hired the best lawyers to represent us; they hired a small company to paint the offices* **(b)** **to hire a car** *or* **a crane** = to pay money to use a car *or* a crane for a time; *he hired a truck to move his furniture* **(c)** **to hire out workers** *or* **cars** *or* **equipment** = to lend workers *or* cars *or* equipment to customers who pay for their use

◇ **hiring** ['haɪərɪŋ] *noun* employing; *hiring*

of new personnel has been stopped; **hiring and firing** = hiring new employees and dismissing them in quick succession; **hiring rate** = rate of pay for employees when first hired; *though the hiring rate is low, pay goes up rapidly during the first year; the hiring rate depends on whether the entrants are skilled or not*

histogram ['hɪstəgræm] *noun* chart *or* diagram with bars set on a base-line, the length of each bar expressing the quantity of an item or unit; *the histogram shows the comparison between the wages of different workers*

hold [həʊld] *verb* **(a)** to own *or* to keep; *he holds 10% of the company's shares;* **you should hold these shares - they look likely to rise** = you should keep these shares and not sell them **(b)** to contain; *the carton holds twenty packets; each box holds 250 sheets of paper; a bag can hold twenty kilos of sugar* **(c)** to make something happen; *to hold a meeting or a discussion; the computer show will be held in London next month; board meetings are held in the boardroom; the AGM will be held on March 24th; the receiver will hold an auction of the company's assets; the accountants held a review of the company's accounting practices* **(d)** *(on telephone)* **hold the line please** = please wait; *the chairman is on the other line - will you hold?* **(e)** to have a certain place; *he holds the position of chairman* (NOTE: **holding - held**)

◊ **hold back** ['həʊld 'bæk] *verb* to wait *or* not to go forward; **he held back from signing the contract until he had checked the details** = he delayed signing the contract until he had checked the details; **payment will be held back until the contract has been signed** = payment will not be made until the contract has been signed

◊ **hold down** ['həʊld 'daʊn] *verb* **(a)** to keep at a low level; *we are cutting margins to hold our prices down* **(b) to hold down a job** = to manage to do a difficult job

◊ **holding company** ['həʊldɪŋ 'kʌmpni] *noun* (i) company which owns more than 50% of the shares in another company; (ii) company which exists only or mainly to own shares in subsidiary companies; *see also* SUBSIDIARY (NOTE: the US English for this is **proprietary company**)

◊ **hold out for** ['həʊld 'aʊt fɔː] *verb* to wait

and ask for; **you should hold out for a 10% pay rise** = do not agree to a pay rise of less than 10%

◊ **hold over** ['həʊld 'əʊvə] *verb* to postpone *or* to put back to a later date; *discussion of item 4 was held over until the next meeting*

◊ **hold to** ['həʊld 'tuː] *verb* not to allow something to change; **we will try to hold him to the contract** = we will try to stop him going against the contract; **the government hopes to hold wage increases to 5%** = the government hopes that wage increases will not be more than 5%

◊ **hold up** ['həʊld 'ʌp] *verb* **(a)** to stay at a high level; *share prices have held up well; sales held up during the tourist season* **(b)** to delay; *the workers are holding up production as a form of protest against poor conditions; payment will be held up until the contract has been signed; the strike will hold up dispatch for some weeks*

◊ **hold-up** ['həʊldʌp] *noun* delay; *the strike caused hold-ups in the dispatch of goods*

QUOTE real wages have been held down; they have risen at an annual rate of only 1% in the last two years

Sunday Times

holiday ['hɒlədeɪ] *noun* **(a) bank holiday** = weekday which is a public holiday when the banks are closed; *New Year's Day is a bank holiday;* **public holiday** = day when all workers rest and enjoy themselves instead of working; **statutory holiday** = holiday which is fixed by law; *the office is closed for the Christmas holiday* **(b)** period when a worker does not work, but rests, goes away and enjoys himself or herself; *to take a holiday or to go on holiday; when is the manager taking his holidays? my secretary is off on holiday tomorrow; he is away on holiday for two weeks;* **the job carries five weeks' holiday** = one of the conditions of the job is that you have five weeks' holiday; **annual holiday** = holiday which is taken once a year; **paid holiday** *or* **holiday with pay** = holiday period for which the worker still receives salary, even if not at work; **the summer holidays** = holidays taken by the workers in the summer when the weather is good and children are not at school; **holiday entitlement** = number of days' paid holiday that a worker has the right to take; *I have used up all my holiday entitlement this year,*

and can only look forward to Christmas;
holiday pay = salary which is still paid
during the holiday

home [həum] *noun* place where a person
lives; *please send the letter to my home
address, not my office*

◊ **homeworker** ['həumwʌkə] *noun*
worker employed by a company but
working at home; *see also* OUTWORKER

◊ **homeworking** ['həumwʌkɪŋ] *noun*
working method where employees work at
home on computer terminals, and send the
finished material back to the central office
by modem; *also called* NETWORKING,
TELEWORKING

hon = HONORARY **hon sec** = honorary
secretary

honorarium [ɒnə'reərɪəm] *noun* money
paid to a professional person, such as an
accountant *or* a lawyer, when he or she does
not ask for a fee (NOTE: plural is **honoraria)**

◊ **honorary** ['ɒnərəri] *adjective* person
who is not paid a salary for the work he or
she does for an organization; *the honorary
secretary of a charity;* **honorary member** =
member who does not have to pay a
subscription

hooking ['hukɪŋ] *noun US* persuading a
worker to watch what other union
members are doing or saying and to report
back to management

horizontal [hɒrɪ'zɒntl] *adjective* flat *or*
going from side to side, not up and down;
horizontal communication =
communication between workers at the
same level in the hierarchy; **horizontal
integration** = joining similar companies *or*
taking over a company in the same line of
business as yourself; **horizontal job
enlargement** = expanding a job to include
new activities *or* responsibilities, but still at
the same level in the organization; *we have
implemented horizontal job enlargement to
increase individual workloads while at the
same time making the work more interesting*
(NOTE: the opposite is **vertical)**

horse trading ['hɔːs 'treɪdɪŋ] *noun* hard
bargaining which ends with someone
giving something in return for a concession
from the other side

hostile ['hɒstaɪl] *adjective* unfriendly,

showing dislike; **a hostile work environment**
= working surroundings which are
unfriendly

hot [hɒt] *adjective* **(a)** very warm; *the staff
complain that the office is too hot in summer
and too cold in winter; the drinks machines
sells coffee, tea and hot soup; switch off the
machine if it gets too hot* **(b)** not safe *or* very
bad; **to make things hot for someone** = to
make it difficult for someone to work *or* to
trade; *customs officials are making things
hot for the drug smugglers;* **he is in the hot
seat** = his job involves making many
difficult decisions **(c) hot cargo provision** =
clause in a contract that allows workers to
refuse to handle products from another
factory where there is an industrial dispute
in progress

hour ['auə] *noun* **(a)** period of time lasting
sixty minutes; **to work a thirty-five hour
week** = to work seven hours a day each
weekday; **we work an eight-hour day** = we
work for eight hours a day, e.g. from 8.30 to
5.30 with one hour for lunch **(b)** sixty
minutes of work; *he earns £4 an hour; we
pay £6 an hour;* **to pay by the hour** = to pay
people a fixed amount of money for each
hour worked; *see also* ANNUAL **(c) extra
hours** = working more hours than are
normal; *she worked three hours extra; he
claimed for extra hours;* **office hours** = time
when an office is open; *do not telephone
during office hours;* **outside hours** *or* **out of
hours** = when the office is not open; *he
worked on the accounts out of hours;*
opening hours = hours when a shop *or*
business is open; **peak hours** *or* **rush hour** =
time when traffic is worst *or* when everyone
is trying to travel to work or from work
back home; *the taxi was delayed in the rush
hour traffic;* **to work unsocial hours** = to
work at times (i.e. in the evening *or* at night
or during public holidays) when most
people are not at work; *she asked for extra
pay for working unsocial hours;* **hours of
work** = time when the staff of an office are
working; *our hours of work are 9.30 to 5.30,
with an hour off for lunch*

◊ **hourly** ['auəli] *adverb* per hour; **hourly-
paid workers** = workers paid at a fixed rate
for each hour worked; **hourly rate** =
amount of money paid for an hour worked

house [haus] *noun* company; *a French
business house; the largest London finance
house; he works for a broking house or a*

publishing house; **house journal** *or* **house magazine** *or US* **house organ** = magazine produced for the workers or shareholders in a company to give them news about the company; *the house journal keeps workers in touch with the plans of senior management;* **house telephone** = internal telephone for calling from one office to another

◊ **house party** ['haʊs 'pɑːti] *noun* method of interviewing candidates, where they are invited to spend a few days in a hotel or other centre, where they are given tests and monitored for interpersonal relations

◊ **housing** ['haʊzɪŋ] *noun* houses and flats for living in; *the company provides housing for senior staff;* **housing benefit** = local government benefit paid to people who cannot pay their rent

HR = HUMAN RESOURCES

HRM = HUMAN RESOURCE MANAGEMENT

HRP = HUMAN RESOURCE PLANNING

HSC = HEALTH AND SAFETY COMMISSION

human ['hjuːmən] *adjective* referring to people; *US* **human factor engineering** = study of people at work and their working conditions; **human relations management** = management based on the importance of ensuring good relations and cooperation in an organization

◊ **human resources (HR)** ['hjuːmən rɪ'sɔːsɪz] *noun* manpower *or* labour which an organization has available; *our human resources must be looked after and developed if we are to raise productivity successfully;* **human resource(s) management (HRM)** = responsibility for an organization's productive use of and constructive dealings with its employees; **human resources manager** = person who is responsible for an organization's

productive use of its workforce; *he was appointed human resources manager because of his experience in manpower planning and recruitment;* **human resource(s) planning (HRP)** = planning the future needs of a company as regards employees, arranging for interviews for candidates, organizing training, etc.

QUOTE clearly a human resources strategy for new technology has to be a flexible strategy
Personnel Management

QUOTE a systematic approach to human resource planning can play a significant part in reducing recruitment and retention problems
Personnel Management

QUOTE effective use and management of human resources hold the key to future business development and success
Management Today

QUOTE HR departments have accepted that if their role is to change, it is far better to be in control of developments than to have them imposed. Typically, it is those departments that are proactively managing their changing role that make the most use of IT and are most likely to have advanced HR systems
People Management

hygiene ['haɪdʒiːn] *noun* being clean *or* being careful that everything is clean and conditions are healthy; **industrial hygiene** *or* **occupational hygiene** = branch of medicine dealing with the health of people at work; *standards of industrial hygiene are improving in line with developments in general medicine*

◊ **hygienic** [haɪ'dʒiːnɪk] *adjective* clean and healthy; **hygienic management** = management theory that good working conditions encourage hard work and productivity

Ii

ID card [aɪ'diː 'kɑːd] *noun* identity card, a plastic card which carries details of the person it belongs to

identification [aɪdentɪfɪ'keɪʃn] *noun* showing who someone is; **visitors must produce proof of identification** = they must prove who they are

idle ['aɪdl] *adjective* (a) not working; *2,000 employees were made idle by the recession;* **idle machinery** *or* **machines lying idle** = machinery not being used; **idle time** = time for which employees are paid, although they are unable to work because of factors beyond their control; *idle time in January was attributed to the temporary closing down of one of the company's factories; workers were laid off to avoid excessive idle time* (b) **idle capital** = capital not being used productively; **money lying idle** *or* **idle money** = money which is not being used to produce interest *or* which is not invested in business

illegal [ɪ'liːgəl] *adjective* not legal *or* against the law; **illegal aliens** *or* **illegal immigrants** = persons who live or work in a country, but have no right to do so; *the farmers employed illegal aliens who were not in a position to complain about their low wages;* **illegal strike** = strike which violates an existing law *or* strike that violates an agreement between employers and unions

◊ **illegality** [ɪlɪ'gæləti] *noun* being illegal

◊ **illegally** [ɪ'liːgəli] *adverb* against the law; *the union was accused of striking illegally*

ill-feeling ['ɪl 'fiːlɪŋ] *noun* bad feeling *or* feeling of being upset; *the management's attitude created a lot of ill-feeling among the junior employees*

ILM = INTERNAL LABOUR MARKET

illness ['ɪlnəs] *noun* state of being ill *or* of not being well; **chronic illness** = illness or condition which lasts for a long time

ILO ['aɪel'əʊ] = INTERNATIONAL LABOUR ORGANIZATION

image ['ɪmɪdʒ] *noun* general idea which the public has of a product *or* a company; *they are spending a lot of advertising money to improve the company's image; the company has adopted a down-market image;* **corporate image** = idea which a company would like the public to have of it; **to promote a corporate image** = to publicize a company so that its reputation is improved

immediate [ɪ'miːdjət] *adjective* happening at once; **immediate dismissal** *or* **summary dismissal** = dismissal without giving the worker any notice (usually, caused by a crime committed by the worker, drunkenness or violent behaviour towards other workers

immigrant ['ɪmɪgrənt] *noun* person who enters a country to live and work; *there is a large immigrant population working without work permits; the influx of immigrants is due to high unemployment in their own countries;* **illegal immigrant** = person who enters a country to live permanently without having the permission of the government to do so

◊ **immigration** [ɪmɪ'greɪʃn] *noun* (a) coming to live and work in a country; **Immigration Laws** = legislation regarding immigration into a country; **Immigration Service** = government department which deals with allowing immigrants to enter and settle in a country; *the Immigration Service is trying to cope with thousands of applications from potential immigrants* (b) office at an airport *or* port of entry, where government officials inspect the papers of people entering the country; *she was held up at Immigration, because her visa was not in order see also* EMIGRATE, EMIGRANT

immobility [ɪmə'bɪlɪti] *noun* not moving from one place to another; **immobility of labour** *or* **of the workforce** = little movement of workers from one area of the country to another

immunity [ɪ'mjuːnəti] *noun* protection against arrest; **immunity from legal action** = not being liable to be sued (such as workers who strike cannot be sued for breach of their contract of employment); **diplomatic immunity** = being outside a country's laws because of being a diplomat; **he was granted immunity from prosecution** = he was told he would not be prosecuted

impaired [ɪm'pəerd] *adjective* (a sense or function) harmed so that it does not work properly; **impaired vision** = eyesight which is not fully clear

◊ **impairment** [ɪm'pəemənt] *noun* condition where a sense or function is harmed so that it does not work properly; *his hearing impairment does not affect his work*

impartial [ɪm'pɑːʃl] *adjective* not biased *or* not prejudiced; *the arbitration board's decision is completely impartial*

impersonal [ɪm'pɜːsnl] *adjective* without any personal touch *or* as if done by machines; *an impersonal style of management*

impingement pay [ɪm'pɪnʒmənt 'peɪ] *noun* extra pay paid to an employee for working when he should be on holiday

implement ['ɪmplɪmənt] **1** *noun* tool *or* instrument used to do some work; *he was hit on the head with a heavy implement* **2** *verb* to put into action; *to implement an agreement or a decision*

◊ **implementation** [ɪmplɪmen'teɪʃən] *noun* putting into action; *the implementation of new rules*

implied [ɪm'plaɪd] *adjective* which is presumed to exist; **implied terms and conditions** = terms and conditions which are not written in a contract, but which are legally taken to be present in the contract

importance [ɪm'pɔːtəns] *noun* having a value *or* mattering a lot; *the bank attaches great importance to the deal*

◊ **important** [ɪm'pɔːtənt] *adjective* which matters a lot; *he left a pile of important papers in the taxi; she has an important meeting at 10.30; he was promoted to a more important job*

impossible [ɪm'pɒsəbl] *adjective* which

cannot be done; *getting skilled staff is becoming impossible; government regulations make it impossible for us to export*

improve [ɪm'pruːv] *verb* to make something better *or* to become better; *we are trying to improve our image with a series of TV commercials; the union negotiators have asked management to take steps to improve working conditions on the shop floor*

◊ **improved** [ɪm'pruːvd] *adjective* better; *the union rejected the management's improved offer*

◊ **improvement** [ɪm'pruːvmənt] *noun* **(a)** getting better; *there is no improvement in the cash flow situation; employees have noticed an improvement in the working environment;* **improvement notice** = order from the Health and Safety Executive, requiring a company to do something to improve working conditions where there has been a breach of the Health and Safety at Work Act **(b)** thing which is better; **improvement on an offer** = making a better offer

◊ **improve on** [ɪm'pruːv ɒn] *verb* to do better than; **he refused to improve on his previous offer** = he refused to make a better offer

◊ **improver** [ɪm'pruːvə] *noun* employee working for very low wages in return for learning by work experience; *the management has a policy of employing improvers where possible so as to cut down on salaries; three months as an improver gave him the necessary confidence to find a better paid position*

QUOTE the management says the rate of loss-making has come down and it expects further improvement in the next few years
                Financial Times

QUOTE we also invest in companies whose growth and profitability could be improved by a management buyout
                       Times

in-basket test *or* **in-tray test** ['ɪnbɑːskɪt 'test *or* 'ɪntreɪ 'test] *noun* method of testing management potential by asking the candidate to deal with a set of problems; *the candidates for the management post had to pass a series of in-basket tests*

incapability [ɪnkeɪpə'bɪlɪti] *noun* being incapable of working properly because of illness or incompetence

COMMENT: in the case of incompetence, if the employee's work does not improve after he has been given time to improve, incapability can be a reason for dismissal

incapacity [ɪnkə'pæsɪti] *noun* **(a)** not being able to do something; **a worker's incapacity for the job** = where a worker is shown to be too incompetent, or too ill, or does not have the right skills, to do a job **(b)** being unable to work because of illness or disability; **incapacity benefit** = benefit paid to people who are unable to work because of illness or disability; *see also* PIW (PERIOD OF INCAPACITY FOR WORK)

incentive [ɪn'sentɪv] *noun* something which encourages staff to work better; **staff incentives** = pay and better conditions offered to workers to make them work better; **tax incentive** = incentive to invest, given by reducing the tax burden; **incentive bonus** *or* **incentive payment** = extra pay offered to a worker to make him work better; **incentive ceiling** = limit on how much can be paid on the basis of results; *an incentive ceiling was introduced to limit bonuses and the possibility of resentment among workers;* **incentive drift** = decrease in the gap between effort and output in production; *short cuts were found to increase productivity and thus cause incentive drift;* **incentive plan** *or* **incentive scheme** = scheme which encourages better work by paying higher commission or bonuses; *incentive schemes are boosting production; the new bonus scheme gives the workers more incentive to achieve production targets;* **individual incentive scheme** = payment scheme whereby an individual is rewarded for improvements in his or her work

◊ **incentivize** [ɪn'sentɪvaɪz] *verb US* = MOTIVATE

QUOTE the right incentives can work when used strategically
Management Today

QUOTE an additional incentive is that the Japanese are prepared to give rewards where they are due
Management Today

incidental [ɪnsɪ'dentl] **1** *adjective* which is not important, but connected with something else; **incidental expenses** = small amounts of money spent at various times in addition to larger amounts **2** *noun* **incidentals** = incidental expenses

include [ɪn'kluːd] *verb* to count something along with other things; *the charge includes VAT; the total comes to £1,000 including freight; the total is £140 not including insurance and freight; the account covers services up to and including the month of June*

◊ **inclusive** [ɪn'kluːsɪv] *adjective* which counts something in with other things; *inclusive of tax; not inclusive of VAT;* **inclusive sum** *or* **inclusive charge** = charge which includes all costs; **the conference runs from the 12th to the 16th inclusive** = it starts on the morning of the 12th and ends on the evening of the 16th

income [ˈɪŋkʌm] *noun* **(a)** money which a person receives as salary *or* dividends; *he makes a good income by doing his basic job and moonlighting;* **annual income** = money received during a calendar year; **disposable income** = income left after tax and national insurance have been deducted; **earned income** = money received as a salary or wages; **earned income allowance** = tax allowance to be set against money earned by the wife or children of the main taxpayer; **fixed income** = income which does not change from year to year; **gross income** = income before tax has been deducted; **net income** = income left after tax has been deducted; **personal income** = income received by an individual person; **private income** = income from dividends *or* interest *or* rent which is not part of a salary; **retained income** = profits which are not paid out to shareholders as dividends; **taxable income** = income on which a person has to pay tax; **unearned income** = money received from interest or dividends; **income bracket** = group of people earning roughly the same income; **lower** *or* **upper income bracket** = groups of people who earn low or high salaries considered for tax purposes; **he comes into the higher income bracket** = he is in a group of people earning high incomes and therefore paying more tax; **people in the middle-income bracket** = people with average incomes, not high or low; **income support** = government benefit paid to low-income earners who are working less than 16 hours per week, provided they can show that they are actively looking for jobs; **income before tax** = gross income before tax has been deducted **(b) the government's incomes policy** = the government's ideas on how incomes should be controlled **(c)** *US* **income statement** = a statement of company expenditure and sales which shows whether the company has made a profit or loss (NOTE: the UK equivalent is the **profit and loss account)**

◊ **income tax** ['ɪŋkʌm tæks] *noun* (i) tax on a person's income (both earned and unearned); (ii) *also US* tax on the profits of a corporation; **income tax form** = form to be completed which declares all income to the tax office; **declaration of income** *or* **income tax return** = statement declaring income to the tax office; *see also* PAYE

> QUOTE there is no risk-free way of taking regular income from your money much higher than the rate of inflation
> *Guardian*

incoming ['ɪnkʌmɪŋ] *adjective* **(a) incoming call** = phone call coming into the office from someone outside; **incoming mail** = mail which comes into an office **(b)** (person) who has recently been elected *or* appointed; *the incoming chairman will be formally introduced at the meeting;* **the incoming board of directors** = the new board which is about to start working

incompatible [ɪnkəm'pætɪbl] *adjective* not able to live *or* work together; *her views and those of the department manager were incompatible; the manager's paternalistic approach was incompatible with the company's more democratic approach*

incompetent [ɪn'kɒmpətənt] *adjective* (person) who cannot do a job well; *the sales manager is quite incompetent; the company has an incompetent sales director*

◊ **incompetence** [ɪn'kɒmpətəns] *noun* being unable to do a job well; *the clerk was fired for gross incompetence; much of the salesmen's incompetence is due to lack of training*

incorrect [ɪnkə'rekt] *adjective* wrong *or* not correct; *the minutes of the meeting were incorrect and had to be changed*

◊ **incorrectly** [ɪnkə'rektli] *adverb* wrongly *or* not correctly; *the package was incorrectly addressed*

increase 1 ['ɪŋkriːs] *noun* **(a)** growth *or* becoming larger; *increase in tax or tax increase; increase in price or price increase; profits showed a 10% increase or an increase of 10% on last year;* **increase in the cost of living** = rise in the annual cost of living **(b)** higher salary; *increase in pay or pay increase; increase in salary or salary increase; the government hopes to hold salary increases to 3%;* **he had two increases last year** = his salary went up twice; **across-the-board increase** = increase which applies to everything *or* everyone; **cost-of-living increase** = increase in salary to allow it to keep up with higher cost of living; **merit increase** = increase in pay given to a worker whose work is good **2** [ɪn'kriːs] *verb* **(a)** to grow bigger *or* higher; *profits have increased faster than the increase in the rate of inflation; the price of oil has increased twice in the past week;* **to increase in price** = to cost more; **to increase in size** *or* **in value** = to become larger *or* more valuable **(b) the company increased his salary to £20,000** = the company gave him a rise in salary to £20,000

increment ['ɪŋkrɪmənt] *noun* regular automatic increase in salary; *annual increment;* **salary which rises in annual increments of £500** = each year the salary is increased by £500

◊ **incremental** [ɪŋkrɪ'mentl] *adjective* which rises automatically in stages; **incremental cost** = cost of making a single extra unit above the number already planned; **incremental increase** = increase in salary according to an agreed annual increment; **incremental salary scale** = salary scale with regular annual salary increases

incumbent [ɪn'kʌmbənt] *noun* person currently filling a position

incur [ɪn'kɜː] *verb* to make yourself liable to; **to incur the risk of a penalty** = to make it possible that you risk paying a penalty; **to incur debts** *or* **costs** = to do something which means that you owe money *or* that you will have to pay costs; *the company has incurred heavy costs in implementing its expansion programme* = the company has had to pay large sums of money

indecision [ɪndɪ'sɪʒn] *noun* not being able to decide; *the unions protested to the management about the indecision over relocation*

◊ **indecisive** [ɪndɪ'saɪsɪv] *adjective* not able to make up one's mind *or* to decide on something important; *he is too indecisive to be a good manager*

◊ **indecisiveness** [ɪndɪ'saɪsɪvnəs] *noun* being indecisive

indenture [ɪn'dentʃə] **1** *noun* **indentures** *or* **articles of indenture** = contract by which an apprentice works for a master for some years to learn a trade **2** *verb* to contract with an apprentice who will work for some years to learn a trade; *he was indentured to a builder*

independent [ɪndɪ'pendənt] *adjective* free, not controlled by anyone; **independent company** = company which is not controlled by another company; **independent contractor** = self-employed person who works for a company, and is paid a fee for providing a service, but is not paid a salary; **independent trader** *or* **independent shop** = shop which is owned by an individual proprietor, not by a chain

in-depth study ['ɪndepθ 'stʌdi] *noun* thorough, painstaking study

index ['ɪndeks] **1** *noun* **(a)** list of items classified into groups or put in alphabetical order; **index card** = small card used for filing; **card index** = series of cards with information written on them, kept in a special order so that the information can be found easily **(b)** regular statistical report which shows rises and falls in prices, etc.; **cost-of-living index** = way of measuring the cost of living, shown as a percentage increase on the figure for the previous year; **retail price index** *or* *US* **consumer price index** = index showing how prices of consumer goods have risen over a period of time, used as a way of measuring inflation and the cost of living (NOTE: plural is **indexes** or **indices**) **2** *verb* to link a payment to an index; *salaries indexed to the cost of living*

◊ **indexation** [ɪndeks'seɪʃn] *noun* linking of something to an index; **indexation of wage increases** = linking of wage increases to the percentage rise in the cost of living (NOTE: no plural)

◊ **index-linked** ['ɪndeks 'lɪŋkt] *adjective* which rises automatically by the percentage increase in the cost of living; *inflation did not affect her as she has an index-linked pension; his pension is index-linked*

indicator ['ɪndɪkeɪtə] *noun* thing which indicates; **government economic indicators** = statistics which show how the country's economy is going to perform in the short or long term

indifference [ɪn'dɪfrəns] *see* RANGE

indirect [ɪndaɪ'rekt] *adjective* not direct; **indirect compensation** = non-financial benefit given by a company to employees (such as sports facilities, a company car, health insurance, etc.); **indirect expenses** *or* **costs** = costs which are not directly related to the amount of items produced (such as cleaning, rent, administration); **indirect labour** = workers who are not directly related to the production of the product; **indirect labour costs** = costs of paying workers (such as secretaries, cleaners), who are not directly involved in making a product; *the salaries of top management constituted one of the firm's increasing indirect costs; in order to reduce costs while maintaining production levels, management cut down on indirect labour;* **indirect taxation** = taxes (such as sales tax) which are not paid direct to the government; *the government raises more money by indirect taxation than by direct*

individual [ɪndɪ'vɪdjʊəl] **1** *noun* one single person; *savings plan tailored to the requirements of the private individual* **2** *adjective* single *or* belonging to one person; *a pension plan designed to meet each person's individual requirements; we sell individual portions of ice cream;* **individual incentive scheme** = payment scheme whereby an individual is rewarded for improvements in his or her work; **individual relations** = relations between employers and individual employees; *US* **Individual Retirement Account (IRA)** = private pension plan, where people can make contributions separate from a company pension plan

individualism [ɪndɪ'vɪdjʊəlɪzm] *noun* belief that society flourishes if each individual is responsible only for himself and his family (as opposed to collectivism)

inducement [ɪn'djuːsmənt] *noun* incentive *or* thing which helps to persuade someone to do something; *bad working conditions in senior management are no inducement to success; they offered him a* *company car as an inducement to stay; high rates of tax are no inducement to work*

> COMMENT: inducement can be a tort, if, say, a union official induces members to take industrial action in contravention of their contracts of employment

induction [ɪn'dʌkʃən] *noun* introduction to a new organization *or* starting a new person in a new job; **induction course** *or* **induction training** = programme intended to help a person entering an organization *or* starting a new job; *the company is organizing a two-day induction course for new employees; the induction course spelt out the main objectives and procedures of the organization*

industrial [ɪn'dʌstrɪəl] *adjective* referring to industry *or* manufacturing work; **industrial accident** = accident which takes place at work (fatal accidents, accidents which cause major injuries, or which prevent a worker from working for more than three days must be reported to the Health and Safety Executive); **industrial action** = steps taken by employees to strengthen their position in making demands on employers; **to take industrial action** = to go on strike or go-slow; *repeated industrial action has crippled the industry; negotiations must succeed if industrial action is to be avoided;* GB **industrial court** = INDUSTRIAL TRIBUNAL; **industrial democracy** = concept where power is shared by workers in an organization *or* industry, in particular, where the workers have a role in the decision-making processes, and can veto proposals by the management; *industrial democracy was part of the political party's manifesto; the union claimed that industrial democracy required all workers to vote on important issues;* **industrial disputes** = conflicts *or* arguments between management and workers; **industrial espionage** = trying to find out the secrets of a competitor's work or products, usually by illegal means; **industrial estate** *or* **industrial park** = area of land near a town specially for factories and warehouses; **industrial health** *or* **industrial hygiene** = branch of medicine dealing with the health of people at work; *standards of industrial hygiene are improving in line with developments in general medicine; the development of industrial health has meant better protection against lung disease in the mining industry;* **industrial injuries** =

injuries which happen to workers at work; **industrial injuries insurance** = government insurance scheme for workers who have accidents at work; **industrial psychology** = study of human behaviour and mental health in the workplace; **industrial relations** = relations between management and workers; **industrial relations audit** = review of all relations between management and workers in a company; **good industrial relations** = situation where management and workers understand each others' problems and work together for the good of the company; **industrial sociology** = study of workers and their attitudes to work and management; **industrial training** = training of new workers to work in an industry; **Industrial Training Boards** = regional government organizations whose responsibility is to provide training facilities for industry in all areas of the country; **industrial tribunal** = court which can decide in industrial disputes if both parties agree to ask it to judge between them, in particular deciding cases of unfair dismissal, work safety, sexual discrimination, etc.

> QUOTE ACAS has a legal obligation to try and solve industrial grievances before they reach industrial tribunals
> *Personnel Today*

> QUOTE Britain's industrial relations climate is changing
> *Personnel Today*

industry ['ɪndəstri] *noun* **(a)** all factories *or* companies *or* processes involved in the manufacturing of products; *all sectors of industry have shown rises in output;* **basic industry** = most important industry of a country (such as coal, steel, agriculture); **a boom industry** *or* **a growth industry** = industry which is expanding rapidly; **heavy industry** = industry which deals in heavy raw materials (such as coal) or makes large products (such as ships or engines); **light industry** = industry making small products (such as clothes, books, calculators); **primary industry** = industry dealing with basic raw materials (such as coal, wood, farm produce); **secondary industry** = industry which uses basic raw materials to produce manufactured goods; **service industry** *or* **tertiary industry** = industry which does not produce raw materials or manufacture products but offers a service (such as banking, retailing, accountancy) **(b)** group of companies making the same type of product; *the aircraft industry; the building industry; the car industry; the food processing industry; the mining industry; the petroleum industry;* **single industry union** = union whose members work in only one industry (such as the mineworkers' union)

◊ **industry-wide** ['ɪndəstri 'waɪd] *adjective* affecting all companies in one industry; *we are expecting industry-wide wage increases for machinists of 10%*

ineffective time [ɪnɪ'fektɪv 'taɪm] *noun (during a time study)* time spent by an operator which does not contribute to production; *the dramatic fall in productivity was due to an increase in ineffective time; the poor profit figures can be put down to too much ineffective time and wastage of raw materials*

inefficiency [ɪnɪ'fɪʃənsi] *noun* lack of efficiency *or* not being able to work quickly and correctly; *the report criticized the inefficiency of the sales staff; the secretary was sacked for inefficiency*

◊ **inefficient** [ɪnɪ'fɪʃənt] *adjective* not efficient *or* not doing a job well; unable to work efficiently and correctly; *inefficient workers waste raw materials and fail to complete tasks on schedule; an inefficient sales director should be sacked*

ineligible [ɪn'elɪdʒɪbl] *adjective* not eligible

◊ **ineligibility** [ɪnelɪdʒə'bɪlɪti] *noun* being ineligible

inequality [ɪnɪ'kwɒlɪti] *noun* state of not being equal; *the workforce has complained about the inequalities of the pension scheme*

inequity [ɪn'ekwɪti] *noun* unfairness, such as unequal pay for the same type of job; *inequity has caused much resentment in the organization, especially when younger staff are being paid more than their seniors for the same type of work*

inexperienced [ɪnɪk'spiːriənst] *adjective* (person) who does not have much experience; *the negotiating team was quite inexperienced in dealing with management negotiators; they have appointed an inexperienced young man as workshop manager*

in flagrante delicto [ɪn flə'grænteɪ dɪ'lɪktəʊ] *Latin phrase meaning* 'in the act of doing something'; *the clerk was caught in flagrante delicto pocketing the petty cash*

inflated [ɪn'fleɪtɪd] *adjective* **inflated salaries** = salaries which are increased without any reason

◊ **inflation** [ɪn'fleɪʃən] *noun* situation where prices rise to keep up with increased production costs; **we have 15% inflation** *or* **inflation is running at 15%** = prices are 15% higher than at the same time last year; *to take measures to reduce inflation; high interest rates tend to increase inflation;* **inflation accounting** = accounting system, where inflation is taken into account when calculating the value of assets and the preparation of accounts; **rate of inflation** *or* **inflation rate** = percentage increase in prices over a twelve-month period; **galloping inflation** *or* **runaway inflation** *or* **soaring inflation** = very rapid inflation which it is almost impossible to reduce; **spiralling inflation** = inflation where price rises make workers ask for higher wages which then increase prices again

◊ **inflationary** [ɪn'fleɪʃnəri] *adjective* which tends to increase inflation; *inflationary trends in the economy;* **the economy is in an inflationary spiral** = in a situation where price rises encourage higher wage demands which in turn make prices rise; **anti-inflationary measures** = measures to reduce inflation

QUOTE the decision by the government to tighten monetary policy will push the annual inflation rate above the year's previous high
Financial Times

QUOTE when you invest to get a return, you want a 'real' return - above the inflation rate
Investors Chronicle

inform [ɪn'fɔːm] *verb* to tell someone officially; *I regret to inform you that your tender was not acceptable; we are pleased to inform you that you have been selected for interview; we have been informed by the Department of Employment that new regulations are coming into force*

◊ **information** [ɪnfə'meɪʃən] *noun* **(a)** details which explain something; *please send me information on* or *about holidays in* *the USA; have you any information on or about deposit accounts? I enclose this leaflet for your information; to disclose a piece of information; to answer a request for information; for further information, please write to Department 27;* **disclosure of information** = giving information to someone, such as the union representatives in collective bargaining, so that they know all the relevant facts about a case before presenting the defence; **disclosure of confidential information** = telling someone information which should be secret **(b) information agreement** = agreement between management and union regarding the information about the company which management agrees to pass to the union on a regular basis; **information overload** = burdening someone with too much information; **information retrieval** = storing and then finding data in a computer; **information system** = system of storing information either manually or by computer; *the information system is so bad that details on staff cannot be found easily; our information system is being computerized;* **information technology** = working with computer data; *information technology has made storage of data about personnel much easier* **(c) information bureau** *or* **information office** = office which gives information to tourists *or* visitors; **information officer** = person whose job is to give information about a company *or* an organization *or* a government department to the public; person whose job is to give information to other departments in the same organization (NOTE: no plural; for one item say **a piece of information**)

informal [ɪnˈfɔːməl] *adjective* not official *or* not formal; **informal warning** = spoken warning to a worker, which is not recorded and cannot be taken into account if the worker is disciplined later; *see also* FORMAL

◊ **informally** [ɪnˈfɔːməli] *adverb* unofficially

infringement [ɪnˈfrɪn(d)ʒmənt] *noun* breaking a law *or* a rule; *infringement of the company's rules*

in-house [ˈɪn ˈhaʊs] *adverb & adjective* working inside a company's building; *the in-house staff; we do all our data processing in-house;* **in-house training** = training given to staff at their place of work

initiative [ɪˈnɪʃɪətɪv] *noun* decision to start something; **to take the initiative** = to decide to do something; **to follow up an initiative** = to take action once someone else has decided to do something; **to lack initiative** = not to be enterprising or go-ahead; *the manager will have to be replaced - he lacks initiative*

injunction [ɪnˈdʒʌŋ(k)ʃən] *noun* court order telling someone not to do something; *he got an injunction preventing the company from selling his car; the company applied for an injunction to stop their rival from marketing a similar product;* **mandatory injunction** = order from a court which compels someone to do something; **prohibitory injunction** = injunction which prevents someone from doing an illegal act

injure [ˈɪn(d)ʒə] *verb* to hurt (someone); *two workers were injured in the fire*

◊ **injury** [ˈɪn(d)ʒəri] *noun* hurt caused to a person; **injury benefit** = money paid to a worker who has been hurt at work; **industrial injuries** = injuries caused to workers at work; **occupational injury** = injury which is caused by a type of work

QUOTE the CBI and TUC are collaborating on a joint project in an effort to reduce the 30 million days lost every year through sickness and occupational injury
People Management

inland [ˈɪnlənd] *adjective* **(a)** inside a country; **inland postage** = postage for a letter to another part of the country; **inland freight charges** = charges for carrying goods from one part of the country to another **(b)** *GB* **the Inland Revenue** = government department dealing with tax; *he received a letter from the Inland Revenue* (NOTE: the US department is the **Internal Revenue Service**)

input [ˈɪnpʊt] **1** *noun* **(a)** what is contributed to an activity *or* project; *the amount of staff input in the company magazine is small* **(b) input of information** *or* **computer input** = data fed into a computer; **input lead** = lead for connecting the electric current to a machine; **input tax** = VAT paid on goods or services which a company buys **2** *verb* **to input information** = to put data into a computer

inquire [ɪnˈkwaɪə] *verb* to ask questions

about something; *he inquired if anything was wrong; she inquired about the mortgage rate;* 'inquire within' = ask for more details inside the office *or* shop

◊ **inquire into** [ɪŋ'kwaɪə 'ɪntʊ] *verb* to investigate *or* to try to find out about something; *we are inquiring into the background of the new supplier*

◊ **inquiry** [ɪŋ'kwaɪəri] *noun* (a) official question; *I refer to your inquiry of May 25th; all inquiries should be addressed to this department* (b) official investigation; *a government inquiry into trading practices;* a commission of inquiry = group of people appointed to investigate something officially

in-service training (INSET) ['ɪnsɜːvɪs 'treɪnɪŋ] *noun* training of staff while they are employed by an organization; *management trainees will draw full salaries during the period of their in-service training*

inside [ɪn'saɪd] **1** *adjective & adverb* in, especially in a company's office or building; *we do all our design work inside;* inside work *or* internal work = work that an operator can do within the period that the machine is working; inside worker = worker who works in the office or factory (not in the open air, not a salesman) **2** *preposition* in; *there was nothing inside the container; we have a contact inside our rival's production department who gives us very useful information*

◊ **insider** [ɪn'saɪdə] *noun* person who works in an organization and therefore knows its secrets; insider dealing *or* insider trading = illegal buying or selling of shares by staff of a company who have secret information about the company's plans

insolvent [ɪn'sɒlvənt] *adjective* not able to pay debts; *the company was declared insolvent*

◊ **insolvency** [ɪn'sɒlvənsi] *noun* not being able to pay debts or wages to employees; *the company was in a state of insolvency* = it could not pay its debts; insolvency practitioner = person who advises insolvent companies (NOTE: no plural. **Insolvent** and **insolvency** are general terms, but are usually applied to companies; individuals are usually described as **bankrupt** once they have been declared so by a court)

inspect [ɪn'spekt] *verb* to make a formal

check to see that regulations are being followed; to examine something in detail; *to inspect a machine or an installation; to inspect the accounts;* to inspect products for defects = to look at products in detail to see if they have any defects

◊ **inspection** [ɪn'spekʃən] *noun* formal check that regulations are being obeyed; close examination of something; *to make an inspection or to carry out an inspection of a machine or an installation; inspection of a product for defects; a machinery inspection to check safety precautions;* to carry out a tour of inspection = to visit various places *or* offices *or* factories to inspect them; to issue an inspection order = to order an official inspection; inspection stamp = stamp placed on something to show it has been inspected

◊ **inspector** [ɪn'spektə] *noun* official who inspects; *the inspectors will soon be round to make sure the building is safe;* inspector of factories *or* factory inspector = government official who inspects factories to see if they are safely run; inspector of taxes *or* tax inspector = official of the Inland Revenue who examines tax returns and decides how much tax people should pay; inspector of weights and measures = government official who inspects weighing machines and goods sold in shops to see if the quantities and weights are correct

◊ **inspectorate** [ɪn'spektərət] *noun* all inspectors; the factory inspectorate = all inspectors of factories

install [ɪn'stɔːl] *verb* to put (a machine) into an office *or* into a factory; *to install new machinery; to install a new data processing system*

◊ **installation** [ɪnstə'leɪʃən] *noun* (a) machines, equipment and buildings; *harbour installations; the fire seriously damaged the oil installations* (b) putting new machines into an office *or* a factory; *to supervise the installation of new equipment*

instalment *or* US **installment** [ɪn'stɔːlmənt] *noun* part of a payment which is paid regularly until the total amount is paid; *the first instalment is payable on signature of the agreement;* the final instalment is now due = the last of a series of payments should be paid now; to pay £25 down and monthly instalments of £20 = to pay a first payment of £25 and the rest in payments of £20 each month; **to miss an instalment** = not to pay an instalment at the right time

institute ['instɪtjuːt] **1** *noun* society *or* organization which represents a particular profession or activity; *the Institute of Personnel Management (IPM);* **research institute** = organization set up to do research **2** *verb* to start a new custom *or* procedure; *to institute a new staff payment scheme*

◊ **institution** [instɪ'tjuːʃən] *noun* organization *or* society set up for a particular purpose; **financial institution** = bank *or* investment trust *or* insurance company whose work involves lending or investing large sums of money

instruct [in'strʌkt] *verb* **(a)** to give an order to someone; **to instruct someone to do something** = to tell someone officially to do something; *he instructed the credit controller to take action; the foreman will instruct the men to stop working* **(b)** to teach

◊ **instruction** [in'strʌkʃən] *noun* order which tells what should be done *or* how something is to be used; *he gave instructions to his stockbroker to sell the shares immediately;* **to await instructions** = to wait for someone to tell you what to do; **to issue instructions** = to tell everyone what to do; **in accordance with** *or* **according to instructions** = as the instructions show; **failing instructions to the contrary** = unless someone tells you to do the opposite; **forwarding instructions** *or* **shipping instructions** = details of how goods are to be shipped and delivered

◊ **instructor** [in'strʌktə] *noun* person who shows how something is to be done; *two new instructors are needed for the training courses; distance learning can be carried out without instructors*

insubordination [insʌbɔːdɪ'neɪʃn] *noun* refusing to do what a person in authority tells you to do

insure [in'ʃuə] *verb* to have a contract with a company where, if regular small payments are made, the company will pay compensation for loss, damage, injury or death; *to insure a house against fire; to insure someone's life; he was insured for £100,000; to insure baggage against loss; to*

insure against bad weather; to insure against loss of earnings; **the life insured** = the person whose life is covered by life assurance; **the sum insured** = the largest amount of money that an insurer will pay under an insurance policy

◊ **insurable** [in'ʃuərəbl] *adjective* which can be insured

insurance [in'ʃuərəns] *noun* **(a)** agreement that in return for regular small payments, a company will pay compensation for loss, damage, injury or death; **to take out insurance against fire** = to pay a premium, so that if a fire happens, compensation will be paid; **to take out insurance on the house** = to pay a premium, so that if the house is damaged compensation will be paid; **the damage is covered by the insurance** = the insurance company will pay for the damage; *repairs will be paid for by the insurance;* **to pay the insurance on a car** = to pay premiums to insure a car **(b)** **accident insurance** = insurance which will pay if an accident takes place; **car insurance** *or* **motor insurance** = insuring a car, the driver and passengers in case of accident; **comprehensive insurance** = insurance which covers against all risks which are likely to happen; **endowment insurance** = situation where a sum of money is paid to the insured person on a certain date or to his heir if he dies before that date; **fire insurance** = insurance against damage by fire; **health insurance** = insurance which pays the cost of treatment for illnesses; **catastrophic health insurance** = health insurance which provides for the high cost of treating severe or lengthy illnesses; **private health insurance** = insurance which will pay for the cost of treatment in a private hospital, not a state one; **life insurance** = situation which pays a sum of money when someone dies; **medical insurance** = insurance which pays the cost of medical treatment, especially when travelling abroad; *the company provides free medical insurance for all employees;* **third-party insurance** = insurance which pays compensation if someone who is not the insured person incurs loss or injury; **whole-life insurance** = insurance where the insured person pays premiums for all his life and the insurance company pays a sum when he dies **(c)** **insurance agent** *or* **insurance broker** = person who arranges insurance for clients; **insurance claim** = asking an insurance company to pay for damage; **insurance company** = company whose business is to receive payments and pay compensation for loss or damage; **insurance contract** = agreement by an insurance company to insure; **insurance cover** = protection guaranteed by an insurance policy; **insurance plan** *or* **insurance scheme** = set of conditions which make up an insurance package; *what type of insurance scheme should be provided for the employees?;* **insurance policy** = written contract which shows the conditions of an insurance; **insurance premium** = payment made by the insured person to the insurer **(d)** *GB* **National Insurance** = state insurance, organized by the government, which pays for medical care, hospitals, unemployment benefits, etc.; **National Insurance contributions** = money paid by a worker and the company each month to the National Insurance

insurer [ɪnˈʃʊərə] *noun* company which insures (NOTE: for life insurance, GB English prefers to use **assurance, assure, assurer)**

intangible [ɪnˈtæn(d)ʒəbl] *adjective* which cannot be touched; **intangible fixed assets** = assets which have a value, but which cannot be seen (such as goodwill, copyrights, patents or trademarks)

integrate [ˈɪntɪɡreɪt] *verb* to link things together to form one whole group

◊ **integration** [ɪntɪˈɡreɪʃən] *noun* bringing several businesses together under a central control; **integration test** = test to show if a person is an employee or a freelancer (by seeing if the work done is an integral part of the company's operations or simply an additional help to the company); **horizontal integration** = joining similar companies *or* taking over a company in the same line of business as yourself; **vertical integration** = joining businesses together which deal with different stages in the production or sale of a product

◊ **integrative bargaining** *or* **negotiation** [ˈɪntɪɡrətɪv ˈbɑːɡənɪŋ *or* nɪɡəʊsɪˈeɪʃn] *noun* bargaining to reach a solution which is beneficial to both sides

intelligence test [ɪnˈtelɪdʒəns ˈtest] *noun* test to assess someone's intellectual ability; *the intelligence tests showed that only some of the applicants were capable of undergoing management training*

◊ **intelligence quotient (IQ)** [ɪnˈtelɪdʒəns ˈkwəʊʃənt] *noun* measure of mental ability according to a comparative scale; *the intelligence test showed he had only an average IQ*

inter- [ˈɪntə] *prefix* between; **inter-bank loan** = loan from one bank to another; **the inter-city rail services are good** = train services between cities are good; **inter-company dealings** = dealings between two companies in the same group; **inter-company comparisons** = comparing the results of one company with those of another in the same product area

interaction [ɪntəˈækʃn] *noun* contact between individuals *or* groups; *there is very little interaction between office staff and manual workers*

◊ **interactive** [ɪntəˈæktɪv] *adjective* **interactive learning** = learning through a computer teaching package, where the student is helped by the course and is taught by making responses to the course; **interactive skills** = skills used when communicating with other people (passing information, giving orders, discussing problems, etc.)

interest group [ˈɪntrəst ˈɡruːp] *noun* group of people who share the same interests (sport, animal welfare, the shareholders of a company, etc.)

interface [ˈɪntəfeɪs] **1** *noun* (i) link between two different computer systems or pieces of hardware; (ii) point where two groups of people come in contact; **human-machine interface** = point of contact between a person and a machine, such as a computer **2** *verb* to meet and act with; *the office micros interface with the mainframe computer at head office*

interfere [ɪntəˈfɪə] *verb* to get involved *or* to try to change something which is not your concern

◊ **interference** [ɪntəˈfɪərəns] *noun* the act of interfering; *the sales department complained of continual interference from the accounts department;* **interference pay** = pay made to pieceworkers who have not had enough work because other workers making parts have been moved to other jobs; **interference time** = time during which a machine is waiting for the operator's attention while he or she is doing something else; *the production manager will calculate how much time is lost through interference time; interference time was caused by having a lot of machines worked by one machinist*

interim ['ɪntərɪm] *noun* **interim agreement** = agreement in collective bargaining, which is designed to keep a strike off while a more long-term agreement is being worked out; *the interim agreement helped provide breathing space while the two sides reconsidered their positions; the interim agreement allowed for a 10% pay rise;* **interim payment** = payment of part of a dividend; **interim relief** = order from an industrial tribunal telling an employer to continue an employee's contract of employment (or reemploy him or her) until a decision has been made on a complaint for unfair dismissal

intermediary [ɪntə'miːdjəri] *noun* person who is the link between parties who do not agree or who are negotiating; *he refused to act as an intermediary between the two directors*

intern ['ɪntɜːn] *noun* person who is undergoing on-the-job training

◊ **internship** ['ɪntɜːnʃɪp] *noun US* probationary period of on-the-job training for newly qualified employees under the guidance of experts; *during his internship he learnt the practical aspects of the job*

internal [ɪn'tɜːnl] *adjective* **(a)** inside a company; **we decided to make an internal appointment** = we decided to appoint an existing member of staff to the post, and not bring someone in from outside the company; **internal alignment** = relationship between positions in an organization in terms of rank and pay; **internal audit** = audit carried out by a department within the company; **internal audit department** *or* **internal auditor** = department *or* member of staff who audits the accounts of the company he works for; **internal growth** = development of a company by growing its existing business with its own finances, as opposed to acquiring other businesses (called 'external growth'); **internal market** = way of operating a large organization, where each manager becomes a separate entrepreneurial unit which is run as if totally independent from the rest of the group; **internal labour market (ILM)** = the workforce already employed in a group, which can be redeployed to other jobs inside the group; **internal promotion** = promotion of someone working in the company already (as opposed to bringing in a new employee from outside); **internal recruitment** = filling vacancies by recruiting staff from inside the company; **internal telephone** = telephone which is linked to other phones in an office **(b)** inside a country; *US* **Internal Revenue Service** = government department which deals with tax

◊ **internally** [ɪn'tɜːnəli] *adverb* inside a company; *the job was advertised internally* (NOTE: the opposite is **external, externally**)

international [ɪntə'næʃənl] *adjective* working between countries; **international call** = telephone call to another country; **international dialling code** = number used to make a telephone call to another country; **international law** = laws governing relations between countries; *US* **international union** = parent union composed of affiliated unions, known as 'locals'

◊ **International Labour Organization (ILO)** [ɪntə'næʃənl 'leɪbə ɔːgənaɪ'zeɪʃn] section of the United Nations, an organization which tries to improve working conditions and workers' pay in member countries

inter partes ['ɪntə 'pɑːtiːz] *Latin phrase* meaning 'between the parties': case heard where both parties are represented; *the court's opinion was that the case should be heard inter partes as soon as possible see also* EX PARTE

interpersonal *adjective* between people; **interpersonal relations** = relations, communications and dealing with people; **interpersonal skills** = skills used when communicating with other people, especially when negotiating

intervene [ɪntə'viːn] *verb* to try to make a change in a system; **to intervene in a dispute** = to try to settle a dispute

◊ **intervention** [ɪntə'venʃən] *noun* **(a)** acting to make a change in a system; *the government's intervention in the labour dispute* **(b)** action taken by an outside agent to change the structure of a large company

interview ['ɪntəvjuː] **1** *noun (in a company)* talking to a person (either someone who is applying for a job or to an employee); *(in general)* asking someone questions (as part of an opinion poll); *we called six people for interview; I have an interview next week or I am going for an interview next week;* **active interview** = interview where the interviewee is encouraged to answer fully the questions asked (as in an open-end interview); **closed interview** = interview where the interviewer asks only fixed questions with 'yes' or 'no' answers; **directed interview** = interview built round specific questions instead of an open discussion; *directed interviews are easier to conduct, but may fail to extract as much as less formal methods of interviewing;* **disciplinary interview** = interview between management and worker to discuss a breach of discipline (the worker may be accompanied by a union representative); **exit interview** = interview with an employee when he or she is leaving an organization to find out his or her views on how the organization is run and reasons for leaving; **guided interview** = GUIDED INTERVIEW **open-ended interview** = interview where the candidate is asked general questions, which make him give reasons for actions, show his feelings, etc.; **passive interview** = interview where the interviewee only answers the questions (as in a closed interview); **structured interview** = interview using preset questions and following a fixed pattern; **unstructured interview** = interview which does not use preset questions and does not follow a fixed pattern (NOTE: the opposite is **directed interview**) **2** *verb* to interview someone for a job = to talk to a person applying for a job to see if he or she is suitable; *we interviewed ten candidates, but did not find anyone suitable*

◊ **interviewee** [ɪntəvjuːˈiː] *noun* person who is being interviewed; *the interviewer did everything to put the interviewee at ease; the interviewees were all nervous as they waited to be called into the interview room*

◊ **interviewer** ['ɪntəvjuːə] *noun* person who is conducting the interview

intimidation [ɪntɪmɪˈdeɪʃn] *noun* threat to harm someone if he does not do what you want

in-tray ['ɪntreɪ] *noun* basket on a desk for letters or memos which have been received and are waiting to be dealt with; **in-tray test** or **in-tray exercise** = method of testing management potential by asking the candidate to deal with a set of problems

intrinsic [ɪnˈtrɪnzɪk] *adjective* **intrinsic motivation** = motivation of staff by satisfying their deepest personal needs; **intrinsic rewards** = non-material rewards of working in a job (such as status, job satisfaction, human interest, etc.); *the intrinsic rewards of the job more than compensated for the low pay; comradeship is one of the intrinsic rewards in this job;* compare EXTRINSIC REWARD

introduce [ɪntrəˈdjuːs] *verb* to make someone get to know a new person or thing; *the office manager introduced his new assistant to the rest of the staff; we are hoping to introduce a new roster system next month;* **to introduce a client** = to bring in a new client and make him known to someone; **to introduce a new product on the market** = to produce a new product and launch it on the market

◊ **introduction** [ɪntrəˈdʌkʃən] *noun* **(a)** **letter of introduction** = letter making someone get to know another person; *I'll give you an introduction to the MD - he's an old friend of mine* **(b)** bringing into use; **the introduction of new technology** = putting new machines (usually computers) into a business or industry

invalidity [ɪnvəˈlɪdɪti] *noun* being disabled; **invalidity benefit** = money paid by the government to someone who is permanently disabled

inventory ['ɪnvəntri] *noun* **US** comprehensive list of certain items; *the manpower inventory helped decide how many workers were needed;* **personal** or **personality inventory** = list of strengths and weaknesses in a worker's personality; *when considering candidates for a post the personnel manager drew up a personality inventory for each one; the manpower inventory helped decide how many workers were needed;* **skills inventory** = list of all the skills, qualifications, etc. of each member of staff, so that they can be redeployed rather than be made redundant if their job ceases to exist

inverse seniority ['ɪnvɜːs siniˈɒrɪti] *noun* scheme which allows for longest-serving workers to be laid off before those most recently recruited; *inverse seniority will help the company benefit from new blood; inverse seniority created ill-feeling among the longer-serving employees*

inverted appraisal [ɪnˈvɜːtɪd əˈpreɪzəl] *noun* appraisal where a subordinate appraises his manager

investigate [ɪnˈvestɪgeɪt] *verb* to examine something which may be wrong

◊ **investigation** [ɪnvestɪˈgeɪʃən] *noun* examination to find out what is wrong; *to conduct an investigation into petty theft in the office*

invite [ɪnˈvaɪt] *verb* to ask someone to do something *or* to ask for something; *to invite someone to an interview; to invite someone to join the board*

◊ **invitation** [ɪnvɪˈteɪʃən] *noun* asking someone to do something; *to issue an invitation to someone to join the board*

IOU [ˈaɪəʊˈjuː] *noun meaning* 'I owe you'; a signed document promising that you will pay back money borrowed; *to pay a pile of IOUs*

IPM = INSTITUTE OF PERSONNEL MANAGEMENT

ipsative test [ˈɪpsətɪv test] *noun* test

where the candidate has to choose between various alternative answers (as in a multiple-choice test)

IRA [aɪɑːˈeɪ] *US* = INDIVIDUAL RETIREMENT ACCOUNT

irrecoverable [ɪrɪˈkʌvərəbl] *adjective* which cannot be recovered; **irrecoverable debt** = debt which will never be paid

irregular [ɪˈregjʊlə] *adjective* not correct *or* not done in the correct way; *irregular documentation; this procedure is highly irregular*

◊ **irregularity** [ɪregjʊˈlærəti] *noun* **(a)** not being regular *or* not being on time; *the irregularity of the postal deliveries* **(b) irregularities** = things which are not done in the correct way and which are possibly illegal; *to investigate irregularities in the share dealings*

IRS [aɪɑːˈes] *US* = INTERNAL REVENUE SERVICE

IT [ˈaɪˈtiː] = INDUSTRIAL TRIBUNAL, INFORMATION TECHNOLOGY

item validity [ˈaɪtəm vəˈlɪdɪti] *noun* extent to which a test item measures what it is supposed to test

itinerant worker [ɪˈtɪnərənt] *noun* worker who moves from place to place, looking for work; *most of the workers hired during the summer are itinerant workers; much of the seasonal work on farms is done by itinerant workers*

Jj

janitor ['dʒænɪtə] *noun US* person who looks after a building, making sure it is clean and that the rubbish is cleared away (NOTE: GB English is **caretaker**)

JIT = JUST-IN-TIME

job [dʒɒb] *noun* **(a)** piece of work; **to do a job of work** = to be given a job of work to do; **to be paid by the job** = to be paid for each piece of work done; **job production** *or* **jobbing production** = production system where different articles are produced each to individual specifications; **job ticket** = document which records when a particular job was started (it is passed from worker to worker as the job progresses) *we are working on six jobs at the moment; the shipyard has a big job starting in August* **(c)** regular paid work; *thousands of jobs will be lost if the factories close down; he is looking for a job in the computer industry; he lost his job when the factory closed; she got a job in a factory; to apply for a job in an office;* **casual job** = job which exists for a short period only; **dead-end job** = job where there are no chances of promotion; **entry level job** = job for which no previous experience is needed; **key job** = very important job; **office job** *or* **white-collar job** = job in an office; **service job** *or* **job in the service sector** = job in an industry which does not make products, but offers a service (such as banking, insurance, transport); **skilled job** = job for which certain skills are needed; **to apply for a job** = to ask to be considered for a job, usually in writing; **to change jobs** = to resign from one job and take another; **to give up one's job** = to resign from one's work; **to lose one's job** = to be sacked or made redundant; **to look for a job** = to try to find work; **to retire from one's job** = to leave work and take a pension; **to be out of a job** = to have no work; **to have a steady job** = to be in a good job, with no chance of being made redundant **(d)** **job analysis** = detailed examination and report on a job to establish what it consists of and what skills are needed for it; *a thorough job analysis will determine what type of person should be recruited;* **job application** *or* **application for a job** = asking for a job in writing; **job application form** = form to be filled in when applying for a job; *you have to fill in a job application form;* **job ceiling** = maximum number of employees employed at a given time; *the recession has lowered the job ceilings in many companies in this area; raising the job ceiling will enable many less qualified workers to find jobs;* **job classification** = describing jobs listed under various grades and establishing the level of pay for each job; **job creation scheme** = government-backed plan to make work for the unemployed; **job cycle** = time taken to complete a particular job; **job description** *or* **job specification** = description of what a job consists of and what skills are needed for it; *the letter enclosed an application form and a job description;* **job design** = decision on what a job should consist of; **job dissatisfaction** = a worker's feeling of not being satisfied with his job; **job enlargement** = expansion of a job by adding further tasks or responsibilities; **job enrichment** = making a job more satisfying for the person doing it; **horizontal job enrichment** = expanding a job to include new skills and responsibilities, but still at the same level in the organization; **vertical job enrichment** = expanding a job so that the worker becomes more involved in the organization of the company; **job evaluation** = judging the value of a particular job to the organization, which can then be used as a basis for pay calculations; *the job was not important in the job evaluation scheme because it was not particularly relevant to the company;* **job grading** = evaluating a job in the context of the whole company; **job factors** = aspects of a job that can be examined and to which scores can be given in job evaluation; *one of the most significant job factors considered in the evaluation was the danger involved in the job;* **job family** = group of jobs having the similar requirements in terms of personnel; **job**

freeze = stopping the recruitment of staff in an organization; *the recession has led to a general job freeze in the area;* **job grading** = arranging jobs in a certain order of importance; *job grading resulted in certain jobs being relegated to a lower grade;* **job holder** = person who has a certain job; **job hopper** = person who changes jobs often; **job hunting** = looking for employment; *he bought a guide to job hunting showing how to write a good CV;* **job loading** = assigning a job a greater degree of responsibility; *job loading increases the self-esteem of workers whose jobs had seemed unimportant before;* **jobs market** = number of job available; **job measurement** = establishing the time necessary for the performance of tasks by a skilled worker; **job offer** *or* **offer of a job** = letter from an employer, offering a job; **job posting** = system of advertising posts internally allowing employees to apply for other jobs within the same organization; **job ranking** = method of assessment where jobs to be assessed are each compared with all the others and a final score for each obtained (also called 'paired comparisons'); **job rotation** = moving of workers from one job to another systematically; *job rotation was instituted to make the work less monotonous;* **job satisfaction** = a worker's feeling of contentment from doing a good job; *there was no job satisfaction in doing repetitive and useless tasks; he gets a lot of job satisfaction from his work, even if the pay is low;* **job security** = feeling which a worker has that he has a right to keep his job, or that his job will continue; **job sharing** = situation where a job is shared by more than one person, each working part-time; *job-sharing has benefited many people needing part-time jobs;* **job simulation exercise** = test where candidates are put through a simulation of the real job; **job specification** = very detailed description of what is involved in a job; **job squeeze** = reducing the numbers of people employed, because of financial restrictions; **job study** = analysis of all aspects of a job which may affect performance; **job title** = official name given to a person in a certain job; *though his job title was Marketing Manager, he actually did a lot of the selling himself; the personnel department found it difficult to give a job title since the job involved a range of responsibilities;* **on-the-job training** = training given to workers at their place of work; **off-the-job training** = training given

to workers away from their place of work (i.e. at a college)

◊ **jobbing** ['dʒɒbɪŋ] *noun* doing small pieces of work; **jobbing gardener** *or* **jobbing printer** = person who does odd jobs in the garden *or* who does small printing jobs

◊ **jobcentre** ['dʒɒb 'sentə] *noun* government office which lists jobs which are vacant; *there was a long queue of unemployed people waiting at the jobcentre*

◊ **jobclub** ['dʒɒbklʌb] *noun* organization which helps its members to find jobs; *since joining the jobclub she has improved her interview techniques and gained self-confidence*

◊ **jobless** ['dʒɒbləs] *noun* **the jobless** = people with no jobs *or* the unemployed (NOTE: takes a plural verb)

◊ **jobseeker** ['dʒɒbsiːkə] *noun* person who is looking for a job

join [dʒɔɪn] *verb* **(a) to join a firm** = to start work with a company; **he joined on January 1st** = he started work on the January 1st **(b) to join an association** *or* **a group** = to become a member of an association *or* a group; *all the staff have joined the company pension plan; he was asked to join the board; Smith Ltd has applied to join the trade association*

joinder ['dʒɔɪndə] *noun* situation where a union *or* person is brought in as a party to unfair dismissal proceedings if such a party has been instrumental in the dismissal through some sort of pressure

joint [dʒɔɪnt] *adjective* **(a)** combined *or* with two or more organizations linked together; **joint commission of inquiry** *or* **joint committee** = commission *or* committee with representatives of various organizations on it; **joint consultation** = established channels for discussion between management and employees where management keeps control by disclosing plans to the employee representatives and then asking them to help put them into practice; *joint consultation helps to reduce the possibility of industrial action;* joint **discussions** = discussions between management and workers; **joint venture** = very large business project where two or more companies join together, often forming a new joint company to manage the project **(b)** one of two or more people who work together *or* who are linked; *joint beneficiary; joint managing director; joint owner; joint signatory;* joint **account** = bank account for two people; **joint ownership** = owning of a property by several owners; **joint and several liability** = situation where someone who has a claim against a group of people can sue them separately or together as a group

journal ['dʒɜːnl] *noun* magazine; **house journal** = magazine produced for the workers in a company to give them news about the company; **trade journal** = magazine produced for people or companies in a certain trade

journeyman ['dʒɜːnɪmən] *noun US* skilled craftsman who has completed his apprenticeship

judge [dʒʌdʒ] **1** *noun* person who decides in a legal case; *the judge sent him to prison for embezzlement* **2** *verb* to make a decision about someone *or* something; *to judge an employee's managerial potential; he judged it was time to call an end to the discussions*

◊ **judgement** *or* **judgment** ['dʒʌdʒmənt] *noun* legal decision *or* official decision of a court; **to pronounce judgement** *or* **to give one's judgement on something** = to give an official or legal decision about something; **judgment debtor** = debtor who has been ordered by a court to pay a debt (NOTE: the spelling **judgment** is used by lawyers)

judicial [dʒuːˈdɪʃəl] *adjective* referring to

the law; **judicial processes** = the ways in which the law works

junior ['dʒuːnjə] **1** *adjective* younger *or* lower in rank; **junior clerk** = clerk, usually young, who has lower status than a senior clerk; **junior management** = managers of small departments *or* deputies to departmental managers; **junior executive** *or* **junior manager** = young manager in a company; **junior partner** = person who has been made a partner more recently than others **2** *noun* **office junior** = young man or woman who does all types of work in an office

just [dʒʌst] *adjective* fair and reasonable; *the employees don't expect miracles, but they do want a just settlement of the dispute; everyone respected the foreman for his just handling of the affair*

just-in-time (JIT) ['dʒʌstɪn'taɪm] *noun* **just-in-time (JIT) production** = making goods to order just before they are needed, so as to avoid having too many goods in stock

justice ['dʒʌstɪs] *noun* **(a)** fair treatment in law; *the employee lost his case for unfair dismissal and felt that justice had not been done* **(b)** fairness and reasonableness; *the union negotiators impressed on the management the justice of their demands*

justify ['dʒʌstɪfaɪ] *verb* to give an excuse for *or* to give a reason for; *the employees' representatives produced a mass of documents to justify their wage claim; the personnel manager was asked to justify the dismissal before the industrial tribunal*

juvenile ['dʒuːvənaɪl] *adjective & noun* young (person); **juvenile labour** = children and other young people employed under special conditions (as in films, etc.)

Kk

K [keɪ] *abbreviation* one thousand; **'salary: £15K+ '** = salary more than £15,000 per annum

Keogh plan [ˈkiːəʊ ˈplæn] *noun US* private pension system allowing self-employed businessmen and professionals to set up pension and retirement plans for themselves

key [kiː] *noun* important; *key industry; key personnel; a key member of our management team; she has a key post in the organization; we don't want to lose any key staff in the reorganization*

kickback [ˈkɪkbæk] *noun* illegal commission paid to someone (especially a government official) who helps in a business deal

knock off [ˈnɒk ˈɒf] *verb (informal)* to stop work

◊ **knock-on effect** [ˈnɒkɒn ɪˈfekt] *noun* effect which an action will have on other situations; *the strike by customs officers has had a knock-on effect on car production by slowing down exports of cars*

know [nəʊ] *verb* **(a)** to learn *or* to have information about something; *I don't know how a computer works; does he know how long it takes to get to the airport? the managing director's secretary does not know where he is* **(b)** to have met someone; *do you know Mr Jones, our new sales director? he knows the African market very well*

◊ **know-how** [ˈnəʊhaʊ] *noun* skill *or* ability in a particular field; knowledge about how something works *or* how something is made; *if we cannot recruit men with the right know-how, we will have to initiate an ambitious training programme; know-how and hard work are the secrets of the company's success*

◊ **knowledge** [ˈnɒlɪdʒ] *noun* what is known; **knowledge-based assessment** = appraisal of an employee based on how much he knows as opposed to the ability he has to put his knowledge into practice

LI

laboratory [lə'bɒrətri] *noun* place where scientific research is carried out; *the product was developed in the company's laboratories; all products are tested in our own laboratories;* **laboratory training** = form of group training method for management trainees, designed to improve social skills and self-confidence through counselling, role-playing and simulation exercises; *laboratory training has been important in improving self-confidence in future salesmen; laboratory training will be used to complement our training in accountancy and marketing*

labour *or US* **labor** ['leɪbə] *noun* **(a)** work; **manual labour** = work done by hand; **to charge for materials and labour** = to charge for both the materials used in a job and also the hours of work involved; **labour is charged at £5 an hour** = each hour of work costs £5 **(b)** workers *or* the workforce; *we will need to employ more labour if production is to be increased; the costs of labour are rising in line with inflation;* **casual labour** = workers who are hired for a short period; **cheap labour** = workers who do not earn much money; **indirect labour** = workers who are not directly related to the production of the product; **local labour** = workers recruited near a factory, not brought in from somewhere else; *it would be cheaper to advertise for local labour and so not pay relocation costs;* **organized labour** = workers who are members of trade unions; **skilled labour** = workers who have special knowledge or qualifications; **slave labour** = workers who are owned and exploited by their employers **(c)** **labour agreement** *or* **labour contract** = legal document which is negotiated between the union and the employer; *after intensive bargaining a labour agreement was drawn up; the new labour contract allows for a higher rate of pay;* **labour costs** *or* **labour charges** = cost of the workers employed to make a product (not including materials or overheads); **indirect labour costs** = cost of wages of

workers (such as secretaries, cleaners) who are not directly involved in making the product; **labour dispute** = conflict *or* disagreement between employer and employees or between the groups who represent them; **labour force** = total number of workers employed in a country *or* industry *or* organization; *the management has made an increased offer to the labour force; we are setting up a factory in the Far East because of the cheap labour force available;* **labour force participation rate** = proportion of people in the labour force who are working; **labour grading** *or* **labour ranking** = arranging jobs in order of importance in an organization, and therefore the pay which is suitable for each job; **labour injunction** = court order requiring an individual or group in an industry to stop certain actions considered damaging to another; **labour laws** *or* **labour legislation** = laws relating to the employment of workers; **labour market** = supply of workers ready *or* available for work; *the labour market has improved for employers since the growth in unemployment; 25,000 school-leavers have just come on to the labour market* = 25,000 people have left school and become available for work; **labour mobility** *or* **mobility of labour** = situation in which workers agree to move from one place to another to get work; **labour relations** = relations between management and workers or between groups that represent them; *labour relations have got worse since management tried to step up production without taking on any more workers;* **labour reserve** = people in the labour force who are not working; **labour shortage** *or* **shortage of labour** = situation where there are not enough workers to fill jobs; **labour stability index** = index showing the percentage of workers who have been in their jobs for more than one year; **labour turnover** *or* **turnover of labour** = movement of workers, with some leaving their jobs and other joining; *US* **labor union** = workers' organization which represents and defends the interests of its members; **labour wastage** = loss of employees over a period of time; *labour wastage in the last five years has been rising owing to an increase in people taking early retirement* **(d)** International Labour Organization **(ILO)** = section of the United Nations which tries to improve working conditions and workers' pay in member countries

◊ **Labor Day** ['leɪbə 'deɪ] *noun* American national holiday celebrated on the first Monday in September

◊ **labourer** ['leɪbərə] *noun* person who does heavy work; **agricultural labourer** = person who does heavy work on a farm; **casual labourer** = worker who can be hired for a short period; **manual labourer** = person who does heavy work with his hands

◊ **labour-intensive** ['leɪbə ɪn'tensɪv] *adjective* (industry) which needs large numbers of workers *or* where labour costs are high in relation to turnover; *as the business became more labour-intensive, so personnel management became more important; with computerization, the business has become much less labour-intensive*

◊ **labour-saving** ['leɪbə 'seɪvɪŋ] *adjective* which saves work *or* which needs little labour; *costs will be cut by the introduction of labour-saving devices*

QUOTE the possibility that British goods will price themselves back into world markets is doubtful as long as sterling labour costs continue to rise faster than in competitor countries
Sunday Times

QUOTE 70 per cent of Australia's labour force is employed in service activity
Australian Financial Review

QUOTE European economies are being held back by rigid labor markets and wage structures
Duns Business Month

lack [læk] **1** *noun* not having enough; **lack of incentive** = not having enough incentive **2** *verb* not to have enough of something; *the industry lacks skilled staff;* **the sales staff lack motivation** = the sales staff are not motivated enough

ladder ['lædə] *noun* series of steps made of wood or metal which can be moved about, and which you can climb; *working his way up the company ladder gave him the discipline to take on further management responsibilities;* **dual ladder** = two career paths in an organization leading to positions of equal importance and open to the same type of employee; **promotion ladder** = series of steps by which people can be promoted; *on his appointment as sales manager, he moved several steps up the promotion ladder*

large [lɑːdʒ] *adjective* very big *or* important; *our company is one of the largest suppliers of computers to the government; he is our largest customer; why has she got an office which is larger than mine?*

◊ **largely** ['lɑːdʒli] *adverb* mainly *or* mostly; *our sales are largely in the home market; they have largely pulled out of the American market*

◊ **large-scale** ['lɑːdʒ 'skeɪl] *adjective* involving large numbers of people *or* large amounts of money; *large-scale investment in new technology; large-scale redundancies in the construction industry*

last [lɑːst] **1** *adjective & adverb* **(a)** coming at the end of a series; *out of a queue of twenty people, I was served last; this is our last board meeting before we move to our new offices; we finished the last items in the order just two days before the promised delivery date;* **last quarter** = period of three months to the end of the financial year **(b)** most recent *or* most recently; *where is the last batch of orders? the last ten orders were only for small quantities;* **last week** *or* **last month** *or* **last year** = the week *or* month *or* year before this one; *last week's sales were the best we have ever had; the sales managers have been asked to report on last month's drop in unit sales; last year's accounts have to be ready in time for the AGM* **2** *verb* to go on *or* to continue; *the boom started in the 1970s and lasted until the early 1980s; the discussions over redundancies lasted all day*

◊ **last in first out (LIFO)** ['lɑːst 'ɪn 'fɜːst 'aʊt] *noun* redundancy policy, where the people most recently appointed are the first to be made redundant

lateral ['lætərəl] *adjective* referring to the side; **lateral relations** = relations between people of the same grade in an organization; *the struggle for promotion has* *soured lateral relations;* **lateral thinking** = way of approaching problems by looking at them from unusual directions; **lateral transfer** = moving an employee to another job at the same level in the organization; *he was pleased with his new job, even though it was a lateral transfer and not a promotion*

law [lɔː] *noun* **(a) laws** = rules made by central government *or* local government *or* a court, by which a country is governed and the activities of people and organizations controlled; **labour laws** = laws concerning the employment of workers **(b) law** = all the laws of a country taken together; **civil law** = laws relating to arguments between individuals and the rights of individuals; **commercial law** = laws regarding business; **company law** = laws which refer to the way companies work; **contract law** *or* **the law of contract** = laws relating to private agreements; **maritime law** *or* **the law of the sea** = laws referring to ships, ports, etc.; **trade union law** = laws concerning the running of trade unions; **law courts** = place where a judge listens to cases and decides who is right legally; **to take someone to law** = to tell someone to appear in court to settle an argument; **inside the law** *or* **within the law** = obeying the laws of a country; **against** *or* **outside the law** = not according to the laws of a country; *the company is operating outside the law;* **to break the law** = to do something which is not allowed by law; *he is breaking the law by selling goods on Sunday; you will be breaking the law if you try to take that computer out of the country without an export licence* **(c)** general rule; **law of effect** = principle that behaviour which is rewarded will be repeated; *payment by results was designed to put the law of effect into practice;* **law of supply and demand** = general rule that the amount of a product which is available is related to the needs of the possible customers; **law of diminishing returns** = general rule that as more factors of production (land, labour and capital) are added to the existing factors, so the amount they produce is proportionately smaller (NOTE: no plural for this meaning)

◊ **lawsuit** ['lɔːsuːt] *noun* case brought to a court; **to bring a lawsuit against someone** = to tell someone to appear in court to settle an argument; **to defend a lawsuit** = to appear in court to state your case

◊ **lawyer** ['lɔːjə] *noun* person who has

studied law and practises law as a profession; *the union has relied heavily on their lawyers for advice during the dispute;* **commercial lawyer** *or* **company lawyer** = person who specializes in company law *or* who advises companies on legal problems; **maritime lawyer** = person who specializes in laws concerning ships

lay [leɪ] *verb* to put; **to lay an embargo on trade with a country** = to forbid trade with a country

◊ **lay off** ['leɪ 'ɒf] *verb* **to lay off workers** = to dismiss workers for a time (until more work is available); *the factory laid off half its workers because of lack of orders*

◊ **lay-off** ['leɪɒf] *noun* action of dismissing a worker for a period of more than four weeks; *the recession has caused hundreds of lay-offs in the car industry;* **disciplinary lay-off** = dismissing a worker for a time as a punishment

QUOTE the company lost $52 million last year, and has laid off close to 2,000 employees

Toronto Star

lazy ['leɪzi] *adjective* (person) who does not want to work; *she is too lazy to do any overtime; he is so lazy he does not even send in his expense claims on time*

leader ['liːdə] *noun* person who manages *or* directs others; *the leader of the construction workers' union or the construction workers' leader; she is the leader of the trade mission to Nigeria; the minister was the leader of the party of industrialists on a tour of American factories*

◊ **leaderless discussion** ['liːdələs dɪs'kʌʃn] *noun* way of assessing candidates for a post, by putting them together in a group and asking them to discuss a problem, without appointing one of them as chairman

◊ **leadership** ['liːdəʃɪp] *noun* **(a)** quality that enables a person to manage *or* administer others; *employees showing leadership potential will be chosen for management training* **(b)** group of people who manage *or* administer an organization; *the elections have changed the composition of the union leadership* (NOTE: no plural)

◊ **leading** ['liːdɪŋ] *adjective* most important; *leading industrialists feel the end* *of the recession is near; leading shares rose on the Stock Exchange; leading shareholders in the company forced a change in management policy; they are the leading company in the field;* **leading indicator** = indicator (such as manufacturing order books) which shows a change in economic trends earlier than other indicators

◊ **lead time** ['liːd 'taɪm] *noun* time between the start of a task and its completion

leak [liːk] *verb* to pass secret information; *the new manager was guilty of leaking confidential information about the organization to the press*

lean [liːn] *adjective* slim (and efficient); **lean management** = style of management, where few managers are employed, allowing decisions to be taken rapidly; **lean production** = production methods which reduce excessive expenditure on staff and concentrate on efficient low-cost manufacturing

leap-frogging ['liːpfrɒgɪŋ] **1** *adjective* **leap-frogging pay demands** = pay demands where each section of workers asks for higher pay to do better than another section, which then asks for further increases in turn **2** *noun* communication which by-passes the official chain of command; *leap-frogging caused much resentment among middle managers who felt left out of decisions*

learning ['lɜːnɪŋ] *noun* process of receiving and assimilating information or skills; *the learning of new skills is hard for our senior employees who are nearing retirement; the trainees all had different learning potentials;* **learning curve** = rate at which skills or knowledge are learnt over a period of time (shown as a curve on a graph); *this learning curve shows how production has become more efficient as the machinists' skills have improved;* **continuous learning** = system of training which continues during an employee's career with a company; **distance learning** = learning in one's own time away from the centre producing the course, by mail, radio, television or by occasional visits to centres; **open learning** = system of flexible training courses which a trainee can start at any time, and which do not require a teacher; **rote learning** *or* **learning by heart** = learning by remembering pieces of information, so as to able to repeat it verbally

leave [liːv] **1** *noun* permission to be away from work; *he was granted leave to go to his uncle's funeral; owing to undermanning, leave will only granted in the most deserving cases;* **six weeks' annual leave** = six weeks' holiday each year; **leave of absence** = being allowed to be away from work; *he was given leave of absence in order to sort out his personal affairs;* **compassionate leave** = time off work granted to an employee to deal with personal or family problems; **maternity leave** = permission given to woman to be away from work to have a baby; **paternity leave** = short period of leave given to a father to be away from work when his wife has a baby; **sick leave** = period when a worker is away from work because of illness; **unpaid leave** = leave during which the worker does not receive any pay; **to go on leave** *or* **to be on leave** = to be away from work; *she is away on sick leave or on maternity leave* **2** *verb* **(a)** to go away from; *he left his office early to go to the meeting; the next plane leaves at 10.20* **(b)** to resign; *he left his job and bought a farm*

◊ **leaver** ['liːvə] *noun* person who has left; **school-leaver** = person who has just left school; **leaver's statement** = official document given to someone who is leaving a company and has recently received statutory sick pay

ledger ['ledʒə] *noun* book in which accounts are written; **payroll ledger** = list of staff and their salaries

legal ['liːgəl] *adjective* **(a)** according to the law *or* allowed by the law; *the company's action in sacking the accountant was completely legal* **(b)** referring to the law; **to take legal action** = to sue someone *or* to take someone to court; **to take legal advice** = to ask a lawyer to advise about a legal problem; **legal adviser** = person who advises clients about the law; **legal costs** *or* **legal charges** *or* **legal expenses** = money spent on fees to lawyers; *the clerk could not afford the legal expenses involved in suing his boss*

◊ **legal aid** ['liːgəl 'eɪd] *noun* legal advice offered by the state; **Legal Aid scheme** = British government scheme where a person with very little money can have legal representation and advice paid for by the state; **Legal Aid Centre** = local office giving advice to clients about applications for Legal Aid and recommending clients to solicitors

◊ **legally** ['liːgəli] *adverb* according to the law; **the contract is legally binding** = according to the law, the contract has to be obeyed; **the directors are legally responsible** = the law says that the directors are responsible

legislation [ledʒɪs'leɪʃən] *noun* laws; **labour legislation** = laws concerning the employment of workers; *labour legislation was changed to the benefit of the workers*

legitimate [lə'dʒɪtəmət] *adjective* allowed by law; *he has a legitimate claim to the property;* **legitimate grievance** = employer's grievance based on an actual violation of a contract of employment; *the worker received no compensation since he had no legitimate grievance; the personnel department considered that the treatment of workers should be such that no legitimate grievance could be claimed*

leisure ['leʒə] *noun* time free from work or other obligations; *the organization is trying to encourage constructive leisure pursuits; the company provides many leisure facilities such as tennis courts and a swimming pool; too much work and not enough leisure had an adverse effect on his family life; there are so few orders coming in that the employees have more leisure;* **leisure activities** = what you do in your spare time

length [leŋθ] *noun* measurement of how long something is; **length of service** = how long someone has been employed by a company

leniency ['liːnɪənsi] *noun* not being strict in dealing with subordinates; *given the worker's good work record, she was treated with leniency by her superior;* **leniency bias** = unjustifiably high rating of an employee's job performance; *leniency bias works against objectivity in performance appraisal*

let go ['let 'gəʊ] *verb (euphemism)* to make someone redundant; to sack someone

letter ['letə] *noun* **(a)** piece of writing sent from one person *or* company to another to give information; **business letter** = letter which deals with business matters; **covering letter** = letter sent with documents to say why they are being sent; **personal letter** *or* **private letter** = letter which deals with personal matters; **standard letter** = letter which is sent without change to various correspondents **(b)** **letter of acknowledgement** = letter which says that something has been received; **letter of application** = letter in which someone applies for a job; *he sent the company a letter of application accompanied by a CV; the personnel manager was sorting through more than fifty letters of application;* **letter of appointment** = formal letter sent to someone, stating that he or she has been offered a job, and giving relevant details; **letter of attorney** = document showing that someone has power of attorney; **letter of complaint** = letter in which someone complains; **letter of dismissal** = official letter notifying someone that he has been dismissed; **letter of introduction** = letter making someone get to know another person; **letter of offer** = letter which offers someone a job; **letter of recommendation** = letter in which the writer recommends someone (for a job); **letter of reference** = letter in which an employer recommends someone for a new job; **letter of resignation** = letter in which a worker resigns from his job **(c)** **airmail letter** = letter sent by air; **express letter** = letter sent very fast; **registered letter** = letter which is noted by the post office before it is sent, so that compensation can be claimed if it is lost **(d)** **to acknowledge receipt by letter** = to write a letter to say that something has been received **(e)** written or printed sign (such as A, B, C, etc.); *write your name and address in block letters or in capital letters*

level ['levl] *noun* position where high is large and low is small; *low level of productivity or low productivity levels; to raise the level of employee benefits; record levels of absenteeism;* **pay levels** *or* **wage levels** = rates of pay for different types of work; **entry level pay** = pay for an entry level job (i.e. one for which no previous experience is needed); **high-level** = very important; *a high-level meeting or decision;* **a decision taken at the highest level** = decision taken by the most important person or group; **low-level** = not very important; *a low-level delegation;* **decisions taken at managerial level** = decisions taken by managers; **manning levels** *or* **staffing levels** = number of people required in each department of a company to do the work efficiently

leverage ['liːvərɪdʒ] *noun* **(a)** influence

which you can use to achieve an aim; *he has no leverage over the chairman* **(b)** borrowing money at fixed interest which is then used to produce more money than the interest paid (NOTE: no plural)

levy ['levi] **1** *noun* money which is demanded and collected by the government; **training levy** = tax to be paid by companies to fund the government's training schemes **2** *verb* to demand payment of a tax *or* an extra payment and to collect it

liability [laɪə'bɪlətɪ] *noun* **(a)** legal responsibility for damage *or* loss, etc.; *the two partners took out insurance to cover employers' liability;* **to accept liability for something** = to agree that you are responsible for something; **to refuse liability for something** = to refuse to agree that you are responsible for something; **contractual liability** = legal responsibility for something as stated in a contract; **employer's liability** = legal responsibility of an employer when employees suffer accidents due to negligence on the part of the employer; **employers' liability insurance** = insurance to cover accidents which may happen at work, and for which the company may be responsible; **limited liability** = situation where someone's liability for debt is limited by law; **limited liability company** = company where a shareholder is responsible for repaying the company's debts only to the face value of the shares he owns **(b)** someone *or* something which represents a loss to a person *or* organization; *the sales director is an alcoholic and has become a liability to the company*

◊ **liable** ['laɪəbl] *adjective* **(a)** **liable for** = legally responsible for; *the customer is liable for breakages; the chairman was personally liable for the company's debts; the garage is liable for damage to customers' cars* **(b)** **liable to** = subject to; *employees' wages are liable to tax*

liaise [lɪ'eɪz] *verb* **to liaise with someone** = to inform someone of what is being done, so that actions are coordinated; *the personnel department will liaise with individual managers regarding certain employees*

◊ **liaison** [lɪ'eɪzən] *noun* keeping someone informed of what is happening; **liaison**

officer = person whose job it is to keep someone else informed of what is happening; *the personnel manager was appointed liaison officer with the unions over relocation*

licence *or US* **license** ['laɪsəns] *noun* **(a)** official document which allows someone to do something; **driving licence** = document which allows someone to drive a car *or* a truck, etc.; *applicants should hold a valid driving licence;* **import licence** *or* **export licence** = documents which allow goods to be exported *or* imported **(b)** **licence agreement** = contractual agreement by which a patent owner *or* copyright owner allows a company to manufacture something and pay a fee for this; **goods manufactured under licence** = goods made with the permission of the owner of the copyright or patent

◊ **license** ['laɪsəns] **1** *noun US* = LICENCE **2** *verb* to give someone official permission to do something; *she is licensed to run an employment agency*

lieu [ljuː] *noun* **in lieu of** = instead of; *she was given two months' salary in lieu of notice* = she was given the salary and asked to leave immediately

life [laɪf] *noun* **(a)** time when a person is alive; **for life** = for as long as someone is alive; *his pension gives him a comfortable income for life;* **life annuity** *or* **annuity for life** = annual payments made to someone as long as he is alive; **life assurance** *or* **life insurance** = insurance which pays a sum of money when someone dies, or at a certain date if he is still alive; *one of the fringe benefits provided by the company is a contribution to a life assurance scheme;* **the life assured** *or* **the life insured** = the person whose life has been covered by the life assurance policy; **life expectancy** = number of years a person is likely to live **(b)** being alive; **quality of life** = general feeling of wellbeing in one's life; **life skills** = skills used in dealing with other people **(c)** period of time something exists; *the life of a loan; during the life of the agreement*

◊ **life-long employment** [['laɪflɒŋ ɪm'plɔɪmənt] *noun* the concept (common in Japan) that a worker who enters a company as a young man will be guaranteed employment by that company for the rest of his working life

LIFO = LAST IN FIRST OUT

lightning strike ['laɪtnɪŋ 'straɪk] *noun* sudden strike; *the lightning strike took the management completely by surprise*

limit ['lɪmɪt] *noun* point at which something must not be passed; *the government has imposed a limit on wage increases; what is the time limit for completion of this particular task?;* **to set limits to imports** *or* **to impose import limits** = to allow only a certain amount of imports; **age limit** = top age at which you are allowed to do a job; *there is an age limit of thirty-five on the post of buyer;* **time limit** = maximum time which can be taken to do something; *to set a time limit for acceptance of the offer*

◊ **limited** ['lɪmɪtɪd] *adjective* restricted *or* not open; **limited liability company** = company where a shareholder is responsible for the company's debts only to the face value of his shares; **private limited company** = company with a small number of shareholders, whose shares are not traded on the Stock Exchange; **public limited company** = company whose shares can be bought on the Stock Exchange (NOTE: private limited company is abbreviated to **Ltd: J. Smith & Sons, Ltd.** Public limited company is abbreviated to **plc: Smith and Jones, plc**) **limited partnership** = registered business where the liability of the partners is limited to the amount of capital they have each provided to the business and where the partners may not take part in the running of the business

line [laɪn] *noun* (**a**) **line of business** *or* **line of work** = type of business or work; *what is his line?* (**b**) series of things, one after another; **to be in line for promotion** = to be the next to be promoted; **to bring someone into line** = to make someone do the same as the others; **line authority** = power to direct others and make decisions regarding the operations of the organization; **line of command** *or* **line management** *or* **line organization** = organization of a business where each manager is responsible for doing what his superior tells him to do; **line manager** = manager responsible to a superior, but with authority to give orders to other employees (**c**) *US* row of people waiting one after the other (NOTE: GB English is **queue**) **to be on the breadline** *or* **on the poverty line** = to be so poor as to have hardly enough to live on (**d**) row of letters *or* figures on a page; **bottom**

line = (i) last line on a balance sheet indicating profit or loss; (ii) final decision on a matter; **the boss is interested only in the bottom line** = he is only interested in the final profit (**e**) short letter; **to drop someone a line** = to send someone a note (**f**) **assembly line** *or* **production line** = production system where the product (such as a car) moves slowly through a factory with new sections added to it as it goes along; *he works on the production line* *or* *he's a production line worker in the car factory* (**g**) **line chart** *or* **line graph** = chart or graph using lines to indicate values; **line printer** = machine which prints information from a computer one line at a time (**h**) **telephone line** = wire along which telephone messages travel; **to be on the line to someone** = to be telephoning someone; **the line is bad** = it is difficult to hear clearly what someone is saying; **a crossed line** = when two telephone conversations get mixed; **direct line** = telephone number which goes direct to someone, without passing through an operator; **the line is engaged** = the person is already speaking on the phone; **outside line** = line from an internal office telephone system to the main telephone exchange

liquidation [lɪkwɪ'deɪʃən] *noun* winding up *or* closing of a company and selling of its assets; **compulsory liquidation** = liquidation which is ordered by a court

list [lɪst] *noun* several items written one after the other; **address list** *or* **mailing list** = list of names and addresses of people and companies; **black list** = list of goods *or* companies *or* countries which are banned for trade; **short list** = list of candidates who can be asked to come for a test *or* interview (drawn up after all applications have been examined and the most obviously unsuitable candidates have been rejected); **waiting list** = list of people waiting for something (an interview, a job, a company car, etc.)

litigate ['lɪtɪgeɪt] *verb* to go to law *or* to bring a lawsuit against someone to have a dispute settled

◊ **litigant** ['lɪtɪgənt] *noun* person who is involved in a civil action in court

◊ **litigation** [lɪtɪ'geɪʃən] *noun* going to law *or* bringing of a lawsuit against someone to have a dispute settled

◊ **litigious** [lɪ'tɪdʒəs] *adjective* (person)

who likes to bring lawsuits against other people

living ['lɪvɪŋ] *noun* **cost of living** = money which a person has to pay for rent, food, heating, etc.; **cost-of-living index** = way of measuring the cost of living which is shown as a percentage increase on the figure for the previous year; **he does not earn a living wage** = he does not earn enough to pay for essentials (food, heat, rent); **to make a living** = to earn enough to pay for one's living expenses; *he makes a good living from selling secondhand cars;* **standard of living** *or* **living standard** = quality of personal home life (amount of food, clothes bought, size of the family car, etc.); *living standards fell as unemployment rose; the living standard in oil-producing countries has risen dramatically*

loading ['ləʊdɪŋ] *noun* assigning work to workers or machines; *the production manager has to ensure that careful loading makes the best use of human resources*

lobby ['lɒbi] *noun* group of people who try to influence MPs, members of town councils, etc.; **the energy-saving lobby** = people who try to persuade MPs to pass laws to save energy

local ['ləʊkəl] **1** *adjective* referring to a particular area, especially one near where a factory *or* an office is based; **local authority** = elected section of government which runs a small area of the country; **local call** = telephone call to a number in the same area as the person making the call; **local collective bargaining** = collective bargaining which takes place in the factory, and not at national level; **local government** = elected administrative bodies which run areas of the country; **local labour** = workers who are recruited near a factory, and are not brought there from a distance; *it would be cheaper to advertise for local labour and avoid relocation costs* **2** *noun* US branch of a national trade union

◊ **locally** ['ləʊkəli] *adverb* in the area near where an office or factory is based; *we recruit all our staff locally*

lock [lɒk] **1** *noun* device for closing a door *or* box so that it can be opened only with a key; *the lock is broken on the petty cash box; I have forgotten the combination of the lock on my briefcase* **2** *verb* to close a door with a key, so that it cannot be opened; *the manager forgot to lock the door of the computer room; the petty cash box was not locked*

◊ **lock out** ['lɒk 'aʊt] *verb* **to lock out workers** = to shut the factory door so that workers cannot get in and so force them not to work until the conditions imposed by the management are met

◊ **lockout** ['lɒkaʊt] *noun* industrial dispute where the management will not let the workers into the factory until they have agreed to the management's conditions

lodge [lɒdʒ] *verb* **to lodge a complaint against someone** = to make an official complaint about someone

long [lɒŋ] *adjective* for a large period of time; **in the long term** = over a long period of time; **long service award** *or* **award for long service** = present given by a company to someone who has worked for them for a long time

◊ **long-distance** ['lɒŋ 'dɪstəns] *adjective* **a long-distance call** = telephone call to a number which is not near

◊ **longhand** ['lɒŋhænd] *noun* handwriting where the words are written out in full and not typed or in shorthand; *applications should be written in longhand and sent to the personnel officer*

◊ **long-range** ['lɒŋ 'reɪn(d)ʒ] *adjective* for a long period of time in the future; **long-range economic forecast** = forecast which covers a period of several years

◊ **long-standing** ['lɒŋ 'stændɪŋ] *adjective* which has been arranged for a long time; *long-standing agreement*

◊ **long-term** ['lɒŋ 'tɜːm] *adjective* for a long time ahead; *the management projections are made on a long-term basis; sound long-term planning will give the company more direction; it is in the company's long-term interests to have a contented staff;* **long-term disability** = disability which lasts or is likely to last a very long time; **Long-Term Disability Plan** = insurance scheme that pays insured workers a proportion of their wages in the event of disablement; **long-term objectives** = aims which will take years to achieve; **long-term planning** = planning for a long time in advance (as in a five-year plan, a seven-year plan, etc.); **long-term unemployed** = people who have had no regular paid work for over twelve months; people with no jobs and no prospect of ever being employed

loose [luːs] *adjective* not packed together; **loose change** = money in coins; **loose rate** = rate applied to a worker earning above the rate earned by other workers in similar jobs requiring similar skills

lose [luːz] *verb* **(a)** not to have something any more; **to lose one's job** = to be made redundant or to be sacked; *he lost his job in the reorganization; she lost her job when the factory closed;* **to lose an order** = not to get an order which you were hoping to get; *during the strike, the company lost six orders to American competitors;* **to lose customers** = to have fewer customers; *their service is so slow that they have been losing customers;* **lost time** = time during which a worker does not work, through no fault of his own; *too much lost time is uneconomical; better logistics will help cut down lost time;* **number of days lost through strikes** = numbers of days which are not worked when workers are on strike **(b)** to have less money; *he lost £25,000 in his father's computer company;* **the pound has lost value** = the pound is worth less

loss [lɒs] *noun* **loss of one's job** = being made redundant; **loss of an order** = not getting an order which was expected; **compensation for loss of earnings** = payment to someone who has stopped

earning money *or* who is not able to earn money; **compensation for loss of office** = payment to a director who is asked to leave a company before his contract ends

low [ləʊ] *adjective* not high *or* not much; *the union claims the wages in the company are too low; she works long hours for a low salary;* **low-paid staff** = staff on low salaries

◊ **lower** ['ləʊə] *adjective* smaller *or* less high; **lower-paid staff** = staff who are paid less than others; **lower limit** = bottom limit; **lower earnings limit** = minimum earnings level at which an employee has to pay National Insurance contributions

loyal ['lɔɪəl] *adjective* (worker) who supports the company he works for

◊ **loyalty** ['lɔɪəltɪ] *noun* **company loyalty** = dedication of staff to the company and its objectives

Ltd ['lɪmɪtɪd] = LIMITED

lump [lʌmp] *noun* **the Lump** *or* **Lump labour** = self-employed workers who are paid a lump sum for a day's work *or* for the amount of work completed (often with a view to avoiding tax); **lump sum** = money paid in one single amount, not in several small sums; *when he retired he received a lump-sum payment of several thousand pounds*

luncheon voucher ['lʌntʃən 'vaʊtʃə] *noun* ticket given by an employer to a worker in addition to his wages, which can be exchanged for food in a restaurant

lying time ['laɪɪŋ 'taɪm] *noun* time between the end of a period of work and the date on which you are paid for it

Mm

MA = MATERNITY ALLOWANCE

machine [məˈʃiːn] *noun* device which works with power from a motor; **copying machine** *or* **duplicating machine** = machine which makes copies of documents; **machine shop** = place where working machines are placed; **machine tools** = tools worked by motors, used to work on wood or metal

◊ **machinery** [məˈʃiːnəri] *noun* **(a)** machines; **idle machinery** *or* **machinery lying idle** = machines not being used; **machinery guards** = pieces of metal to prevent workers from getting hurt by the moving parts of a machine **(b)** organization *or* system; *the administrative machinery needs reviewing; the machinery for awarding pay increases*

◊ **machinist** [məˈʃiːnɪst] *noun* person who works *or* controls a machine

magazine [mægəˈziːn] *noun* paper, usually with pictures, which comes out regularly, every month or every week; **house magazine** = magazine produced for the workers in a company to give them news of the company's affairs; **trade magazine** = magazine produced for people or companies in certain trades

main [meɪn] *adjective* most important; *main office; main building; one of our main customers*

maintain [meɪnˈteɪn] *verb* **(a)** to keep something going *or* working; *to maintain good relations with the employees' representatives; to maintain contact with an overseas market* **(b)** to keep something working at the same level; *the company has maintained the same volume of business in spite of the recession; to maintain an interest rate at 5%;* **to maintain a dividend** = to pay the same dividend as the previous year

◊ **maintenance** [ˈmeɪntənəns] *noun* **(a)** keeping things going *or* working; *maintenance of contacts; maintenance of supplies* US **maintenance of membership** = requirement that employees who are union members must remain so for the full duration of their employment in an organization; **maintenance factors** = elements at work which create employee dissatisfaction when they are not adequately provided; *the reason for the strike was the lack of maintenance factors such as decent rest periods* **(b)** keeping a machine in good working order; **maintenance contract** = contract by which a company keeps a piece of equipment in good working order; *we offer a full maintenance service* **(c)** keeping a person alive and well

major [ˈmeɪdʒə] *adjective* important; *there is a major risk of fire*

majority [məˈdʒɒrəti] *noun* **(a)** larger group than all others; *the majority of union members voted for the strike;* **the board accepted the proposal by a majority of three to two** = three members of the board voted to accept and two voted against; **majority vote** *or* **majority decision** = decision made after a vote according to the wishes of the largest group **(b)** number of votes by which a person wins an election; *he was elected shop steward with a majority of three hundred*

make [meɪk] **1** *noun* type of product manufactured; *Japanese makes of cars; a standard make of equipment; what make is the new computer system?* **2** *verb* **(a)** to produce *or* to manufacture; *to make a car or to make a computer; the workmen spent ten weeks making the table; the factory makes three hundred cars a day;* **make-whole remedy** = way of compensating an employee for his or her bad treatment in violation of employment legislation; *make-whole remedies are often considered insufficient by aggrieved workers* **(b)** to sign *or* to agree; *to make a deal or to make an agreement;* **to make a bid for something** = to offer to buy something; **to make a payment** = to pay; **to make a deposit** = to pay money as a deposit **(c)** to earn *or* to increase in value; *he makes £50,000 a year or £25 an hour*

◊ **make good** ['meɪk 'gʊd] *verb* **(a)** to repair; *the company will make good the damage* **(b)** to compensate for; *to make good a loss*

◊ **make up** ['meɪk 'ʌp] *verb* to compensate for something; **to make up a loss** *or* **to make up the difference** = to pay extra so that the loss or difference is covered

◊ **make-work practices** ['meɪk wɜːk 'præktɪsɪs] *noun* methods of creating work for people who would otherwise have no work; *make-work practices are boosting morale in areas badly hit by the recession; make-work practices at least provide practical work experience*

man [mæn] **1** *noun* person *or* ordinary worker; *all the men went back to work yesterday;* **right-hand man** = main assistant **2** *verb* to provide the workforce for something; *to man a shift; to man an exhibition; the exhibition stand was manned by three salesgirls; see also* MANNED, MANNING *and note at* PERSON

◊ **man-hour** ['mæn 'aʊə] *noun* work done by one worker in one hour; *one million man-hours were lost through industrial action; there are two hundred man-hours of work still to be done, which will take ten workers twenty hours to complete*

◊ **Man Friday** ['mæn 'fraɪdeɪ] *noun* male employee who does a variety of tasks

◊ **man-to-man ranking** ['mæn tə 'mæn 'ræŋkɪŋ] *noun* arranging employees in order according to their skills or other criteria

manage ['mænɪdʒ] *verb* **(a)** to direct *or* to be in charge of an organization or part of one; *a competent and motivated person is required to manage an important department in the company; he has been recruited to manage a branch office in the north of the country;* **managing change** = managing the way changes in the working environment are implemented and how they affect the workforce **(b)** **to manage to** = to be able to do something; *did you manage to see the head buyer? she managed to write six orders and take three phone calls all in two minutes*

management ['mænɪdʒmənt] *noun* **(a)** directing *or* administering a business; *to study management; good management or efficient management; bad management or inefficient management; a management graduate or a graduate in management;* **management of change** = managing the way changes in the working environment are implemented and how they affect the workforce; **human resource(s) management (HRM)** = management and administration of the recruitment, welfare and training of employees in an organization and responsibility for an organization's productive use of its employees; **line management** = organization of a business where each manager is responsible for doing what his superior tells him to do; **personnel management** = management *or* administration of the recruitment, welfare and training of employees in an organization; **product management** = directing the making and selling of a product as an independent item; **management accountant** = accountant who prepares specialized information for managers so that they can make decisions; **management accounts** = financial information (on sales, costs, credit, profitability) prepared for a manager; **management audit** = listing of all the managers in an organization with information about their skills and experience; *the management audit helped determine how many more managers needed to be recruited;* **management committee** = committee which manages a club, a pension fund, etc.; **management consultant** = person who gives professional advice on how to manage a business; *the company has advertised for a management consultant, specializing in personnel matters, to advise on manpower planning;* **management course** = training course for managers; **management development** = selecting and training future managers; *the management development programme consisted of an outside college course and work experience in all the major departments;* **management games** = problems which are given to trainee managers to solve as part of a training course; *the management game run on a computer, demanded decisions in marketing strategy;* **management by exception** = management system where deviations from the plan are located and corrected; **management by objectives (MBO)** = way of managing a business by involving all employees in the objectives of the organization as a whole, planning work for the staff and testing to see if it is completed correctly and on time; **management by walking around (MBWA)** = way of managing, where the manager moves round the shop floor, discusses problems with the staff and learns from them; **management ratio** = number of managers for every hundred employees in an organization; *there was a very high management ratio since there was more planning and less manual work than in most companies;* **management science** = skill and knowledge which can be applied to management; *he studied management science at a polytechnic;* **management style** *or* **style of management** = way in which managers work, in particular the way in which they treat their employees; **management team** = a group of managers working together on a problem or project; **management techniques** = ways of managing a business; **management training** = training managers by making them study problems and work out ways of solving them; **management trainee** = young person being trained to be a manager; *the management trainees were first sent on a short accountancy course* **(b)** group of managers or directors; *management has decided to give an overall pay increase;* **top management** = the main directors of a company; **middle management** = the department managers of a company who carry out the policy set by the directors and organize the work of a group of workers

manager ['mænɪdʒə] *noun* **(a)** person who administers an organization *or* a department; *all new trainees must report to the departmental manager; relations are improving between the managers of rival branches; the personnel manager is responsible for negotiations with the union;* **accounts manager** = head of the accounts department; **area manager** = manager who is responsible for the company's work (usually sales) in an area; **general manager** = manager in charge of administration in a large company; **human resources manager** = person who is responsible for an organization's productive use of its workforce; **junior manager** = young manager in a company; **personnel manager** = head of the personnel department, the person who organizes and co-ordinates the recruitment, welfare and training of staff; **trainee manager** = young member of staff being trained to be a manager **(b)** person in

charge of a branch or shop; *Mr Smith is the manager of our local Lloyds Bank; the manager of our Lagos branch is in London for a series of meetings;* **bank manager** = person in charge of a branch of a bank; **branch manager** = person in charge of a branch of a company

◊ **manageress** ['mænɪdʒəres] *noun* woman who runs a shop, or a department

◊ **managerial** [mænə'dʒɪərɪəl] *adjective* referring to managers; *managerial staff have a special canteen; the training officer is looking for managerial talent among the new recruits;* **to be appointed to a managerial position** = to be appointed a manager; **decisions taken at managerial level** = decisions taken by managers

◊ **managerial grid** [mænə'dʒɪərɪəl 'grɪd] *noun* type of management training in which trainees attempt to solve a number of problems in groups, and thus discover their individual strengths and weaknesses

◊ **managership** ['mænɪdʒəʃɪp] *noun* job of being a manager; *after six years, he was offered the managership of a branch in Scotland*

managing ['mænɪdʒɪŋ] *adjective* **managing director** = director who is in charge of a whole company; **chairman and managing director** = managing director who is also chairman of the board of directors

> QUOTE the management says that the rate of loss-making has come down and it expects further improvement in the next few years
> *Financial Times*

> QUOTE the research director will manage and direct a team of graduate business analysts reporting on consumer behaviour throughout the UK
> *Times*

> QUOTE the No. 1 managerial productivity problem in America is managers who are out of touch with their people and out of touch with their customers
> *Fortune*

mandate ['mændeɪt] *verb* to give instructions to someone who will represent you in negotiations

◊ **mandating** [mæn'deɪtɪŋ] *noun* giving instructions to a representative

mandatory ['mændətəri] *adjective* **mandatory injunction** = order from a court which compels someone to do something; **mandatory issues** = bargaining issues that directly affect employees' jobs; **mandatory meeting** = meeting which all members have to attend

manifest ['mænɪfest] **1** *adjective* obvious *or* apparent; **manifest content** = apparent meaning of words used by one person to another; *the manifest content of the boss' talk to us was congratulatory, but, reading between the lines, we could tell he was angry* **2** *noun* list of goods in a shipment; **passenger manifest** = list of passengers on a ship or plane

manned [mænd] *adjective* with someone working on it; *the switchboard is manned twenty-four hours a day; the stand was manned by our sales staff*

◊ **manning** ['mænɪŋ] *noun* people who are needed to do a work process; **manning agreement** *or* **agreement on manning** = agreement between the company and the workers about how many workers are needed for a certain job; *the union is not pleased with the manning agreement, since it considers the numbers of workers needed to be an underestimate;* **manning levels** = number of people required in each department of a company to do the work efficiently; *manning levels are rising as the output rises* (NOTE: no plural)

manpower ['mænpaʊə] *noun* number of workers in a country *or* industry *or* organization; *we will have to increase our manpower if production targets are to be met; in a labour-intensive industry, manpower is the most important resource;* **manpower audit** = listing all the employees in an organization with details of their skills and experience; *a complete manpower audit was needed to decide what recruitment or training should be carried out to meet future requirements;* **manpower forecasting** = forecasting how many and what type of workers will be needed, and how many will be available; *manpower forecasting is difficult since the future production plans of the company are still unclear;* **manpower needs** *or* **manpower requirements** = number of workers needed; **manpower planning** = planning to anticipate manpower

requirements and trying to meet them as closely as possible; **manpower shortage** *or* **shortage of manpower** = lack of workers

QUOTE the shake-out of manpower from traditional employment areas has generally increased the overall productivity of those at work

Personnel Management

manual ['mænjʊəl] **1** *adjective* done by hand *or* done using the hands; **manual labour** *or* **manual work** = heavy work done by hand; **manual labourer** = person who does heavy work with his or her hands; **manual worker** = employee who works with his or her hands **2** *noun* book of instructions, showing what procedures to follow; **strike manual** = book showing how to conduct a strike; **service manual** = book showing how to service a machine; **user's manual** = book showing someone how to use something

manufacture [mænjʊ'fæktʃə] **1** *verb* to make a product for sale, using machines; *manufactured goods; the company manufactures spare parts for cars* **2** *noun* making a product for sale, using machines

margin ['mɑːdʒɪn] *noun* **(a)** difference between the money received when selling a product and the money paid for it; **gross margin** = percentage difference between the unit manufacturing cost and the received price; **net margin** = percentage difference between received price and all costs, including overheads **(b)** extra space *or* time allowed; **margin of error** = number of mistakes which are accepted in a document *or* in a calculation; **safety margin** = time *or* space allowed for something to be safe

◊ **marginal** ['mɑːdʒɪnəl] *adjective* **marginal cost** = cost of making a single extra unit above the number already planned

marital status ['mærɪtəl 'steɪtəs] *noun* condition of being married or not; *the application form asked the candidate's age, sex, and marital status*

market ['mɑːkɪt] *noun* demand for a certain type of product *or* service; **the labour market** = number of workers available for work; **25,000 graduates have come on to the labour market** = they have become available for work because they have left college; **market forces** = influences from the market on the sales of a product; **market rate** = normal price in the market; *we pay the market rate for secretaries or we pay secretaries the market rate*

married ['mærɪd] *adjective* joined as husband and wife; **married staff** = staff who have wives or husbands

mass [mæs] *noun* (a) large group of people; **mass redundancies** = making a large number of workers redundant at the same time; **mass unemployment** = unemployment of large numbers of workers (b) large number; *we have a mass of letters or masses of letters to write; they received a mass of orders or masses of orders after the TV commercials*

◊ **mass-produce** [mæsprə'djuːs] *verb* to manufacture identical products in large quantities; *to mass-produce cars*

◊ **mass production** [mæsprə'dʌkʃən] *noun* manufacturing large quantities of identical products; *mass production has resulted in high levels of specialization*

master ['mɑːstə] *noun* (a) skilled worker, qualified to train apprentices; *a master craftsman;* **master and servant** = employer and employee; **the law of master and servant** = employment law (b) main *or* original; **master budget** = budget prepared by amalgamating budgets from various profit and cost centres (sales, production, marketing, administration, etc.) to provide a main budget for the whole company; **master contract** = industry-wide contract between a group of employers and the unions; **master copy of a file** = main copy of a computer file, kept for security purposes (c) further university degree; **Master of Business Administration (MBA)** = degree awarded to graduates who have completed a further course in business studies

◊ **mastermind** ['mɑːstəmaɪnd] *verb* to have the main ideas behind a scheme; to be in charge of a project

◊ **masterminding** ['mɑːstəmaɪndɪŋ] *noun* type of interview where the interviewer influences the interviewee who accepts his or her views; *masterminding resulted in interviews revealing little of the real discontent on the shop floor*

maternity [mə'tɜːnəti] *noun* becoming a mother; **maternity allowance (MA)** = government benefit paid to women who are not eligible for statutory maternity pay; **maternity benefit** = government aid paid to an employee when she is unable to work during late pregnancy and after having given birth to a child; **maternity leave** = permission for a woman to be away from work to have a baby; **notice of maternity absence** = statutory notice given by a worker that she is going to be absent from work to have a baby; **statutory maternity pay (SMP)** = payment made by an employer to an employee who is on maternity leave; **maternity pay period (MPP)** = period of eighteen weeks when statutory maternity pay is paid

matrix organization ['meɪtrɪks ɔːgənaɪ'zeɪʃn] *noun* flexible organization structure where authority depends on the expertise needed for a particular task and overall responsibility is shared between several persons; *the study found that matrix organizations were best suited to unstable environments requiring flexibility*

maturity [mə'tjʊərəti] *noun* **maturity curves** = rate of pay increases based on age and length of service; *maturity curves are not a feature of our pay structure since seniority is no guarantee of real contribution;* **amount payable on maturity** = amount received by the insured person when the policy becomes mature

maximization [mæksɪmaɪ'zeɪʃən] *noun* making as large as possible; *profit maximization or maximization of profit*

◊ **maximize** ['mæksɪmaɪz] *verb* to make as large as possible; *the cooperation of the workforce will be needed if we are to maximize production; he is paid on results, and so has to work flat out to maximize his earnings*

maximum ['mæksɪməm] **1** *noun* largest possible number *or* price *or* quantity; **up to a maximum of £10** = no more than £10 (NOTE: plural is **maxima**) **2** *adjective* largest possible; *maximum income tax rate or maximum rate of tax; maximum load; maximum production levels; maximum price*

MBA = MASTER OF BUSINESS ADMINISTRATION degree awarded to graduates who have completed a further course in business studies

MBO = MANAGEMENT BY OBJECTIVES

MBWA = MANAGEMENT BY WALKING AROUND

MD ['em 'di:] = MANAGING DIRECTOR *the MD is in his office; she was appointed MD of a property company*

means [mi:nz] *plural noun* **(a)** way of doing something; *bank transfer is the easiest means of payment* **(b)** money *or* resources; *the company has the means to launch the new product; such a level of investment is beyond the means of a small private company;* he has private means = he has income from dividends *or* interest *or* rent which is not part of his salary

◊ **means test** ['mi:nz 'test] **1** inquiry into how much money someone earns to see if he is eligible for state benefits **2** *verb* to find out how much money someone has in savings and assets; *all applicants will be means-tested*

measure ['meʒə] **1** *noun* **(a)** way of calculating size *or* quantity *or* value; **inspector of weights and measures** = government inspector who inspects weighing machines and goods sold in shops to see if the quantities and weights are correct; **as a measure of the manager's performance** = as a way of judging if the manager's performance is good or bad **(b)** type of action; **to take measures to prevent something happening** = to act to stop something happening; **to take crisis** *or* **emergency measures** = to act rapidly to stop a crisis developing; **disciplinary measures** = action taken to control or punish bad behaviour by employees; **an economy measure** = an action to save money; **as a precautionary measure** = to prevent something taking place; **preventive measures** = actions taken to prevent something from taking place; **safety measures** = actions to make sure that something is safe **2** *verb* **(a)** to find out the size *or* quantity of something; to be of a certain size *or* quantity; *to measure the size of a package; a package which measures 10cm by 25cm or a package measuring 10cm by 25cm;* **measured day work** = payment scheme where payment for a day's work depends on a specified level of output being achieved; **measured performance** = work performance which is measured in

quantitative terms **(b)** to measure the department's performance = to judge how well the department has done

mechanic [mɪ'kænɪk] *noun* person who works with engines *or* machines; *a car mechanic*

◊ **mechanical** [mɪ'kænɪkəl] *adjective* worked by a machine; *a mechanical pump*

◊ **mechanism** ['mekənɪzəm] *noun* action of a machine *or* system; *a mechanism to slow down inflation; the company's salary review mechanism*

◊ **mechanistic** [mekə'nɪstɪk] *adjective* very formal and structured; *it is a typical mechanistic organization with rigid rules and procedures*

mediate ['mi:dɪeɪt] *verb* to try to make the two sides in an argument come to an agreement; *to mediate between the manager and his staff; the government offered to mediate in the dispute*

◊ **mediation** [mi:dɪ'eɪʃən] *noun* attempt by a third party to make the two sides in an argument agree; *the employers refused an offer of government mediation; the dispute was ended through the mediation of union officials; mediation by some third party is the only hope for ending the dispute*

◊ **mediator** ['mi:dɪeɪtə] *noun* **official mediator** = government official who tries to make the two sides in an industrial dispute agree

medical ['medɪkəl] **1** *adjective* referring to the study or treatment of illness; **medical certificate** = paper signed by a doctor, giving a patient permission to be away from work *or* not to do certain types of work; **medical examination** = examination of a person by a doctor to find out his or her state of health; **medical inspection** = examining a place of work to ensure working conditions are not harmful to workers; **medical insurance** = insurance which pays the cost of medical treatment for illness; *the company contributes towards the employees' private medical insurance schemes;* **he resigned for medical reasons** = he resigned because he was too ill to work **2** *noun* = MEDICAL EXAMINATION *all new staff have to pass a medical*

meet [mi:t] *verb* **(a)** to come together with someone; *to meet a negotiating committee;*

to meet an agent at his hotel; the two sides met in the lawyer's office **(b)** to be satisfactory for; *to meet a customer's requirements;* **to meet the conditions of an agreement** = to fulfil the conditions; **to meet the demand for a new product** = to fill the demand for a product; **to meet the union's demands** = to agree to what the union is asking for **(c)** to pay for; *to meet someone's expenses; the company will meet your expenses; he was unable to meet his mortgage repayments*

◊ **meeting** ['miːtɪŋ] *noun* **(a)** coming together of a group of people; *a meeting between union representatives and employers;* **Annual General Meeting (AGM)** = meeting of all the shareholders when a company's financial situation is discussed with the directors; **Extraordinary General Meeting (EGM)** = special meeting of shareholders to discuss an important matter which cannot wait until the next AGM (such as a change in the company's articles of association) **(b) to hold a meeting** = to organize a meeting of a group of people; *the meeting will be held in the committee room;* **to open a meeting** = to start a meeting; **to conduct a meeting** = to be in the chair for a meeting; **to close a meeting** = to end a meeting; **to address a meeting** = to speak to a meeting; **to put a resolution to a meeting** = to ask a meeting to vote on a proposal

◊ **meetings room** ['miːtɪŋz 'ruːm] *noun* special room in which meetings are held

member ['membə] *noun* **(a)** person who belongs to a group *or* a society *or* an organization; *every employer is a member of the employers' federation; union members voted unanimously to strike; several members were expelled from the union for not paying their dues* **(b)** organization which belongs to a society; *the member companies of a trade association*

◊ **membership** ['membəʃɪp] *noun* **(a)** belonging to a group *or* organization; *membership of a trade union is not compulsory, but is strongly encouraged on the shop floor; to get into the meeting he had to show his membership card; he was expelled from the union for not paying his membership fees;* **membership of a pension scheme** = belonging to a pension scheme; **membership group** = group of which a

certain person is a member **(b)** all the members of a group; *the union membership was asked to vote for the new president*

memorandum *or* **memo** [memə'rændəm *or* 'meməʊ] *noun* short message sent from one person to another in the same organization; *the foreman sent a memorandum to the personnel department, reminding them of the need to recruit new machinists; I sent the managing director a memo about your complaint;* **memorandum (and articles) of association** = legal documents setting up a limited company and giving details of its name, aims, authorized share capital, conduct of meetings, appointment of directors, and registered office

◊ **memo pad** ['meməʊ 'pæd] *noun* pad of paper for writing short notes

mentor ['mentɔː] *noun* person who is respected and looked up to by less experienced members of staff

merit ['merɪt] *noun* quality which deserves reward; *the pay increase is based on seniority rather than merit;* **merit award** *or* **merit bonus** = extra payment to reward good work; *a merit bonus can encourage the better workers, but will discourage those who feel they cannot reach the required level;* **merit increase** = increase in pay given to someone because his or her work is good; **merit rating** = assessment of an employee on the basis of the qualities needed for a certain type of work, and assigning a grade

◊ **meritocracy** [merɪ'tɒkrəsi] *noun* society *or* organization where advancement is based on a person's natural ability rather than on his or her background

method ['meθəd] *noun* way of doing something; *a new method of making something or of doing something; what is the best method of payment? his organizing methods are out of date; their manufacturing methods or production methods are among the most modern in the country;* **method study** = study of the way in which something is done; **time and method study** = examining the way in which something is done to see if a cheaper or quicker way can be found

mid- [mɪd] *prefix* middle; **from mid-1996** = from the middle of 1996; *the factory is closed until mid-July*

◇ **mid-career crisis** ['mɪd kə'riːə 'kraɪsɪs] *noun* point in the middle of someone's career when he or she has to decide what to do in the future

◇ **mid-month** ['mɪd 'mʌnθ] *adjective* taking place in the middle of the month; *mid-month accounts*

◇ **mid-week** ['mɪd 'wiːk] *adjective* which happens in the middle of a week; *the mid-week lull in sales*

middle ['mɪdl] *adjective* in the centre *or* between two points; **middle management** = department managers in a company, who carry out the policy set by the directors and organize the work of a group of workers; **middle manager** = manager of a department in a company, answerable to a senior manager or director

migrant ['maɪgrənt] *noun* person who moves from one place *or* country to another, usually to work; **migrant worker** = worker who moves from place to place looking for work; *migrant workers were working illegally without work permits; during the summer thousands of migrant workers cross the border to work on the harvest*

◇ **migration** [maɪ'greɪʃn] *noun* moving from one place *or* country to another, usually to work

militant ['mɪlɪtənt] *adjective* & *noun* (person) who very actively supports and works for a cause; *the more militant shop stewards have urged the workers to strike* (NOTE: the opposite is **moderate**)

◇ **militancy** ['mɪlɪtənsi] *noun* being militant

military leave ['mɪlɪtri 'liːv] *noun US* unpaid leave or absence from work by workers who are in the armed forces or who have to do their military service

milk round ['mɪlk 'raʊnd] *noun* visiting of universities and colleges by employers, in order to find promising new employees

QUOTE as the annual milk round gets under way, many students are more interested in final exams than in job hunting
Personnel Management

minimal ['mɪnɪməl] *adjective* the smallest possible; *there was a minimal quantity of imperfections in the batch; the head office exercises minimal control over the branch offices*

◇ **minimize** ['mɪnɪmaɪz] *verb* (a) to make something as small as possible; *the company is attempting to minimize its labour costs by only hiring workers when they are needed; unemployment was minimized by giving more people part-time work* (b) to make something seem not very important; *do not minimize the risks involved; he tends to minimize the difficulty of the project*

◇ **minimum** ['mɪnɪməm] **1** *noun* smallest possible quantity *or* price *or* number; *to keep expenses to a minimum; to reduce the risk of a loss to a minimum* (NOTE: plural is **minima** or **minimums**) **2** *adjective* smallest possible; **minimum payment** = smallest payment necessary; **minimum pay** *or* **minimum wage** = lowest hourly wage which a company can legally pay its workers

minor ['maɪnə] *adjective* less important; **a minor official** = person in a low position in a government department

◇ **minority** [maɪ'nɒrəti] *noun* (a) number *or* quantity which is less than half of the total; *a minority of the union members opposed the motion; a small minority of workers voted to remain at work;* **to be in the minority** = section of the population from a certain racial group, which does not make up the majority of the population (b) small number of people in a larger group, who may suffer discrimination; *the government's legislation plans to protect minorities from discrimination at work*

minute ['mɪnɪt] *noun* **the minutes of the meeting** = notes of what happened at a meeting, written by the secretary; **to take the minutes** = to write notes of what happened at a meeting; **(minute of) failure to agree** = official record of a meeting which states that the two sides did not reach an agreement

misappropriate [mɪsə'prəʊprɪeɪt] *verb* to use illegally money which is not yours, but with which you have been trusted

◇ **misappropriation** [mɪsəprəʊprɪ'eɪʃən] *noun* illegal use of money by someone who is not the owner but who has been trusted to look after it

miscarriage of justice [mɪs'kærɪdʒ əv 'dʒʌstɪs] *noun* decision wrongly *or* unjustly reached by a court *or* decision which goes against the rights of a party in a case, in such a way that the decision may be reversed on appeal

misconduct [mɪs'kɒndʌkt] *noun* illegal action by an employee, action which can harm someone, such as disobeying instructions; **gross misconduct** = very bad behaviour by a worker, which is a fair reason for dismissal (such as drunkenness, theft, etc.); *he was dismissed for gross misconduct;* **professional misconduct** = behaviour by a member of a profession (such as a lawyer *or* accountant *or* doctor) which the body regulating that profession considers to be wrong; **wilful misconduct** = doing something which harms someone while knowing it is wrong

misdemeanour [mɪsdə'miːnə] *noun* minor crime; *to commit a misdemeanour*

mismanage [mɪs'mænɪdʒ] *verb* to manage badly

◊ **mismanagement** [mɪs'mænɪdʒmənt] *noun* bad management; *the company failed because of the chairman's mismanagement*

misrepresentation [mɪsreprɪzen'teɪʃən] *noun* wrongly reporting facts; **fraudulent misrepresentation** = giving someone wrong information in order to cheat him

mistake [mɪ'steɪk] *noun* wrong action *or* wrong decision; **to make a mistake** = to do something wrong; *the shop made a mistake and sent the wrong items; there was a mistake in the address; she made a mistake in addressing the letter;* **spelling mistake** = mistake in spelling a word; **typing mistake** = mistake made when typing; **by mistake** = in error *or* wrongly; *they sent the wrong items by mistake; she put my letter into an envelope for the chairman by mistake*

misunderstanding [mɪsʌndə'stændɪŋ] *noun* lack of agreement *or* mistake; *there was a misunderstanding over the pay deal*

misuse 1 [mɪs'juːs] *noun* wrong use; *misuse of funds or of assets;* **misuse of authority** = using one's authority in a wrong way **2** [mɪs'juːz] *verb* **to misuse funds** = to use funds in a wrong way (especially funds which do not belong to you)

mobile ['məʊbaɪl] *adjective* which can move about; **mobile workforce** = workers who move from place to place to get work

◊ **mobility** [mə'bɪləti] *noun* being able to move from one place to another; **labour mobility** *or* **mobility of labour** = situation in which workers agree to move from one place to another to get work, or change skills within the same organization; *acute unemployment dramatically increased mobility of labour;* **blocked mobility** = limited potential for promotion that is not dependent on educational background of the employee; **geographical mobility** = ability of workers to move from place to place to find work; **occupational mobility** = extent to which workers can move from one type of occupation to another; **professional mobility** *or* **skills mobility** = ability of workers to move from one type of job to another within the same organization; **mobility allowance** = addition to normal salary paid to a worker who is willing to travel to different places of work

model ['mɒdl] **1** *noun* something which can be copied; *the Swedish model of industrial relations;* **economic model** = computerized plan of a country's economic system, used for forecasting economic trends **2** *adjective* which is a perfect example to be copied; *a model agreement*

moderate ['mɒdərət] **1** *adjective* **(a)** not too large; *the trade union made a moderate claim; the government proposed a moderate increase in the tax rate* **(b)** not holding very extreme views; *a moderate trade union leader* (NOTE: the opposite is **militant**) **2** *verb* to make less strong *or* less large; *the union was forced to moderate its claim*

modify ['mɒdɪfaɪ] *verb* to change *or* to make something fit a different use; *the management modified its proposals; this is the new modified union agreement*

◊ **modification** [mɒdɪfɪ'keɪʃən] *noun* change; *to make or to carry out modifications to the plan; the union negotiators pressed for modifications to the contract*

momentum [mə'mentəm] *noun* movement forwards; **to gain** *or* **gather momentum** = to move faster; *the strike is gaining momentum* = more workers are joining the strike; **to lose momentum** = to move more slowly

Monday morning feeling ['mʌndeɪ 'mɔːnɪŋ 'fiːlɪŋ] *noun* feeling slightly ill or miserable on going to work on Monday morning

monitor ['mɒnɪtə] *verb* to check *or* to examine how something is working; *he is monitoring the progress of union negotiations; how do you monitor the performance of the workforce?*

month [mʌnθ] *noun* one of twelve periods which make a year; *the company pays him £100 a month; he earns £2,000 a month; bills due at the end of the current month;* **calendar month** = whole month as on a calendar; **paid by the month** = paid once each month; **to give a customer two months' credit** = to allow a customer to pay not immediately, but after two months

◊ **month end** [mʌnθ 'end] *noun* the end of a calendar month, when accounts have to be drawn up; *month-end accounts*

◊ **monthly** ['mʌnθli] **1** *adjective* happening every month *or* which is received every month; *monthly statement; monthly payments; he is paying for his car by monthly instalments; my monthly salary cheque is late;* **monthly ticket** = ticket for travel which is good for one month **2** *adverb* every month; *to pay monthly; the account is credited monthly*

moonlight ['muːnlaɪt] *verb (informal)* to do a second job for cash (often in the evening) as well as a regular job

◊ **moonlighter** ['muːnlaɪtə] *noun* person who moonlights

◊ **moonlighting** ['muːnlaɪtɪŋ] *noun* doing a second job; *he makes thousands a year from moonlighting*

morale [mɒ'rɑːl] *noun* feeling of confidence *or* satisfaction; *morale has been high since the new targets have been met; workers' morale is low due to the threat of unemployment;* **to boost morale** = to increase the workers' feelings of confidence

motion ['məʊʃən] *noun* **(a)** moving about; **motion study** = study of the movements of workers performing tasks in order to improve efficiency; **time and motion study** = study in an office *or* factory of the time taken to do certain jobs and the movements workers have to make to do them, in order

to improve efficiency; *motion studies will be carried out to see if human and material resources can be more effectively used; as a result of the motion study, several workers were made redundant* **(b)** proposal which will be put to a meeting to be voted on; *to propose or to move a motion; the meeting voted on the motion; to speak against or for a motion; the motion was carried or was defeated by 220 votes to 196;* **to table a motion** = to put forward a proposal for discussion by putting details of it on the table at a meeting

motivate ['məʊtɪveɪt] *verb* to give someone a good reason *or* incentive to do something; *the company tried to motivate workers with the promise of bonus payments;* **highly motivated sales staff** = sales staff who are very eager to sell

◊ **motivation** [məʊtɪ'veɪʃən] *noun* encouragement *or* good reason *or* incentive to do something; *the payment by results scheme increased motivation and raised productivity considerably;* **the sales staff lack motivation** = the sales staff are not motivated enough (NOTE: no plural)

◊ **motivational** [məʊtɪ'veɪʃənəl] *adjective* referring to motivation; **motivational factors** = aspects of a job or an organization which encourage employees to work hard; *a bonus system based on production targets was a strong motivational factor; a high commission should be a strong motivational factor for the salesmen*

movement ['muːvmənt] *noun* **(a)** changing position; **free movement of labour within the EU** = principle that workers from any country of the EU can move to another country to obtain work **(b)** group of people working towards the same aim; *the labour movement; the trade union movement*

MPP = MATERNITY PAY PERIOD

multiple ['mʌltɪpl] *adjective* many; **multiple chain promotion plan** = system of linking each position in an organization to several others from which promotion may be made, or to which workers may be promoted; **multiple-employer bargaining** = bargaining between the employers' associations and the unions; **multiple hurdles selection** = method of selecting candidates for a job by requiring that they should pass a series of tests; *the multiple* *hurdle system very efficiently eliminates a large number of candidates;* **multiple management** = management system where committees of middle managers advise top management on company policy

multiskilling [mʌltɪˈskɪlɪŋ] *noun* working system, where workers are trained to work in various types of job, and none are kept on the same type of work for very long, so as to allow flexibility in the deployment of the workforce

mutuality [mjuːtʃʊˈælɪti] *noun* right of a trade union to bargain on behalf of its members and so take a part in the running of the company; **mutuality agreement** = agreement between management and the union, by which the management agrees not to make changes to the conditions of work without consulting the union

Nn

narrative ['nærətɪv] *noun* description of something as a story; **narrative appraisal** = type of performance appraisal where the employee's performance is described with illustrations of specific points about it

nation ['neɪʃən] *noun* country and the people living in it

◊ **national** ['næʃənl] **1** *adjective* referring to a particular country; **national agreement** = agreement between employers and a union at national level (i.e., covering the whole country); **national executive (committee)** = main committee running a trade union; *GB* **National Insurance** = state insurance which pays for medical care, hospitals, unemployment benefits, etc.; **National Insurance contributions (NIC)** = money paid into the National Insurance scheme by the employer and the worker; **national union** = central union organization which coordinates local branches; **National Vocational Qualifications (NVQs)** = system of examinations and qualifications in vocational subjects for people who are in employment but who want to acquire extra skills related to their current job (run alongside traditional academic studies and of equal value to the traditional qualifications) **2** *noun* person who is a citizen of a state; **foreign nationals** = people who are citizens of other countries, not this one; **EU nationals** = people who are citizens of countries which are members of the EU

◊ **nationality** [næʃə'næləti] *noun* **he is of British nationality** = he is a British citizen

◊ **nationwide** [neɪʃən'waɪd] *adjective* all over a country; *the union called for a nationwide strike*

natural ['nætʃrəl] *adjective* normal; *it was natural for the workers to feel aggrieved when the management decided to change production methods without consultation;* **natural wastage** = losing workers because they resign or retire, not through redundancy or dismissals; *the company is hoping to avoid redundancies and reduce its staff by natural wastage*

NAV = NET ASSET VALUE

NCVQ = NATIONAL COUNCIL FOR VOCATIONAL QUALIFICATIONS a government body set up to validate the system of national qualifications in vocational subjects

needs [niːdz] *noun* what is necessary; **needs assessment** *or* **assessment of needs** = analysis of an organization's manpower requirements which can form the basis of training plans; *needs assessment pointed to a level of manpower requirements which the company could not finance*

negative ['negətɪv] *noun* meaning 'No'; *his reply was in the negative;* **false negative** = exclusion of a suitable candidate by a screening process (NOTE: the opposite is **positive**)

neglect [nɪ'glekt] **1** *noun* not doing a duty; **wilful neglect** = intentionally not doing something which it is your duty to do (NOTE: no plural) **2** *verb* **to neglect to do something** = to forget *or* omit to do something which has to be done; *he neglected to return his income tax form*

◊ **neglected** [nɪ'glektɪd] *adjective* not well looked after; **neglected business** = company which has not been actively run by its owners and could therefore do better

negligence ['neglɪdʒəns] *noun* (i) lack of proper care *or* not doing a duty (with the result that a person *or* property is harmed); (ii) not doing a job properly when one is capable of doing it; *the foreman was sacked for negligence US* **contributory negligence** = negligence partly caused by the plaintiff and partly by the defendant, resulting in harm done to the plaintiff; **criminal negligence** = acting recklessly with the result that harm is done to other people;

gross negligence = act showing very serious neglect of duty towards other people; **professional negligence** = failing to carry out one's duties properly (on the part of a professional person) (NOTE: no plural)

◊ **negligent** ['neglɪdʒnt] *adjective* showing negligence *or* not taking proper care

◊ **negligently** ['neglɪdʒntli] *adverb* in a way which shows negligence

◊ **negligible** ['neglɪdʒəbl] *adjective* very small *or* not worth bothering about

negotiable [nɪ'gəʊʃəbl] *adjective* which can be discussed so that an agreement is reached; *the employer's offer was not negotiable, so when it was turned down a strike seemed inevitable; all part of the offers are negotiable, with the exception of the new manning levels; the salary for the job is negotiable*

◊ **negotiate** [nɪ'gəʊʃɪeɪt] *verb* to negotiate with someone = to discuss a problem formally with someone, so as to reach an agreement; *the management refused to negotiate with the union;* to negotiate terms and conditions *or* to negotiate a contract = to discuss and agree the terms of a contract; **negotiating committee** = group of representatives of management or unions who negotiate a wage settlement; to go back to the negotiating table = to start negotiations again after a break; *the two sides discussed the proposals, and, a week later, the management negotiators returned to the negotiating table with improved proposals;* negotiating team = group which negotiates for one party in negotiations; *the union negotiating team asked for further time to consider the management's proposals*

◊ **negotiation** [nɪgəʊʃɪ'eɪʃən] *noun* discussion of terms and conditions to reach an agreement; **contract under negotiation** = contract which is being discussed; **a matter for negotiation** = something which must be discussed before a decision is reached; **to enter into negotiations** *or* **to start negotiations** = to start discussing a problem; **to resume negotiations** = to start discussing a problem again, after talks have stopped for a time; **to break off negotiations** = to refuse to go on discussing a problem; **to conduct negotiations** = to negotiate; **a breakdown in negotiations** = stopping talking because no agreement has been reached, after negotiations have been in

progress for some time; **a resumption of negotiations** = starting negotiations again, after talks have stopped for a time; **negotiations broke down after six hours** = discussions stopped because no agreement was possible; **pay negotiations** *or* **wage negotiations** = discussions between management and workers about pay

◊ **negotiator** [nɪ'gəʊʃɪeɪtə] *noun* person who discusses with the aim of reaching an agreement; **an experienced union negotiator** = member of a union who has a lot of experience of discussing terms of employment with management

QUOTE initial salary is negotiable around $45,000 per annum
Australian Financial Review

QUOTE after three days of tough negotiations, the company reached agreement with its 1,200 unionized workers
Toronto Star

nepotism ['nepətɪzm] *noun* giving preferential treatment to someone who is a relative *or* friend (especially giving a job to a member of the family who is less well qualified than other candidates); *the staff talked about nepotism when the training officer selected his nephew for management training; so as not to be accused of nepotism, the sales manager refused to take his son into the department as a salesman*

net [net] **1** *adjective* pay *or* price, etc. after all deductions have been made; **net asset value (NAV)** *or* **net worth** = total value of a company after deducting the money owed by it (it is the value of shareholders' capital plus reserves and any money retained from profits); **net income** *or* **net salary** = person's income which is left after taking away tax and other deductions; *a net salary is considerably less than a gross salary, due to the tax rate;* **net profit** = result where income from sales is more than all expenditure; **net profit before tax** = profit of a company after expenses have been deducted but before tax has been paid **2** *adverb* after deductions have been made; *his salary is paid net* **3** *verb* to earn as a net salary *or* profit; *he netted over £30,000 last year* (NOTE: opposite is **gross)**

network ['netwɜːk] **1** *noun* system which links different points together; **network**

analysis = way of planning and controlling large projects (such as PERT or Critical Path Analysis); **a network of distributors** *or* **a distribution network** = series of points *or* warehouses from which goods are sent all over a country; **computer network** = computer system where several micros are linked so that they all draw on the same database **2** *verb* to link together in a network

◊ **networking** ['netwɜːkɪŋ] *noun* **(a)** working method where employees work at home on computer terminals, and send the finished material back to the central office by modem **(b)** keeping in contact with former colleagues, school friends, etc., so that all the members of the group can help each other in their careers

neutrality laws [njuˈtrælɪti lɔːz] *noun US* laws relating to discrimination which must be observed by organizations

new [njuː] *adjective* recent *or* not old; **under new management** = with a new owner

◊ **news** [njuːz] *noun* information about things which have happened; *business news; financial news; financial markets were shocked by the news of the devaluation*

◊ **newsletter** ['njuːzletə] *noun* printed sheet *or* pamphlet *or* small newspaper sent to members of an organization giving them news of the organization; **company newsletter** = printed sheet *or* small newspaper giving news about a company

◊ **newssheet** ['njuːzʃiːt] *noun* leaflet distributed by an organization, giving the latest news about itself

next of kin ['nekst əv 'kɪn] *noun* nearest member of the family (to be contacted if a worker dies or is involved in an accident, etc.)

NI = NATIONAL INSURANCE

NIC = NATIONAL INSURANCE CONTRIBUTIONS

night [naɪt] *noun* period of time from evening to morning; **night shift** = shift which works at night; *there are thirty men on the night shift; he works nights or he works the night shift; night work is paid at time and a half*

No = NUMBER

no-attention job [ˈnəʊəˈtenʃn ˈdʒɒb] *noun* job that can be done with minimal concentration; *no-attention jobs create stress because of the boredom they produce*

no-claims bonus ['nəʊkleɪmz 'bəʊnəs] *noun* reduction of premiums on an insurance policy because no claims have been made

nominal ['nɒmɪnl] *adjective* **(a)** very small (payment); *the employment agency makes a nominal charge for its services* **(b)** **nominal group technique** = group method of drawing out ideas from people on a specific topic; *nominal group methods are used when representatives from all the sales and production departments are considering new product ideas*

nominate ['nɒmɪneɪt] *verb* to suggest someone *or* to name someone for a job; *the supervisor will probably nominate his most efficient worker for promotion;* **to nominate someone to a post** = to appoint someone to a post without an election

◊ **nomination** [nɒmɪˈneɪʃən] *noun* act of nominating someone for a job; *he is celebrating his nomination as marketing director*

◊ **nominee** [nɒmɪˈniː] *noun* person who is nominated for a job (NOTE: a person may be nominated to a position without any other candidates being considered, or without the post being advertised; the word implies a personal choice, rather than selection by a committee. In other cases, it is better to use the words **appoint, appointment, appointee**)

non- [nɒn] *prefix* not

◊ **non-analytical** ['nɒn ænəˈlɪtɪkl] *adjective* **non-analytical job evaluation** = way of evaluating a job, by giving each job a rank within the organization (as opposed to the analytical system, where each job is evaluated according to a points system)

◊ **non-conformance** ['nɒn kənˈfɔːməns] *noun* act of not conforming; *he was criticized for non-conformance with the regulations*

◊ **non-contributory** [nɒn kənˈtrɪbjutəi] *adjective* **non-contributory pension plan** *or* **scheme** = pension scheme where company, not the employee, pays all contributions; *the company pension scheme is non-contributory*

◊ **non-directed interview** or **non-directive interview** ['nɒn daɪ'rektɪd or 'nɒn daɪ'rektɪv] noun interview which is not conducted round certain fixed questions, and which therefore encourages open discussion; *non-directed interviews give candidates a good chance to show their creative potential;* **non-directive counselling** = giving professional advice to others on personal matters, without following a fixed form, but rather through open discussion of problems

◊ **non-executive director** ['nɒnɪgzekjʊtɪv daɪ'rektə] noun director who attends board meetings and gives advice, but does not work full-time for the company

◊ **non-exempt employee** ['nɒn ɪg'zempt] adjective person whose wages are subject to minimum wage legislation

◊ **non-resident** ['nɒn 'rezɪdənt] noun person who is not considered a resident of a country for tax purposes; *he has a non-resident bank account*

◊ **non-taxable** ['nɒn 'tæksəbl] adjective which is not subject to tax; *non-taxable income*

◊ **non-union** ['nɒn 'juːnjən] adjective **company using non-union labour** = company employing workers who do not belong to trade unions

◊ **non-verbal communication** ['nɒn 'vɜːbəl kəmjʊnɪ'keɪʃn] noun communicating a message, using facial expressions or body language, but without speaking; *in negotiations, interpreting non-verbal communication is just as important as listening to what people say*

norm [nɔːm] noun the usual quantity or the usual rate; *the output from this factory is well above the norm for the industry or well above the industry norm*

◊ **normal** ['nɔːməl] adjective usual or which happens regularly; *now that the strike is over we hope to resume normal service as soon as possible;* **normal working** = working in the usual way; *normal working will be resumed as soon as the men return to work on Monday*

◊ **normally** ['nɔːməli] adverb in the usual way; *the production line is working normally again after the stoppage*

◊ **normative** ['nɔːməntɪv] adjective believing that everything should be agreed in writing and should then be binding on all parties

◊ **norms** [nɔːmz] noun values of an organization or of society; *the induction period will familiarize workers with the norms of the organization*

no-smoking ['nəʊ 'sməʊkɪŋ] adjective **no-smoking office** = office where smoking is not allowed

no-strike agreement or **no-strike clause** ['nəʊ 'straɪk] noun agreement or clause where the workers promise never to strike

notary public ['nəʊtəri 'pʌblɪk] noun lawyer who has the authority to witness documents and spoken statements, making them official (NOTE: plural is **notaries public**)

notice ['nəʊtɪs] noun **(a)** piece of written information; *the company secretary pinned up a notice about the pension scheme* **(b)** official warning that a contract is going to end or that terms are going to be changed; *the union has given notice that they will call a strike next week unless their demands are met;* **until further notice** = until different instructions are given; *you must pay £200 on the 30th of each month until further notice;* **at short notice** = with very little warning; **strike notice** = warning that a strike will take place; **without notice** = with no warning; **without prior notice** = with no advance warning; **to give advance notice of** = to inform someone officially that something will happen several weeks in the future; **notice of appearance** = lodging by the employer of a document to confirm his intention to defend an application by an employee to an industrial tribunal **(c)** (i) written announcement that a worker is leaving his job on a certain date; (ii) time between the announcement that a worker is leaving and the date of his leaving; **notice period** or **period of notice** = time stated in the contract of employment which the worker or company has to allow between resigning or being fired and the worker actually leaving his job (an employee has to give at least one week's notice and an employer has to give between one week and twelve weeks' notice, depending on the employee's length of service); *we require three months' notice; he gave six months' notice; we gave* him three months' wages in lieu of notice; **she gave in** or **handed in her notice** = she resigned; **he is working out his notice** = he is working during the time between resigning and actually leaving the company

◊ **noticeboard** ['nəʊtɪsbɔːd] noun board fixed to a wall where notices can be put up; did you see the new list of prices on the noticeboard?

notify ['nəʊtɪfaɪ] verb **to notify someone of something** = to tell someone something formally; the management were notified of the union's decision

◊ **notification** [nəʊtɪfɪ'keɪʃən] noun informing someone of something; all members of staff have received notification of the change in the hours of work

nuisance ['njuːsəns] noun something which causes harm or inconvenience to someone or to property

nursery ['nɜːsəri] noun special room or building where babies and small children can be looked after (not necessarily on the company's premises); the company offers nursery provision to its staff compare CRECHE

NVQ = NATIONAL VOCATIONAL QUALIFICATION

Oo

O & M = ORGANIZATION AND METHODS

OAP [əʊeɪ'piː] = OLD AGE PENSIONER

object [əb'dʒekt] *verb* to refuse to do something *or* to say that you do not accept something; *the secretaries object to having to make coffee for their bosses; the union negotiators object to a clause in the contract* (NOTE: you object **to** something)

◊ **objection** [əb'dʒekʃən] *noun* **to raise an objection to something** = to object to something; *the union delegates raised an objection to the wording of the agreement*

objective [əb'dʒektɪv] **1** *noun* aim *or* target; *our recruitment objectives are to have well-qualified and well-placed staff;* **to achieve one's objectives** = to do what you set out to do; *the company has achieved almost all its objectives;* **long-term objective** *or* **short-term objective** = aim which you hope to achieve within a few years or a few months; *what are the long-term objectives of the pay scheme?;* **objective setting** = planning targets (e.g. for negotiations); *see also* MANAGEMENT BY OBJECTIVES **2** *adjective* considered from a general point of view not from that of the person involved; *you must be objective in assessing the performance of the staff; to carry out an objective survey of the department's performance;* **objective test** = test where each question has only one possible answer (NOTE: opposite is **subjective)**

obligation [ɒblɪ'geɪʃən] *noun* duty to do something; **to be under an obligation to do something** = to feel it is your duty to do something; *there is no obligation to help out in another department; we are under no obligation to do what the sales manager wants*

◊ **obligatory** [ɒ'blɪgətəri] *adjective* necessary according to the law or rules; *each member of the sales staff has to pass an obligatory medical examination*

observe [ɒb'zɜːv] *verb* **(a)** to obey (a rule *or* a law); *failure to observe the correct procedure; all members of the association should observe the code of practice* **(b)** to watch *or* to notice what is happening; *officials have been instructed to observe the conduct of the ballot for union president*

◊ **observance** [ɒb'zɜːvəns] *noun* doing what is required by a law; *the company's observance of the law concerning discrimination*

◊ **observation** [ɒbzə'veɪʃn] *noun* noticing what is happening

◊ **observational method** [ɒbzə'veɪʃnl 'meθəd] *noun* way of evaluating the performance of workers, by watching them work and observing their conduct with others

◊ **observer** [ɒb'zɜːvə] *noun* person who observes; *two official observers attended the election meeting*

obsolescence [ɒbsə'lesəns] *noun* situation where a worker no longer has the knowledge or skill to perform efficiently *or* where a machine is out-of-date; **built-in obsolescence** *or* **planned obsolescence** = situation where the manufacturer designs his products to become out of date so that the customers can be pressed to replace them with new models; **managerial obsolescence** = situation where managers cannot keep up with the latest technology or are not as well-qualified as more junior staff

◊ **obsolescent** [ɒbsə'lesənt] *adjective* becoming out of date

◊ **obsolete** ['ɒbsəliːt] *adjective* no longer used; *when the office was equipped with word-processors the typewriters became obsolete*

obstacle ['ɒbstəkl] *noun* thing which prevents you from doing something; *we still have to overcome several important obstacles in our negotiations with the union*

obstruct [ɒb'strʌkt] *verb* to get in the way *or* to stop something progressing; *the intransigence of the unions is obstructing the company's modernization plans*

occupation [ɒkju'peɪʃən] *noun* **(a)** job *or* work; *what is her occupation? his main occupation is house building; it is not a well-paid occupation;* **occupations** = types of work; *people in professional occupations have higher salaries than manual workers* **(b)** living *or* staying in a place; *the occupation of the factory by the strikers*

◊ **occupational** [ɒkju'peɪʃənl] *adjective* referring to a job; **occupational accident** = accident which takes place at work; *the number of occupational accidents has decreased owing to better preventive measures;* **occupational association** = organization which represents people doing a certain type of work and defends their interests; **occupational deafness** = deafness caused by noise at work (as in someone using a pneumatic drill); **occupational disease** = disease which affects people in certain jobs; *lung illnesses among miners are some of the worst forms of occupational disease;* **occupational family** = groups of jobs having the same personnel requirements; *for jobs in certain occupational families, finding qualified staff is going to be difficult;* **occupational group** = category of job *or* profession; **occupational hazards** = dangers which apply to certain jobs; *heart attacks are one of the occupational hazards of managers;* **occupational health** *or* **occupational hygiene** = branch of medicine dealing with the health of people at work; **occupational injury** = injury which is caused by a type of work; **occupational mobility** = extent to which workers can move from one type of occupation to another; *occupational mobility is increasing because of rising unemployment in some areas;* **occupational pension** = pension received by a worker after retirement, paid from a pension scheme set up by the past employer; **Occupational Pensions Board (OPB)** = government body set up to oversee and validate occupational pension schemes; **occupational pension scheme** = pension scheme where the worker gets a pension from the company he has worked for; **occupational psychology** = study of the behaviour of people at work; **occupational sick pay (OSP)** = extra payments made by an employer to a member of staff who is sick, above the statutory sick pay; **occupational therapy** = light work or hobbies used as a means of treatment, especially for handicapped or mentally ill patients and during the recovery period after an illness or operation

QUOTE occupational classifications need to be kept up to date if planners are to remain fully informed about the changing job market
Employment Gazette

QUOTE the area of competence of an occupation is defined as the field of competence required to conduct the associated tasks
Employment Gazette

occupy ['ɒkjupaɪ] *verb* **(a)** to live *or* work in a property (such as an office); *the office occupied by the personnel manager; the company occupies three floors of an office block* **(b) to occupy a post** = to be employed in a job **(c)** to take up a certain amount of time; *interviewing new staff occupied most of the day* **(d)** to stay in a property as a protest; *the strikers occupied the factory*

QUOTE employment in professional occupations increased by 40 per cent between 1974 and 1983, while the share of white-collar occupations in total employment rose from 44 per cent to 49 per cent
Sydney Morning Herald

odd [ɒd] *adjective* **odd numbers** = numbers (like 17 or 33) which cannot be divided by two; *odd-numbered buildings or buildings with odd numbers are on the south side of the street;* **odd jobs** = small pieces of work, not connected to each other, and paid for individually; *we have a number of odd jobs needing doing, but nothing adding up to full-time employment;* **to do odd jobs** = to do various pieces of work

◊ **odd-job-man** [ɒd'dʒɒbmæn] *noun* person who does various pieces of work

off [ɒf] **1** *adverb* not working *or* not in operation; *the agreement is off; they called the strike off* **2** *preposition* **(a)** away from work; *to take time off work; to take three days off; we give the staff four days off at Christmas; it is the secretary's day off tomorrow* **(b)** *US* **off the books** = not declared to the tax authorities; *some of the staff are paid off the books*

offence _or US_ **offense** [ə'fens] _noun_ crime _or_ act which is against the law; **traffic offences** = offences committed by drivers of vehicles; **to be charged with an offence** = to be accused formally of having committed a crime; _the manager was charged with three serious offences;_ **to commit an offence** = to carry out a crime

◊ **offender** [ə'fendə] _noun_ person who breaks a law _or_ regulation; _when we investigated who was making private calls during the working hours, the worst offender was the personnel manager_

offer ['ɒfə] **1** _noun_ statement that a company is willing to do something; **conditional offer** = job offer which depends on certain conditions being met (such as passing a medical); **unconditional offer** = job offer with no conditions _or_ provisions attached; **offer of employment** _or_ **job offer** _or_ **offer of a job** = letter from an employer, offering a job; **he received six offers of jobs** _or_ **six job offers** = six companies told him he could have a job with them; **to make someone an offer** = to propose something to someone; _the management made the union an improved offer;_ **to make someone an offer he can't refuse** = to make an offer to someone which is so attractive that he cannot turn it down; **to accept an offer** _or_ **to take up an offer** = to say 'yes' _or_ to agree to an offer; **to turn down an offer** = to refuse something which has been offered **2** _verb_ **to offer someone a job** = to tell someone that he can have a job in your company; _he was offered a job as sales manager with Smith Ltd_

office ['ɒfɪs] _noun_ **(a)** building _or_ set of rooms where a company works _or_ where business is done; **branch office** = less important office, usually in a different town or country from the main office; **head office** _or_ **main office** = office building where the board of directors works and meets; _GB_ **registered office** = office address of a company which is officially registered with the Companies' Registrar **(b)** **office block** _or_ **a block of offices** = building which contains only offices; **office boy** = young man who works in an office, usually taking messages from one department to another; _he worked his way up from office boy to general manager in ten years;_ **office hours** = time when an office is open; _open during normal office hours; do not telephone during office hours; the manager can be reached at home_

out of office hours; **office junior** = young man or woman who does all types of work in an office; _we are looking for extra office space;_ **office staff** = people who work in offices; **office worker** = person who works in an office **(c)** room where someone works and does business; _come into my office; the personnel manager's office is on the third floor_ **(d)** **employment office** = office which finds jobs for people; **general office** = main administrative office in a company **(e)** post _or_ position; _he holds or performs the office of treasurer;_ **to take office** = to start to work in a certain position; **compensation for loss of office** = payment to a director who is asked to leave a company before his contract ends

◊ **office-bearer** ['ɒfɪs 'beərə] _noun_ person who holds an office, especially person who is a member of a union council and holds the office of secretary or treasurer, etc.

officer ['ɒfɪsə] _noun_ **(a)** person who has an official position; **fire safety officer** = person responsible for fire safety in a building; **information officer** = person who gives information about a company _or_ about a government department to the public; **personnel officer** = head of the personnel department _or_ person who organizes and co-ordinates the recruitment, welfare and training of staff; **training officer** = person who deals with the training of staff; **the company officers** _or_ **the officers of a company** = the main executives _or_ directors of a company; _the information officer provided an outline history of the organization; the company officers are working on the development plan for the next ten years_ **(b)** official (usually unpaid) of a club _or_ society, etc.; _the election of officers of an association_

official [ə'fɪʃəl] **1** _adjective_ **(a)** from a government department or organization; _he left official documents in his car; she received an official letter of explanation;_ **speaking in an official capacity** = speaking officially; **to go through official channels** = to deal with officials, especially when making a request **(b)** formal _or_ done or approved by a person in authority; _this is the union's official policy; the complaint was written on official company notepaper;_ **official dispute** = industrial action approved by a trade union; **official strike** = strike which has been approved and is directed by a trade union; **the strike was made official** = the local strike was approved by the trade union's main office **2**

noun person who holds public office *or* who is working in a government department; *airport officials inspected the shipment; government officials stopped the import licence;* **high official** *or* **high-ranking official** = important person in a government department; **minor official** = person in a low position in a government department; *some minor official tried to stop my request for building permission;* **top official** = very important person in a government department; **union officials** = paid organizers in a trade union

◊ **officialese** [əfɪʃə'liːz] *noun* language used in government documents which can be difficult to understand

◊ **officially** [ə'fɪʃəli] *adverb* according to what is said in public; *officially he knows nothing about the problem, but unofficially he has given us a lot of advice about it*

off-the-job training ['ɒfðədʒɒb 'treɪnɪŋ] *noun* training given to workers away from their place of work (such as at a college or school); *after a period of off-the-job training he is in line for promotion*

old [əʊld] *adjective* having existed for a long time; *the company is 125 years old next year; we have decided to get rid of our old computer system and install a new one*

◊ **old age** ['əʊld 'eɪdʒ] *noun* period when a person is old; **old age pension** = government pension given to a person who is past retirement age; **old age pensioner (OAP)** = person who receives an old age pension

◊ **old boy network** ['əʊld 'bɔɪ 'netwɜːk] *noun* using long-standing key contacts to appoint people to jobs *or* to get a job *or* to do business; *see also* NETWORKING

◊ **old-fashioned** ['əʊld 'fæʃənd] *adjective* out of date *or* not modern; *he still uses an old-fashioned typewriter*

ombudsman ['ɒmbʊdzmən] *noun* **(a)** official who investigates complaints by the public against government departments; *the ombudsman is investigating reports of bureaucratic incompetence* **(b)** management employee who is given the freedom to move around the workplace to locate and remedy unfair practices (NOTE: plural is **ombudsmen)**

COMMENT: there are in fact several ombudsmen: the main one is the

Parliamentary Commissioner, who is a civil servant. The Banking Ombudsman and the Insurance Ombudsman are independent officials who investigate complaints by the public against banks or insurance companies

omnibus agreement ['ɒmnɪbəs ə'griːmənt] *noun* agreement which covers many different items; **omnibus test** = test which covers various subjects

on [ɒn] *preposition* **(a)** being a member of a group; *to sit on a committee; she is on the boards of two companies; we have 250 people on the payroll; she is on our full-time staff* **(b)** in a certain way; *he is still on probation; she is employed on very generous terms* **(c)** at a time; *we work 7 hours a day on weekdays; the shop is closed on Wednesday afternoons; the whole staff has the day off on May 24th* **(d)** doing something; *the director is on holiday; she is in the States on business; the switchboard operator is on duty from 6 to 9*

◊ **on call** ['ɒn 'kɔːl] *adverb* ready to be called to work at any time; *we must have an engineer on call twenty-four hours a day;* **on-call pay** = pay for being on call outside normal working hours; *the on-call pay was not enough to compensate for being on call all night;* **on-call time** = time outside normal working hours when an employee is standing by, ready for work

◊ **on-going** ['ɒn 'gəʊɪŋ] *adjective* which is continuing; *on-going discussions*

◊ **on line** *or* **online** [ɒn'laɪn] *adverb* linked directly to a mainframe computer; *the sales office is on line to the warehouse; we get our data on line from the stock control department*

on-the-job training ['ɒnðədʒɒb 'treɪnɪŋ] *noun* training given to workers at their place of work; *on-the-job training provides trainees with practical instruction that can be immediately put into practice*

one-man ['wʌn 'mæn] *adjective* **one-man business** *or* **firm** *or* **company** *or* **operation** = business run by one person alone with no staff or partners

◊ **one-off** ['wʌn 'ɒf] *adjective* done or made only once; *one-off payment*

◊ **one-sided** ['wʌn 'saɪdɪd] *adjective* which favours one side and not the other in a negotiation; *the shop floor workers* *accused the union negotiators of having given in to a one-sided agreement*

onerous ['ɒnərəs] *adjective* heavy *or* needing a lot of effort or money; *the duties of the senior managers are particularly onerous during the present crisis*

o.n.o. = OR NEAR OFFER

OPB = OCCUPATIONAL PENSIONS BOARD

open ['əupən] **1** *adjective* **(a)** at work *or* not closed; *the store is open on Sunday mornings; our offices are open from 9 to 6; they are open for business every day of the week* **(b)** ready to accept something; **the job is open to all applicants** = anyone can apply for the job; **we will keep the job open for you until you have passed your driving test** = we will not give the job to anyone else, and will wait until you have passed your test **(c) open ad** = advertisement for a job where the applicant can apply to the employer directly, without having to go through a third party, such as an agency; *open ads can be used for recruitment when additional staff are required urgently;* **open communication** = freedom of people to communicate what they like to whoever they like within an organization; *the policy of open communication is an aid to decision-making as it creates a wider source of expertise to be tapped;* **open day** = day when an organization is open to interested candidates who may wish to inspect the organization and discuss career possibilities; *he went to the charity's open day to see what training they demanded for fund-raising work; at the open day last week, preliminary interviews were held with candidates to see if their backgrounds were right for the company;* **open-door system** = system in which supervisors are always available at work to talk to employees; **open learning** = system of flexible training courses which a trainee can start at any time, and which do not require a teacher; *open learning can be fitted round the employee's work schedule;* **open shop** = workplace where employees can be employed whether they are members of a union or not; **open system** = flexible type of organization, which allows employees freedom to work in their own way; *an open system can allow employees to choose their own working hours;* **open union** = union which accepts members from a wide range of jobs **2** *verb* **(a)** to start a new business; *she has opened a shop in the High Street; we have opened an office in London* **(b)** to start work *or* to be at work; *the office opens at 9 a.m.; we open for business on Sundays* **(c)** to begin; **to open negotiations** = to begin negotiating; *he opened the discussions with a description of the product; the chairman opened the meeting at 10.30*

◊ **open-ended** *or US* **open-end** ['əupən 'endɪd *or* 'əupən 'end] *adjective* with no fixed limit *or* with some items not specified; *the candidate was offered an open-ended contract with a good career plan;* **open-ended interview** = interview where the candidate is asked general questions, which make him give reasons for actions, show his feelings, etc.

◊ **opening** ['əupənɪŋ] *noun* **(a)** act of starting a new business; *the opening of a new branch; the opening of a new market or of a new distribution network* **(b) opening hours** = hours when a shop *or* business is open **(c) job openings** = jobs which are empty and need filling; *we have openings for office staff*

◊ **openness** ['əupənnəs] *noun* being honest, not hiding anything; *openness in discussing company problems with staff*

◊ **open-plan office** ['əupənplæn 'ɒfɪs] *noun* large room divided into smaller working spaces with no fixed divisions between them

operate ['ɒpəreɪt] *verb* **(a)** to work; *the new terms of service will operate from January 1st;* **operating costs** *or* **running costs** = cost of the day-to-day organization of a company; **computer operating system** = the main program which operates a computer **(b)** to make something work *or* function; **to operate a machine** = to make a machine work; *he is learning to operate the new telephone switchboard*

◊ **operation** [ɒpə'reɪʃən] *noun* **(a)** business organization and work; *the company's operations in West Africa; he heads up the operations in Northern Europe;* **operations review** = examining the way in which a company or department works to see how it can be made more efficient and profitable; **a franchising operation** = selling licences to trade as a franchise **(b) in operation** = working *or* being used; *the system will be in operation by June; the new* *system came into operation on June 1st;* **to put a plan into operation** = to start a plan working

◊ **operational** [ɒpə'reɪʃənl] *adjective* **(a)** referring to how something works; **operational budget** = expenditure which is expected to be made in running a business *or* an office; **operational planning** = planning how something is to be run; **operational research** = study of a method of working to see if it can be made more efficient and cost-effective **(b) the system became operational on June 1st** = the system began working on June 1st

◊ **operative** ['ɒpərətɪv] **1** *adjective* referring to the working of a system; **to become operative** = to start working; *the new system has been operative since June 1st* **2** *noun* person who operates a machine which makes a product

◊ **operator** ['ɒpəreɪtə] *noun* **(a)** person who works a machine; *a keyboard operator* **(b)** person who works a telephone switchboard; *switchboard operator; to call the operator or to dial the operator; to place a call through or via the operator*

opportunity [ɒpə'tjuːnəti] *noun* situation where you can do something successfully; **employment opportunities** *or* **job opportunities** = new jobs being available; *the increase in export orders has created hundreds of job opportunities;* **equality of opportunity** = situation where everyone, regardless of sex, race, class, etc., has the same opportunity to get a job; **to seize an opportunity** = to take advantage of an opportunity as soon as it appears; **to miss out on an opportunity** = not to be able to take advantage of an opportunity; *see also* EQUAL OPPORTUNITIES

◊ **opportunistic** [ɒpɔːtjuː'nɪstɪk] *adjective* done when the opportunity arises; **opportunistic thefts in offices** = thefts committed when valuables are left lying around

QUOTE the group is currently undergoing a period of rapid expansion and this has created an exciting opportunity for a qualified accountant
Financial Times

oppose [ə'pəʊz] *verb* to try to stop something happening; to vote against something; *a minority of union members opposed the deal*

opposite number ['ɒpəzɪt 'nʌmbə] *noun* person who has a similar job in another company; **John is my opposite number in Smith's** = John has the same job in Smith's as I have here

opt out ['ɒpt 'aʊt] *verb* to decide not to do something

optional ['ɒpʃənl] *adjective* not necessary according to rules; *attendance at staff meetings is optional, although the management encourages employees to attend*

oral ['ɔːrəl] *adjective* referring to speech, as opposed to writing; **oral warning** = first stage of disciplinary measures, where a worker is told by the supervisor that his or her work is unsatisfactory and must be improved; *after being given his second oral warning he knew he would be fired for absenteeism; after an oral warning from her supervisor, she received a written warning from the personnel director*

order ['ɔːdə] **1** *noun* **(a)** arrangement of records (filing cards, invoices, etc.); **alphabetical order** = arrangement by the letters of the alphabet (A, B, C, etc.); **chronological order** = arrangement by the order of the dates; *the reports are filed in chronological order;* **numerical order** = arrangement by numbers; *put these invoices in numerical order;* **in order of merit** = placing employees in order according to their qualities **(b)** working arrangement; **machine in full working order** = machine which is ready and able to work properly; **the telephone is out of order** = the telephone is not working; **is all the documentation in order?** = are all the documents valid and correct? **(c)** instruction, telling someone to do something; **standing order** = order written by a customer asking a bank to pay money regularly to an account **2** *verb* **(a)** to tell someone to do something; *the management ordered the workforce to leave the factory* **(b)** to put in a certain way; *the address list is ordered by country; that filing cabinet contains personnel records ordered by name*

ordinary ['ɔːdnri] *adjective* normal *or* not special; **ordinary member** = person who pays a subscription to belong to an organization such as a club

organ ['ɔːgən] *noun* journal *or* magazine;

house organ = magazine produced for the workers *or* shareholders in a company to give them news about the company

organic organization [ɔː'gænɪk ɔːgənaɪ'zeɪʃən] *noun* type of organization with little formality in its structure and procedures

organization [ɔːgənaɪ'zeɪʃən] *noun* **(a)** way of arranging something so that it works efficiently; *the chairman handles the organization of the AGM; the organization of the group is too centralized to be efficient; the organization of the head office into departments;* **organization and methods (O & M)** = systematic examination of how an office works, suggesting how it can be made more efficient; *we need better organization and methods to improve our use of labour and machinery;* **organization chart** = list of people working in various departments, showing the areas of responsibility and relationships between personnel; *the organization chart shows that the company has too many chiefs and too few indians;* **organization man** = manager who works happily in a large organization; **organization pyramid** = structure of an organization with many employees at lower levels and fewer at the top; **organization theory** = study of the structure and function of organizations; **line organization** = organization of a business where each manager is responsible for doing what his superior tells him to do; **matrix organization** = flexible organization structure where authority depends on the expertise needed for a particular task and overall responsibility is shared between several persons **(b)** group or institution which is arranged for efficient work; **a government organization** = official body, run by the government; **an employers' organization** *or* **a trade union organization** = group of employers or trade unions with similar interests

◊ **organizational** [ɔːgənaɪ'zeɪʃənl] *adjective* referring to the way in which something is organized; *the paper gives a diagram of the company's organizational structure;* **organizational change** = change in the way something is organized; **organizational climate** = general feeling in an organization; *the organizational climate will improve as soon as workers are allowed to take part in decision-making;* **organizational development** = form of

management training designed to affect the whole organization as well as the individual employees; **organizational iceberg** = official or apparent system of an organization, as opposed to the way the organization is really run

◊ **organize** ['ɔːgənaɪz] *verb* to arrange things *or* people in a certain way so that they work more efficiently; *the company is organized into six profit centres; the group is organized by sales areas;* **organized labour** = workers who are members of trade unions which represent them and defend their interests; **organizing committee** = group of people who work together to persuade workers to unite *or* strike *or* to protect workers' interests

◊ **organogram** [ɔː'gænəʊgræm] *noun* = ORGANIZATION CHART

QUOTE working with a client base which includes many major commercial organizations and nationalized industries
Times

QUOTE we organize a rate with importers who have large orders and guarantee them space at a fixed rate so that they can plan their costs
Lloyd's List

QUOTE governments are coming under increasing pressure from politicians, organized labour and business to stimulate economic growth
Duns Business Month

oriented *or* **orientated** ['ɔːrɪentɪd *or* 'ɔːrɪenteɪtɪd] *adjective* working in a certain direction; *a market-orientated approach*

orientation [ɔːrɪən'teɪʃn] *noun* introduction of new employees into an organization; *the orientation programme included a talk by the chairman on the history of the company and its products; lack of proper orientation can cause much distress in the first days of a new job*

originating application [ə'rɪdʒɪneɪtɪŋ æplɪ'keɪʃn] *noun* form by which an employee begins the process of complaint to an industrial tribunal

ostracism ['ɒstrəsɪzm] *noun* rejection of a member or members of a group by others;

the fate of non-strikers was ostracism by their former colleagues

◊ **ostracize** ['ɒstrəsaɪz] *verb* to reject and refuse to have anything to do with a member or members of a group; *workers who carried on working were ostracized after the strike ended; see also* COVENTRY

out [aʊt] *adverb* on strike; *the workers have been out on strike for four weeks; as soon as the management made the offer, the staff came out; the shop stewards called the workforce out*

◊ **outcome** ['aʊtkʌm] *noun* result; *what was the outcome of the discussion?*

◊ **outfit** ['aʊtfɪt] *noun* small, sometimes badly run, company; *they called in a public relations outfit; he works for some finance outfit*

◊ **out-house** ['aʊthaʊs] *adjective* working outside a company's buildings; *the out-house staff; we do all our data processing out-house*

◊ **outing** ['aʊtɪŋ] *noun* trip away from the place of work; **staff outing** = trip by the staff to celebrate something away from the office; **works outing** = trip taken by the workers of a factory

◊ **outline** ['aʊtlaɪn] **1** *noun* general description, without giving many details; *they drew up the outline of a plan or an outline plan* **2** *verb* to make a general description; *the chairman outlined the company's plans for the coming year*

◊ **out of court** [aʊt əv 'kɔːt] *adverb & adjective* **a settlement was reached out of court** = a dispute was settled between two parties privately without continuing a court case; *they are hoping to reach an out-of-court settlement*

◊ **out of date** [aʊt əv 'deɪt] *adjective & adverb* old-fashioned *or* no longer modern; *their computer system is years out of date; they are still using out-of-date equipment*

◊ **out of pocket** [aʊt əv 'pɒkɪt] *adjective & adverb* having paid out money personally; *the deal has left me out of pocket;* **out-of-pocket expenses** = amount of money to pay a worker back for money of his own spent on company business

◊ **out of work** ['aʊt əv 'wɜːk] *adjective & adverb* with no job; *the recession has put millions out of work; the company was set up by three out-of-work engineers*

◊ **outplacement** ['aʊtpleɪsmənt] *noun* help in finding another job, given by an employer to an employee who has been made redundant; **group outplacement** = situation where several employees are dealt with together in being given help to find other jobs after being made redundant

◊ **output** ['aʊtpʊt] **1** *noun* **(a)** amount which a company *or* a person *or* a machine produces; *output has increased by 10%; 25% of our output is exported;* **output per hour** = amount produced in one hour; **output-based bonus** *or* **output bonus** = extra payment for increased production **(b)** information which is produced by a computer **2** *verb* to produce (by a computer); *the printer will output colour graphs; that is the information outputted from the computer*

◊ **outside** ['aʊtsaɪd] *adjective & adverb* not in a company's office or building; **to send work to be done outside** = to send work to be done in other offices; **outside office hours** = when the office is not open; **outside line** = line from an internal office telephone system to the main telephone exchange; *you dial 9 to get an outside line;* **outside worker** = worker who does not work in a company's offices; *our headquarters are very small since we employ mainly outside workers*

◊ **outsourcing** ['aʊtsɔːsɪŋ] *noun* obtaining services from specialist bureaux or other companies, rather than employing full-time members of staff to provide them

> QUOTE organizations in the public and private sectors are increasingly buying in specialist services - or outsourcing - allowing them to cut costs and concentrate on their core business activities
>
> *Financial Times*

outstrip [aʊt'strɪp] *verb* to become larger than something else; *wage increases are outstripping inflation*

◊ **outvote** [aʊt'vəʊt] *verb* to defeat in a vote; **the chairman was outvoted** = the majority voted against the chairman

◊ **outwork** ['aʊtwɜːk] *noun* work which a company pays someone to do at home

◊ **outworker** ['aʊtwɜːkə] *noun* person who works at home for a company

over- ['əʊvə] *prefix* more than; **shop which**

caters for the over-60s = shop which has goods which appeal to people who are more than sixty years old

◊ **overachiever** [əʊvəə'tʃiːvə] *noun* person who tries too hard and achieves more than he is really capable of; *overachievers on the management course were encouraged to slow down*

◊ **overall** [əʊvər'ɔːl] *adjective* covering *or* including everything; **although some divisions traded profitably, the company reported an overall fall in profits** = company reported a general fall in profits; **overall performance** = performance of a worker relating to the whole job, and not simply to part of it; **overall plan** = plan which covers everything; *the company's overall plan included a new recruitment programme*

◊ **overcome** [əʊvə'kʌm] *verb* to beat something after a struggle; *to overcome obstacles on the way to reaching agreement*

◊ **overemployment** [əʊvəɪm'plɔɪmənt] *noun* situation where there is a shortage of labour in a certain area or industry

◊ **overhaul** [əʊvə'hɔːl] *verb* to examine something carefully and make changes so that it works better; *to overhaul the company's union agreements*

◊ **overhead** ['əʊvəhed] **1** *adjective* **overhead costs** *or* **expenses** = money spent on the day-to-day cost of a business; **overhead budget** = plan of probable overhead costs **2** *noun* **overheads** *or US* **overhead** = costs of the day-to-day running of a business; *secretaries' salaries are now a significant part of overheads*

◊ **overlearning** [əʊvə'lɜːnɪŋ] *noun* continuing the learning process beyond the level of skill needed; *the training manager found that without overlearning, skills were easily lost*

◊ **overmanned** [əʊvə'mænd] *adjective* having more workers than necessary

◊ **overmanning** [əʊvə'mænɪŋ] *noun* having more workers than are needed to do a company's work; *the answer to our overmanning problem must be redundancies*

◊ **overpaid** [əʊvə'peɪd] *adjective* paid too much; *our staff are overpaid and underworked*

◊ **overproduce** [əʊvəprə'djuːs] *verb* to produce too much

◊ **overproduction** [əʊvəprə'dʌkʃən] *noun* manufacturing too much of a product

◊ **overqualified** [əʊvə'kwɒlɪfaɪd] *adjective* having too many skills for a job; *with a degree in business studies he is overqualified to be an ordinary shop floor worker*

◊ **overrepresent** [əʊvərepri'zent] *verb* to give one group more representatives than another; *the female workers are overrepresented on the management committee*

◊ **override** [əʊvə'raɪd] *verb* not to do something which has been decided; *to override an order*

◊ **overrule** [əʊvə'ruːl] *verb* to decide against something which has been decided; *to overrule a decision*

◊ **overrun** [əʊvə'rʌn] *verb* to go beyond a certain limit; *the workers overran the time limit set by the production manager*

◊ **overseas** [əʊvə'siːz] *adjective & adverb* across the sea *or* to foreign countries; *management trainees knew that they would be sent overseas to learn about the export markets; some workers are going overseas to find new jobs;* **an overseas call** = phone call from or to another country; **the overseas division** = section of a company dealing with trade with other countries

◊ **oversee** [əʊvə'siː] *verb* to supervise

◊ **overseer** ['əʊvəsiə] *noun* person who supervises other workers

◊ **overstaffed** [əʊvə'stɑːft] *adjective* with more workers than are needed to do the work of the company

overtime ['əʊvətaɪm] **1** *noun* hours worked beyond the normal working time; *he worked six hours' overtime last week; the overtime rate is one and a half times normal pay; workers are doing overtime to earn extra pay;* **overtime ban** = order by a trade union which forbids overtime work by its members; **overtime pay** = pay for extra time worked **2** *adverb* **to work overtime** = to work longer hours than in the contract of employment

QUOTE overtime working by operatives in manufacturing industries rose in January to 14.54 million hours a week after allowing for normal seasonal influences

Employment Gazette

overturn [əʊvə'tɜːn] *verb (of a tribunal)* **to overturn a decision** = to cancel a decision made previously

overwork [əʊvə'wɜːk] *noun* **he is suffering from overwork** = he has too much work and this is making him ill

overworked [əʊvə'wɜːkt] *adjective* having too much work to do; *our staff complain of being underpaid and overworked*

own [əʊn] *verb* to have *or* to possess; *he owns 50% of the shares;* **a state-owned industry** = industry which is nationalized

◊ **owner** ['əʊnə] *noun* person who owns something; **homeowner** = person who owns the house or flat where he lives; **sole owner** = person who owns something by himself; **owner-occupier** = person who owns and lives in a house

◊ **ownership** ['əʊnəʃɪp] *noun* act of owning something; **common** *or* **collective ownership** = situation where a business is owned by the workers who work in it; **homeownership** = being the owner of the house or flat in which you live; **public ownership** *or* **state ownership** = situation where an industry is nationalized; **private ownership** = situation where a company is owned by private shareholders (NOTE: no plural)

Pp

P11 ['piː ɪ'levən] working sheet, showing the employer's calculations in deducting tax from an employee's pay

P11D ['piː ɪ'levən 'diː] form showing expenses paid to directors

P14 ['piː fɔː'tiːn] form sent by an employer to the Inland Revenue at the end of a tax year, giving a summary of pay and deductions of an individual employee

P35 ['piː θɜːtɪ 'faɪv] annual declaration of pay, tax and other deductions for all employees, sent by the employer to the Inland Revenue

P45 ['piː fɔːtɪ 'faɪv] form given to an employee who leaves a company, showing how much tax has been deducted from his salary

P60 ['piː 'sɪkstɪ] certificate showing pay and tax deducted for each individual employee, sent to each employee at the end of the tax year

PA ['piː'eɪ] = PERSONAL ASSISTANT

p.a. = PER ANNUM

PABX = PRIVATE AUTOMATIC BRANCH EXCHANGE

pacemaker ['peɪsmeɪkə] *noun* organization which helps another to change by giving advice or offering support

package ['pækɪdʒ] *noun* (a) group of different items joined together in one deal; **pay package** *or* **salary package** *or* **reward package** *or US* **compensation package** = total of all money and benefits given to an employee (salary, bonuses, company car, pension plans, medical insurance, etc.); *the job carries an attractive salary package;* **package deal** = agreement where several different items are agreed at the same time; *we are offering a package deal which*

includes the whole office computer system, staff training and hardware maintenance (b) piece of computer software; *a payroll package*

> QUOTE the remuneration package will include an attractive salary, profit sharing and a company car
> *Times*

> QUOTE are remuneration and benefits packages flexible enough?
> *Personnel Management*

paid [peɪd] *adjective* money has been given (a) **paid educational leave** = time away from work for an employee to study; **paid holiday** *or* **paid leave** = holiday *or* time away from work when the worker's wages are still paid even though he is not working; *he was entitled to paid holiday three months after joining the company* (b) **paid assistant** = assistant who receives a salary; **well-paid job** = job with a high salary

◊ **paid-up** ['peɪd 'ʌp] *adjective* paid in full; **paid-up policy** = life insurance policy based on premiums which have already been paid

paired comparisons ['peəd kəm'pærɪzənz] *noun* method of assessment where jobs to be assessed are each compared with all others and a final score for each obtained (also called 'job ranking'); *having observed the work performance of ten men, the supervisor used paired comparisons to rank performance*

panel ['pænl] *noun* group of people; **panel of experts** = group of people who give advice on a problem; **panel interview** = interview conducted by a group of people, not just by a single interviewer; **consumer panel** = group of consumers who report on goods they have used so that the manufacturer can improve the goods, or use the consumers' reports in his advertising

paperwork ['peɪpəwɜːk] *noun* office work,

especially writing memos and filling in forms; *exporting to Russia involves a large amount of paperwork* (NOTE: no plural)

parachute ['pærəʃuːt] *noun* **golden parachute** = large, usually tax-free, sum of money given to an executive who retires from a company before the end of his service contract

parity ['pærəti] *noun* being equal; **pay parity** *or* **wage parity** = earning the same pay for the same job; **the female staff want parity with the men** = they want to have the same rates of pay and perks as the men; *the company showed it did not believe in parity by always assigning women to lower positions than men* (NOTE: no plural)

Parkinson's Law ['pɑːkɪnsnz 'lɔː] *noun* law, based on wide experience, that in business the amount of work increases to fill the time available for it

parte ['pɑːteɪ] *see* EX PARTE

partial ['pɑːʃəl] *adjective* not complete; **partial disability** = situation where a worker is partly disabled, as so is eligible for less benefit; **partial disablement** = being disabled to such an extent that you can only do part of your normal work

participate [pɑːˈtɪsɪpeɪt] *verb* to take part in an activity *or* enterprise; *the staff are encouraged to participate actively in the company's decision-making processes*

◊ **participation** [pɑːtɪsɪˈpeɪʃən] *noun* taking part; *the workers are demanding more participation in the company's affairs; participation helps to make an employee feel part of the organization;* **participation rate** = proportion of a group that is active in some way; *what is the participation rate in this department's fund-raising efforts?;* **employee participation** *or* **worker participation** = sharing by the employees in the company's planning and decision-making (as in works councils, quality circles, etc.); **financial participation** = holding by employees of shares in the company they work for

◊ **participative** [pɑːˈtɪsɪpeɪtɪv] *adjective* where both sides take part; *we do not treat management-worker relations as a participative process;* **participative management** = management of an organization *or* department with the active participation of the staff

> QUOTE for those not yet participating there is the motivation of becoming future beneficiaries
> *Personnel Management*

> QUOTE employee share ownership programmes (ESOPs) are now among the fashionable ways of providing employee participation and motivation
> *Personnel Management*

partner ['pɑːtnə] *noun* person who works in a business and has an equal share in it with other partners; *he became a partner in a firm of solicitors;* **active partner** *or* **working partner** = partner who works in a partnership; **sleeping partner** = partner who has a share in a business but does not work in it; **junior partner** *or* **senior partner** = person who has a small or large part of the shares in a partnership

◊ **partnership** ['pɑːtnəʃɪp] *noun* **(a)** unregistered business where two or more people share the risks and profits equally; **to go into partnership with someone** to join with someone to form a partnership; **to offer someone a partnership** *or* **to take someone into partnership with you** = to have a working business and bring someone in to share it with you; **to dissolve a partnership** = to bring a partnership to an end **(b) limited partnership** = registered business where the liability of the partners is limited to the amount of capital they have each provided to the business and where the partners may not take part in the running of the business

part-owner [pɑːtˈəʊnə] *noun* someone who owns part of something (such as a worker who has shares in the company he works for)

part-time [pɑːtˈtaɪm] *adjective & adverb* not working for the whole working day; *she only works part-time as she has small children to look after; it is a part-time job that involves two days' work a week; he is trying to find part-time work when the children are in school; we are looking for part-time staff to work our computers;* **part-time employee** *or* **part-time worker** = employee who works between 8 and 16 hours per week; **part-time work** *or* **part-time employment** = work for part of a working day (officially, between 8 and 16 hours per week)

◊ **part-timer** [pɑːt'taɪmə] *noun* person who works part-time

QUOTE part-timers currently make up just under 24 per cent of the workforce
Personnel Management

QUOTE are remuneration and benefit packages flexible enough to allow the integration of part-time and full-time jobs and the growing movement between the two?
Personnel Management

party ['pɑːti] *noun* (a) organization *or* person involved in a legal dispute *or* legal agreement; *how many parties are there to the contract?; the company is not a party to the agreement* (b) **third party** = any third person, in addition to the two main people involved in a contract; **third party insurance** *or* **third party policy** = insurance to cover damage to any person who is not one of the people named in the insurance contract (that is, not the insured person nor the insurance company)

pass [pɑːs] **1** *noun* permit to allow someone to go into a building; *you need a pass to enter the ministry offices; all members of staff must show a pass* **2** *verb* (a) to be successful; *he passed his typing test; she has passed all her exams and is now a qualified accountant* (b) to move something on to someone else; **to pass the buck** = to move a problem *or* responsibility on to someone else to deal with; *it has got to the point that there is so much buck-passing that none of the problems get solved*

paternalism [pə'tɜːnəlɪzm] *noun* used to describe a 'fatherly' style of management where the employer is overprotective towards his employees

◊ **paternalistic** [pətɜːnə'lɪstɪk] *adjective* being overprotective towards the employees; **paternalistic management style** = way of managing, where the employer takes all the decisions and tries to keep the loyalty of the workforce by giving them special treatment

paternity leave [pə'tɜːnəti 'liːv] *noun* short period of leave given to a father to be away from work when his wife has a baby

pattern bargaining ['pætən 'bɑːgənɪŋ] *noun* bargaining between unions and an employer, in which the unions refer to past collective agreements made with employers

pay [peɪ] **1** *noun* (a) salary *or* wage *or* money given to someone for regular work; **back pay** = salary which has not been paid; **basic pay** = normal salary without extra payments; **call-back pay** = pay given to a worker who has been called back to work after his normal working hours; **half pay** = half one's normal salary; **profit-related pay** = pay (including bonuses) which is linked to profit; **severance pay** = money paid as compensation to an employee who loses his job through no fault of his own; **take-home pay** = pay left after tax and insurance have been deducted; **holidays with pay** = holiday which a worker can take by contract and for which he is paid; **unemployment pay** = dole *or* money given by the government to someone who is unemployed (b) **pay cheque** = cheque (usually paid monthly) which pays a salary to a worker; **pay day** = day on which wages are paid to workers (usually Friday for workers paid once a week, and during the last week of the month for workers who are paid once a month); **pay differentials** = differences between one worker's wage and another's in similar types of jobs; **pay freeze** = period when wages are not allowed to be increased; **pay negotiations** *or* **pay talks** = discussions between management and workers about pay increases; **pay package** = salary and other benefits offered with a job; *the job carries an attractive pay package;* **pay packet** = envelope containing the pay slip and the cash pay; **pay parity** = earning the same pay for the same job; **pay review** = re-examination by the employer of an employee's pay; *I'm soon due for a pay review and hope to get a rise;* **pay review body** = independent organization which examines pay scales of groups of workers and recommends increases; **pay rise** = increase in pay; *the dockers are hoping for a 10% pay rise;* **pay round** = annual series of wage bargaining negotiations in various industries; **pay slip** *or* **pay statement** = piece of paper showing the full amount of a worker's pay, and the money deducted as tax, pension and insurance contributions; *every month employees received itemized pay statements with all deductions shown* **2** *verb* (a) to give money to buy an item or a service; *how much did you pay to have the office cleaned?* (b) to give a worker money for work done; *the workforce has not been* *paid for three weeks; we pay good wages for skilled workers; how much do they pay you per hour?;* **to be paid by the hour** = to get money for each hour worked; **to be paid at piece-work rates** = to get money for each piece of work finished (NOTE: **paying - paid**)

◊ **payable** ['peɪəbl] *adjective* which is due to be paid; *wages are payable every month*

◊ **pay as you earn (PAYE)** ['peɪæzjʊ 'ɜːn] *GB* tax system, where income tax is deducted from the salary before it is paid to the worker

◊ **pay-as-you-go** ['peɪæzjʊ 'gəʊ] *US* = PAY AS YOU EARN

◊ **paycheck** ['peɪtʃek] *noun* salary cheque given to an employee

◊ **PAYE** ['piːeɪwaɪ 'iː] = PAY AS YOU EARN

◊ **payment** ['peɪmənt] *noun* **(a)** giving money; *payment in cash or cash payment; payment by cheque; payment of interest or interest payment;* **payment in kind** = paying by giving goods or food, but not money; **payment by results (PBR)** = money given which increases with the amount of work done or goods produced; *payment by results is not popular with the workers, who would prefer more security;* **payment scheme** *or* **payment system** = method used by an organization to pay staff; *the personnel manager has devised a payment scheme which is both fair and motivating;* **payment structure** = wage *or* salary levels in an organization **(b)** money paid; **back payment** = paying money which is owed; **incentive payments** = extra pay offered to an employee to encourage him to work better; **a one-off payment** = a single payment, made once only and not repeated

◊ **pay off** ['peɪ 'ɒf] *verb* to pay all the money owed to someone and terminate his employment; *the company was taken over, the factory closed and all the workers paid off*

◊ **payroll** ['peɪrəʊl] *noun* (i) list of people employed and paid by a company; (ii) money paid by a company in salaries; *the company has 250 on the payroll; the organization has a weekly payroll of £10,000;* **payroll administration** = administering the salaries and NIC payments for employees and claims for their expenses; **payroll clerk** = person employed to administer the payment of employees; **payroll costs** = running costs of payroll administration, as well as the actual salaries themselves; **payroll ledger** = list of staff and their salaries; **payroll tax** = tax paid by an employer on each employee employed by the company

PBR = PAYMENT BY RESULTS

peak [piːk] **1** *noun* highest point; *he has reached the peak of his career;* **peak season** = period when a company is busiest; **peak unemployment** = period when unemployment is as its highest level **2** *verb* to reach the highest point; *he peaked early and never achieved his ambition of becoming managing director; demand peaks in August, after which sales usually decline; unemployment seems to have peaked and is now beginning to fall*

peer [pɪə] *noun* person who is the same age or at the same level as someone else; *the personnel director and his peers believed in a strict chain of authority, but the younger managers wanted a more flexible approach;* **peer group** = group of people of the same age, doing the same sort of job, with the same background; **peer group appraisal** = appraisal of a worker by his peer group

peg [peg] *verb* to hold something at a certain point; **to peg prices** = to fix prices to stop them rising; **to peg wage increases to the cost-of-living index** = to limit increases in wages to the increases in the cost-of-living index; *the government will try to peg prices to avoid a rise in inflation; production was pegged at two hundred units per month*

penalty ['penlti] *noun* punishment (such as a fine, suspension without pay, written warning, etc.) which is imposed if something is not done; *there are stiff penalties for workers who are persistently late;* **to impose a penalty on someone** = to make someone pay a fine, to suspend someone, etc., as a punishment; **financial penalty** = penalty in the form of a fine, money deducted from wages, etc.; **penalty clause** = clause which lists the penalties which will be imposed if the terms of the contract are not fulfilled; *the contract contains a penalty clause which fines the company 1% for each week beyond the completion date*

◊ **penalize** ['piːnəlaɪz] *verb* to punish *or* to

fine; *they were penalized for bad time-keeping*

pendulum arbitration ['pendjələm ɑːbɪ'treɪʃn] *noun* method of arbitration, where each side makes a proposal, and the arbitrator chooses one of them, which then becomes binding on both parties

pension ['penʃən] **1** *noun* **(a)** money received regularly after retirement as part of either a private *or* government scheme; *though he received his pension at sixty-five, he still went on working part-time;* **to draw a pension** = to receive a pension; **retirement pension** *or* **old age pension** = state pension given to a man who is over 65 or and woman who is over 60; **full pension** = maximum pension allowed; **government pension** *or* **state pension** = pension paid by the state; **occupational pension** = pension which is received by an employee after retirement, paid by the pension fund set up by the company which employed him or her; **contracted out pension scheme** = private pension scheme which gives benefits at least as high as the state scheme; **portable pension** = pension entitlement which can be moved (as a worker changes jobs) from one company to another without loss; **widow's pension** = state pension paid to a widow aged 45 or older when her husband died **(b) pension book** = book with vouchers entitling the bearer to be paid a weekly pension; **pension contributions** = money paid by a company or worker into a pension fund; **pension entitlement** = amount of pension which someone has the right to receive after retirement; **pension fund** = accumulation of money from regular contributions by employees and employers which provides employees with pensions after retirement; **the Pensions Ombudsman** = government official · who arbitrates in disputes over pensions and the administration of pension funds **(c) pension plan** *or* **pension scheme** = plan worked out by an insurance company which arranges for a worker to pay part of his salary over many years and receive a regular payment when he retires; **company pension scheme** = pension which is organized by a company for its staff; *he decided to join the company's pension scheme;* **contributory pension scheme** = scheme where the worker has to pay a proportion of his salary; **graduated pension scheme** = pension scheme where the benefit

is calculated as a percentage of the salary of each person in the scheme; **non-contributory pension scheme** = scheme where the employer pays in all the money on behalf of the worker; **personal pension plan** = pension plan which applies to one worker only, usually a self-employed person, not to a group; **portable pension plan** = pension plan which a worker can carry from one company to another as he changes jobs **2** *verb* **to pension someone off** = to ask someone to retire and take a pension; *after the takeover, six senior managers were pensioned off*

◊ **pensionable** ['penʃənəbl] *adjective* able to receive a pension; **pensionable age** = age after which someone can take a pension; **pensionable earnings** = salary at the moment of retirement, on which the pension is calculated

◊ **pensioner** ['penʃənə] *noun* person who receives a pension; **old age pensioner (OAP)** = person who receives the retirement pension

QUOTE new forms of pension plan are likely to be set up for some major British companies in the next few months
Personnel Management

QUOTE the stock market crash had little effect on company pension schemes
Personnel Today

QUOTE the company operated a policy of retiring women when they reached pensionable age
Personnel Today

per [pɜː] *preposition* **(a)** at a rate of; **per day** *or* **per diem** = for each day; **per hour** = for each hour; *see the rate is £5 per hour; he makes about £250 per month;* **we pay £10 per hour** = we pay £10 for each hour worked; **per month** = for each month; *he makes about £250 per month;* **per head** = for each person; *allow £15 per head for expenses; representatives cost on average £25,000 per head per annum;* **per week** = for each week; **per year** = PER ANNUM **(b)** out of; *the rate of imperfect items is about twenty-five per thousand; the birth rate has fallen to twelve per hundred*

◊ **per annum** ['pər 'ænəm] *adverb* in a year; *what is his total income per annum?; she earns over £10,000 per annum*

◊ **per capita** ['pə 'kæpɪtə] *adjective* &

adverb for each person; **average income per capita** *or* **per capita income** = average income of one person; **per capita expenditure** = total money spent divided by the number of people involved; *the per capita income is much higher in the more prosperous parts of the country; output per capita has risen with the introduction of newer machinery*

perform [pə'fɔːm] *verb* to do well or badly; **how did he perform at the interview?** = did he do well or badly at the interview?

◊ **performance** [pə'fɔːməns] *noun* way in which someone *or* something acts; *his overall performance has improved considerably since he went on a management training course;* **performance appraisal** = assessment of the quality of a person's work in a job; **performance of personnel against objectives** = how personnel have worked, measured against the objectives set; **performance rating** = evaluating a person's work by giving it a certain grade; **performance review** = study of a worker's performance to determine how it can be improved; **job performance** = doing a job well or badly; **performance-based assessment** = assessment of a worker's knowledge and skills as shown in his work (as opposed to 'knowledge-based assessment'); **performance pay** *or* **performance-related pay (PRP)** = pay which is linked to the worker's performance of his duties; **performance-related pay system** = system of payment for increased productivity (such as merit pay, financial participation schemes, etc.)

QUOTE fortunately there has been a move towards more objective measures of performance when assessing and developing staff
Personnel Management

period ['pɪərɪəd] *noun* length of time; *for a period of time* or *for a period of months* or *for a six-year period; output over a period of three months;* **period of disqualification** = period during which a pregnant woman cannot claim statutory sick pay (11 weeks before giving birth); **period of entitlement** = period during which a worker can claim statutory sick pay; **period of incapacity for work (PIW)** = period when a worker has been away from work because of sickness for four consecutive days (and then becomes eligible for SSP); **period of notice** =

time stated on a contract of employment which the employer *or* employee has to allow between resigning or being fired and actually leaving the job; *a three months period of notice is usually required of both parties;* **accounting period** = period of time at the end of which the firm's accounts are made up; **base period** = time that an employee must work before becoming eligible for state unemployment insurance benefits; **reference period** = period which is used as a base for comparisons; *see also* COOLING OFF, PROBATIONARY, SLACK, TRIAL

◊ **periodic** [pɪərɪ'ɒdɪk] *adjective* from time to time; *a periodic review of staff salaries*

peripheral [pə'rɪfərəl] *adjective* **peripheral workers** = workers who are hired as necessary (part-timers or workers on short-term contracts) as opposed to 'core' workers who are permanent

perk [pɜːk] *noun (informal)* extra item given by a company to workers in addition to their salaries (such as company cars, private health insurance)

QUOTE a perks-for-all programme, when used with management conviction, can be the key to keeping a loyal and effective workforce
Management Today

permanent ['pɜːmənənt] *adjective* which will last for a long time *or* for ever; *he has found a permanent job; she is in permanent employment; the permanent staff and part-timers;* **permanent health insurance (PHI)** = long-term insurance which gives an income during periods of disability; **permanent night shift** = shift which only works at night (as opposed to the alternating system)

◊ **permanency** ['pɜːmənənsi] *noun* being permanent

◊ **permanently** ['pɜːmənəntli] *adverb* for ever

permission [pə'mɪʃən] *noun* being allowed to do something; **to ask for permission to do something** = to ask someone in authority to allow you to do something; *he asked the manager's permission to take a day off;* **to give someone permission to do something** = to allow someone to do something; **verbal permission** = telling someone that he is allowed to do something; **written permission** = document which allows someone to do something

permit 1 ['pɜːmɪt] *noun* official document which allows someone to do something; **residence permit** = official document allowing a foreigner to live in a country; **work permit** = official document which allows someone who is not a citizen to work in a country; *he worked in a restaurant for a year without a work permit* **2** [pə'mɪt] *verb* to allow someone to do something; *this document permits you to stay in the country for six months*

per pro ['pɜː 'prəʊ] = PER PROCURATIONEM with the authority of; *the secretary signed per pro the manager*

perquisites ['pɜːkwɪzɪts] *plural noun (formal)* = PERKS

persistent unemployment [pə'sɪstənt ʌnɪm'plɔɪmənt] *noun* unemployment which is constant, owing to lack of skills *or* lack of jobs

person ['pɜːsn] *noun* (a) someone *or* man *or* woman; *an insurance policy which covers a named person;* **the persons named in the contract** = people whose names are given in the contract; **the document should be witnessed by a third person** = someone who is not named in the document should witness it; **person specification** = form of job description which gives the ideal personal qualities needed for the job and a description of the ideal candidate for the job (b) **in person** = someone himself *or* herself; **this important package is to be delivered to the chairman in person** = the package has to be given to the chairman himself (and not to his secretary, assistant, etc.); **he came to see me in person** = he himself came to see me (NOTE: to avoid using the words 'man' or 'woman' or 'girl' in advertisements (and so to avoid criticism on the grounds of sexism), it is common to use the word **person: chairperson, sales person, person Friday,** etc.)

◊ **person-to-person call** ['pɜːsn tə 'pɜːsn 'kɔːl] *noun* telephone call where you ask the operator to connect you with a particular person

◊ **personal** ['pɜːsənl] *adjective* (a) referring to one person; **personal allowances** = part of a person's income which is not taxed; *the accountant took into account the employee's personal allowances when calculating his take-home pay;* **personal assets** = moveable assets which belong to a person; **personal call** = telephone call where you ask the operator to connect you with a particular person; **personal contract** = contract negotiated between an employer and a single employee (as opposed to a collective contract, negotiated with a group of employees); **personal effects** *or* **personal property** = things which belong to someone; **personal income** = income received by an individual person before tax is paid; **apart from the family shares, he has a personal shareholding in the company** = he has shares which he owns himself; **the car is for his personal use** = the car is for him to use himself; **personal pension plan** *or* **personal pension scheme** = pension plan or scheme which applies to one worker only, usually someone who is self-employed (b) private; *I want to see the director on a personal matter;* **personal assistant (PA)** = person employed to be a general help to a particular manager; *she was an invaluable personal assistant with her knowledge of languages and business; after four years in the typing pool she was promoted to be PA to the Sales Director*

◊ **personality** [pɜːsə'nælɪti] *noun* a person's character or general nature; **personality clash** = situation where two members of staff with strong personalities cannot work together; **personality test** = test to assess a person's character; *we give all the salesmen a personality test to see how they can communicate with potential customers; his personality test showed he was a particularly aggressive individual*

◊ **personally** ['pɜːsnəli] *adverb* in person; *he personally opened the envelope; she wrote to me personally*

personnel [pɜːsə'nel] *noun* people who work in a certain place or for a certain organization; *the company is famous for the way it looks after its personnel; the personnel of the warehouse or the warehouse personnel have voted to strike;* **the personnel department** = section of the company which deals with the staff; **personnel development** = selection and training of employees for particular jobs in an organization; **personnel management** = management *or* administration of the recruitment, welfare and training of employees in an organization; *personnel management is becoming more important as companies realize the importance of making the best use of their human resources;* **personnel manager** *or* **personnel officer** *or* **head of personnel** = head of the personnel department, the person who organizes and co-ordinates the recruitment, welfare and training of staff

QUOTE personnel management will increasingly be concerned with facilitating change, whether in skill development, attitude change or cultural accommodation
Personnel Management

QUOTE managers should realise you need a strategic view of personnel management
Personnel Today

QUOTE pensions are very much on the personnel agenda at present
Personnel Management

PERT = PROGRAMME EVALUATION AND REVIEW TECHNIQUE

PEST = POLITICAL, ECONOMIC, SOCIAL, TECHNICAL analysis of the environment in which a company works, under these headings

Peter principle ['pi:tə 'prɪnsəpl] *noun* law, based on wide experience, that people are promoted until they occupy positions for which they are incompetent

petty ['peti] *adjective* not important; **petty theft** = stealing small items (as in an office: it can be the reason for summary dismissal)

phase [feɪz] *noun* period *or* part of something which takes place; *the first phase of the expansion programme*

◊ **phase in** ['feɪz 'ɪn] *verb* to bring something in gradually; *the new system of pension contributions will be phased in over the next two months*

◊ **phase out** ['feɪz 'aut] *verb* to remove something gradually; *Smith Ltd will be phased out as a supplier of spare parts*

PHI = PERMANENT HEALTH INSURANCE

physical (examination) ['fɪzɪkl] *noun* medical examination; *all the candidates have to pass a physical examination; though his qualifications for the job were good, he was rejected after failing the physical*

picket ['pɪkɪt] **1** *noun* striking worker who stands at the gate of a factory to try to persuade other workers not to go to work; **flying pickets** = pickets who travel round the country to picket other places of work; **picket line** = line of pickets at the gate of a factory; *to man a picket line or to be on the picket line;* **to cross a picket line** = to go into a factory to work, even though pickets are trying to prevent workers from going in **2** *verb* **to picket a factory** = to put pickets at the gate of a factory to try to prevent other workers from going to work

◊ **picketing** ['pɪkɪtɪŋ] *noun* act of standing at the gates of a factory to prevent workers going to work; **lawful picketing** = picketing which is allowed by law; **mass picketing** = picketing by large numbers of pickets; **peaceful picketing** = picketing which does not involve fighting; **secondary picketing** = picketing of another factory, not directly connected with the strike, to prevent it supplying the striking factory *or* receiving supplies from it

piece [pi:s] *noun* small part of something; *to sell something by the piece; the price is 25p the piece*

◊ **piece rate** ['pi:s 'reɪt] *noun* rate of pay for a product produced *or* for a piece of work done and not paid for at an hourly rate; *to earn piece rates;* **piece rate wages** = pay based on the number of units produced

◊ **piecework** ['pi:swɜːk] *noun* work for which workers are paid for the products produced *or* the piece of work done and not at an hourly rate

pilferage *or* **pilfering** ['pɪlfərɪdʒ *or* 'pɪlfərɪŋ] *noun* stealing small amounts of money *or* small items from an office *or* shop

pink slip ['pɪŋk 'slɪp] *noun US* official letter of dismissal given to an employee (in place of a final interview)

PIW = PERIOD OF INCAPACITY FOR WORK

place [pleɪs] **1** *noun* where something is *or* where something happens; **place of birth** =

place where someone was born; **place of work** = office or factory, etc. where people work; **to take place** = to happen; *the negotiations will take place in the company's offices; the meeting took place in our offices;* **meeting place** = room or area where people can meet **2** *verb* **to place staff** = to find jobs for staff; **how are you placed for work?** = have you enough work to do?

◊ **placement** ['pleɪsmənt] *noun* putting someone in a job; **placement service** = office which specializes in finding jobs (such as for students leaving college)

plaintiff ['pleɪntɪf] *noun* person who starts a legal action against someone

plan [plæn] **1** *noun* **(a)** scheme or organized way of doing something; *the department has been asked to make plans for future expansion; the personnel department has a plan for the development of a new pay system;* **business plan** = document drawn up to show how a business is planned to work, with cash flow forecasts, sales forecasts, etc. (often used when trying to raise a loan, or when setting up a new business); **contingency plan** = plan which will be put into action if something happens which no one expects to happen; **grand plan** or **master plan** = main or original plan, covering many different departments **(b)** way of saving or investing money; **pension plan** = plan worked out by an insurance company which arranges for a worker to pay part of his salary over many years and receive a regular payment when he retires; *he has joined the company pension plan* **2** *verb* to organize carefully how something should be done; **to plan for an increase in staff costs** = to change a way of doing things because you think there will be an increase in staff costs

◊ **planning** ['plænɪŋ] *noun* making plans or organizing how something should be done in the future; *setting up a new incentive scheme with insufficient planning could be a disaster; the long-term planning or short-term planning of the project has been completed;* **career planning** = examining the way in which career opportunities are available, leading to advice on which careers to pursue or how to further an employee's existing career; **manpower planning** = planning to get the right number of workers in each job; **planning permission** = official document allowing a person or

company to plan new buildings on empty land

> QUOTE the benefits package is attractive and the compensation plan includes base, incentive and car allowance totalling $50,000+
> *Globe and Mail (Toronto)*

plant [plɑːnt] *noun* **(a)** industrial machinery and equipment; **plant-hire firm** = company which lends large machines (such as cranes and tractors) to building companies (NOTE: no plural) **(b)** large factory; *they are planning to build a car plant near the river; to set up a new plant; they closed down six plants in the north of the country; he was appointed plant manager*

PLC or **Plc** [piːelˈsiː] = PUBLIC LIMITED COMPANY

pluralism ['plʊərəlɪzm] *noun* belief that the way to achieve good industrial relations is to acknowledge that various groups of workers have different requirements and make different demands, and that compromises have to be reached (as opposed to 'unitarism'); *pluralism is making more employees feel they are part of the organization*

plus [plʌs] **1** *preposition* **(a)** added to; *his salary plus commission comes to more than £25,000; production costs plus overheads are higher than revenue* **(b)** more than; **a salary of £100,000 plus** = a salary of more than £100,000 **2** *noun* a good or favourable point; *his marketing experience is a definite plus*

poaching ['pəʊtʃɪŋ] *noun* enticing employees to work for another organization or enticing members of a union to join another union; *the company was accused of poaching staff from its rival*

pocket ['pɒkɪt] *noun* **pocket calculator** or **pocket diary** = calculator or diary which can be carried in the pocket; **to be £25 in pocket** = to have made a profit of £25; **to be £25 out of pocket** = to have lost £25; **out-of-pocket expenses** = amount of money to pay back a worker for his own money which he has spent on company business

point [pɔɪnt] *noun* **(a)** place or position; *at what point in your career did you decide to change companies?;* **assembly point** or

meeting point = place where people can meet (as at a railway station, or for checking during fire drill); **starting point** = place where something starts; *the salary scale is £6,000 to £9,000, and the starting point on the scale will depend on the appointee's experience; she took her experiences in management as the starting point for her article in the house journal* (b) mark *or* grade; **points system** = system whereby points are given to items in order to evaluate them; *salesmen are awarded points for good timekeeping and neatness, as well as sales performance; the personnel department uses a points system for performance appraisals; a points system can be used in evaluating candidates for a job*

police [pli:s] *noun* description of what has happened in the past; **police record** *or* **criminal record** = note of previous crimes for which someone has been convicted

policy ['pɒlɪsi] *noun* (a) decisions on the general way of doing something; ideas of a person *or* organization which have an effect on future planning; *we have a policy of only hiring qualified staff; the company's policy of good employee relations has paid off in high productivity; the government policy on wages or government wages policy has been criticized by the unions;* **company policy** = the company's agreed plan of action *or* the company's way of doing things; *what is the company policy on hiring part-time staff? it is against company policy to employ secretaries in the sales department; our policy is to submit all employment contracts to the legal department;* **fiscal policy** = a government's policy regarding taxes; **pricing policy** = a company's policy in giving prices to its products (b) **insurance policy** = document which shows the conditions of an insurance contract; **accident policy** = insurance contract against accidents; **all-risks policy** = insurance policy which covers risks of any kind, with no exclusions; **comprehensive** *or* **all-in policy** = insurance which covers all risks; **policy holder** = person who is insured by an insurance company; **to take out a policy** = to sign the contract for insurance and start paying the premiums; *she took out a life insurance policy*

polite [pə'laɪt] *adjective* behaving in a pleasant way; *we stipulate that our salesgirls must be polite to customers; we had a polite letter from the MD*

◊ **politely** [pə'laɪtli] *adverb* in a pleasant way; *she politely answered the customers' questions*

polygraph ['pɒlɪgrɑːf] *noun* lie detector, a machine which tells if a person is lying by recording physiological changes which take place while the person is being interviewed

◊ **polygraphy** [pə'lɪgrəfi] *noun* using a polygraph to check members of staff

pool [pu:l] *noun* (a) **typing pool** = group of typists, working together in a company, offering a secretarial service to several departments (b) unused supply; *a pool of unemployed labour or of expertise*

poor [pɔː] *adjective* (a) without much money; *the company tries to help the poorest members of staff with soft loans* (b) not very good; *poor performance by office staff; poor organization of working methods*

◊ **poorly** ['pɔːli] *adverb* badly; **poorly-paid staff** = staff with low wages

population [pɒpjʊ'leɪʃən] *noun* number of people who live in a country *or* in a town; *Paris has a population of over one million; the working population of the country has fallen by 10%;* **population growth** = increase in the population; **population trends** = developments in the size and make-up of the population; *to assess the future employment market, the personnel department studied population trends; judging by present population trends, there will be a labour shortage in five years' time;* **the working population** = people who are in paid employment

portable ['pɔːtəbl] *adjective* which can be carried; **portable pension** = pension entitlement which a worker can take with him from one company to another as he changes jobs

QUOTE from 1 July new provisions concerning portable pensions will come into effect
Personnel Management

position [pə'zɪʃən] *noun* (a) point of view; *what is the union's position on the issue of the closed shop?;* **bargaining position** = statement of position by one group during negotiations (b) job *or* paid work in a company; *to apply for a position as manager; we have several positions vacant; all the vacant positions have been filled; she retired from her position in the accounts department;* **he is in a key position** = he has an important job; **position of authority** = job where the employee has authority over other employees; **position of trust** = job where the employee is trusted with money *or* confidential documents, etc.

positive ['pɒzətɪv] *adjective & noun* meaning 'yes'; **positive discrimination** = giving more favourable treatment to a minority to help them be more equal; *the company's policy of positive discrimination is to enable more women to reach senior management posts;* **positive vetting** = close examination of a person working with secret information who may not be reliable; **false positive** = inclusion of an unsuitable candidate by a screening process (NOTE: opposite is **negative)**

post [pəʊst] *noun* job *or* paid work in a company; *to apply for a post as cashier; we have three posts vacant; all our posts have been filled; we advertised three posts in the 'Times'*

◊ **posting** ['pəʊstɪŋ] *noun* appointment to a job; *he has been offered an overseas posting;* **posting and bidding** = advertising a job internally so that employees can apply for it

post- [pəʊst] *prefix* meaning after; **post-entry closed shop** = closed shop which applies to workers after they have joined a company; **post-industrial experience** = experience after working in industry

potential [pə'tenʃəl] **1** *adjective* possible; **he is a potential managing director** = he is the sort of man who could become managing director **2** *noun* a person's ability to become something in the future; *the training manager is always on the lookout for trainees with management potential; though he has the potential he is much too lazy to take a management training course;* **potential review** = study of a worker's performance to determine what direction his or her career should take in the organization; **earning potential** = amount of money which someone should be able to earn *or* amount of dividend which a share is capable of earning

power ['paʊə] *noun* **(a)** strength *or* ability; **bargaining power** = strength of one person *or* group when discussing prices *or* wages; **earning power** = amount of money someone should be able to earn; *he is such a fine designer that his earning power is considerable;* **purchasing power** = quantity of goods which can be bought by a group of people *or* with a sum of money; **union power** = strength of a union to affect management or government decisions **(b)** force *or* legal right; *as chief executive he wields enormous power; his new post gives him a lot of power over personnel in his department;* **executive power** = right to act as director *or* to put decisions into action; **power of attorney** = legal document which gives someone the right to act on someone's behalf in legal matters; **power struggle** = fight between people or groups to obtain control of something; *there was a power struggle in the boardroom, and the finance director had to resign*

p.p. ['piː'piː] *verb* = PER PROCURATIONEM **to p.p. a letter** = to sign a letter on behalf of someone; *the secretary p.p.'d the letter while the manager was at lunch*

PR ['piː'ɑː] = PUBLIC RELATIONS

practice ['præktɪs] *noun* way of doing things; *his practice was to arrive at work at 7.30 and start counting the cash;* **business practices** *or* **industrial practices** *or* **trade practices** = ways of managing *or* working in business, industry or trade; **restrictive practices** = ways of working which make people less free (such as trade unions stopping workers from doing certain jobs *or* companies not allowing customers a free choice of product); **standard practice** = the usual way of doing things; *it's standard practice to pass an envelope with money in it to the director's secretary;* **code of practice** = rules drawn up by an association which the members must follow when doing business

precautions [prɪ'kɔːʃənz] *plural noun* care taken to avoid something unpleasant; *to take precautions to prevent thefts in the office; the company did not take proper fire precautions;* **fire precautions** = care taken to avoid damage or casualties by fire; **safety precautions** = actions to try to make sure that something is safe

precondition [priːkənˈdɪʃn] *noun* condition set before something happens, such as a condition set by one side before joining negotiations; *management has agreed to talks without preconditions*

predecessor [ˈpriːdisesə] *noun* person who had a job *or* position before someone else; *he took over from his predecessor last May; she is using the same office as her predecessor*

predictive validity [priˈdɪktɪv vəˈlɪditi] *noun* assessing the validity of selection tests, by comparing the employee's performance in tests with his subsequent job performance

preferential [prefəˈrenʃəl] *adjective* showing that something is preferred more than another; **preferential shop** = agreement with a union that management will give first chance of new jobs to members of the union; *a preferential shops system is resented by applicants who do not wish to become members of the union;* **preferential treatment** = good treatment given to someone in power *or* to someone who is a friend of the person giving the treatment; *he gets preferential treatment because he's the MD's nephew*

prejudice [ˈpredʒudis] **1** *noun* **(a)** bias *or* unjust feelings against someone; **racial prejudice** = feelings against someone because of his or her race; *they investigated claims of racial prejudice in hiring staff; the immigrant felt forced to give up his job because of racial prejudice on the shop floor; the company found a deep-seated prejudice against new training methods on the part of the older managers* **(b)** harm done to someone; **without prejudice** = without harming any interests (words written on a letter to indicate that the writer is not legally bound to do what he offers to do in the letter) **2** *verb* to harm; *to prejudice someone's claim*

◊ **prejudiced** [ˈpredʒudist] *adjective* biased *or* with unjust feelings against someone; *the company was accused of being prejudiced against women*

preliminary [priˈlɪmɪnəri] *adjective* early,

happening before anything else; **preliminary hearing** = first meeting of an industrial tribunal where the tribunal decides if it is competent to hear the case

premium [ˈpriːmjəm] *noun* **(a) insurance premium** = annual payment made by the insured person *or* a company to an insurance company; *you pay either an annual premium of £360 or twelve monthly premiums of £32* **(b) premium bonus** = extra payment to an employee for taking less than the standard time for a task; **premium pay** *or* **premium rate** = rate of payment for overtime work

present [ˈpreznt] *adjective* **(a)** happening now; *the shares are too expensive at their present price; what is the present address of the company?* **(b)** being there when something happens; *only six directors were present at the board meeting*

preside [priˈzaɪd] *verb* to be chairman; *to preside over a meeting; the meeting was held in the committee room, Mr Smith presiding*

◊ **president** [ˈprezidənt] *noun* chief executive of a company *or* a club; *he was elected president of the sports club; after many years on the board, A.B. Smith has been appointed president of the company* (NOTE: in GB, president is sometimes a title given to a non-executive former chairman of a company; in the USA, the president is the main executive director of a company)

pressure [ˈpreʃə] *noun* something which forces you to do something; **to put pressure on someone to do something** = to try to force someone to do something; *the group tried to put pressure on the government to act; the banks put pressure on the company to reduce its borrowings;* **pressure group** = group of people who try to influence the government *or* the local town council, etc.

prevention [priˈvenʃn] *noun* steps to prevent something happening; **accident prevention** = measures taken to prevent accidents

preventive [priˈventɪv] *adjective* **preventive measures** = actions taken to prevent something from taking place

previous [ˈpriːvjəs] *adjective* which happens earlier; *list all previous positions with the salaries earned*

price [praɪs] **1** *noun* money which has to be paid to buy something; **Retail Price(s) Index (RPI)** = index which shows how prices of consumer goods have increased or decreased over a period of time; *our wage increases have closely followed the retail price index; the retail price index has risen at a lower rate than wages* **2** *verb* to give a price to a product; **to price oneself out of the market** = to ask for such a high salary that you cannot get a job

primary ['praɪmərɪ] *adjective* basic; **primary group** = group which is small enough to allow the members to interact informally; **primary labour market** = market for workers with specific skills; **primary negotiating demands** = initial demands made by one side in a negotiation, which are in fact not negotiable; *US* **primary boycott** = pressure put on an employer by workers directly involved in an industrial dispute; **primary industry** = industry dealing with basic raw materials (such as coal, wood, farm produce); *see also* SECONDARY

principal ['prɪnsəpl] **1** *noun* **(a)** person or company which is represented by an agent; *the agent has come to London to see his principals* **(b)** money invested or borrowed on which interest is paid; *to repay principal and interest* **2** *adjective* most important; *the principal shareholders asked for a meeting; the company's principal asset is its design staff*

principle ['prɪnsəpl] *noun* basic point or general rule; **in principle** = in agreement with a general rule; **agreement in principle** = agreement with the basic conditions of a proposal

priority [praɪ'ɒrɪtɪ] *noun* **to have priority** = to have the right to be first

private ['praɪvət] *adjective* **(a)** belonging to a single person, not a company or the state; **letter marked 'private and confidential'** = letter which must not be opened by anyone other than the person it is addressed to; **private secretary** = secretary who works for one manager or director only, and deals with personal and confidential matters **(b) in private** = away from other people; *he asked to see the managing director in private; in public the union said it would never go back to the*

negotiating table, but in private they were already having discussions with the company representatives

◊ **privately** ['praɪvətlɪ] *adverb* away from other people; *the deal was negotiated privately*

privilege ['prɪvɪlɪdʒ] *noun* advantage associated with a certain position or situation; *using the company jet is a privilege given only to top management*

proactive ['prəʊæktɪv] *adjective* taking the initiative in doing something (as opposed to reacting to events)

> QUOTE HR departments have accepted that if their role is to change, it is far better to be in control of developments than to have them imposed. Typically, it is those departments that are proactively managing their changing role that make the most use of IT and are most likely to have advanced HR systems
> *People Management*

probation [prə'beɪʃən] *noun* trial period for a new employee; *the accountant was appointed on three months' probation at the end of which he was not found to be satisfactory*

◊ **probationary** [prə'beɪʃənərɪ] *adjective* while someone is being tested; **probationary employee** = employee who is still on probation; **probationary period** = period during which a new employee is on probation; *during the probationary period the employee may be dismissed without notice; the probationary period is three months, after which the management may decide not to keep the worker, or alternatively, may offer an employment contract*

◊ **probationer** [prə'beɪʃənə] *noun* person who is on probation

problem ['prɒbləm] *noun* thing to which it is difficult to find an answer; *the company suffers from cash flow problems or staff problems;* **to solve a problem** = to find an answer to a problem; *problem solving is the test of a good manager;* **problem area** = area of a company's work which is difficult to run; *overseas sales is one of our biggest problem areas*

QUOTE everyone blames the strong dollar for US trade problems, but they differ on what should be done
Duns Business Month

procedure [prə'si:dʒə] *noun* method used *or* steps taken when something is done; *the management complained that the unions did not follow the proper procedure; induction mainly consists of introducing recruits to the company's work procedures;* **this procedure is very irregular** = this is not the set way to do something; **appeals procedure** = way in which an employee can appeal against a decision; **complaints procedure** *or* **grievance procedure** = way in which a trade union formally presents complaints to management; *the trade union has followed the correct complaints procedure;* **disciplinary procedure** = way of warning a worker officially that he or she is breaking the rules of a company; **dismissal procedures** = correct way to dismiss someone, following the rules in the contract of employment

◊ **procedural** [prə'si:dʒərəl] *adjective* referring to procedure; **procedural agreement** = agreement between a trade union and management on procedure to be followed during negotiations *or* bargaining

QUOTE the procedural 'gentleman's agreement' approach was not sufficient to sustain individual employees against workplace industrial action
Personnel Management

QUOTE this was a serious breach of disciplinary procedure and the dismissal was unfair
Personnel Management

proceedings [prə'si:dɪŋz] *plural noun* **appeal proceedings** = formal hearing of an appeal by a tribunal; **legal proceedings** = legal action *or* lawsuit; **to take** *or* **to institute proceedings against someone** = to start a legal action against someone

process ['prəʊses] **1** *noun* series of steps *or* stages that make up an activity; *we are beginning the process of shortlisting the candidates who have replied to the advertisement;* **process chart** = diagram which shows all the stages involved in a job *or* project in correct order; **decision-making processes** = ways in which decisions are

reached; **process skills** = skills in organizing, problem-solving, decision-making, etc. **2** *verb* **(a) to process figures** = to sort out information to make it easily understood; *the sales figures are being processed by our accounts department; data is being processed by our computer* **(b)** to deal with an administrative task in the usual routine way; *it takes some time to process an insurance claim; she is processing all the job applications*

production [prə'dʌkʃən] *noun* **(a)** showing something; **on production of** = when something is shown; *the case will be released by the customs on production of the relevant documents; goods can be exchanged only on production of the sales slip* **(b)** making *or* manufacturing of goods for sale; *production will probably be held up by industrial action; we are hoping to speed up production by installing new machinery; higher production is rewarded with higher pay;* **production bonus** = extra payment made for each job *or* task completed after a certain production target has been reached; **production curve** = extent to which output varies according to how long the worker has been working; **production management** = supervising a factory *or* a production process; **production manager** = person who supervises a production process; **production targets** = amounts of work which are fixed by the production manager as the target for each worker *or* shift; **production transfer** = transferring employees from jobs in which manpower requirements are declining to jobs where manpower requirements are on the increase

◊ **productivity** [prɒdʌk'tɪvɪti] *noun* rate of output per worker *or* per machine in a factory; *bonus payments are linked to productivity; the company is aiming to increase productivity; productivity has fallen or risen since the company was taken over;* **productivity agreement** = agreement between a union and management to make wage increases dependent on increases in productivity; **productivity audit** = review of a company's productivity and its relationship with its workers; **productivity bargaining** = bargaining between a union and management to agree on the level of productivity to be achieved; **productivity bonus** = extra payments made to workers because of increased productivity; **productivity drive** = extra effort to increase productivity

QUOTE the shake-out of manpower from traditional employment areas has generally increased the overall productivity of those at work
Personnel Management

QUOTE though there has been productivity growth, the absolute productivity gap between many British firms and their foreign rivals remains
Sunday Times

profession [prə'feʃən] *noun* **(a)** work which needs special skills learnt over a period of time, and tested by examinations; *personnel management is now more widely recognized as a profession; the managing director is an accountant by profession* **(b)** group of specialized workers; **the legal profession** = all lawyers; **the medical profession** = all doctors

◊ **professional** [prə'feʃənl] **1** *adjective* **(a)** referring to one of the professions; *the accountant sent in his bill for professional services; we had to ask our lawyer for professional advice on the contract; the professional institute awards diplomas;* **a professional man** *or* **professional woman** = man *or* woman who works in one of the professions (such as a lawyer, doctor, accountant); **professional body** = organization which trains, validates and organizes examinations for its members; **professional indemnity** = insurance against claims taken out by companies providing professional services, such as accountants, surveyors, etc.; **professional negligence** = failing to carry out one's duties properly (on the part of a professional person); **professional qualifications** = documents showing that someone has successfully finished a course of study which allows him or her to work in one of the professions; **professional traits** = characteristics (skills, knowledge, agreement with aims of a professional organization) which mark the true professional **(b)** fully qualified in a profession *or* skill; *she's a professional photographer* **(c)** with an attitude that shows that someone is an expert *or* skilled; *his work is very professional; they did a very professional job in designing the new office; his behaviour was not very professional* **2** *noun* skilled person *or* person who does skilled work for money

◊ **professionalism** [prə'feʃənlɪzm] *noun* showing a professional attitude; *his sales*

reports show a lack of professionalism which could be remedied by a period of in-house training

proficiency [prə'fɪʃənsi] *noun* skill *or* being capable of doing something; *her proficiency in languages should help in the export department; to get the job he had to pass a proficiency test*

◊ **proficient** [prə'fɪʃənt] *adjective* capable of doing something well; *she is quite proficient in accountancy*

profile ['prəʊfaɪl] *noun* brief description; *he asked for a company profile of the possible partners in the joint venture; his CV provided a profile of his education and career to date;* **job profile** = description of a job

profit ['prɒfɪt] *noun* money gained from a sale which is more than the money spent

◊ **profit and loss account (P&L account)** ['prɒfɪt ənd 'lɒs ə'kaʊnt] *noun* statement of a company's expenditure and income over a period of time, almost always one calendar year, showing whether the company has made a profit or loss; **consolidated profit and loss account** = profit and loss accounts of the holding company and its subsidiary companies, grouped together into a single profit and loss account (NOTE: the US equivalent is the **profit and loss statement** or **income statement**)

◊ **profit centre** ['prɒfɪt 'sentə] *noun* person *or* department which is considered separately for the purposes of calculating a profit

◊ **profit-related** ['prɒfɪt rɪ'leɪtɪd] *adjective* linked to profit; *profit-related pay*

◊ **profit-sharing scheme** ['prɒfɪtʃeərɪŋ 'skiːm] *noun* scheme by which employees (either all of them, or only certain selected categories) are entitled to get a share of the profits of the organization they work for; *the company runs a profit-sharing scheme; profit-sharing schemes encourage employees to identify more closely with the company*

programme *or* *US* **program** ['prəʊgræm] **1** *noun* **(a)** plan of things which will be done; *we are initiating a new recruitment programme; the personnel manager has drawn up a training programme;* **program evaluation and review**

technique (**PERT**) = way of planning and controlling a large project, concentrating on scheduling and completion on time (**b**) computer program = set of instructions for a computer to follow; *a program for selecting and retrieving information about personnel* **2** *verb* to write a program for a computer; **to program a computer** = to install a program in a computer; **programmed instruction** *or* **programmed learning** = course of instruction carried out by each trainee at his or her own speed (NOTE: the spelling **program** is often used in British English when referring to computers)

progress 1 ['prəʊgres] *noun* movement of work forward; *to report on the progress of the work or of the negotiations;* **to make progress** = to move forward in one's work; **in progress** = which is being done but is not finished; *negotiations in progress; work in progress* **2** [prə'gres] *verb* to move forward *or* to go ahead; *the contract is progressing through various departments*

◊ **progress chaser** ['prəʊgres 'tʃeɪsə] *noun* person whose job is to check that work is being carried out on schedule *or* that orders are being fulfilled on time, etc.

progression [prə'greʃn] *noun* moving forward in stages; **automatic wage progression** = automatic increase in wages according to the time a person has worked in the organization

progressive [prə'gresɪv] *adjective* which moves forward in stages; **progressive taxation** = tax which increases as a percentage of income as a person's income increases

prohibition [prəʊhɪb'ɪʃn] *noun* forbidding something; **prohibition notice** = notice from the Health and Safety Executive telling a company to stop doing something which is dangerous

prohibitory [prəʊ'hɪbɪtəri] *adjective* **prohibitory injunction** = injunction which prevents someone from doing an illegal act

projective [prə'dʒektɪv] *adjective* **projective listening** = imagining the effects of one's own words on other people in order to improve direct communication skills; *the sales manager trained his trainee salesmen in projective listening;* **projective test** = test of personality, where a candidate

is asked to describe what he sees in certain shapes

promote [prə'məʊt] *verb* to give someone a more important job *or* to move someone to a higher grade; *he was promoted from salesman to sales manager*

◊ **promotion** [prə'məʊʃn] *noun* moving an employee to a more important job *or* to a higher grade; *the job offers good promotion chances or promotion prospects; he ruined his chances of promotion when he argued with the managing director; he didn't regard his new job as promotion, since the pay was no higher;* **internal promotion** *or* **promotion from within** = promotion of someone working in the company already (as opposed to bringing in a new employee from outside); **to get promotion** = to be promoted; **to earn promotion** = to work hard and efficiently and so be promoted; **to be passed over for promotion** = not to be promoted when other employees on the same level are promoted

proprietor [prə'praɪətə] *noun* owner of a business; *he is the proprietor of a hotel or a hotel proprietor; the proprietor of the restaurant would only employ experienced staff*

◊ **proprietress** [prə'praɪətrəs] *noun* woman owner; *she is the proprietress of an advertising consultancy*

prosecute ['prɒsɪkjuːt] *verb* to bring (someone) to court to answer a criminal charge; *he was prosecuted for embezzlement*

◊ **prosecution** [prɒsɪ'kjuːʃn] *noun* (i) party who brings a criminal charge against someone; (ii) lawyers representing the party bringing a criminal charge against someone; *the costs of the case will be borne by the prosecution;* **prosecution counsel** *or* **counsel for the prosecution** = lawyer acting for the prosecution; *see also* DEFENCE

prospect 1 *noun* ['prɒspekt] (**a**) **prospects** = future possibilities for a person *or* organization; *he left the job because it had no prospects; what are his prospects of promotion or his promotion prospects?;* **career prospects** = possibilities of advancement in a career; **his job prospects are good** = he is very likely to find a job (**b**) possibility that something will happen; *there is no prospect of negotiations coming to an end soon* **2** *verb* [prə'spekt] to look for; *to prospect customers*

◊ **prospective** [prə'spektɪv] *adjective* person who could be appointed to a job; *we are interviewing prospective candidates next week*

protect [prə'tekt] *verb* to defend something against harm; *the workers are protected from unfair dismissal by government legislation*

◊ **protection** [prə'tekʃən] *noun* act of protecting; *the new legislation offers some protection against unscrupulous employers*

◊ **protective** [prə'tektɪv] *adjective* which protects; **protective award** = award made to a worker who was made redundant without the company following the normal consultation procedures or the normal notice period; **protective clothing** = clothes (hats, gloves, goggles, etc.) which protect a worker from dangerous substances

protest 1 ['prəʊtest] *noun* statement *or* action to show that you do not approve of something; *to stage a protest against low rates of pay;* **protest march** *or* **protest demonstration** = march *or* demonstration organized to protest against something; **sit-down protest** = action by members of the staff who occupy their place of work and refuse to leave; **in protest at** = showing that you do not approve of something; *the staff occupied the offices in protest at the low pay offer;* **to do something under protest** = to do something, but say that you do not approve of it **2** [prə(ʊ)'test] *verb* **to protest against something** = to say that you do not approve of something; *the staff are protesting against the ban on smoking in the office* (NOTE: GB English is **to protest against something**, but US English is **to protest something**)

proven ['prəʊvən] *adjective* which has been proved by time; *a man of proven experience*

provident ['prɒvɪdənt] *adjective* which provides benefits in case of illness *or* old age, etc.; *a provident fund; a provident society*

provision [prə'vɪʒən] *noun* **(a)** providing; **to make provision for** = to see that something is allowed for in the future; **there is no provision for** *or* **no provision has been made for car parking in the plans for the office block** = the plans do not include space for cars to park; *the management accepted*

the provision of a creche **(b) provisions** = money put aside in accounts for anticipated expenditure where the timing or amount of expenditure is uncertain (if the expenditure is not certain to occur at all, then the money set aside is called a 'contingent liability')

◊ **provisional** [prə'vɪʒənl] *adjective* temporary *or* not final or permanent; *he was given a provisional posting to see if he could manage a larger department*

◊ **provisionally** [prə'vɪʒnəli] *adverb* not finally; *the contract has been accepted provisionally*

proviso [prə'vaɪzəʊ] *noun* condition; *we are signing the contract with the proviso that the terms can be discussed again after six months*

proximate cause ['prɒksɪmət 'kɔːz] *noun* the direct cause (of an accident)

proxy ['prɒksi] *noun* **(a)** document which gives someone the power to act on behalf of someone else; *to sign by proxy;* **proxy form** *or* **proxy card** = form which a shareholder receives with his invitation to attend an AGM, which he fills in if he wants to appoint a proxy to vote for him on a resolution; **proxy vote** = votes made by proxy; *the proxy votes were all in favour of the board's recommendation* **(b)** person who acts on behalf of someone else; *to act as proxy for someone*

PRP = PERFORMANCE-RELATED PAY

psychology [saɪ'kɒlədʒi] *noun* study of the mind and its processes; **industrial psychology** = study of human behaviour and mental health in the workplace

◊ **psychological test** [saɪkə'lɒdʒɪkl] *noun* way of assessing the principal traits of a person's character; *the result of the psychological test showed that she was prone to depression*

◊ **psychologist** [saɪ'kɒlədʒɪst] *noun* doctor who specializes in the study of the mind and of mental processes; *studies by psychologists have shown the influence of work stress on production-line workers*

psychometric [saɪkə'metrɪk] *adjective* referring to psychometrics

◊ **psychometrics** [saɪkə'metrɪks] *noun* way of measuring ability and personality where the result is shown as a number on a scale; *psychometrics can be successfully applied to recruitment processes*

psychosometric [saɪkəsə'metrɪk] *adjective* **psychosometric tests** = tests to measure psychological traits in candidates

public ['pʌblɪk] **1** *adjective* referring to all the people in general; **public holiday** = day when all workers rest and enjoy themselves instead of working; *because he has no proper contract he doesn't get paid on public holidays;* **public liability insurance** = insurance against claims by members of the public **2** *noun* **the public** *or* **the general public** = the people; **in public** = in front of everyone; *in public he said that the company would soon be in profit, but in private he was less optimistic* (NOTE: no plural)

◊ **public relations (PR)** ['pʌblɪk rɪ'leɪʃənz] *plural noun* building up and keeping good relations between an organization *or* a group and the public *or* its employees, so that people know and think well of what the company is doing; *the company's internal public relations were improved by setting up the house journal; good public relations means explaining the company objectives to the employees;* **a public relations exercise** = a campaign to improve public relations

pull out ['pʊl 'aʊt] *verb* to stop being part of a deal *or* agreement; *our Australian partners pulled out of the talks*

punctual ['pʌŋktjʊəl] *adjective* tending to arrive at a place at the right time

◊ **punctuality** [pʌŋktjʊ'ælɪti] *noun* tendency to arrive at a place at the right time

punitive [pju:nɪtɪv] *adjective* which punishes; **punitive damages** = heavy damages awarded to show that the court feels the defendant has behaved badly towards the plaintiff; **punitive measures** = measures to punish someone

put back ['pʊt 'bæk] *verb* to change to a later time; *we had to put back the meeting because the leader of the management team was ill*

◊ **put in** ['pʊt 'ɪn] *verb* **to put an ad in a paper** = to have an ad printed in a newspaper; **the union put in a 6% wage claim** = the union asked for a 6% increase in wages

◊ **put off** ['pʊt 'ɒf] *verb* to arrange for something to take place later than planned; *the meeting was put off for two weeks; he asked if we could put the visit off until tomorrow*

◊ **put out** ['pʊt 'aʊt] *verb* to send out; *to put work out to freelancers; we put all our typing out to a bureau;* **to put work out to contract** = to decide that work should be done by a company on a contract, rather than employ members of staff to do it

pyramid ['pɪrəmɪd] *noun* shape like a triangle with a wide bottom rising to a point at the top; **organization pyramid** = structure of an organization with many employees at lower levels and fewer at the top

Qq

QC = QUALITY CIRCLE

quadruplicate [kwɒ'druːplɪkət] *noun* **in quadruplicate** = with the original and three copies; *the application form should be completed in quadruplicate*

qualification [kwɒlɪfɪ'keɪʃ(ə)n] *noun* **(a)** formal document *or* proof which recognizes that a person has completed a specialized course of study *or* has a special skill; *job-hunting is difficult if you have no qualifications; even with a university degree, he still did not have the right qualifications for the job;* **professional qualifications** = documents which show that someone has successfully finished a course of study which allows him to work in one of the professions **(b) period of qualification** = time which has to pass before someone qualifies for something

◊ **qualify** ['kwɒlɪfaɪ] *verb* **(a) to qualify for** = to be considered to be entitled to; *she qualifies for unemployment pay* **(b) to qualify as** = to follow a specialized course and pass examinations so that you can do a certain job; *she has qualified as an accountant; he will qualify as a solicitor next year*

◊ **qualified** ['kwɒlɪfaɪd] *adjective* having formal recognition of skill in a particular activity *or* having passed special examinations in a subject; *she is a qualified accountant; we have appointed a qualified designer to supervise the new factory project; she was the best-qualified candidate;* **highly qualified** = with very good results in examinations; *all our staff are highly qualified; they employ twenty-six highly qualified engineers*

◊ **qualifying** ['kwɒlɪfaɪɪŋ] *adjective* **qualifying day** = working day for which a worker is eligible to receive statutory sick pay; **qualifying earnings** = money earned on which national insurance contributions have been paid (such earnings qualify the worker for incapacity benefit); **qualifying period** = time which has to pass before something qualifies for a grant *or* subsidy, etc.; *there is a six-month qualifying period before you can get a grant from the local authority*

quality ['kwɒləti] *noun* what something is like *or* how good or bad something is; **quality assurance standards** = guaranteed levels of product quality which can be checked by the company; **quality circle (QC)** = group of workers in a company who meet to discuss quality controls and working practices; **quality control** = checking that the quality of a product is good; *our new profit-related incentive scheme has motivated the workforce to improve quality control;* **total quality management (TQM)** = management style which demands commitment to maintain and improve quality throughout the workforce; **quality controller** = person who checks the quality of a product; **quality of working life (QWL)** = general satisfaction with one's life at work, including the environment, career structure and pay

quantifiable ['kwɒntɪfaɪəbl] *adjective* which can be quantified; *the effect of the change in the discount structure is not quantifiable;* **quantifiable objectives** = objectives for which it is possible to give measures to gauge if they have been reached

quarter ['k(w)ɔːtə] *noun* period of three months; **first quarter** *or* **second quarter** *or* **third quarter** *or* **fourth quarter** *or* **last quarter**

= periods of three months from January to the end of March *or* from April to the end of June *or* from July to the end of September *or* from October to the end of the year; *his commission is paid by the quarter; the instalments are payable at the end of each quarter; the first quarter's rent is payable in advance;* **quarter day** = day at the end of a quarter, when rents *or* fees, etc. should be paid

COMMENT: in England, the quarter days are 25th March (Lady Day), 24th June (Midsummer Day), 29th September (Michaelmas Day) and 25th December (Christmas Day)

◊ **quarterly** ['k(w)ɔːtəli] *adjective & adverb* happening every three months *or* happening four times a year; *there is a quarterly charge for electricity; the bank sends us a quarterly statement; we agreed to pay the rent quarterly or on a quarterly basis;* **quarterly statement of contributions** = statement issued by a pension company which shows how much has been paid into a pensions scheme over the last quarter

QUOTE corporate profits for the first quarter showed a 4 per cent drop from last year's final three months
Financial Times

QUOTE economists believe the economy is picking up this quarter and will do better still in the second half of the year
Sunday Times

question ['kwestʃ(ə)n] **1** *noun* **(a)** words which need an answer; *the managing director refused to answer questions about redundancies; the training manager prepared a series of questions to test the trainees' reactions in different sales situations;* **open-ended question** = question in a questionnaire which allows a respondent to answer in some detail as he or she likes without having simply to say 'yes' or 'no' **(b)** problem; **to raise a question** = to mention a problem and expect it to be discussed; *he raised the question of moving to less expensive offices; the main question is that of the cost of the training programme; the board discussed the question of redundancy payments* **2** *verb* **(a)** to ask questions; *the police questioned the accounts staff for four hours; she questioned the chairman on the company's investment policy* **(b)** to query *or* to suggest that something may be wrong; *we all question how accurate the computer printout is*

◊ **questionnaire** [k(w)estʃə'neə] *noun* printed list of questions, especially used in surveys; *questionnaires were handed to the staff asking them about their attitudes to work conditions; the personnel department sent round questionnaires to other companies, asking them how they organized their information systems*

queue [kjuː] **1** *noun* **(a)** line of people waiting one behind the other; **dole queue** = line of people waiting to collect their unemployment money (NOTE: US English is **line**) **(b)** series of documents (such as orders, application forms) which are dealt with in order; **his case went to the end of the queue** = his case was dealt with last **2** *verb* to form a line one after the other for something; *the candidates queued outside the interviewing room*

quid pro quo [kwɪd prəʊ 'kwəʊ] *noun* money paid *or* action carried out in return for something; *he agreed to repay the loan early, and as a quid pro quo the bank released the collateral*

quit [kwɪt] *verb* to resign *or* to leave (a job); *he quit after an argument with the managing director; several of the managers are quitting to set up their own company*

quorum ['kwɔːrəm] *noun* minimum number of people who have to be present at a meeting to make it valid; **to have a quorum** = to have enough members present for a meeting to go ahead

QWL = QUALITY OF WORKING LIFE

Rr

R&D ['ɑːrən'diː] = RESEARCH AND DEVELOPMENT *the R&D department; the company spends millions on R&D*

race ['reɪs] *noun* group of people who are different because of skin colour, hair, eyes, etc.; **Race Relations Act 1976** = British act which makes racial discrimination in employment an offence

◊ **racial** ['reɪʃəl] *adjective* of or referring to a person's race; **racial discrimination** = treating a person differently (usually worse) because of his or her race; *the organization was accused of racial discrimination in selecting managers*

◊ **racism** *or* **racialism** ['reɪsɪzm *or* 'reɪʃəlɪzm] *noun* belief in racist ideas *or* actions based on racist ideas; *she accused the company of racism in their appointments to the management committee*

◊ **racist** ['reɪsɪst] *adjective* (person) believing that people of certain racial or ethnic groups are inferior

raiding ['reɪdɪŋ] *noun* enticing workers to work for another organization *or* enticing members of a union to join another union; *raiding is on the increase now that skilled labour is so scarce in this industry*

raise [reɪz] **1** *noun US* increase in salary; *he asked the boss for a raise; she got her raise last month* (NOTE: GB English is **rise**) **2** *verb* to increase *or* to make higher; *the organization will raise wages if inflation gets worse; this increase in production will raise the standard of living in the area*

random ['rændəm] *adjective* done without making any special choice; **random check** = check on items taken from a group without any special choice; **random inspection** = inspection carried out without any particular choice and without warning; **random sample** = sample for testing taken without any choice; **random sampling** = choosing samples for testing without any special selection; **at random** = without special choice; *the chairman picked out two salesmen's reports at random*

range [reɪn(d)ʒ] **1** *noun* series of items within certain limits; *there are a whole range of alternatives for the new salary scheme;* **range of salaries** *or* **salary range** = list of salaries paid, from the lowest to the highest; *the salary range is £5,000 - £7,000;* **range of indifference** = top area of a salary scale, where the salaries are so high that salary increases are no longer an incentive to perform better **2** *verb* to vary *or* to be different; *the company's salary scale ranges from £5,000 for a trainee to £50,000 for the managing director*

rank [ræŋk] **1** *noun* position in a company *or* an organization; *all managers are of equal rank; promotion means moving up from a lower rank;* **the lower ranks** = workers in less important jobs; **in rank order** = in order according to position of importance; *after the test the candidates were placed in rank order according to their results* **2** *verb* **(a)** to classify in order of importance; *candidates are ranked in order of their test results* **(b)** to be in a certain position; **all managers rank equally** = all managers have the same status in the company

◊ **rank and file** ['ræŋk ənd 'faɪl] *noun* ordinary members of a trade union; *the rank and file of the trade union membership; the decision was not liked by the rank and file;* **rank-and-file members** = ordinary members

◊ **ranking** ['ræŋkɪŋ] **1** *adjective* in a certain position; *he is the top-ranking or the senior-ranking official in the delegation* = the member of the delegation who occupies the highest official post **2** *noun* arranging into a list in order of quality *or* importance *or* quantity; *job ranking was carried out according to the relative importance of each job in the organization;* **factor ranking** = method of grading jobs in relation to factors such as 'training' or 'effort'; **ranking system** = way of calculating the value of jobs and sorting them into different levels

rate [reɪt] **1** *noun* **(a)** degree *or* level; **rate of taxation** *or* **tax rate** = proportion of a particular sum of money (such as a salary) which must be paid in tax; *he pays income tax at the highest rate* **(b)** money charged for time worked *or* work completed; **all-in rate** = price which covers all items in a purchase (such as delivery, tax and insurance, as well as the goods themselves); **daily rate** = money paid for one day's work; **fixed rate** = charge which cannot be changed; **flat rate** = charge which always stays the same; *a flat-rate increase of 10%; he is paid a flat rate of £2 per thousand;* **full rate** = full charge, with no reductions; **the going rate** = the usual *or* the current rate of payment; **hourly rate** = money paid for one hour's work; **the market rate** = normal price in the market; *we pay the going rate or the market rate for typists;* **overtime rate** = money paid for working overtime; **reduced rate** = specially cheap charge; **standard rate** = the normal rate, which everyone receives; **weekly rate** = money paid for one week's work **(c)** amount *or* number *or* speed compared with something else; *they work at the rate of five completed units per hour; the rate of increase in redundancies;* **absenteeism rate** = percentage of the workforce which is away from work with no good excuse; *the rate of absenteeism or the absenteeism rate always increases in fine weather;* **accident frequency rate** = number of accidents involving injury *or* death during a specified number of man-hours; **unemployment rate** *or* **rate of unemployment** = number of people out of work, shown as a percentage of the total number of people available for work **2** *verb* **to rate someone highly** = to value someone *or* to think someone is very good

QUOTE the unions had argued that public sector pay rates had slipped behind rates applying in private sector employment
Australian Financial Review

ratify ['rætɪfaɪ] *verb* to approve officially; *the agreement has to be ratified by the board*

◊ **ratification** [rætɪfɪ'keɪʃən] *noun* official approval; *the agreement has to go to the board for ratification*

rating ['reɪtɪŋ] *noun* assessing something by assigning a certain grade; **merit rating** = judging how well a worker does his work, so that he can be paid according to merit; **efficiency rating** = evaluation of an employee's efficiency in performing a job; **performance rating** = evaluating a person's work by giving it a certain grade; *some of the most confident workers had surprisingly low performance ratings;* **rating scale** = series of grades used in performance rating; **rating standard** = international standard of work efficiency for piece workers

ratio ['reɪʃɪəʊ] *noun* mathematical expression to show the relationship between two amounts; *with less manual work available, the ratio of workers to managers is decreasing; what is the ratio of foreign workers to British workers in the company?*

rationalization [ræʃnəlaɪ'zeɪʃən] *noun* streamlining *or* making more efficient

◊ **rationalize** ['ræʃnəlaɪz] *verb* to streamline *or* to make more efficient; *the organization is trying to rationalize its salary scales*

rat race ['ræt 'reɪs] *noun* competition for success in business *or* in a career; *he decided to get out of the rat race and buy a small farm*

raw [rɔː] *adjective* in the original state *or* not processed; **raw data** = data as it is put into a computer, without being analyzed; **raw labour** = unskilled workers; *because too high a proportion of the local workforce was raw labour, the company had to recruit from further afield*

reach [riːtʃ] *verb* to come to; **to reach an agreement** = to agree; **to reach a decision** = to decide; *the two parties reached an agreement over the terms for the contract; the board reached a decision about closing the factory*

readjust [riːə'dʒʌst] *verb* to adjust again; *to readjust salary scales*

readvertise [riː'ædvətaɪz] *verb* to advertise again; **to readvertise a post** = to put in a second advertisement for a vacant post; *all the candidates failed the test, so we will just have to readvertise*

◊ **readvertisement** [riːəd'vɜːtɪsmənt] *noun* second advertisement for a vacant post

real [rɪəl] *adjective* **(a)** true *or* not an imitation; **real earnings** *or* **real income** *or* **real**

wages = income which is available for spending after tax, etc. has been deducted, corrected for inflation; *his real income is low owing to the high level of taxation;* in real terms = actually *or* really; *wages have gone up by 3% but with inflation running at 5% that is a fall in real terms* (b) real time = time when a computer is working on the processing of data while the problem to which the data refers is actually taking place; **real-time system** = computer system where data is inputted directly into the computer which automatically processes it to produce information which can be used immediately

QUOTE real wages have been held down dramatically: they have risen as an annual rate of only 1% in the last two years

Sunday Times

reapply [riːə'plaɪ] *verb* to apply again; *when he saw that the job had still not been filled, he reapplied for it*

◊ **reapplication** ['riːæplɪ'keɪʃən] *noun* second application for a job

reappoint ['riːə'pɔɪnt] *verb* to appoint someone again; *he was reappointed chairman for a further three-year period*

◊ **reappointment** ['riːə'pɔɪntmənt] *noun* being reappointed; *the board decided to offer him reappointment for a further two years at the end of his fixed-term contract*

reason ['riːzn] *noun* thing which explains why something has happened; *the company gave no reason for the sudden closure of the factory; the personnel officer asked him for the reason why he was late again*

◊ **reasonable** ['riːzənəbl] *adjective* (a) sensible *or* not annoyed; *the manager of the shop was very reasonable when she tried to explain that she had left her credit cards at home;* **reasonable behaviour** = way of approach by an employer when making workers redundant; **duty of reasonable care** = duty of an employer to look after the safety of his employees and not act negligently (b) moderate *or* not expensive; *the union has decided to put in a reasonable wage claim*

reassess [riːə'ses] *verb* to assess again; *the manager was asked to reassess the department staff, after the assessments were badly done by the supervisors*

◊ **reassessment** [riːə'sesmənt] *noun* new assessment

reassign [riːə'saɪn] *verb* to assign again; to assign someone to a new position; *after six years as branch manager she has been reassigned to the headquarters staff*

◊ **reassignment** [riːə'saɪnmənt] *noun* new assignment

reassure [riːə'ʃuə] *verb* to make someone calm *or* less worried; *the manager tried to reassure her that she would not lose her job*

rebuke [rɪ'bjuːk] *noun* criticising someone for doing something

receipt [rɪ'siːt] *noun* (a) paper showing that money has been paid *or* that something has been received; *he had to sign a receipt for his payment; she signed a receipt for an advance on wages* (b) act of receiving something; **to acknowledge receipt of a letter** = to write to say that you have received a letter; *we acknowledge receipt of your letter of the 15th* (NOTE: no plural for this meaning)

receiver [rɪ'siːvə] *noun* **official receiver** = government official who is appointed to run a company which is in financial difficulties, to pay off its debts as far as possible, and to close it down; *the court appointed a receiver for the company; the company is in the hands of the receiver*

reception [rɪ'sepʃən] *noun* place (in a hotel *or* office) where visitors register *or* say who they have come to see; *all candidates should report to reception;* **reception desk** = desk where customers *or* visitors check in

◊ **receptionist** [rɪ'sepʃənɪst] *noun* person in a hotel *or* office who meets guests *or* clients, answers the phone, etc.

recession [rɪ'seʃən] *noun* fall in trade *or* in the economy; *several firms have closed factories because of the recession*

COMMENT: there are various ways of deciding if a recession is taking place: the usual one is when the GNP falls for three consecutive quarters

recipient [rɪ'sɪpɪənt] *noun* person who receives; *the recipient of an allowance from the company*

reckonable year ['rekənəbl] *noun* year in

which full NICs have been paid (used to calculate the state retirement pension)

recognize ['rekəgnaız] *verb* (a) to know someone *or* something because you have seen *or* heard them before; *I recognized his voice before he said who he was; do you recognize the handwriting on the application form?* (b) **to recognize a union** = to accept that a union can act on behalf of staff; *although all the staff had joined the union, the management refused to recognize it*

◊ **recognition** [rekəg'nıʃən] *noun* act of recognizing; **recognition of a trade union** *or* **union recognition** = act of agreeing that a union can act on behalf of staff in a company; **to grant a trade union recognition** = to recognize a trade union; **recognition agreement** = document which sets out the terms under which a union is recognized, and the ways in which management and union will work together in the future

recommend [rekə'mend] *verb* to say that someone *or* something is good; *I certainly would not recommend Miss Smith for the job; the management consultant recommended a different form of pay structure*

◊ **recommendation** [rekəmen'deıʃən] *noun* saying that someone *or* something is good; *we appointed him on the recommendation of his former employer;* **to make a recommendation** = to suggest that something should be done

reconsider [ri:kən'sıdə] *verb* to think again about a decision which has already been made; *the union asked management to reconsider their decision on closing the factory; the interim agreement will provide a breathing space while both sides reconsider their positions*

reconcile ['rekənsaıl] *verb* to make two things agree; *to reconcile different points of view*

record 1 ['rekɔːd] *noun* (a) documents which give information; *the names and addresses of members of staff are kept in the company's records; we find from our records that Mr Smith was employed by us from 1972 to 1975; the personnel department keeps records of all payments to staff;* **police record** = note of previous crimes for which someone has been convicted; *he did not say*

that he had a police record; **personnel records** = details of members of staff (b) history of past performance; *the salesman's record of service or service record; he has a very poor timekeeping record; the company has an excellent record of productivity;* **record of achievement** = document given to someone who has finished a course of instruction, showing achievement in class, exam results, etc.; **track record** = success or failure of a company *or* salesman in the past; *he has a good track record as a salesman; the company has no track record in the computer market* (c) report of something which has happened; *the chairman signed the minutes as a true record of the last meeting;* **for the record** *or* **to keep the record straight** = to note something which has been done; *for the record, I would like these sales figures to be noted in the minutes;* **on record** = correctly reported; *the chairman is on record as saying that profits are set to rise;* **to go on record as stating** = to state emphatically, so that it can be noted **2** [rı'kɔːd] *verb* to note *or* to report; **to record a complaint** = to listen to a complaint and make notes of it; *your complaint has been recorded and will be investigated*

recreation [rekrı'eıʃn] *noun* leisure time; *giving the shift workers half an hour recreation in the middle of the morning has resulted in improved productivity*

◊ **recreational** [rekrı'eıʃnl] *adjective* referring to recreation; **recreational facilities** = sports centres, football pitches, gymnasia, etc., provided by a company for the staff

recruit [rı'kru:t] **1** *noun* new member of staff; *the induction programme for recruits begins on Wednesday* **2** *verb* **to recruit new staff** = to search for and appoint new staff; *in the busy season we always recruit more temporary staff; they are recruiting staff for their new store; a new manager was recruited with experience in dealing with personnel matters*

◊ **recruitment** *or* **recruiting** [rı'kru:tmənt *or* rı'kru:tıŋ] *noun* the recruitment of new staff = searching for and appointing new staff to join a company; *which section in personnel deals with recruitment and selection?;* **graduate recruitment** = recruitment of graduates for traineeships in a company; **recruitment ratio** = ratio of the number of people appointed to jobs to the number of candidates applying; *the recruitment ratio is low in departments where a high level of skills is required; the sudden demand for a large number of new workers has led to the lowering of the recruitment ratio*

QUOTE greater pressure to identify and attract the most able people at all levels has led to the development of recruitment advertising into a highly sophisticated industry
Personnel Management

QUOTE some companies are still able to meet most of their needs by recruiting experienced people already in the industry
Personnel Management

QUOTE employers were asked about the nature of the jobs on offer and of the people they recruited to fill them
Employment Gazette

red circling [red 'sɜːklɪŋ] *noun* paying staff at a higher rate, even if their jobs have been downgraded

◊ **red circle rate** ['red sɜːkl 'reɪt] *noun* pay rate that is above the minimum rate for an employee's evaluated level

◊ **red tape** ['red 'teɪp] *noun* rules and regulations which creates a lot of paperwork; *the appointment of the new manager has been held up by red tape in the personnel office*

redeploy [riːdɪ'plɔɪ] *verb* to move workers from one place to another *or* to give workers totally different jobs to do; *we closed the design department and redeployed the workforce in the publicity and sales departments*

◊ **redeployment** [riːdɪ'plɔɪmənt] *noun* moving workers from one place of work to another or from one job to another

reduce [rɪ'djuːs] *verb* to make smaller *or* lower; *we have made some staff redundant to reduce overmanning;* **to reduce salaries** = to lower the level of salaries; **to reduce staff** = to sack employees in order to have a smaller number of staff

◊ **reduction** [rɪ'dʌkʃən] *noun* lowering (of quantities, prices, etc.); *working only part-time will mean a significant reduction in* take-home pay; *staff reductions were made necessary by the fall in the order book;* **manpower reductions** = reducing the number of employees; **reduction of manning levels** = reducing the number of employees needed in certain jobs; **reduction of working hours** = reducing the number of hours worked

redundancy [rɪ'dʌndənsi] *noun* **(a)** dismissal of a person whose skills are no longer needed; **redundancy pay** *or* **redundancy payment** = payment made to a worker to compensate for losing his job; **compulsory redundancy** = situation where an employee is made redundant by the company; **mass redundancies** = making a large number of people redundant at the same time; **voluntary redundancy** = situation where the worker asks to be made redundant **(b)** person who has lost a job because he is not needed any more; *the takeover caused 250 redundancies*

◊ **redundant** [rɪ'dʌndənt] *adjective* **(a)** (ability *or* skill) which is no longer needed *or* is useless; *retraining can help workers whose old skills have become redundant* **(b)** (person) who loses his job because his skills are no longer needed; **to make someone redundant** = to decide that a worker is not needed any more; **redundant staff** = staff who have lost their jobs because they are not needed any more; *several members of staff were made redundant during the recession*

QUOTE when Mrs C. was made redundant at 59 and 10 months she lost ten-twelfths of her redundancy pay
Personnel Management

re-employ [riːɪm'plɔɪ] *verb* to employ someone again

◊ **re-employment** [riːɪm'plɔɪmənt] *noun* employing someone again

re-engage [riːɪn'geɪdʒ] *verb* to re-employ a person, but not necessarily in the same job

◊ **re-engagement** [riːɪn'geɪdʒmənt] *noun* employing someone again, but not necessarily in the same job

referee [refə'riː] *noun* person (such as a former employer) who can give a report on someone's character *or* ability *or* job performance, etc.; *he chose his former* *headmaster as referee; she gave the name of her boss as a referee; when applying please give the names of three referees*

◊ **reference** ['refərəns] *noun* **(a)** written report on someone's character *or* ability *or* job performance, etc.; *her former boss wrote her a reference or gave her a reference; all applicants for the post are asked to supply references; she got the job on the strength of two excellent references;* **negligent reference** = written reference from an employer which could mislead another employer about a worker; **letter of reference** = letter in which an employer *or* former employer recommends someone for a job; *he enclosed letters of reference from his two previous employers* **(b)** person who reports on someone's character *or* ability, etc.; *he gave the name of his former manager as reference; please use me as a reference if you wish;* **character reference** = report showing the strength of someone's character **(c)** **reference group** = group used as a comparison with another group; **reference period** = period which is used as a base for comparisons

QUOTE the reference has to be accurate and opinion must be clearly separated from the facts
Personnel Management

refresher course [rɪ'freʃə 'kɔːs] *noun* course of study designed to revive skills or knowledge in people who have forgotten them or are out of practice; *refresher courses were given to some of the workers who had not used this type of machinery for some time; he went on a refresher course in bookkeeping*

refreshment [rɪ'freʃmənt] *noun* food and drink; **refreshment time** *or* **refreshment break** = rest time during work when the workers can have something to eat or drink; *see also* COFFEE BREAK, TEA BREAK

region ['riːdʒən] *noun* large area of a country; **in the region of** = about *or* approximately; *he was earning a salary in the region of £25,000*

register ['redʒɪstə] **1** *noun* official list; *people on the register of electors;* **to be on the unemployment register** = to be officially classified as unemployed **2** *verb* to write something in an official list; *after he was*

made redundant he registered at the unemployment office; to register a fall in the numbers of unemployed teenagers;* **registered as unemployed** = person who has not job, has registered for unemployment benefit and is actively looking for work; **registered disabled person** = person who is registered with the Department for Employment as handicapped

registrar [redʒɪs'trɑː] *noun* person who keeps official records

regular ['regjʊlə] *adjective* which happens *or* comes at the same time each day *or* each week *or* each month *or* each year; **regular income** = income which comes in every week or month; *she works freelance so she does not have a regular income;* **regular staff** = full-time staff

regulation [regjʊ'leɪʃən] *noun* **regulations** = laws *or* rules; *the new member was warned not to break union regulations about overtime; the organization is a typical bureaucracy with hundreds of rules and regulations; have you read the fire regulations or safety regulations?*

rehabilitation [riːhəbɪlɪ'teɪʃn] *noun* making someone fit for work again (after illness, period in prison, etc.); **rehabilitation centre** = centre where people who have been out of work for some time (because of illness or unemployment, etc.) can be trained to reenter the work environment

COMMENT: by the Rehabilitation of Offenders Act, 1974, a person who is convicted of an offence, and then spends a period of time without committing any other offence, is not required to reveal that he has a previous conviction

rehire [riː'haɪə] *verb* to take someone back as a member of staff after he or she has been made redundant or has left the company

reimburse [riːɪm'bɜːs] *verb* **to reimburse someone his expenses** = to pay someone back for money which he has spent; *you will be reimbursed for your expenses or your expenses will be reimbursed*

◊ **reimbursement** [riːɪm'bɜːsmənt] *noun* paying back money; **reimbursement of expenses**

reinstate [riːɪn'steɪt] *verb* to re-employ

someone in the same job (from which he was dismissed); *the union demanded that the sacked workers should be reinstated*

◊ **reinstatement** [ri:ɪn'steɪtmənt] *noun* putting someone back into a job from which he was dismissed; **reinstatement order** = order by a tribunal to an employer to give a dismissed person his job back

reject [rɪ'dʒekt] *verb* to refuse to accept *or* to say that something is not satisfactory; *the union rejected the management's proposals; he will probably reject the conditions attached to the job offer; three out of the four candidates were rejected by the selection board*

◊ **rejection** [rɪ'dʒekʃən] *noun* refusal to accept; *after the union's rejection of the offer, management came back with new redundancy terms*

relations [rɪ'leɪʃənz] *noun* **(a)** dealing (with other people *or* other organizations); *we try to maintain good relations with our customers; relations between management and workforce have never been good in this factory;* **to break off relations with someone** = to stop dealing with someone; **collective relations** = relations between employers associations and trade unions; **industrial relations** *or* **labour relations** = relations between management and workers; *the company has a history of bad labour relations* **(b)** **public relations (PR)** = building up and keeping good relations between an organization and the public *or* its employees, so that people know and think well of what the company is doing; **public relations department** = section of a company which deals with relations with the public; **a public relations exercise** = a campaign to improve public relations; **public relations officer (PRO)** = official who deals with relations with the public

release [rɪ'li:s] **1** *noun* **(a)** end to an employee's contract with an organization; *he was offered early release so that he could take up his new job* **(b)** **block-release** = permission for an employee to attend a series of courses outside his place of work; **day release** = arrangement where a company allows a worker to go to college to study for one day each week; *the junior sales manager is attending a day release course* **(c)** **press release** = sheet giving news about something which is sent to

newspapers and TV and radio stations so that they can use the information in it **2** *verb* to end an employee's contract early

relevant ['reləvənt] *adjective* which has to do with what is being discussed or the current situation; *the new secretary does not have any relevant experience*

reliable [rɪ'laɪəbl] *adjective* which can be trusted; **a reliable test** = a test which always gives correct results

◊ **reliability** [rɪlaɪə'bɪləti] *noun* being reliable

relief [rɪ'li:f] *noun* **(a)** person who takes the place of another, who is sick or on holiday; *a relief manager has been sent from headquarters; the bus carrying relief workers was late;* **relief shift** = shift which comes to take the place of another shift, usually the shift between the day shift and the night shift **(b)** help; **tax relief** = allowing someone to pay less tax on certain parts of his income

◊ **relieve** [rɪ'li:v] *verb* to come to work to take the place of another worker at the end of a shift; *the shift will be relieved at 06.30*

relocate [ri:lə'keɪt] *verb* to establish an organization in a new place; to be established in a new place; *if the company moves down south, all the managerial staff will have to relocate or to be relocated*

◊ **relocation** [ri:lə'keɪʃn] *noun* establishing an organization *or* a worker in a new place; *the company will pay all relocation expenses;* **relocation allowance** = special payment given to a worker who agrees to move to another town to work; **relocation expenses** = payment of expenses involved when a worker has to move house because his place of work has changed, or when a new employee has to move house to join the company

QUOTE for some employees company relocation will have the same effect as redundancy
Personnel Today

QUOTE a firm of relocation experts was called in to assist in the mechanics, especially for house sales and purchases
Personnel Today

remedial transfer [rɪ'mi:diəl 'trænzfə]

noun transferring an employee to another more suitable job after he or she has not performed well in the present position; *the personnel manager and the supervisor discussed the possibility of a remedial transfer for a staff member who was doing badly in his present position*

removal [rɪ'muːvəl] *noun* (a) moving to a new house *or* office; **removal** *or* **removals company** = company which specializes in moving the contents of a house *or* an office to a new building; *staff are allowed removal expenses on joining the company* (b) sacking someone (usually a director) from a job; *the removal of the managing director is going to be very difficult*

remunerate [rɪ'mjuːnəreɪt] *verb* to pay someone for doing something; *the company refused to remunerate them for their services*

◊ **remuneration** [rɪmjuːnə'reɪʃən] *noun* payment for services; *the job is interesting but the remuneration is low; she receives a small remuneration of £400 a month; no one will work hard for such poor remuneration;* **remunerations committee** = committee of senior executives or non-executive directors who decide on directors' salaries; **remunerations consultant** = adviser who gives advice on wage and salary structures

◊ **remunerative**   [rɪ'mjuːnərətɪv] *adjective* (job) which pays well; *he is in a highly remunerative job*

renew [rɪ'njuː] *verb* to continue something for a further period of time; *his contract was renewed for a further three years;* **to renew an insurance policy** = to pay the premium for another year's insurance

◊ **renewal** [rɪ'njuːəl] *noun* act of renewing; *renewal of a contract; his contract is up for renewal in January;* **renewal notice** = note sent by an insurance company asking the insured person to renew the insurance; **renewal premium** = premium to be paid to renew an insurance policy

reopen [riː'əupən] *verb* to open again; *the management agreed to reopen discussions with the union*

◊ **reopening** [riː'əupənɪŋ] *noun* opening again; **reopening clause** = clause in an agreement between a union and an employer which allows the union to reopen discussions on a particular issue during the term of the agreement

reorganize [riː'ɔːgənaɪz] *verb* to organize in a new way

◊ **reorganization** [riːɔːgənaɪ'zeɪʃən] *noun* new way of organizing; *his job was downgraded in the office reorganization or in the reorganization of the office*

repeat [rɪ'piːt] *verb* to do or say something again; **repeated absences from work** = being absent from work again and again

repetitive   [rɪ'petɪtɪv] *adjective* which happens again and again; **repetitive strain injury** *or* **repetitive stress injury (RSI)** = pain in the arm felt by someone who performs the same movement many times over a certain period, as when keyboarding; **repetitive work** = work which involves repeating the same task over and over again; *supervisors try to introduce some variation into the work pattern since repetitive work leads to boredom; psychologists claim that repetitive work can be just a stressful as more demanding but varied work*

replace [rɪ'pleɪs] *verb* to put someone in the place of someone else; *they replaced the foreman with a younger man; we are replacing all our salaried staff with freelancers*

◊ **replacement** [rɪ'pleɪsmənt] *noun* (a) act of putting someone in the place of another; **replacement rate** = proportion of an organization's manpower that is replaced every year; *the high replacement rate can be put down to dissatisfaction with working conditions* (b) person who replaces someone; *my secretary leaves us next week, so we are advertising for a replacement*

report   [rɪ'pɔːt] **1** *noun* statement describing what has happened *or* describing a state of affairs; *the personnel manager read the reports of the training sessions; the chairman has received a report on the union claim;* **accident report** = report of an accident which has taken place at work; **monthly activity report** = report by a department on what has been done during the past month; **annual report** = report of a company's financial situation at the end of a year, sent to all the shareholders; **confidential report** = secret document which must not be shown to other people; **medical report** = report by a doctor on the medical condition of an employee; **progress report** =

document which describes what progress has been made **2** *verb* **(a)** to make a statement describing something; *each manager reports on the progress made by the new recruits during their first six weeks in the department; he reported seeing the absentee in a shop* (NOTE: in this meaning, you **report something** or **report on something** or **report doing something**) **(b)** to **report to someone** = to be responsible to *or* to be under someone; *he reports direct to the managing director; the salesmen report to the sales director* **(c)** to go to a place *or* to attend; *he reported for work at the usual time; you are asked to report for an interview at 11.00; please report to our London office for training;* to **report sick** = to state officially that you are sick and so cannot work; **reporting pay** = guaranteed pay for employees who report for work whether there is work for them to do or not; *the reporting pay system can be a drain on the company's resources when the order book is low*

◊ **reportable accident** [rɪ'pɔːtəbl 'æksɪdənt] *noun* accident which causes death, or which makes a worker stay away from work for more than three days

QUOTE the successful candidate will report to the area director for profit responsibility for sales of leading brands

Times

represent [reprɪ'zent] *verb* to act on behalf of someone; *he sent his solicitor and accountant to represent him at the meeting; three managers represent the workforce in discussions with the directors; which sector of the workforce does he represent on the committee?*

◊ **representation** [reprɪzen'teɪʃən] *noun* **(a)** having someone to act on your behalf; *the ordinary shop floor workers want representation on the committee;* **employee representation** = having representatives of the employees on committees or boards **(c)** complaint made on behalf of someone; *the managers made representations to the board on behalf of the hourly-paid members of staff*

◊ **respresentational rights** [reprɪzen'teɪʃənəl 'raɪts] *noun* rights of a union to represent workers in dealings with management

◊ **representative** [reprɪ'zentətɪv] *noun* person who acts on someone's behalf; *he*

sent his solicitor and accountant to act as his representatives at the meeting; the board refused to meet the representatives of the workforce; **staff representative** = person who represents the staff on a committee; **union representative** = person who represents a union on a committee

reprimand ['reprɪmɑːnd] **1** *noun* official criticism given to an employee; *after receiving one reprimand he knew he would be sacked for further absenteeism* **2** *verb* to criticize someone officially; *he was reprimanded by the manager*

repudiate [rɪ'pjuːdɪeɪt] *verb* to refuse to accept; **to repudiate an agreement** *or* **a contract** = to refuse to perform one's obligations under an agreement *or* contract

◊ **repudiation** [rɪpjuːdɪ'eɪʃən] *noun* refusal to accept; refusal to perform one's obligations under an agreement *or* contract

request [rɪ'kwest] *noun* asking for something; **on request** = if asked for; *we will send samples on request or 'samples available on request'*

requirement [rɪ'kwaɪəmənt] *noun* what is needed; **entry requirement** = qualifications which a beginner needs to start a job; **job requirement** = qualifications or experience needed to start a job; **manpower requirements** = number of workers needed; **to meet the requirements of a job** = to have the right qualifications or experience for a job

requisition [rekwɪ'zɪʃən] **1** *noun* official order for something; **requisition form** = form sent to the personnel department from a department in an organization asking for a new employee to be found to fill a vacancy; *the requisition form should contain all details of the job specification and terms of employment offered* **2** *verb* to put in an official order for something

research [rɪ'sɜːtʃ] *noun* trying to find out facts *or* information; **research and development (R & D)** = scientific investigation which leads to making new products or improving existing products; *the company spends millions on research and development;* **research and development costs** = the costs involved in R & D

resent [rɪ'zent] *verb* to feel annoyed about

something; *the secretaries resent having to make coffee for their bosses; the rest of the office resented his promotion to manager*

◊ **resentful** [rɪ'zentfʊl] *adjective* feeling annoyed about something; *the junior members of staff feel resentful that the managers have a separate dining room*

◊ **resentment** [rɪ'zentmənt] *noun* feeling of annoyance at something; *the resentment of the unions at their treatment by management ended in a series of one-day strikes*

residence ['rezɪdəns] *noun* act of living *or* operating officially in a country; **residence permit** = official document allowing a foreigner to live in a country; *after living and working illegally for some time he has finally applied for a residence permit; she was granted a residence permit for one year*

◊ **resident** ['rezɪdənt] *noun* person *or* company considered to be living or operating in a country for official or tax purposes; **non-resident** = person *or* company which is not officially resident in a country; *she was granted a non-resident visa*

residual [rɪ'zɪdjʊəl] *adjective* remaining after everything else has gone; **residual unemployment** = unemployment amongst people who are not capable of doing the work available

resign [rɪ'zaɪn] *verb* to give up a job; *he resigned from his post as treasurer; he has resigned with effect from July 1st; she resigned as finance director*

◊ **resignation** [rezɪg'neɪʃən] *noun* act of giving up a job; *he wrote his letter of resignation to the chairman;* **to hand in** *or* **to give in** *or* **to send in one's resignation** = to resign from a job

resolution [rezə'luːʃən] *noun* decision to be discussed at a meeting; **to put a resolution to a meeting** = to ask a meeting to vote on a proposal; *the meeting passed or carried or adopted a resolution to go on strike; the meeting rejected the resolution or the resolution was defeated by ten votes to twenty; a resolution was passed to raise salaries by six per cent*

resolve [rɪ'zɒlv] *verb* to decide to do something; *the meeting resolved that a strike ballot should be held*

resources [rɪ'sɔːsɪz] *plural noun* (a) **financial resources** = supply of money for something; *the costs of the London office are a drain on the company's financial resources; the company's financial resources are not strong enough to support the cost of the research programme;* **the cost of the new project is easily within our resources** = we have enough money to pay for the new project (b) strengths *or* advantages of a person *or* organization; **human resources** = workforce available to do a certain job; **human resources management** = responsibility for an organization's productive use of and constructive dealings with its employees; **human resources manager** = person who is responsible for an organization's productive use of its workforce; *we must improve our human resources if productivity is to be increased; emigration has reduced the country's manpower resources; he was appointed human resources manager because of his experience in manpower planning and recruitment*

QUOTE clearly a human resources strategy for new technology has to be a flexible strategy
Personnel Management

QUOTE a systematic approach to human resource planning can play a significant part in reducing recruitment and retention problems
Personnel Management

QUOTE effective use and management of human resources hold the key to future business development and success
Management Today

respondent [rɪ'spɒndənt] *noun* employer who is defending a case brought before the Industrial Tribunal by an employee

responsibility [rɪspɒnsə'bɪləti] *noun* (a) being responsible for doing a job *or* for the care of someone or something; *the manager has overall responsibility for the welfare of the workers in his department* (b) **responsibilities** = duties; *he finds the responsibilities of being managing director too heavy*

◊ **responsible** [rɪ'spɒnsəbl] *adjective* (a) **responsible for** = directing *or* being in charge of doing a certain job; *he is responsible for the staff in his department; the fire safety* *officer is responsible for seeing that all staff are out of a building if a fire breaks out* **(b) responsible to someone** = being under someone's authority; *he is directly responsible to the managing director* **(c)** (person) who is sensible *or* who can be trusted; **responsible job** = job where important decisions have to be taken *or* where the employee has many responsibilities; *he is looking for a responsible job in marketing*

◊ **responsibly** [rɪ'spɒnsɪbli] *adverb* in a responsible way; *the staff acted very responsibly when the fire broke out*

responsive [rɪ'spɒnsɪv] *adjective* (person) who listens and does what someone asks; *the personnel manager was responsive to her request for compassionate leave;* **responsive listening** = listening carefully and responding to what another person says; *the personnel manager's responsive listening made the trainee feel that he understood her problems*

restart [riː'stɑːt] *verb* to start something again; *negotiations will restart tomorrow;* **restart interview** = interview given to someone who is unemployed, with the aim of advising him or her on means of getting back to work

restraint [rɪ'streɪnt] *noun* control; **pay restraint** *or* **wage restraint** = keeping increases in wages under control

restrict [rɪ'strɪkt] *verb* to limit *or* to impose controls on; *we are restricted to twenty staff by the size of our offices*

◊ **restrictive** [rɪ'strɪktɪv] *adjective* which limits; **restrictive covenant** = clause in a contract which prevents someone from doing something; **restrictive practices** = ways of working which make people less free (such as trade unions stopping workers from doing certain jobs *or* companies not allowing customers a free choice of product); *as part of a policy of restrictive practices he refused to do anything which was not laid down in his contract of employment; restrictive practices in industry mean that employers will not be able to afford to take on more labour;* **restrictive trade practices** = arrangement between companies to fix prices *or* to share the market, etc.

restructuring [riː'strʌktʃərɪŋ] *noun*

reorganizing the financial basis (of a company)

result [rɪ'zʌlt] **1** *noun* something which happens because of something else; *the company doubled its sales force with the result that sales rose by 26%;* **payment by results** = being paid for profits *or* increased sales **2** *verb* **(a) to result in** = to produce as a result; *the doubling of the sales force resulted in increased sales; the extra orders resulted in overtime work for all the factory staff* **(b) to result from** = to happen because of something; *we have to fill several vacancies resulting from the recent internal promotions*

resume [rɪ'zjuːm] *verb* to start again; *the discussions resumed after a two hour break*

résumé *or* **resume** ['rezjʊmeɪ] *noun US* summary of a person's life story with details of education and work experience sent to a prospective employer by someone looking for a job (NOTE: GB English is **curriculum vitae**)

resumption [rɪ'zʌm(p)ʃən] *noun* starting again; *we expect an early resumption of negotiations* = we expect negotiations will start again soon; **resumption of work** = starting work again after a strike, an accident, etc.

retain [rɪ'teɪn] *verb* **(a)** to keep; **retained earnings** *or* **retained profit** = amount of profit after tax which a company does not pay out as dividend to the shareholders, but keeps within the business **(b) to retain a lawyer to act for a company** = to agree with a lawyer that he will act for you (and pay him a fee in advance)

◊ **retainer** [rɪ'teɪnə] *noun* money paid in advance to someone so that he will work for you, and not for someone else; *we pay him a retainer of £1,000*

retention [rɪ'tenʃn] *noun* **employee retention** = keeping employees on the staff, and not losing them to rival firms; **retention bonus** = bonus payment paid to workers who are obliged to stay on to close down a business, where their colleagues will have been eligible for redundancy payments; **retention profile** = analysis of all employees who join at the same date, showing how many leave each year, expressed as a percentage of the original total

QUOTE a systematic approach to human resource planning can play a significant part in reducing recruitment and retention problems
Personnel Management

retire [rɪ'taɪə] *verb* **(a)** to stop work and take a pension; *she retired with a £6,000 pension; the founder of the company retired at the age of 85; the shop is owned by a retired policeman* **(b)** to make a worker stop work and take a pension; *they decided to retire all staff over 50*

◊ **retiral** [rɪ'taɪərəl] *noun* *US* = RETIREMENT

◊ **retiree** [rɪtaɪə'riː] *noun* person who has retired or is about to retire

◊ **retirement** [rɪ'taɪəmənt] *noun* (i) act of retiring from work; (ii) period when a person is retired; *he is looking forward to his retirement; older staff are wondering what they will do in retirement;* **early retirement** = scheme where a company encourages employees to retire earlier than usual, and receive financial compensation for this; **to take early retirement** = to leave work before the usual age; **flexible retirement scheme** = scheme where employees can choose the age at which they retire (between certain age limits, 55 and 65, for example); **retirement age** = age at which a worker can retire on full pension (in the UK usually 65 for men and 60 for women, though it is illegal to discriminate between the two); **retirement date** = date on which someone retires and takes a pension; **retirement pension** = pension paid to a person who has reached retirement age; *in two years he will be eligible for his retirement pension* (NOTE: no plural)

QUOTE the company operated a policy of retiring women when they reached pensionable age
Personnel Today

QUOTE companies are equalizing retirement ages for men and women
Personnel Management

retrain [riː'treɪn] *verb* to train someone for a new job, or to do the same job in a more modern way

◊ **retraining** [riː'treɪnɪŋ] *noun* act of training again; *the shop is closed for staff retraining; he had to attend a retraining*

session; *retraining is necessary to keep up with new production methods*

QUOTE employers will have to invest more - and more effectively - in training and retraining those they already employ
Employment Gazette

retroactive [retrəʊ'æktɪv] *adjective* which takes effect from a time in the past; *retroactive pay rise; they got a pay rise retroactive to last January*

◊ **retroactively** [retrəʊ'æktɪvli] *adverb* going back to a time in the past

returner [rɪ'tɜːnə] *noun* person who comes back to work after being away for a time; **women returners** = women who return to full-time work after having had children

review [rɪ'vjuː] **1** *noun* general examination; **wage review** *or* **salary review** = examination of salaries *or* wages in a company to see if the workers should earn more; *she had a salary review last April* = her salary was examined (and increased) in April; **under review** = being examined; *our wage and salary structure is currently under review* **2** *verb* to examine something generally; **to review salaries** = to look at all salaries in a company to decide on increases; *his salary will be reviewed at the end of the year; the company has decided to review freelance payments in the light of the rising cost of living*

revoke [rɪ'vəʊk] *verb* to cancel; *to revoke a decision or a clause in an agreement*

reward [rɪ'wɑːd] **1** *noun* money or other gains from effort; *the present given to the retiring manager was a reward for many years loyal service to the company; although the job is very demanding, the rewards are considerable;* **reward package** = total of all money and benefits given to an employee (salary, bonuses, company car, pension plans, medical insurance, etc.); **reward review** = study of a worker's performance to determine his correct pay level **2** *verb* to give a person something in return for effort *or* achievement; *the work is hard and not very rewarding financially*

QUOTE an additional incentive is that the Japanese are prepared to give rewards where they are due
Management Today

rid [rɪd] *verb* **to get rid of something** = to throw something away because it is useless; *the department has been told to get rid of twenty staff*

right [raɪt] *noun* legal title to something; *right of renewal of a contract; she has a right to the property; he has no right to the patent; the staff have a right to know how the company is doing;* **right of appeal** = right to challenge a decision of a tribunal; **right to manage** = right which a management has to take decisions without necessarily taking the opinions of the employees into account; **right to strike** = legal title for workers to stop working if they have a good reason for it; **right to work** = right of an adult person to find work; **civil rights** = rights and privileges of each individual according to the law; **human rights** = rights of individual men and women to basic freedoms, such as freedom of speech, freedom of association

◊ **right-hand man** [raɪthænd 'mæn] *noun* most important subordinate or assistant

rigid ['rɪdʒɪd] *adjective* not flexible *or* which cannot be changed; *the economy is being held back by rigid labour laws; the employees complained that the management was too rigid in interpreting the rule book*

rise [raɪz] **1** *noun* **(a)** increase; *there needs to be an increase in salaries to keep up with the rise in the cost of living; the recent rise in unemployment has been linked to the increased suicide rate* **(b)** **pay rise** *or* **salary rise** = increase in salary; *she asked her boss for a rise; he had a 6% rise in January* (NOTE: US English for this meaning is **raise**) **2** *verb* to move upwards *or* to become higher; *salaries are rising faster than inflation* (NOTE: **rising - rose - has risen**)

roadshow ['rəʊdʃəʊ] *noun* travelling exhibition where companies have stands to show what they do in order to attract potential trainees

robot ['rəʊbɒt] *noun* machine which can be programmed to work like a person; *the car is made by robots*

◊ **robotics** [rəʊ'bɒtɪks] *noun* study of robots *or* making of robots

role [rəʊl] *noun* part played by someone in a workplace *or* organization; *the manager is more effective in his role as employer than as salesman; it is easier for an outsider to play the role of mediator in the dispute;* **role model** = someone whose behaviour is copied; **role play** *or* **role playing** = training technique where trainees play different roles (salesman, customer, manager, junior, etc.) in order to get a better understanding of people and to improve their powers of communication; *role-playing sessions are used to improve the salesmen's approach to customers; role-playing was used as part of the management training programme to stimulate board meetings*

QUOTE role playing designed to simulate work situations: for example, candidates may be asked to stand in for a fictional manager who has been taken sick
Sunday Times

roll call ['rəʊl 'kɔːl] *noun* calling out the names of employees to see if their are present (as during a fire in an office or factory)

rolling budget ['rəʊlɪŋ 'bʌdʒɪt] *noun* budget which moves forward on a regular basis (such as a budget covering a twelve-month period, which moves forward each month or quarter)

roster *or* **rota** ['rɒstə *or* 'rəʊtə] *noun* list showing when different members of staff will do certain duties; *we are drawing up a new roster for Saturday afternoon work;* **duty roster** = list of times showing when each person is on duty at those times

rotate [rəʊ'teɪt] *verb* to do tasks in turns; *the shifts are rotated every fortnight;* **rotating shifts** = system where workers take turns in working different shifts; *rotating shifts can be unpopular with workers who do not want to break their routine*

◊ **rotation** [rəʊ'teɪʃən] *noun* taking turns; *to avoid monotony, the workers do the different tasks in rotation;* **to fill the post of chairman by rotation** = each member of the group is chairman for a period then gives the post to another member; **job rotation** = moving of workers from one job to another systematically

routine [ruː'tiːn] **1** *noun* normal *or* regular way of doing something; *he follows a daily routine - he takes the 8.15 train to London, then the bus to his office, and returns by the same route in the evening; refitting the* *conference room has disturbed the office routine* **2** *adjective* normal *or* which happens regularly; *they carried out a routine check of the fire equipment; members of staff have routine medical examinations*

RSI = REPETITIVE STRAIN INJURY

rule [ruːl] **1** *noun* **(a)** general way of conduct; **as a rule** = usually; *as a rule, we do not give discounts over 20%;* **company rules** = general way of working in a company; *it is a company rule that smoking is not allowed in the offices; the rules of the organization are explained during the induction sessions* **(b)** **to work to rule** = to work strictly according to the rules agreed by the company and union, and therefore to work very slowly **2** *verb* **(a)** to give an official decision; *the commission of inquiry ruled that the company was in breach of contract; the judge ruled that the documents had to be deposited with the court* **(b)** to be in force; *the current ruling agreement is being redrafted*

◊ **rule book** [ˈruːlbʊk] *noun* list of rules by which union members work in an organization, agreed between the union and management

◊ **ruling** [ˈruːlɪŋ] *noun* decision; *the inquiry gave a ruling on the case; according to the ruling of the court, the contract was illegal*

rumour clinic [ˈruːmə ˈklɪnɪk] *noun US* information service for employees which corrects false rumours which might be circulating in an organization; *installing a rumour clinic is an important part of the management's internal public relations*

run [rʌn] *verb* to manage *or* to organize; *she runs the personnel department; they run a staff sports club; he is running a multimillion-pound company*

◊ **running** [ˈrʌnɪŋ] *noun* **running costs** *or* **running expenses** *or* **costs of running a business** = money spent on the day-to-day cost of keeping a business going

Ss

sabbatical [sə'bætɪkl] *noun & adjective* paid *or* unpaid time off, for the purposes of research *or* study *or* travel; *the union claimed sabbatical leave for every six years worked; she is due for a sabbatical next year*

sack [sæk] **1** *noun* **to get the sack** = to be dismissed from a job **2** *verb* **to sack someone** = to dismiss someone from a job; *he was sacked after being late for work; he was warned that he would be sacked for further unpunctuality; they decided to sack all the workers responsible for the damage to the machinery*

◊ **sackable offence** ['sækəbl ə'fens] *noun* behaviour which automatically means dismissal; *being drunk in the office is a sackable offence here*

◊ **sacking** ['sækɪŋ] *noun* dismissal from a job; *the union protested against the sackings*

s.a.e. = STAMPED ADDRESSED ENVELOPE *send your application form to the personnel officer, with an s.a.e. for reply*

safeguard ['seɪfgɑːd] *verb* to protect; *to safeguard the interests of the shareholders*

safety ['seɪfti] *noun* **(a)** freedom from danger *or* risk; **safety audit** = check of the workplace to see how safety regulations are being implemented; **safety committee** = committee set up to examine the health and safety policy of a particular company; **safety offence** = behaviour which can cause a hazard; **safety officer** = official who inspects places of work and work methods to make sure that they are safe; **to take safety precautions** *or* **safety measures** = to act to make sure something is safe; **safety regulations** = rules to make a place of work safe for the workers; **safety representative** = trade union representative for health and safety problems **(b) fire safety** = making a place of work safe for the workers in case of fire and through fire prevention methods; **fire safety officer** = person in a company responsible for seeing that the workers are safe if a fire breaks out

salary ['sæləri] *noun* (i) regular payment for work done, made to an employee usually as a cheque at the end of each month; (ii) amount paid to an employee, shown as a monthly, quarterly or yearly total; *she got a salary increase in June; the company froze all salaries for a six-month period; if I get promoted, my salary will go up; the salary may be low, but the fringe benefits attached to the job are good;* **annual salary** = salary for one year's work; **basic salary** = normal salary without extra payments; **gross salary** = salary before tax is deducted; **net salary** = salary which is left after deducting tax and national insurance contributions; **starting salary** = amount of payment for an employee when starting work; *he was appointed at a starting salary of £10,000;* **salary bands** = all salaries at certain levels; *the pay structure is made up five salary bands;* **salary cut** = sudden reduction in salary; *the staff were asked to take a cut in salary;* **salary cheque** = monthly cheque by which an employee is paid; **salary club** = meeting of representatives from various companies to discuss the salary structure in an industry; **salary deductions** = money which a company removes from salaries to give to the government as tax, national insurance contributions, etc.; **salary differential** = difference between one employee's salary and another's in similar types of jobs; *salary differentials between employees with similar qualifications and experience cause much discontent; any salary differentials should be justified by differences in experience or responsibility;* **salary expectations** = how the employee hopes his salary will increase; **salary-related pension scheme** = pension scheme where the pension received is based on the final salary of the contributor; **salary review** = examination of salaries in a company to see if workers should earn more; *she had a salary review last April or her salary was reviewed last April;* **scale of salaries** *or* **salary scale** = table showing salaries for different jobs in the same company, with several grades at each level; **the company's salary structure** = organization of salaries in a company, with different rates for different types of job

◊ **salaried staff** ['sælərɪd 'stɑːf] *noun* employees who receive regular fixed payments, as opposed to those who are paid for the time worked, or the tasks completed; *the company has 250 salaried staff; we are cutting down on salaried staff as an economy measure; the sales department has few salaried staff, as most of the salesmen are on commission*

QUOTE the union of hotel and personal service workers has demanded a new salary structure and uniform conditions of service for workers in the hotel and catering industry
Business Times (Lagos)

sales [seɪlz] *noun* money received for selling something *or* number of items sold; *sales have risen over the first quarter;* **sales analysis** = examining the reports of sales to see why items have or have not sold well; **sales budget** = plan of probable sales; **sales campaign** = planned work to achieve higher sales; **sales conference** *or* **sales meeting** = meeting of sales managers, representatives, publicity staff, etc., to discuss results and future sales plans; **sales department** = section of a company which deals in selling the company's products or services; **sales executive** = person in a company in charge of sales; **sales force** = group of salesmen; **sales manager** = person in charge of a sales department; **sales representative** *or* **sales rep** = person who sells an organization's products *or* services

◊ **salesclerk** ['seɪlzklɑːk] *noun US* person who sells goods to customers in a store

◊ **salesgirl** ['seɪlzgɜːl] *noun* girl who sells goods to customers in a store

◊ **saleslady** ['seɪlzleɪdi] *noun* woman who sells goods to customers in a store

◊ **salesman** ['seɪlzmən] *noun* man who sells an organization's products *or* services to customers; *salesmen are paid a basic salary plus commission* (NOTE: plural is **salesmen**)

◊ **salesmanship** ['seɪlzmənʃɪp] *noun* art of selling *or* of persuading customers to buy

◊ **saleswoman** ['seɪlzwʊmən] *noun* woman in a shop who sells goods to customers (NOTE: plural is **saleswomen**)

QUOTE the wage agreement includes sales clerks and commission sales people in stores in Toronto
Toronto Star

sampling ['sɑːmplɪŋ] *noun* **(a)** testing a product by taking a small amount; *a sampling of European Union produce;* **acceptance sampling** = testing a small sample of a batch to see if the whole batch is good enough to be accepted; **activity sampling** = observation of tasks and their performances, carried out at random intervals **(b)** testing the reactions of a small group of people to find out the reactions of a larger group of consumers; **random sampling** = choosing samples for testing without any special selection

sanction ['sæŋ(k)ʃən] **1** *noun* **(a)** permission; *you will need the sanction of the local authorities before you can knock down the office block* **(b)** penalty *or* punishment; *the government is considering imposing trade sanctions;* **automatic sanction** = penalty which is applied automatically, outside the legal process, to an employee taking part in industrial action **2** *verb* to approve; *the board sanctioned the expenditure of £1.2m on the development project*

sandwich course ['sændwɪʃ 'kɔːs] *noun* course of study where students at a college *or* institute spend a period of time working in a factory *or* office as part of their course

satisfaction [sætɪs'fækʃən] *noun* feeling of being happy *or* good feeling of happiness and contentment; *he finds great satisfaction in the job even though the pay is bad;* **job satisfaction** = a worker's feeling that he is happy in his place of work and pleased with the work he does

◊ **satisfy** ['sætɪsfaɪ] *verb* **(a)** to give satisfaction *or* to please; *the training officer was not satisfied with the courses offered by the local college;* **to satisfy a client** = to make a client pleased with what he has purchased **(b)** to fill (the requirements for a job, etc.); *he did not satisfy the entry requirements of the Civil Service*

save-as-you-earn (SAYE) ['seɪvæzjuː 'ɜːn] *noun GB* scheme where workers can save money regularly by having it deducted automatically from their wages and invested in National Savings

SAYE ['es eɪ waɪ 'iː] = SAVE-AS-YOU-EARN

scab [skæb] *noun informal & pejorative* worker who goes on working when there is a strike

scale [skeɪl] **1** *noun* system which is graded into various levels; **scale of salaries** *or* **salary scale** = list of salaries showing different levels of pay in different jobs in the same company; *he was appointed at the top end of the salary scale;* **incremental scale** = salary scale with regular annual salary increases; **sliding scale** = set of numbers which rises gradually according to other values *or* quantity *or* time, etc. **2** *verb* **to scale down** *or* **to scale up** = to lower *or* to increase in proportion

◊ **scalar** ['skeɪlɑː] *adjective* working according to a scale; **scalar principle** = principle that employees should only communicate with their seniors through the established hierarchy

schedule ['ʃedjuːl] **1** *noun* **(a)** timetable *or* plan of time drawn up in advance; **to be ahead of schedule** = to be early; **to be on schedule** = to be on time; **to be behind schedule** = to be late; **to have a heavy schedule of meetings** = to have a large number of meetings arranged **(b)** additional documents attached to a contract; **tax schedules** = six types of income as classified in the Finance Acts for British tax; **Schedule A** = schedule under which tax is charged on income from land *or* buildings; **Schedule B** = schedule under which tax is charged on income from woodlands; **Schedule C** = schedule under which tax is charged on profits from government stock; **Schedule D** = schedule under which tax is charged on income from trades *or* professions, interest and other earnings not derived from being employed; **Schedule E** = schedule under which tax is charged on income from salaries *or* wages *or* pensions; **Schedule F** = schedule under which tax is charged on income from dividends **2** *verb* **(a)** to list officially; *scheduled prices or scheduled charges* **(b)** to plan the time when something will happen; *the meeting is scheduled for 2.30 p.m.*

scheme [skiːm] *noun* plan *or* arrangement *or* way of working; *the new payment scheme is based on reward for individual effort;* **bonus scheme** = scheme by which workers

can earn bonuses (such as for exceeding targets, completing a task within the deadline, etc.); **pension scheme** = plan worked out by an insurance company which arranges for a worker to pay part of his salary over many years and receive a regular payment when he retires

school-leaver ['skuːl'liːvə] *noun* person who has left school and has not yet found a job; *many school-leavers find it difficult to get jobs because they do not have any qualifications or experience; unemployment figures are high because of the large number of school-leavers coming onto the job market*

scientific management ['saɪəntɪfɪk 'mænɪdʒmənt] *noun* school of management which believes in the rational use of resources in order to maximize output, thus motivating workers to earn more money; *as an engineer by training he is a great believer in scientific management*

scope [skəʊp] *noun* range of subjects being dealt with; *the scope of an agreement*

screen [skriːn] *verb* **to screen candidates** = to examine candidates to see if they are completely suitable

◊ **screening** ['skriːnɪŋ] *noun* **the screening of candidates** = examining candidates to see if they are suitable for a job; *the recruitment process includes three days' intensive screening to ensure that the right person is selected*

search [sɜːtʃ] **1** *noun* **executive search** = looking for new managers for organizations, usually by approaching managers in their existing jobs and asking them if they want to work for another company **2** *verb* **(a)** to look for something; *the company is searching for a formula which will be acceptable to the unions* **(b)** to examine thoroughly; *members of staff were searched as they left the building*

season ['siːzn] *noun* **(a)** one of four parts which a year is divided into (spring, summer, autumn, winter) **(b)** a period of time when something usually takes place; **tourist season** *or* **holiday season** = period when there are many people on holiday; **busy season** *or* **high season** = period when a company is busy; **peak season** = period when a company is busiest; **slack season** = period when a company is not very busy;

dead season or low season = time of year when there are few tourists about

◊ **seasonal** ['si:zənl] adjective which lasts for a season or which only happens during a particular season; **the demand for this item is very seasonal; seasonal variations in sales patterns; seasonal employment** or **seasonal work** = job which is available at certain times of the year only (such as in a ski resort); **seasonal unemployment** = unemployment which appears at certain times of the year; **there is seasonal unemployment in the hotel trade during the winter when tourism falls off; seasonal workers** = workers who are employed for a few months during the high season

◊ **seasonally** ['si:znəli] adverb **seasonally adjusted figures** = statistics which are adjusted to take account of seasonal variations

second [sɪ'kɒnd] verb to lend a member of staff to another organization for a fixed period of time; **she was seconded to the Ministry of Trade for a period of three years**

secondary ['sekəndri] adjective **(a)** second in importance; **secondary group** = group which is small enough to allow its members to interact informally; **secondary sector** = industries which use basic raw materials to make manufactured goods **(b)** **secondary action** or **secondary strike** or **secondary picketing** = industrial action aimed at a company which is not a party to an industrial dispute, to prevent it supplying a striking factory or receiving supplies from it; US **secondary boycott** = pressure put on an employer by those not directly involved in an industrial dispute; see also PRIMARY

◊ **secondee** [sɪkɒn'di:] noun person who is seconded to another job

secondment [sɪ'kɒn(d)mənt] noun being seconded to another job for a period; **he is on three years' secondment to an Australian college**

secret ['si:krət] **1** adjective which is not known by many people; **the management signed a secret deal with a foreign supplier; secret ballot** = election where the voters vote in secret **2** noun something which is hidden or which is not known by many people; **to keep a secret** = not to tell secret information which you have been told

secretary ['sekrətri] noun **(a)** person who helps to organize work or types letters or files documents or arranges meetings, etc. for someone; **my secretary deals with incoming orders; his secretary phoned to say he would be late; secretary and personal assistant** or US **executive secretary** = secretary to a top-level member of an organization (a director, or senior manager) **(b)** official of a company or society; **company secretary** = person who is responsible for a company's legal and financial affairs; **general secretary** = head official of a trade union **(c)** member of the government in charge of a department; **Education Secretary; Foreign Secretary** US **Secretary of the Treasury** or **Treasury Secretary** = senior member of the government in charge of financial affairs

◊ **Secretary of State** ['sekrətri əv 'steɪt] noun **(a)** GB member of the government in charge of a department **(b)** US senior member of the government in charge of foreign affairs (the UK equivalent is the **Foreign Secretary**)

◊ **secretarial** [sekrə'teərɪəl] adjective referring to the work of a secretary; **their secretarial duties are not onerous, just boring; secretarial work is seen as a step towards management positions; he is looking for secretarial work; we need extra secretarial help to deal with the mailings; secretarial college** = college which teaches typing, shorthand and word-processing; **secretarial course** = course of study for secretaries; **she is taking a secretarial course**

sector ['sektə] noun part of the economy or the business organization of a country; **all sectors of the economy suffered from the fall in the exchange rate; technology is a booming sector of the economy; public sector** = nationalized industries and public services; **primary sector** = industries dealing with basic raw materials (such as coal, wood, farm produce); **private sector** = all companies which are owned by private shareholders, not by the state; **the expansion is funded completely by the private sector; salaries in the private sector have increased faster than in the public**

QUOTE government services form a large part of the tertiary or service sector
Sydney Morning Herald

secure [sɪ'kjuə] adjective safe or which cannot change; **secure job** = job from which you are not likely to be made redundant

◊ **security** [sɪ'kjuərəti] *noun* **(a) job security** = being able to rely on a steady job and the income which comes from it; *during a recession, most people find job security more important than job satisfaction; there is little job security in the current economic climate of rising unemployment;* **security of employment** = feeling by a worker that he has the right to keep his job until he retires; **security of tenure** = right to keep a job, provided that certain conditions are met **(b)** being protected; **security guard** = person who protects an office *or* factory against burglars; **office security** = protecting an office against theft

select [sɪ'lekt] *verb* to choose; *the board will meet to select three candidates for a second interview*

◊ **selection** [sɪ'lekʃən] *noun* choosing someone for a job; *assessment of candidates for final selection will depend on tests and interviews;* **selection board** *or* **selection committee** = committee which chooses a candidate for a job; **selection procedure** = general method of choosing a candidate for a job; **selection test** = test to assess whether someone should be selected for a job *or* for training, etc.

> QUOTE the Employment and Appeals Tribunal looked at each selection to see if it was in fact fair
> *Personnel Management*

> QUOTE engineering employers have been told they may need to revise their criteria for selecting trainees over the next few years
> *Personnel Management*

self- [self] *prefix* referring to oneself; **self-administered pension scheme** = scheme where the trustees actively administer the funds, and are responsible for its performance

◊ **self-appraisal** *or* **self-assessment** ['selfə'preɪzəl *or* 'selfə'sesmənt] *noun* a person's own assessment of his or her capabilities and character; *the application forms contain room for a short self-appraisal; candidates are asked to write a two-page self-assessment as part of the job application; self-assessment can be an embarrassing process for many applicants*

◊ **self-confidence** ['self'kɒnfɪdəns] *noun* feeling confident in your own ability; *after a month of successful sales, his self-confidence improved dramatically; her lack of self-confidence was obvious at the interview*

◊ **self-confident** ['self'kɒnfɪdənt] *adjective* (person) who is confident in his or her own ability; *the trainee was self-confident to the point of arrogance*

self-employed ['selfɪm'plɔɪd] **1** *adjective* working for yourself or not on the payroll of a company; *a self-employed engineer; he worked for a bank for ten years but is now self-employed* **2** *noun* **the self-employed** = people who work for themselves

> QUOTE especially notable was the very high proportion of managers in casual jobs who were self-employed
> *Employment Gazette*

self-image ['self'ɪmɪdʒ] *noun* idea that a person has about his *or* her own character and abilities; *several months of practical experience in sales improved his self-image and self-confidence*

◊ **self-instruction** ['selfɪn'strʌkʃən] *noun* teaching oneself; *he learnt the language at home, entirely through self-instruction*

◊ **self-made man** *or* **woman** ['selfmeɪd 'mæn *or* 'wʊmən] *noun* person who is rich and successful because of his own work, not because he inherited money or position

◊ **self-managing work team** ['selfmænɪdʒɪŋ 'wɜːk 'tiːm] *see* AUTONOMOUS WORKING GROUP

◊ **self-regulation** ['selfregjʊ'leɪʃən] *noun* regulation of an industry by itself, through a committee which issues a rulebook and makes sure that members of the industry follow the rules

◊ **self-starter** ['self'stɑːtə] *noun* person who can be relied on to take the initiative in a new situation without asking for instructions

◊ **self-taught** ['self'tɔːt] *adjective* (person) who has taught himself

sellout ['selaʊt] *noun* giving in to demands in exchange for financial concessions; *a sellout to the management*

semi- ['semi] *prefix* half

◊ **semi-skilled** ['semi'skɪld] *adjective* **semi-skilled workers** = workers who have had some training

◊ **semi-retired** ['semɪrɪ'taɪəd] *adjective* having retired on a pension, but still working part-time

seminar ['semɪnɑː] *noun* teaching of a small class of advanced students; *he attended a seminar on direct selling; she is running a seminar for senior managers*

senior ['siːnjə] *adjective* older; in a higher rank; (worker) who has been employed longer than another; **a decision taken at a senior level** = a decision taken by directors or senior managers; **senior management** = people who manage an organization and make the most important decisions; *after heading a department for two years, she will soon move into a senior management position;* **senior manager** *or* **senior executive** = manager *or* director who has a higher rank than others; **senior partner** = most important partner in a firm of solicitors *or* accountants; **John Smith, Senior** = the older John Smith (i.e. the father of John Smith, Junior)

◊ **seniority** [siːnɪ'ɒrəti] *noun* being of higher rank; being an employee of the company longer; *seniority is no guarantee of ability;* **inverse seniority** = scheme which allows for longest-serving workers to be laid off before those most recently recruited; **seniority system** = way in which employees can gain seniority in an organization; **the managers were listed in order of seniority** = the manager who had been an employee the longest was put at the top of the list

sensitivity training [sensɪ'tɪvɪti 'treɪnɪŋ] *noun* development of character and awareness by social interaction in small groups; *sensitivity training has helped him to be forceful without offending others in the department*

separation [sepə'reɪʃən] *noun US* leaving a job (resigning, retiring, or being fired or made redundant); *the interviewer asked the candidate whether the separation mentioned in his CV was due to resignation, redundancy or dismissal; the exit interviews attempted to find out what employees really felt about separation*

sequester *or* **sequestrate** [sɪ'kwestə *or* 'sekwəstreɪt] *verb* to take and keep (property) because a court has ordered it; *the union was fined for contempt of court and its funds have been sequestrated*

◊ **sequestration** [sekwes'treɪʃən] *noun* taking and keeping of property on the order of a court, especially seizing property from someone who is in contempt of court; *the union's property is being kept under sequestration*

◊ **sequestrator** ['sekwəstreɪtə] *noun* person who takes and keeps property on the order of a court

SERPS = STATE EARNINGS-RELATED PENSION SCHEME

serve [sɜːv] *verb* to work; *she served ten years as an accounts clerk;* **to serve an apprenticeship** = to work with a skilled workman for a legally agreed period in order to learn from him

service ['sɜːvɪs] *noun* **(a)** work done by an employee for his or her employer or company; *after a lifetime's service to the company he was rewarded with a generous golden handshake;* **length of service** = number of years someone has worked; **service agreement** *or* **service contract** = contract between an employer and an employee showing all conditions of work; *the service agreement says very little about hours of work; he worked unofficially with no service contract* **(b)** **services** = work done *or* tasks performed by a person for an employer *or* by a person or company for a client; *customer services is a division of the sales department;* **service industry** = industry which does not make products, but offers a service (such as banking, insurance, transport)

session ['seʃən] *noun* meeting *or* period when a group of people meets; *the morning session or the afternoon session will be held in the conference room;* **briefing session** = meeting between managers and staff where the staff are informed of decisions, plans, etc.; **closing session** = last part of a meeting *or* conference; **opening session** = first part of a meeting *or* conference; **training session** = meeting where staff are trained

settle ['setl] *verb* to solve a problem *or* dispute; *the employer will have to settle the matter with the union or there will be a strike;* **to settle a claim** = to agree to pay what is asked for; *the insurance company refused to settle his claim for storm damage*

◊ **settlement** ['setlmənt] *noun* solution to a problem *or* dispute; *both sides have everything to gain from a quick settlement of the dispute; there could be a settlement if the workforce agree to a ten per cent pay rise;* **to effect a settlement between two parties** = to bring two parties together to make them agree; **out-of-court settlement** = settling a dispute between two parties privately without continuing a court case; **wage settlement** = agreement on wages reached after negotiations

seven-point plan ['sevən 'pɔint 'plæn] *noun* list of items used in assessing the potential of job candidates

COMMENT: the seven points are: physical appearance, educational qualifications, general intelligence level, special skills (not necessarily connected to his current employment), outside interests, mental and emotional disposition, personal and family circumstances

severance pay ['sevərəns 'pei] *noun* money paid as compensation to an employee who loses his job through no fault of his own

sex [seks] *noun* one of two groups (male and female) into which people can be divided; **sex discrimination** = treating men and women in different ways (usually favouring men); *the company was accused of sex discrimination in its appointment of managers; sex discrimination has made it difficult for women to reach managerial posts in the organization;* **Sex Discrimination Act 1975, 1986** = British Acts of Parliament which ban discrimination on grounds of sex

◊ **sexism** ['seksizm] *noun* belief that one sex is superior to the other

◊ **sexist** ['seksist] *adjective* showing a belief that one sex is superior to the other; *he was reprimanded for making sexist remarks about the secretaries*

◊ **sexual** ['seksjuəl] *adjective* relating to sex; **sexual discrimination** = SEX DISCRIMINATION **sexual harassment** = making unpleasant sexual gestures, comments, or approaches to someone

shakeout ['ʃeikaut] *noun* complete change, where weak *or* inefficient people or companies are removed

◊ **shakeup** ['ʃeikʌp] *noun* total reorganization; *the managing director ordered a shakeup of the sales departments*

QUOTE the shakeout of manpower from traditional employment areas has generally increased the overall productivity of those at work
Personnel Management

share [ʃeə] **1** *noun* one of many parts into which a company's capital is divided; **'A' shares** = ordinary shares with limited voting rights; **'B' shares** = ordinary shares with special voting rights (often owned by the founder of the company and his family); **ordinary shares** = normal shares in a company, which have no special benefits or restrictions; **preference shares** = shares (often with no voting rights) which receive their dividend before all other shares and are repaid first (at face value) if the company goes into liquidation; **share certificate** = document proving that someone owns shares; **share issue** = selling new shares in a company to the public; **share option scheme** = arrangement where a worker has regular deductions made against his pay against the right to buy shares in the company at a fixed low price at a later date; **share ownership scheme** *or* **share incentive scheme** = scheme whereby employees in a company can buy shares in it and so share in the profits; *share ownership schemes help employees to identify more closely with the company they work for* **2** *verb* to divide something up among several people; *to share the profits among the senior executives*

◊ **shareholder** ['ʃeəhəuldə] *noun* person who owns shares in a company; *to call a shareholders' meeting;* **shareholders' equity** = ordinary shares owned by shareholders in a company

◊ **sharing** ['ʃeəriŋ] *noun* dividing up; **job sharing** = situation where a job is shared by more than one person, each working part-time; **profit sharing** = dividing profits among workers; *the company operates a profit-sharing scheme;* **work-sharing** = system where two or more part-timers share one job, each doing part of the work

shed [ʃed] *verb* to lose; **to shed staff** = to lose staff by making them redundant

sheet [ʃiːt] *noun* **sheet of paper** = piece of

paper; **time sheet** = paper showing when a worker starts work and when he leaves work in the evening

shelve [ʃelv] *verb* to postpone *or* to put back to another date; *the project was shelved; discussion of the problem has been shelved*

shift [ʃɪft] *noun* (i) group of workers who work for a period, and then are replaced by another group during one 24-hour period; (ii) period of time worked by a group of workers; **alternating shift system** = system where two groups of workers work day or night shifts, and after a certain period, change round; **continuous shift system** = system where groups of workers work shifts throughout the week, including weekends; **day shift** = shift worked during the daylight hours (from early morning to late afternoon); **discontinuous shift system** = working system where three groups of workers work morning, noon and night shifts, but do not work at weekends; **double day shift** = system of working two shifts during the day time (as from 8.00 a.m. to 2.00 p.m, and then 2.00 p.m. to 8.00 p.m.); **to work double shifts** = to work with two shifts of workers on duty; **they work double shifts** = two groups of workers are working shifts together; **evening shift** = shift which works from 6.00 p.m. to 10.00 or 11.00 p.m. (usually manned by part-timers); **fixed shift system** = system where workers are given fixed hours of work under a shift system; **morning shift** = shift which works during the morning (typically from 7.00 or 8.00 a.m. to lunchtime); **night shift** = shift worked during the night; *there are 150 men on the day shift; he works the day shift or night shift; we work an 8-hour shift; the management is introducing a shift system or shift working;* **permanent night shift** = shift which only works at night (as opposed to the alternating system); **three shift system** = system of working with three shifts (morning, afternoon and evening or night shifts); **shift transfer** = changing an employee's shift or working hours

◊ **shift work** [ˈʃɪft ˈwɜːk] *noun* system of work in a factory with shifts

shoddy [ʃɒdi] *adjective* of bad quality; *shoddy workmanship*

shop [ʃɒp] *noun* **(a)** place where goods are stored and sold; **retail shop** = shop where goods are sold only to the public; **shop assistant** = person who serves customers in a shop (NOTE: US English usually uses **store**) **(b)** place where goods are made *or* workshop; **machine shop** = place where working machines are kept; **repair shop** = small factory where machines are repaired **(c)** **closed shop** = system where an organization agrees to employ only union members in certain jobs *or* in certain places of work; *the union is asking the management to agree to a closed shop;* **open shop** = workplace where employees can be employed whether they are members of a union or not; *US* **union shop** = place of work where it is agreed that all workers must be members of a union

◊ **shop floor** [ˈʃɒp ˈflɔː] *noun* place where goods are manufactured; **shop floor workers** = manual workers and technical workers (as opposed to office workers); **on the shop floor** = in the factory *or* in the works *or* among the ordinary workers; *the feeling on the shop floor is that the manager does not know his job*

◊ **shop steward** [ˈʃɒp ˈstjuəd] *noun* elected trade union official who represents workers in day-to-day negotiations with the management; *the shop steward was elected because of his experience in pay bargaining*

short [ʃɔːt] *adjective* for a small period of time; **in the short term** *or* **in the short run** = in the near future *or* quite soon

◊ **shortage** [ˈʃɔːtɪdʒ] *noun* lack *or* not having enough; *we employ part-timers to make up for staff shortages;* **acute shortage** = very severe shortage for a period of time; **chronic shortage** = shortage which continues for a period of time; *a chronic shortage of skilled staff;* **labour shortage** *or* **manpower shortage** *or* **shortage of manpower** = lack of workers

◊ **shorthanded** [ʃɔːtˈhændɪd] *adjective* without enough staff; *we are rather shorthanded at the moment*

◊ **shortlist** [ˈʃɔːtlɪst] **1** *noun* list of some of the better people who have applied for a job, who can be asked to come for a test or an interview; *to draw up a shortlist; he is on the shortlist for the job* **2** *verb* to make a shortlist; *four candidates have been shortlisted; shortlisted candidates will be asked for an interview*

◊ **short-range** [ʃɔːtˈreɪn(d)ʒ] *adjective*

short-range forecast = forecast which covers a period of a few months

◊ **short-staffed** [ʃɔːt'stɑːft] *adjective* with not enough staff; *we are rather short-staffed at the moment*

◊ **short-term** [ʃɔːt'tɜːm] *adjective* for a short period in the future; *we need to recruit at once to cover our short-term manpower requirements;* **on a short-term basis** = for a short period; **short-term forecast** = forecast which covers a period of a few months; **short-term contract** = contract of employment for a short period (such as six months)

◊ **short time** [ʃɔːt'taɪm] *noun* reduced working hours (officially, giving less than half a normal week's pay); *several machinists will be on short time as long as the shortage of orders lasts; the company has had to introduce short-time working because of lack of orders*

show of hands [ʃəʊ əv 'hændz] *noun* vote where people show by raising their hands which way they have voted; *the motion was carried on a show of hands*

shut [ʃʌt] **1** *adjective* closed *or* not open; *the office is shut on Saturdays* **2** *verb* to close; *to shut a shop or a warehouse*

◊ **shut down** [ʃʌt 'daʊn] *verb* **to shut down a factory** = to make a factory stop working for a time; *the offices will shut down for Christmas; six factories have shut down this month*

◊ **shutdown** [ʃʌtdaʊn] *noun* shutting of a factory

◊ **shutout** [ʃʌtaʊt] *noun* locking of the door of a factory *or* office to stop the staff getting in

sick [sɪk] *adjective* ill *or* not well; **to be off sick** = to be away from work because you are ill; **to report sick** = to say officially that you are ill and cannot work; **sick building syndrome** = condition where many people working in a building feel ill or have headaches, caused by blocked air-conditioning ducts in which stale air is recycled round the building, often carrying allergenic substances or bacteria; **sick leave** = time when a worker is away from work on full pay, because of illness or injury; **sick pay** = pay paid to a worker who is sick and unable to work; **statutory sick pay (SSP)** =

state pay made by an employer to a worker who is sick (the payments are claimed back by the employer against his NI contributions; SSP is paid for working days, called 'qualifying days', up to a maximum of 28 weeks)

◊ **sickness** [sɪknəs] *noun* being ill; **sickness benefit** = payment made by the government or private insurance to someone who is ill and cannot work; *the sickness benefit is paid monthly*

side [saɪd] *noun* **on the side** = separate from your normal work, and hidden from your employer; *he works in an accountant's office, but he runs a construction company on the side; her salary is too small to live on, so the family lives on what she can make on the side*

◊ **sideline** [saɪdlaɪn] *noun* business which is extra to your normal work; *he runs a profitable sideline selling postcards to tourists*

sign [saɪn] *verb* to write your name in a special way on a document to show that you have written it or approved it; *the new recruit was asked to sign the contract of employment*

◊ **signature** [sɪgnətʃə] *noun* person's name written by him or herself on a cheque, document, etc.; *the contract of employment had the personnel director's signature at the bottom*

◊ **sign on** [saɪn 'ɒn] *verb* **(a)** to start work, by signing your name on a contract of employment; **to sign on (for the dole)** = to register as unemployed **(b)** to give someone a job by offering a signed contract of employment; *we are signing on more workers next month*

silver circle rate [sɪlvə 'sɜːkl 'reɪt] *noun* US system whereby pay increases are based on length of service; *the silver circle rate is partly designed to encourage employees to stay with firm a long time*

similar work [sɪmɪlə 'wɜːk] *noun* work done by men and women in the same organization which has equal value

simulation [sɪmjʊ'leɪʃn] *noun* imitation of a real-life situation for training purposes; *the simulation exercises for trainee air hostesses include applying first-aid treatment to passengers*

sinecure ['sɪnɪkjuə] *noun* job which is well-paid but involves very little work; *his job in his father's firm was little more than a sinecure*

single ['sɪŋgl] *adjective* **(a)** one alone; **single door policy** = organization of a personnel department, where various personnel officers are of equal rank and can each deal with any problem that arises; **single industry union** = union whose members work in only one industry (such as the mineworkers' union); **single table bargaining (STB)** = bargaining at one table, with several unions taking part on behalf of all workers employed by a company; **single union agreement** = agreement between management and one union, by which that union will represent all workers in the company, whatever type of job they do; *see also* STATUS **(b)** one (person) alone; unmarried; *marital status: single*

sit-down ['sɪtdaun] *adjective* **sit-down protest** *or* **sit-down strike** = strike where the workers stay in their place of work and refuse to work or to leave; *they staged a sit-down strike but were forced to leave the premises by the police*

◊ **sit-in** ['sɪtɪn] *noun* strike where the workers stay in their place of work and refuse to work or leave (NOTE: plural is **sit-ins)**

site [saɪt] **1** *noun* place where something is built; *we have chosen a site for the new factory; the supermarket is to be built on a site near the station;* **building site** *or* **construction site** = place where a building is being constructed; *all visitors to the site must wear safety helmets;* **green field site** = site for a factory which is in the country, and not surrounded by other buildings; **site engineer** = engineer in charge of a building being constructed; **site foreman** = foreman in charge of workers on a building site **2** *verb* **to be sited** = to be placed; *the factory will be sited near the motorway*

sitting ['sɪtɪŋ] *noun (informal)* **'sitting next to Nellie'** = training method, where a new employee learns a manual process by sitting beside an experienced worker who shows how the work is done

situation [sɪtjuˈeɪʃən] *noun* job; **situations vacant** = section of a newspaper where jobs are advertised; **situations wanted** = section of a newspaper where workers advertise for jobs *or* offer services

◊ **situational** [sɪtjuˈeɪʃənəl] *adjective* referring to a situation; **situational interview** *or* **situation-based interview** = interview where a candidate is asked specific questions about situations which may occur in a job; **situational test** = test where a candidate is placed in certain imaginary situations and is asked to react to them

skeleton staff ['skelɪtn 'stɑːf] *noun* few staff left to carry on essential work while most of the workforce is away; **skeleton service** = service provided by skeleton staff

skill [skɪl] *noun* ability to do something because of training; *we are badly in need of technical skills now that we have computerized the production line; the training officer is initiating a large-scale training programme so that the workers can acquire new skills; she has acquired some very useful office management skills; he will have to learn some new skills if he is going to direct the factory; he was not appointed because he didn't have the skills required for the job;* **core skills** = basic skills, which are needed by everyone; **skill centre** = centre which gives adults accelerated vocational training; **skills inventory** = list of all the skills, qualifications, etc. of each member of staff, so that they can be redeployed rather than be made redundant if their job ceases to exist; **skill shortages** = lack of workers with certain skills

◊ **skilled** [skɪld] *adjective* having learnt certain skills; **skilled workers** *or* **skilled labour** = workers who have special skills *or* who have had long training; *unemployment and job vacancies exist side by side in the area because of the lack of skilled labour*

> QUOTE Britain's skills crisis has now reached such proportions that it is affecting the nation's economic growth
> *Personnel Today*

> QUOTE we aim to add the sensitivity of a new European to the broad skills of the new professional manager
> *Management Today*

slack [slæk] *adjective* **(a)** lazy *or* not busy; *business is slack at the end of the week; the foreman decided to tighten up on slack workers* **(b)** **slack period** = time between finishing a job and starting another one

◊ **slacken off** ['slækən 'ɒf] *verb* to become less busy

◊ **slackness** ['slæknəs] *noun* being lazy; *she got fired for general slackness and unpunctuality*

sleeping partner ['sli:pɪŋ 'pɑːtnə] *noun* partner who has a share in the business but does not work in it

sliding ['slaɪdɪŋ] *adjective* which rises in steps; **sliding scale** = set of numbers which rises gradually according to other values *or* quantity *or* time, etc.; *wages on the sliding scale were dependent on the retail price index*

slip [slɪp] *noun* small piece of paper; **pay slip** = piece of paper showing the full amount of a worker's pay, and the money deducted as tax, pension and insurance contributions; *US* **pink slip** = official letter of dismissal given to an employee (in place of a final interview)

slow [sləʊ] *adverb* **to go slow** = to protest against management by working slowly

◊ **slow down** ['sləʊ 'daʊn] *verb* to stop rising *or* moving *or* falling; *the management decided to slow down production*

◊ **slowdown** ['sləʊdaʊn] *noun* becoming less busy; *a slowdown in the company's expansion*

slush fund ['slʌʃ 'fʌnd] *noun* money kept to one side to give to people to persuade them to do what you want

smoking ['sməʊkɪŋ] *noun* action of smoking cigarettes, pipes or cigars; *smoking is forbidden in the computer room;* **no smoking office** = office where smoking is not allowed

SMP = STATUTORY MATERNITY PAY

social ['səʊʃəl] *adjective* referring to society in general; **Social Charter** *see* EUROPEAN SOCIAL CHARTER **Social Chapter** = additional section of the Maastricht Treaty which commits signatory states to the promotion of employment, improved working conditions, dialogue between management and labour, development of human resources, and the fight against exclusion; **social costs** = ways in which something will affect people; *the report examines the social costs of building the factory in the middle of the town;* **social dumping** = making a company competitive in the international field by reducing pay and living standards for its workers; **social fund** = DHSS fund which provides one-off grants to low-income families; **social partners** = employers and trade unions, working together; **social security** *or* **social insurance** = government scheme where employers, employees and the self-employed make regular contributions to a fund which provides unemployment pay, sickness pay and retirement pensions; **Social Security Act 1975** = act creating benefits for victims of industrial accidents and diseases, and disablement benefits; **social security contributions** *or* **tax** = money paid towards social security; *she never worked but lived on social security for years; he receives weekly social security payments*

◊ **socio-economic** ['səʊsɪəʊ iːkə'nɒmɪk] *adjective* referring to social and economic conditions; **socio-economic groups** = groups in society divided according to income and position

◊ **socio-technical system** ['səʊsɪəʊ 'teknɪkl 'sɪstəm] *noun* system that studies the interaction of people and machines, in order to improve efficiency

software ['sɒftweə] *noun* computer programs (as opposed to machines); *the new software package for personnel records made the department more efficient*

sole [səʊl] *adjective* only; **sole trader** = person who runs a business by himself but has not registered it as a company

solemn ['sɒləm] *adjective* **solemn and binding agreement** = agreement which is not legally binding, but which all parties are supposed to obey

solidarity [sɒlɪ'dærɪti] *noun* loyalty of members of a group to each other; *union solidarity meant that members of other unions were unwilling to cross picket lines*

solution [sə'luːʃən] *noun* answer to a problem; *to look for a solution to the company's manpower crisis; we think we have found a solution to the problem of getting skilled staff*

solve [sɒlv] *verb* **to solve a problem** = to

find an answer to a problem; *the new rates of pay should solve some of our short-term recruitment problems*

sort out [sɔːt'aʊt] *verb* to put into order; to settle (a problem); *did you sort out the accounts problem with the auditors?*

sought after ['sɔːt 'ɑːftə] *adjective* which everyone wants to have; *her skills are widely sought after*

sour [saʊə] *verb* to make things become unpleasant; *the struggle for promotion has soured relations in the department*

source [sɔːs] *noun* place where something comes from; *you must declare income from all sources to the tax office; income which is taxed at source* = where the tax is removed before the income is paid

span of control ['spæn əv kən'trəʊl] *noun* number of subordinates whom a person supervises or administers at the workplace; *the job has a large amount of responsibility with a wide span of control; too wide a span of control can lead to inefficient supervision*

spare [speə] *adjective* extra *or* not being used; *to use up spare capacity* = to make use of time or space which has not been fully used; *spare time* = time when you are not at work, used for amusement, hobbies, etc.; *he built himself a car in his spare time*

spate [speɪt] *noun* sudden rush; *a spate of dismissals or of resignations*

specialist ['speʃəlɪst] *noun* person who deals with one particular type of skill *or* product *or* area of study; *we need a manager who can grasp the overall picture rather than a narrow specialist; she is a specialist in financial planning and not used to the problems of running a small business from home*

◊ **specialization** *or* US **specialism** [speʃəlaɪ'zeɪʃən *or* 'speʃəlɪzm] *noun* study of one particular subject *or* concentration on one particular type of work

◊ **specialize** ['speʃəlaɪz] *verb* to deal with one particular type of skill *or* product *or* service; *after working in all the departments, he finally decided to specialize in distribution*

specify ['spesɪfaɪ] *verb* to state clearly

what is needed; *candidates are asked to specify which of the three posts they are applying for*

◊ **specification** [spesɪfɪ'keɪʃən] *noun* detailed information about what is needed *or* about a product to be supplied; *job specification* = very detailed description of what is involved in a job; *person specification* = form of job description which gives the ideal personal qualities needed for the job and a description of the ideal candidate for the job

spirit ['spɪrɪt] *noun* general mood; *team spirit* = general mood of a team, expressed as loyalty to the team, with motivation coming from working in a team

split [splɪt] *adjective* which is divided into parts; *split shift* = form of shift working where shifts are split into two shorter periods; *split vote* = vote where part of a group votes in one way, and another part votes in a different way, so dividing a block vote

sponsor ['spɒnsə] **1** *noun* **(a)** person who recommends another person for a job; *without having the managing director as sponsor he would never have got the job in marketing* **(b)** company which pays money to help research *or* to help a sport *or* to help someone go on a training course **2** *verb* to recommend someone for a job; to pay for someone to go on a training course; *six of the management trainees have been sponsored by their companies*

◊ **sponsorship** ['spɒnsəʃɪp] *noun* act of sponsoring; *the training course could not be run without the sponsorship of several major companies*

spouse [spaʊs] *noun* husband *or* wife; *all employees and their spouses are invited to the staff party*

squeeze [skwiːz] *noun* control carried out by reducing amounts of money available; *credit squeeze* = period when lending by the banks is restricted by the government; *job squeeze* = reducing the numbers of people employed, because of financial restrictions

SSP = STATUTORY SICK PAY **SSP1** = form given to workers who are not eligible for statutory sick pay, so that they can claim sickness benefits

staff [stɑːf] **1** *noun* people who work for a company *or* for an organization; **to be on the staff** *or* **a member of staff** *or* **a staff member** = to be employed permanently by a company; **ancillary staff** = staff who are not administrators, production staff or sales staff (such as cleaners, porters, canteen staff, etc.); **counter staff** = sales staff who work behind counters; **junior staff** = younger members of staff; people in less important positions in a company; **salaried staff** = staff earning salaries, as opposed to ordinary workers or to part-time workers; **senior staff** = older members of staff; people in more important positions in a company; *see also* ANCILLARY, SALARIED, SKELETON **staff agency** = agency which looks for office staff for companies; **staff appointment** = a job on the staff; **staff assessments** = reports on how well members of staff are working; **staff association** = society formed by members of staff of a company to represent them to the management and to organize entertainments; **staff canteen** = restaurant which belongs to a factory or office, where the staff can eat; **staff club** = club for the staff of a company, which organizes staff parties, sports and meetings; **staff function** = work in an organization which is not directly linked to production of goods or services for sale; **staff management** = management *or* administration of the employees of an organization; **staff status** = enjoying special perks which are given to some members of staff and not to others (NOTE: **staff** refers to a group of people and so is often followed by a verb in the plural) **2** *verb* to employ workers; *the department is staffed by skilled part-timers; they are having difficulty in staffing the factory*

◊ **staffer** ['stɑːfə] *noun US* member of the permanent staff

◊ **staffing** ['stɑːfɪŋ] *noun* providing workers for a company; **staffing levels** = numbers of members of staff required in a department of a company for it to work efficiently; **the company's staffing policy** = the company's views on staff - how many are needed for each department *or* if they should be full-time or part-time *or* what the salaries should be, etc.

staggered ['stægəd] *adjective* (holidays, working hours) arranged so that they do not all begin and end at the same time;

staggered holidays help the tourist industry; we have a staggered lunch hour so that there is always someone on the switchboard; **staggered day work** = working arrangement where groups of workers start and finish work at intervals of 30 minutes or one hour

stakeholder ['steɪkhəʊldə] *noun* person with an interest in a company (with money invested, or employees, customers, suppliers, etc.)

stamp [stæmp] **1** *noun* small piece of gummed paper which you buy from a post office to pay for national insurance contributions **2** *verb* to put a national insurance stamp on (a card, etc.); to put a postage stamp on (an envelope); **stamped addressed envelope (s.a.e.)** = envelope with your own address written on it and a stamp stuck on it to pay for the return postage; *send three copies of the application form with a stamped addressed envelope for reply*

stand in for ['stænd 'ɪn fə] *verb* to take someone's place; *Mr Smith is standing in for the chairman, who is ill*

◊ **stand off** ['stænd 'ɒf] *verb* to reduce workers' hours of work because of shortage of work

standard ['stændəd] **1** *noun* normal quality *or* normal quantity which other things are judged against; *the standard of craftsmanship in the factory is higher than elsewhere in the industry;* **standard of living** *or* **living standards** = quality of personal home life (such as amount of food or clothes bought, size of family car, etc.); *the standard of living has risen dramatically over the last few years;* **performance standard** *or* **standard of performance** = measure of performance needed to reach a certain level, as in the NVQ system; **production standards** = quality of production; **up to standard** = of acceptable quality; *this batch is not up to standard or does not meet our standards* **2** *adjective* normal *or* usual; **standard agreement** *or* **standard contract** = normal printed contract form; **standard hour** = unit of time used to establish the normal time which a job *or* task is expected to take, and used later to compare with the actual time taken; **standard industrial classification (SIC)** = international scheme for classifying industries into groups for statistical purposes; **standard letter** = letter which is sent without any change to various correspondents; **standard performance** = average output which is achieved by an experienced worker; **standard rate of taxation** = basic rate of income tax which rises as income moves above a certain level; **standard time system** = method of payment whereby a worker is paid on the basis of units of work performed, each of which has an agreed standard time which is established after work study

standby ['stæn(d)baɪ] *noun* **standby duty** = waiting to see if you are needed or if an emergency happens; **standby pay** = wages paid when a worker is on standby

standing ['stændɪŋ] *adjective* **standing committee** = permanent committee which always examines the same problem; **standing order** = order written by a customer asking a bank to pay money regularly to an account; **standing orders** = rules *or* regulations which regulate the conduct of any body, such as a council

standstill ['stæn(d)stɪl] *noun* situation where work has stopped; *production is at a standstill; the strike brought the factory to a standstill*

start [stɑːt] **1** *noun* beginning of something; **cold start** = starting a new business *or* opening a new shop where there was none before **2** *verb* to begin; **to start legal proceedings against someone** = to start begin legal proceedings

◊ **starter** ['stɑːtə] *noun* young person who is starting in a job for the first time; *see also* SELF-STARTER

◊ **starting** ['stɑːtɪŋ] *noun* **starting date** = date on which something starts; **starting salary** = salary for an employee when he starts work with a company

state [steɪt] *noun* government of a country; **state enterprise** = company run by the state; **state earnings-related pension scheme (SERPS)** = state pension which is additional to the basic retirement pension and is based on average earnings over a worker's career; **state pension** = pension paid by the state; **state sickness benefit** = sick pay for self-employed people or others who are not eligible to receive statutory sick pay

statistics [stə'tɪstɪks] *plural noun* facts *or* information in the form of figures; *the statistics on unemployment did not take school-leavers into account; according to government statistics, the number of unskilled workers has increased by ten per cent*

status ['steɪtəs] *noun* importance *or* position in a group; *the status of new recruits depends on whether they have a degree or not; as productivity increased, so the production manager's status increased within the company;* **marital status** = condition of being married or not; **single status** = arrangement where managers and ordinary staff all enjoy the same conditions of work, pay structures, recreational facilities, etc., with no extra perks for anyone; **status agreement** = part of a collective agreement which defines the rights and obligations of each of the parties involved; **loss of status** = becoming less important in a group; **status symbol** = something which shows how important its owner is; *the chairman's Rolls Royce is simply a status symbol*

◊ **status quo** ['steɪtəs 'kwəʊ] *noun* existing structure and procedures in an organization; *the union tried to alter the status quo by forcing the management to change its policies; the contract does not alter the status quo;* **status quo clause** = clause in an agreement by which the management guarantees that workers will not be worse off under any new working conditions proposed

statute ['stætjuːt] *noun* law made by parliament; **statute book** = list of laws passed by parliament; **statute law** = established written law, especially an Act of Parliament; **statute of limitations** = law which allows only a certain amount of time (a few years) for someone to claim damages or property

statutory ['stætjʊtəri] *adjective* which is laid down by law; *there is a statutory period of probation of thirteen weeks; are all the employees aware of their statutory rights?;* **statutory holiday** = holiday which is fixed by law; **statutory instrument** = order (which has the force of law) made under authority granted to a minister by an Act of Parliament; **statutory maternity pay (SMP)** = payment made by an employer to an employee who is on maternity leave; **statutory notice period** time stated in the contract of employment which the worker or company has to allow between resigning or being fired and the worker actually leaving his job (an employee has to give at least one week's notice and an employer has to give between one week and twelve weeks' notice, depending on the employee's length of service); **statutory sick pay (SSP)** = benefit paid to eligible employees who cannot work because they are sick

STB = SINGLE TABLE BARGAINING

steady ['stedi] *adjective* continuing in a regular way; *he has a steady job in the supermarket*

step [step] *noun* **(a)** type of action; **to take steps to prevent something happening** = to act to stop something happening **(b)** movement; *becoming assistant to the MD is a step up the promotion ladder*

◊ **step up** ['step 'ʌp] *verb* to increase; *to step up industrial action; the company has stepped up production of the latest models* (NOTE: **stepping - stepped**)

◊ **stepped** [stept] *adjective* rising in steps according to quantity; *the civil service has a stepped payment system divided into various grades;* **stepped pay system** = system of payment for work according to rising levels of performance

steward ['stjuəd] *noun* **shop steward** = elected union representative of workers, who represents their complaints to the management

stiff [stɪf] *adjective* harsh *or* difficult; *there are stiff penalties for not complying with the law*

stipulate ['stɪpjuleɪt] *verb* to demand that a condition be put into a contract; *the new manager stipulated that the contract run for five years*

◊ **stipulation** [stɪpju'leɪʃən] *noun* condition in a contract; *the contract has a stipulation that the new manager has to serve a three-month probationary period*

stock [stɒk] *noun* **(a)** quantity of goods for sale; **opening stock** = details of stock at the beginning of an accounting period; **closing stock** = details of stock at the end of an accounting period; **stock control** = making sure that enough stock is kept and that

quantities and movements of stock are noted; **stock level** = quantity of goods kept in stock; *we try to keep stock levels low during the summer;* **stock valuation** = estimating the value of stock at the end of an accounting period **(b)** **stocks and shares** = shares in ordinary companies; **stock certificate** = document proving that someone owns stock in a company; **stock options** = opportunity for senior managers to buy shares in the company they work for at a later date and at a cheap price

stop [stɒp] **1** *noun* end of an action; *work came to a stop when the company could not pay the workers' wages* **2** *verb* **(a)** not to do anything any more; *the work force stopped work when the company could not pay their wages; the office staff stop work at 5.30* **(b)** **to stop someone's wages** = to take money out of someone's wages; *we stopped £25 from his pay because he was late;* **to stop a cheque** *or* **to stop payment on a cheque** = to ask a bank not to pay a cheque you have written

◊ **stoppage** ['stɒpɪdʒ] *noun* **(a)** **work stoppages** = act of stopping work because of industrial action; *frequent stoppages are holding up the production line* **(b)** money take from a worker's wage packet for insurance, tax, etc.

QUOTE the commission noted that in the early 1960s there was an average of 203 stoppages each year arising out of dismissals

Employment Gazette

strategy ['strætədʒi] *noun* plan of future action; *what is the strategy of the personnel department to deal with long-term manpower requirements? part of the company's strategy to meet its marketing objectives is a major recruitment and retraining programme*

◊ **strategic** [strə'tiːdʒɪk] *adjective* based on a plan of action; **strategic planning** = planning the future work of a company

streamline ['striːmlaɪn] *verb* to make (something) more efficient *or* more simple; *to streamline the accounting system; to streamline distribution services*

◊ **streamlined** ['striːmlaɪnd] *adjective* efficient *or* rapid; *streamlined production; the company introduced a streamlined system of distribution*

◊ **streamlining** ['stri:mlaɪnɪŋ] *noun* making efficient

stress [stres] *noun* nervous tension or worry, caused by overwork, difficulty with managers, etc.; *people in positions of responsibility suffer from stress-related illnesses; the new work schedules caused too much stress on the shop floor;* **stress management** = way of coping with stress-related problems at work

◊ **stressful** ['stresfʊl] *adjective* (situation) which causes stress; *psychologists claim that repetitive work can be just a stressful as more demanding but varied work*

> QUOTE manual and clerical workers are more likely to suffer from stress-related diseases. Causes of stress include the introduction of new technology, job dissatisfaction, fear of job loss, poor working relations with the boss and colleagues, and bad working conditions
> *Personnel Management*

stretch [stretʃ] *verb* to pull out *or* make longer; **he is not fully stretched** = his job does not make him work as hard as he could

strike [straɪk] **1** *noun* **(a)** organized stopping of work by workers (in order to strengthen their position in bargaining with management *or* because of lack of agreement with management *or* because of orders from a union); *if the union's demands are not met in full, the entire workforce will go on strike; we hope that the negotiations will rule out the possibility of a strike;* **all-out strike** = complete strike by all workers; **general strike** = strike of all the workers in a country; **hunger strike** = strike where a prisoner refuses to take any food, in protest against something; **industry-wide strike** = strike which affects a whole industry and not just individual firms; **lightning strike** = strike which is called suddenly, and only lasts a short time; **official strike** = strike which has been approved and is directed by a trade union; **protest strike** = strike in protest at a particular grievance; **sit-down strike** = strike where workers stay in their place of work and refuse to work or leave; **sympathy strike** = strike to show that workers agree with another group of workers who are on strike; *workers in the electricity industry staged a sympathetic strike on behalf of the miners;* **token strike** =

short strike to show that workers have a grievance; **unofficial strike** = strike by local workers, which has not been approved by the main union; **wildcat strike** = lightning strike organized by workers without the main union office knowing about it **(b) to try to avert a strike** = to try to prevent a strike from taking place; **to take strike action** = to go on strike; **strike ballot** *or* **strike vote** = vote by workers to decide if a strike should be held; **strike call** = demand by a union for a strike; *the strike call came when it was clear to the union that the management would never give in to the wage demands;* **strike committee** = group of employees representing various parts of an organization formed to organize a strike; **no-strike agreement** *or* **no-strike clause** = (clause in an) agreement where the workers say that they will never strike; **strike fund** = money collected by a trade union from its members, used to pay strike pay; **strike notice** = advance notice that a strike will take place on a certain date; **strike pay** = wages paid to striking workers by their trade union; *strike pay was not sufficient for the strikers to support their families during the strike* **(c) to come out on strike** *or* **to go on strike** = to stop work; *the office workers are on strike for higher pay;* **to call a strike** = to ask union members to strike; **to call off a strike** = to tell union members to stop striking and go back to work; **to call the workforce out on strike** = to tell the workers to stop work; *the union called its members out on strike;* **the strike was made official** = the local strike was approved by the trade union's main office **2** *verb* **(a)** to stop working because there is no agreement with management; *to strike for higher wages or for shorter working hours; to strike in protest against bad working conditions;* **to strike in sympathy with the postal workers** = to strike to show that you agree with the postal workers who are on strike **(b) to strike a bargain with someone** = to come to an agreement (NOTE: **striking - struck**)

◊ **strikebound** ['straɪkbaʊnd] *adjective* not able to work *or* to move because of a strike; *six ships are strikebound in the docks*

◊ **strikebreaker** ['straɪkbreɪkə] *noun* worker who goes on working while everyone else is on strike

◊ **striker** ['straɪkə] *noun* worker who is on strike

QUOTE the strike ended after four days and the employees returned to work in a surprisingly good atmosphere, despite loss of money

Personnel Management

structure ['strʌktʃə] **1** *noun* way in which something is organized; *the leaflet lays out the career structure within the organization;* **price structure** = way in which prices are arranged for a series of products; **the company's salary structure** = organization of salaries in a company with different rates of pay for different types of job **2** *verb* to arrange in a certain way; *to structure a meeting;* **structured interview** = interview built around fixed questions instead of a general discussion

◊ **structural** ['strʌktʃərəl] *adjective* referring to a structure; **structural unemployment** = unemployment caused by the changing structure of an industry *or* society; *structural unemployment in the north can be linked to the decline of the cotton industry*

◊ **structuring** ['strʌktʃərɪŋ] *noun* bringing order into an organization

study ['stʌdi] **1** *noun* **(a)** examining something carefully; *the company has asked the consultants to prepare a study of new production techniques; he has read the government study on sales opportunities;* **case study** = study of a particular situation to illustrate general principles; **to carry out a feasibility study on a project** = to examine the costs and possible profits to see if the project should be started; **time study** = study of the time taken to finish a certain piece of work; **time and motion study** = study in an office *or* factory of the movements of workers as they perform tasks to try to improve efficiency of production **(b)** learning something from books *or* from attending classes; **study leave** = time off work to allow a worker to follow a course **2** *verb* **(a)** to examine (something) carefully; *we are studying the possibility of setting up an office in New York* **(b)** to learn something from books *or* from classes; *he is studying the principles of personnel management*

style [staɪl] *noun* way of doing *or* making something; **management style** *or* **style of management** = way in which managers work, in particular the way in which they treat their employees

sub [sʌb] *noun informal* wages paid in advance

sub- [sʌb] *prefix* under *or* less important

◊ **subcontract 1** [sʌb'kɒntrækt] *noun* contract between the main contractor for a whole project and another firm who will do part of the work; *they have been awarded the subcontract for all the electrical work in the new building we will put the electrical work out to subcontract* **2** [sʌbkən'trækt] *verb* to agree with a company that they will do part of the work for a project; *the electrical work has been subcontracted to Smith Ltd*

◊ **subcontractor** [sʌbkən'træktə] *noun* company which has a contract to do work for a main contractor

subject to ['sʌbdʒɪkt 'tu] *adjective* depending on; **the contract is subject to government approval** = the contract will be valid only if it is approved by the government

subjective [səb'dʒektɪv] *adjective* considered from the point of view of the person involved, and not from any general point of view; *his assessments of the performance of his staff is quite subjective;* **subjective test** = test where the examiner evaluates the answers according to his own judgement (as opposed to an objective test) (NOTE: opposite is **objective**)

submit [səb'mɪt] *verb* to put (something) forward to be examined; *the union has submitted a claim for a ten per cent wage increase*

subordinate [sə'bɔːdɪnət] *noun* person in a lower position in an organization; *part of the manager's job is to supervise the training of his subordinates; his subordinates find him difficult to work with*

subsidize ['sʌbsɪdaɪz] *verb* to help by giving money; **subsidized accommodation** = cheap accommodation which is partly paid for by an employer

subsistence [səb'sɪstəns] *noun* minimum amount of food, money, housing, etc., which a person needs; **subsistence allowance** = money paid by a company to cover the cost of hotels, meals, etc., for a member of staff who is travelling on business

substandard [sʌb'stændəd] *adjective* not of the necessary quality *or* quantity to meet a standard; *the workers were criticized for substandard performance*

substantive agreement ['sʌbstæntɪv ə'gri:mənt] *noun* agreement between management and unions relating to pay, working hours, etc.

substitute ['sʌbstɪtju:t] **1** *noun* person who takes the place of someone else **2** *verb* to take the place of someone else

succeed [sək'si:d] *verb* **(a)** to do what was planned; *she succeeded in passing her shorthand test; they succeeded in putting their rivals out of business* **(b)** to follow (someone); *Mr Smith was succeeded as chairman by Mr Jones*

◊ **success** [sək'ses] *noun* getting a good result *or* getting the desired result; *he has been looking for a job for six months, but with no success*

◊ **successful** [sək'sesful] *adjective* having got the desired result; *the successful candidates will be advised by letter*

◊ **successfully** [sək'sesfəli] *adverb* well *or* getting the desired result; *he successfully negotiated a new contract with the unions*

◊ **successor** [sək'sesə] *noun* person who takes over from someone; *Mr Smith's successor as chairman will be Mr Jones*

suggestion [sə'dʒestʃən] *noun* proposal *or* idea which is put forward; **suggestion box** = place in a company where members of staff can put forward their ideas for making the company more efficient and profitable; **suggestion scheme** = system whereby employees can make suggestions on how the organization should be run more efficiently *or* profitably; *the suggestions scheme takes the form of a monthly meeting where employees can offer ideas for improvement of production techniques*

suitable ['su:təbl] *adjective* convenient *or* which fits; *we had to readvertise the job because there were no suitable candidates*

sum [sʌm] *noun* quantity of money; *a sum of money was stolen from the personnel office; she received the sum of £500 in compensation;* **lump sum** = money paid in one payment, not in several small payments

summary ['sʌməri] *adjective* done rapidly, without notice; **summary dismissal** = dismissal without giving the worker any notice (usually because of a crime committed by the worker, drunkenness or violent behaviour towards other workers)

◊ **summarily** ['sʌmərəli] *adverb* done rapidly, without notice; *she was summarily dismissed*

Sunday trading laws ['sʌndi 'treɪdɪŋ 'lɔ:z] *noun* regulations which govern business activities on Sundays (NOTE: the US equivalent is **Blue Laws)**

superannuation [su:pərænju'eɪʃn] *noun* pension paid to someone who is too old *or* ill to work any more; **superannuation plan** *or* **scheme** = pension plan *or* scheme

superior [su:'pɪərɪə] *noun* more important person; *each manager is responsible to his superior for accurate reporting of sales*

supervise ['su:pəvaɪz] *verb* to watch carefully to see that work is done well; *the move to the new offices was supervised by the administrative manager; she supervises six girls in the accounts department*

◊ **supervision** [su:pə'vɪʒən] *noun* being supervised; *new staff work under supervision for the first three months; she is very experienced and can be left to work without any supervision; the cash was counted under the supervision of the finance manager*

◊ **supervisor** ['su:pəvaɪzə] *noun* person who supervises; *the supervisor was asked to write a report on the workers' performance*

◊ **supervisory** [su:pə'vaɪzəri] *adjective* as a supervisor; *the supervisory staff have asked for a pay rise; he works in a supervisory capacity;* **supervisory board** = board of directors which deals with general policy and planning (as opposed to the executive board, which deals with day-to-day running of the company in a two-tier system)

supplement ['sʌplɪmənt] **1** *noun* thing which is added; *the company gives him a supplement to his pension* **2** *verb* to add; *we will supplement the warehouse staff with six part-timers during the Christmas rush*

◊ **supplementary** [sʌplɪ'mentəri] *adjective* in addition to; **supplementary**

benefit = extra payments from the government to unemployed people drawing unemployment pay; **supplementary training** = training to increase workers' efficiency; *supplementary training is needed to sharpen up performance*

surplus ['sɜːpləs] *noun* more of something than is needed; *profit figures are lower than planned because of surplus labour; some of the machines may have to be sold off as there is surplus production capacity; we are proposing to put our surplus staff on short time;* **surplus to requirements** = not needed any more

surrender [sə'rendə] **1** *noun* giving up of an insurance policy before the contracted date for maturity; **surrender value** = value of a life insurance policy if the policyholder decides to surrender it **2** *verb* **to surrender a policy** = to give up an insurance policy before the date on which it matures

suspend [səs'pend] *verb* **(a)** to stop doing something for a time; *they agreed to suspend the discussions for a week* **(b)** to stop (someone) working for a time; *he was suspended on full pay while the police investigations were going on*

◊ **suspension** [səs'penʃən] *noun* **(a)** stopping something for a time; *suspension of negotiations* **(b)** stopping someone working for a period; **suspension on full pay** = laying off a worker with full pay for a period; **suspension without pay** = laying off a worker without pay as a penalty

sweated labour ['swetɪd 'leɪbə] *noun* **(a)** people who work hard for very little money; *of course the firm makes a profit - it*

employs sweated labour; *most of the immigrant farmworkers are sweated labour* **(b)** hard work which is very badly paid

◊ **sweatshop** ['swetʃɒp] *noun* factory using sweated labour

sympathy ['sɪmpəθi] *noun* feeling sorry because someone else has problems; *the manager had no sympathy for his secretary who complained of being overworked;* **sympathy strike** = strike to show that workers agree with another group of workers who are on strike; **to strike in sympathy** = to stop work to show that you agree with another group of workers who are on strike; *the postal workers went on strike and the telephone engineers came out in sympathy*

◊ **sympathetic** [sɪmpə'θetɪk] *adjective* showing sympathy; **sympathetic strike** = sympathy strike

system ['sɪstəm] *noun* **(a)** arrangement *or* organization of things which work together; *what system is being used for filing data on personnel? our recruitment system must be defective since we have no suitable applicants;* **filing system** = way of putting documents in order for easy reference **(b)** **computer system** = set of programs, commands, etc., which run a computer **(c)** **systems analysis** = using a computer to analyse how an organization works and suggest how it could be improved; **systems analyst** = person who specializes in systems analysis; **systems management** = directing and controlling all the basic operations in an organization in order to achieve its basic objectives

Tt

table ['teɪbl] *noun* **(a)** piece of furniture with a flat top and legs; **bargaining table** = table where negotiators sit; *the arbitrators are trying to get the parties to return to the bargaining table;* **round table discussions** = discussions involving several parties who sit round the same table **(b)** list of information such as figures *or* facts, set out in columns; *the table shows all the employees and their monthly pay for the last year;* **table of organization** = diagram showing a list of people working in various departments, with their areas of responsibility and relationships between personnel; **actuarial tables** = lists showing how long people of certain ages are likely to live

tactic ['tæktɪk] *noun* way of doing things so as to be at an advantage; *the union leaders met to decide on their tactics in the struggle with management; the directors planned their tactics before going into the meeting with the union representatives*

take [teɪk] *verb* to receive *or* to get; **the shop takes £2,000 a week** = the shop receives £2,000 a week in cash sales; **he takes home £250 a week** = his salary, after deductions for tax, etc., is £250 a week

◊ **take back** ['teɪk 'bæk] *verb* **to take back dismissed workers** = to allow former workers to join the company again

◊ **take-home pay** ['teɪkhəum 'peɪ] *noun* pay received, after tax and insurance, etc., have been deducted

◊ **take on** ['teɪk 'ɒn] *verb* to agree to employ someone; *to take on more staff*

◊ **take over** ['teɪk 'əuvə] *verb* **(a)** to start to do something in place of someone else; *Miss Black took over from Mr Jones on May 1st; the new chairman takes over on July 1st;* **the take-over period is always difficult** = the period when one person is taking over work from another **(b) to take over a company** = to buy (a business) by offering to buy most of its shares; *the buyer takes over the company's liabilities; the company was taken over by a large multinational*

◊ **takeover** ['teɪkəuvə] *noun* buying a business; *the takeover of the company meant that the new management changed the existing pay structure; after the takeover several of the managers were made redundant*

◊ **take up** ['teɪk 'ʌp] *verb* to accept; **to take a new post** = to start a new job

tangible ['tæn(d)ʒəbl] *adjective* **tangible assets** *or* **property** = assets which are visible (such as machinery, buildings, furniture, jewellery, etc.); **tangible fixed assets** = assets such as land, buildings, plant and equipment, etc.

talks ['tɔːks] *plural noun* discussions; **to hold talks with someone** = to discuss with someone; *the talks will resume tomorrow; the talks broke down late last night*

tardiness ['tɑːdɪnəs] *noun (formal)* being late *or* unpunctual; *tardiness and poor performance were both responsible for this year's bad profit figures*

target ['tɑːgɪt] **1** *noun* something to aim for; **production targets** = amount of units a factory is expected to produce; **sales targets** = amount of sales a representative is expected to achieve; *production targets give workers more incentive and raise output; the personnel department complained that setting unrealistic sales targets was causing stress among the salesmen* **2** *verb* to aim at; **to target a market** = to plan to sell goods in a certain market; *an advertising campaign which targets teenagers*

task [tɑːsk] *noun* work which has to be done; *the job involves some tasks which are unpleasant and others which are more rewarding; the candidates are given a series of tasks to complete within a time limit;* **task bonus** = extra payment for a task completed on time; *task bonuses are paid to motivate workers to complete vital jobs on schedule;* **task force** = special group of workers *or* managers who are brought together to work on a project or solve a problem; *a task force has been put together to solve the critical production problems;* **task payment system** *or* **task system of pay** = payment system where workers are paid for each task completed on time; *slower workers dislike the introduction of a task payment system*

> QUOTE inner city task forces were originally set up in spring 1986 by the Department of Employment
> **Employment Gazette**

tax [tæks] **1** *noun* **(a)** regular payments made by citizens of a country to the central *or* local government to pay for government services; *earnings are considerably reduced by tax deductions;* **capital gains tax (CGT)** = tax on capital gains; **capital transfer tax** = tax on gifts or bequests of money or property; **corporation tax** = tax on profits made by companies; **income tax** = tax on salaries and wages; **land tax** = tax on the amount of land owned; **value added tax (VAT)** = tax on goods and services, added as a percentage to the invoiced sales price; **windfall tax** = special tax on unexpected profits **(b)** *(forms of tax)* **ad valorem tax** = tax calculated according to the value of the goods taxed; **back tax** = tax which is owed; **basic tax** = tax paid at the normal rate; **direct tax** = tax paid directly to the government (such as income tax); **indirect tax** = tax paid to someone who then pays it to the government (such as VAT); **to levy a tax** *or* **to impose a tax** = to make a tax payable; *the government has imposed a 15% tax on petrol;* **to lift a tax** = to remove a tax; *the tax on company profits has been lifted;* **exclusive of tax** = not including tax **(c)** **tax abatement** = reduction of tax; **tax adjustments** = changes made to tax; **tax adviser** *or* **tax consultant** = person who gives advice on tax problems; **tax allowance** *or* **allowances against tax** = part of the income which a person is allowed to earn and not pay tax on; **tax avoidance** = trying (legally) to minimize the amount of tax to be paid; **tax bracket** = percentage level of tax; **in the top tax bracket** = paying the highest level of tax; **tax code** = number given to indicate the amount of tax allowances a person has; **tax collector** = person who collects taxes which

are owed; **tax concession** = allowing less tax to be paid; **tax credit** = part of a dividend on which the company has already paid tax, so that the shareholder is not taxed on it again; **tax deductions** = (i) money removed from a salary as tax; (ii) *US* business expenses which can be claimed against tax; **tax deducted at source** = tax which is removed from a salary or interest taken away before the money is paid out; **tax evasion** = trying illegally not to pay tax; **tax exemption** = (i) being free from payment of tax; (ii) *US* part of income which a person is allowed to earn and not pay tax on; **tax form** = blank form to be filled in with details of income and allowances and sent to the tax office each year; **tax haven** = country where taxes are low, encouraging companies to set up their main offices there; **tax inspector** *or* **inspector of taxes** = official of the Inland Revenue who examines tax returns and decides how much tax someone should pay; **tax loophole** = legal means of not paying tax; **tax relief** = allowing someone not to pay tax on certain parts of his income; **tax return** *or* **tax declaration** = completed tax form, with details of income and allowances; **tax schedules** = six types of income as classified in the Finance Acts for British tax; *see also* SCHEDULE **tax shelter** = financial arrangement (such as a pension scheme) where investments can be made without tax; **tax year** = twelve month period on which taxes are calculated (in the UK, 6th April to 5th April of the following year) **2** *verb* to make someone pay a tax *or* to impose a tax on something; *to tax businesses at 50%; income is taxed at 35%; luxury items are heavily taxed*

◊ **taxable** ['tæksəbl] *adjective* which can be taxed; **taxable items** = items on which a tax has to be paid; **taxable income** = income on which a person has to pay tax

◊ **taxation** [tæk'seɪʃən] *noun* act of taxing; **direct taxation** = taxes (such as income tax) which are paid direct to the government; **indirect taxation** = taxes (such as sales tax) which are not paid direct to the government; *the government raises more money by indirect taxation than by direct;* **double taxation** = taxing the same income twice; **double taxation agreement** *or* **treaty** = agreement between two countries that citizens pay tax in one country only

◊ **tax-deductible** ['tæksdɪ'dʌktəbl] *adjective* which can be deducted from an income before tax is calculated; *the manager's travelling expenses are tax-deductible; these expenses are not tax-deductible* = tax has to be paid on these expenses

◊ **tax-exempt** ['tæksɪg'zem(p)t] *adjective* not required to pay tax; (income *or* goods) which are not subject to tax

◊ **tax-free** ['tæks 'friː] *adjective* on which tax does not have to be paid

◊ **taxpayer** ['tækspeɪə] *noun* person *or* company which has to pay tax; *basic taxpayer or taxpayer at the basic rate*

tea break ['tiː breɪk] *noun* rest time during work when the workers can drink coffee or tea

teaching machine ['tiːtʃɪŋ məˈʃiːn] *noun* machine (usually a specially programmed computer) which can be used to teach skills without an instructor

team [tiːm] *noun* group of people who work together and cooperate to share work and responsibility; **management team** = group of all the managers working in the same company; **sales team** = all representatives, salesmen and sales managers working in a company; **team briefing** = regular briefing session by a manager for a team, useful for the rapid communication of information to all the members of the team, and also for keeping the manager aware of the feelings and problems of the team; **team building** = training sessions designed to instil cooperation and solidarity in a group of workers who work together as a team; **team rate** = pay rate for a group of people working together; **team spirit** = general mood of a team, expressed as loyalty to the team, with motivation coming from working in a team

◊ **teamwork** ['tiːmwɜːk] *noun* group effort applied to work; *teamwork is encouraged by rewarding the efforts of the workers as a whole, rather than individually; teamwork is more suitable for this organization, since the problems we are faced with demand a high level of cooperation*

TEC = TRAINING AND ENTERPRISE COUNCIL

technical ['teknɪkəl] *adjective* referring to

scientific methods of production; *the document gives all the technical details on the new computer;* **technical college** = college which offers courses of further education in technical subjects; *some of our management trainees study business courses at the local technical college; the technical college runs a foundation course in product management*

◊ **technician** [tek'nɪʃən] *noun* person who is specialized in industrial work; *computer technician;* **laboratory technician** = person who deals with practical work in a laboratory

◊ **technique** [tek'niːk] *noun* skilled way of doing a job; *the company has developed a new technique for processing steel; he has a special technique for answering complaints from customers;* **management techniques** = skill in managing a business; **marketing techniques** = skill in marketing a product

◊ **technological** [teknə'lɒdʒɪkəl] *adjective* referring to technology; **the technological revolution** = changing of industry by introducing new technology

◊ **technology** [tek'nɒlədʒi] *noun* applying scientific knowledge to industrial processes; **information technology** = working with data stored on computers; **the introduction of new technology** = putting new electronic equipment into a business or industry; **technology transfer** = application of technology developed by one company in another company

teleworking ['telɪwɜːkɪŋ] *noun* working method where employees work at home on computer terminals, and send the finished material back to the central office by modem; *also called* HOMEWORKING, NETWORKING

◊ **teleworker** ['telɪwɜːkə] *noun* person who works at home, especially one using a computer linked to the main office

temp [temp] **1** *noun* temporary secretary or other office worker; *we have had two temps working in the office this week to clear the backlog of letters;* **temp agency** = office which deals with finding temporary staff for offices **2** *verb* to work as a temporary secretary

◊ **temping** ['tempɪŋ] *noun* working as a temporary secretary; *she can earn more money temping than from a full-time job*

temperature ['temprətʃə] *noun* measurement of heat in degrees

COMMENT: acceptable working temperatures vary with the type of work involved. Heavy work can be done at lower temperatures than sedentary office work, where the recommended ambient temperature should not be lower than 19°

temporary ['temprəri] *adjective* which only lasts a short time; *the students took on temporary jobs during the summer; she had to accept a temporary reduction in pay while she took time off work; he has a temporary post with a construction company; he has a temporary job as a filing clerk or he has a job as a temporary filing clerk;* **temporary contract** = contract of employment for a short period only; **temporary employment** *or* **temporary work** = full-time work which does not last for more than a few days or months; **temporary staff** *or* **temporary employees** *or* **temporary workers** = staff who are employed for a short time; *we need to recruit temporary staff for the busy summer season; he is a temporary employee and has no chance of a permanent position*

◊ **temporarily** ['temprərəli] *adverb* lasting only for a short time

QUOTE by comparison with permanent workers, temporary workers are more likely to be female
Employment Gazette

QUOTE regional analysis shows that the incidence of temporary jobs was slightly higher in areas where the rate of unemployment was above average
Employment Gazette

tender ['tendə] **1** *noun* offer to do something for a certain price; *a successful tender or an unsuccessful tender;* **competitive tender** = form of tender where different organizations are asked to tender for a contract, especially for government or local government work; **to put a project out to tender** *or* **to ask for** *or* **to invite tenders for a project** = to ask contractors to give written estimates for a job; **to put in a tender** *or* **to submit a tender** = to make an estimate for a job **2** *verb* **to tender one's resignation** = to give in one's resignation

tentative ['tentətɪv] *adjective* not certain; *they reached a tentative agreement over the proposal; we suggested Wednesday May 10th as a tentative date for the next meeting*

◊ **tentatively** ['tentətɪvli] *adverb* without being sure; *we tentatively suggested Wednesday as the date for our next negotiating meeting*

tenure ['tenjə] *noun* **(a)** right to hold a post permanently; **security of tenure** = right to keep a job provided certain conditions are met; **he has tenure** = he has a permanent job, from which he cannot be sacked or made redundant **(b)** time when a position is held; *during his tenure of the office of chairman*

term [tɜːm] *noun* **(a)** period of time; **short-term** *or* **in the short term** = for a period of months; **long-term** *or* **in the long term** = for a long period of time; **medium-term** *or* **in the medium term** = for a period of one or two years **(b)** period of time when something is legally valid; *the term of a lease; the term of the loan is fifteen years;* **term of office** = period when someone holds an office; *during his term of office as chairman* **(c)** **terms** = conditions *or* duties which have to be carried out as part of a contract *or* arrangements which have to be agreed before a contract is valid; *he refused to agree to some of the terms of the contract; by or under the terms of the contract, the company is responsible for all damage to the property; to negotiate for better terms;* **terms and conditions of employment** = conditions set out in a contract of employment; *after their interviews for the job, the candidates considered the terms of employment offered*

QUOTE companies have been improving communications, often as part of deals to cut down demarcation and to give everybody the same terms of employment
Economist

terminal ['tɜːmɪnl] **1** *adjective* at the end; **terminal assessment** = assessment of a trainee at the end of the course (as opposed to continuous assessment which is carried out during the course); **terminal illness** = illness where the patient is not likely to live more than six months; **terminal leave** = leave at the end of a fixed contract of employment **2** *noun* **computer terminal** = keyboard and screen by which information can be put into a computer or called up from a database

terminate ['tɜːmɪneɪt] *verb* **(a)** to end (something) *or* to bring (something) to an end; *his employment was terminated* **(b)** to dismiss; *to terminate an employee*

◊ **termination** [tɜːmɪ'neɪʃən] *noun* **(a)** bringing to an end; **termination clause** = clause which explains how and when a contract can be terminated **(b)** end to a contract of employment; leaving a job (resigning, retiring, or being fired or made redundant); *both employer and employee agreed that termination is the only way of solving the problem;* **termination allowance** *or* **termination pay** = payment to an employee who loses a job through no fault of his own; **termination clause** = clause which explains how and when a contract can be ended

tertiary ['tɜːʃəri] *adjective* **tertiary industry** = service industry, industry which does not produce or manufacture anything but offers a service (such as banking, retailing or accountancy); **tertiary sector** = section of the economy containing the service industries

test [test] **1** *noun* examination to assess someone; *candidates have to take a battery of tests;* **aptitude test** = test designed to measure someone's ability to use his or her skills in the future (as opposed to an attainment test); **attainment test** = test designed to measure the skills which someone is currently using (as opposed to an aptitude test); **intelligence test** = test to assess someone's intellectual ability; **personality test** = test to assess a person's character; **trade test** = test designed to assess someone's ability to do a certain job; *to assess candidates we use trade tests and personality tests* **2** *verb* to examine someone to assess his ability to do a job

◊ **testee** [tes'tiː] *noun* examinee, person who is being tested

◊ **tester** ['testə] *noun* examiner, person who tests someone

◊ **testing** ['testɪŋ] *noun* examining a person to see if he can do a job

testimonial [testɪ'məʊnjəl] *noun* written report about someone's character *or* ability; *to write someone a testimonial;* **unsolicited testimonial** = letter praising someone *or* a product, without the writer having been asked to write it

theft [θeft] *noun* stealing; *we have brought in security guards to protect the store against theft; they are trying to cut their losses by theft; to take out insurance against theft*

| COMMENT: theft from other employees is a reason for dismissal, but theft of office property may be less serious

think tank ['θɪŋktæŋk] *noun* group of experts who advise *or* put forward plans

threshold ['θreʃ(h)əʊld] *noun* limit *or* point at which something changes; **threshold agreement** = agreement which ensures automatic pay increases triggered by rises in the cost of living; *threshold agreements help workers weather the sharp rise in inflation;* **pay threshold** = point at which pay increases because of a threshold agreement; **tax threshold** = point at which another percentage of tax is payable; *the government has raised the minimum tax threshold from £6,000 to £6,500*

throw out [θrəʊ 'aʊt] *verb* **(a)** to reject *or* to refuse to accept; *the union negotiators threw out the management offer* **(b)** to get rid of (something which is not wanted); *he was thrown out of the company for disobedience*

time [taɪm] *noun* **(a)** period when something takes place (such as one hour, two days, fifty minutes, etc.); **time study** = study of the time taken to finish a certain piece of work; **time and motion study** = study in an office *or* factory of the movements of workers as they perform tasks to try to improve efficiency of production; **time and motion expert** = person who analyzes time and motion studies and suggests changes in the way work is done; *the time and motion study led to radical changes both in factory layout and work methods; we need to call in the time and motion people to find out where the delays are being caused in the production line* **(b)** hour of the day (such as 9.00, 12.15, ten o'clock at night, etc.); **closing time** = time when a shop or office stops work; **lunch time** = time in the middle of the day when people have lunch (for most British offices, from about 12.30 to 1.30, or from 1 to 2 p.m.); **opening time** = time when a shop or office starts work **(c)** hours worked; **he is paid time and a half on Sundays** = he is paid the normal rate plus 50% extra when he works on Sundays; **basic time** = normal time taken to do a job, established by work study; **double time** = time for which work is paid at twice the normal rate; *she is on double time on Sundays;* **full-time** = working for the whole normal working day; **on-call time** = time outside normal working hours when an employee is standing by, ready for work; **overtime** = hours worked beyond the normal working time; **part-time** = not working for a whole working day; **leisure time** *or* **spare time** = time when you are not at work, used for amusement, hobbies, etc.; *see also* ALLOWED TIME, COMPRESSED TIME, JUST-IN-TIME, SHORT TIME

◊ **time clock** ['taɪm 'klɒk] *noun* machine which records when a worker arrives for work and leaves, and punches the times in his card

◊ **time-card** *or US* **time-clock card** ['taɪm 'kɑːd *or* 'taɪm'klɒk 'kɑːd] *noun* card which is put into a timing machine when a worker clocks in *or* clocks out, and records the time when he starts and stops work

◊ **time-keeping** ['taɪmkiːpɪŋ] *noun* being on time for work; *he was warned for poor or bad time-keeping* (NOTE: no plural)

◊ **time limit** ['taɪm 'lɪmɪt] *noun* period during which something should be done; **to keep within the agreed time limits** = to complete work by the time agreed; *the work was finished within the time limit allowed; the time limit on applications to the industrial tribunal is three months*

◊ **time off** ['taɪm 'ɒf] *noun* time away from work granted to an employee to attend to private affairs; *the sales manager was given time off to settle the details of his divorce; we only give people time off in very deserving cases, because we have so much work going through; the management offered her time off in lieu of overtime pay;* **time off for union work** = agreed amount of time which an employer can allow a union official to work on union duties during normal working hours

◊ **time rate** ['taɪm 'reɪt] *noun* rate for work which is calculated as money per hour *or* per week, and not money for work completed

◊ **time saving** ['taɪm 'seɪvɪŋ] **1** *adjective* which saves time; *a time-saving device* **2** *noun* trying to save time; *the management is keen on time saving*

◊ **time scale** ['taɪm 'skeɪl] *noun* time which will be taken to complete work; *our time scale is that all work should be completed by the end of August; he is working to a strict time scale*

◊ **time sheet** ['taɪm 'ʃiːt] *noun* paper showing when a worker starts work in the morning and leaves work in the evening

◊ **time span** ['taɪm 'spæn] *noun* amount of time from when something starts to when it ends; **time span of discretion** = way of showing the amount of responsibility given to an employee, by only checking his or her work at long intervals (checking at shorter intervals indicated a lack of confidence)

◊ **time work** ['taɪm 'wɜːk] *noun* work which is paid for at a rate per hour *or* per day, not per piece of work completed

tip [tɪp] **1** *noun* money given to someone who has helped you; *I gave the taxi driver a 10 cent tip; the staff are not allowed to accept tips* **2** *verb* to give money to someone who has helped you; *he tipped the receptionist £5* (NOTE: **tipping - tipped**)

title ['taɪtl] *noun* **job title** = name given to a person in a certain job; *he has the title 'Chief Executive'*

token ['təʊkən] *noun* thing which acts as a sign *or* symbol; **token strike** = short strike (perhaps for half a day) to show that workers have a grievance; **token woman** = woman who is a member of a committee to show that women are being represented

tool [tuːl] *noun* instrument used for doing manual work (such as a hammer, screwdriver); **to down tools** = to go on strike

top [tɒp] **1** *adjective* at the highest point *or* most important place; **a top executive** *or* **top manager** = a main director; **top-flight** *or* **top-ranking** = in the most important position; *top-flight managers can earn very high salaries; top-ranking marketing managers can earn higher salaries abroad;* **top management** = the people who manage *or* administer an organization and make all important decisions; *after heading a department for two years she was promoted to a top management position* **2** *noun* highest point *or* most important place; **top-down information** = system of passing information down from management to the workforce; **top-down planning** = methods of planning, where decisions are taken at executive level, and passed down to the workforce without any consultation

◊ **top-hat pension plan** ['tɒp 'hæt 'penʃən 'plæn] *noun* special extra pension scheme for senior managers

tort [tɔːt] *noun* civil wrong done by one person to another and entitling the victim to claim damages; **economic tort** = economic harm done to one of the paries in an industrial dispute (such as when shops stewards induce workers to take industrial action and so harm the company's finances)

total ['təʊtl] *adjective* complete, with everything added together; **total quality management (TQM)** = management style which demands commitment to maintain and improve quality throughout the workforce (with control of systems, quality, inspection of working practices, etc.); **total systems approach** = way of organizing a large company, in which the systems in each section are all seen as part of the total corporate system

touch [tʌtʃ] *verb* to **touch base** = to make contact with someone to see how things are going

TQM = TOTAL QUALITY MANAGEMENT

track record ['træk 'rekɔːd] *noun* success or failure of a company *or* salesman in the past; *he has a good track record as a secondhand car salesman; we are looking for someone with a track record in the computer market*

trade [treɪd] *noun* particular type of business; people *or* companies dealing in the same type of product *or* service; **trade association** = group which links together companies in the same trade; **Trades Council** = regional body which brings together representatives of several trade unions in a particular area to discuss possible joint action; **trade cycle** = period during which trade expands, then slows down and then expands again; **trade dispute** = dispute between employers and employees or between the groups that represent them; *lower rates for overtime than last year will almost certainly provoke a trade dispute;* **the trade press** = newspapers and magazines dealing with a certain

industry; **trade test** = test designed to assess someone's ability to do a certain job; *in assessing candidates we use both trade tests and personality tests*

◊ **trade off** ['treɪd 'ɒf] *verb* to give up one demand made in negotiating against a concession from the other side

◊ **trade-off** ['treɪdɒf] *noun* exchanging one thing for another as part of a business deal

◊ **trade union** *or* **trades union** ['treɪd 'juːnjən *or* 'treɪdz 'juːnjən] *noun* workers' organization which represents its members in discussions with employers about wages and conditions of employment; *both the trade union representatives and the management side hope to be able to avert a strike; the trade union is negotiating with the management for a shorter working week; he has applied for trade union membership or he has applied to join a trades union;* **Trades Union Congress** = organization linking all British trade unions (NOTE: although **Trades Union Congress** is the official name for the organization, **trade union** is commoner than **trades union** in GB English. US English is **labor union)**

◊ **trade unionist** ['treɪd 'juːnjənɪst] *noun* member of a trade union

train [treɪn] *verb* to teach (someone) to do something; to learn how to do something; *he trained as an accountant; the company has appointed a trained lawyer as its managing director*

◊ **trainee** [treɪ'niː] *noun* person who is learning to work in an organization; *she's a trainee solicitor; office staff with leadership potential are selected for courses as trainee managers; we employ a trainee accountant to help in the office at peak periods; graduate trainees come to work in the laboratory when they have finished their courses at university;* **graduate trainee** = person in a graduate training scheme; **management trainee** *or* **trainee manager** = young member of staff being trained to be a manager; **trainee-centred learning** = training process where the trainee is expected to do research and carry out group projects, rather than listen to lectures

◊ **traineeship** [treɪ'niːʃɪp] *noun* post of trainee

◊ **trainer** ['treɪnə] *noun* person who trains staff

◊ **training** ['treɪnɪŋ] *noun* instruction in particular skills; *after six months' training he thought of himself as a professional salesman; some of the secretaries need training in dealing with customer enquiries; there is a ten-week training period for new staff; the shop is closed for staff training see also* COLD STORAGE, LABORATORY **graduate training scheme** = training scheme for graduates; **industrial training** = training of new workers to work in an industry; **in-house training** = training given to staff at their place of work; **management training** = training staff to be managers, by making them study problems and work out solutions to them; **on-the-job training** = training given to workers at their place of work; **off-the-job training** = training given to workers away from their place of work (such as at a college or school); **vocational training** = training for a particular career which a person wants to take up; **training board** = government organization set up for each industry to provide training for the workers in the industry; *training boards are especially effective in the north where development is held up because of lack of necessary skills;* **training centre** = government-run organization which trains adults in job skills; *several of our workers are at a training centre to learn how to operate the new machinery;* **training college** = college which provides training for particular professions; *she did a six-month typing course at a training college;* **training credit scheme** = scheme by which young people get vouchers to pay for training; **Training and Enterprise Council (TEC)** = group of local businessmen and training executives, which aims to increase skills learning by using local training establishments, such as further education colleges, to provide courses for local students; **Training, Enterprise and Education Directorate** = British government organization which is responsible for training schemes for workers; **training levy** = formerly, a tax to be paid by companies to fund the government's training schemes; **training officer** = person who deals with the training of staff; **training session** = meeting where staff are trained; **training ship** = ship used for training seamen; **training unit** = special group of teachers *or* instructors who organize training for companies

QUOTE the scale of training clearly required it to be off-the-job
Personnel Management

QUOTE trainee managers developed basic operational skills as well as acquiring a broad business education
Personnel Management

QUOTE in addition, more employers are to be encouraged to become training providers in inner city areas
Employment Gazette

transactional analysis [træn'zækʃənl ə'nælɪsɪs] *noun* method of developing new attitudes and behaviour with reference to certain unconscious rules adopted by people while communicating with others; *transactional analysis sessions have helped many of our managers deal more effectively with subordinates*

transfer 1 ['trænsfə] *noun* **(a)** moving an employee to another job in the same organization; *he applied for a transfer to our branch in Scotland* **(b)** bank transfer = moving money from a bank account to an account in another country; **credit transfer** *or* **transfer of funds** = moving money from one account to another **2** [træns'fɜː] *verb* **(a)** to move an employee to another job in the same organization; *the accountant was transferred to our Scottish branch* **(b)** to move money from one account to another

transitional [træn'zɪʃənl] *adjective* **transitional unemployment** = period where someone is out of work for a short time between two jobs

trashcan hypothesis ['træʃkæn haɪ'pɒθəsɪs] *noun US* tendency to assign any miscellaneous job to the personnel department

travel ['trævl] *noun* moving of people from one place to another *or* from one country to another; *business travel is a very important part of our overhead expenditure;* **travel allowance** = special payment made to a worker who has to travel in order to carry out his work; **travel expenses** = money spent on travelling and hotels for business purposes

trial ['traɪəl] *noun* **(a)** court case to judge a person accused of a crime; *he is on trial or is* *standing trial for embezzlement* **(b)** test to see if something is good; **on trial** = being tested; *the product is on trial in our laboratories;* **to take someone on a trial basis** = to take on a new member of staff for a short time, to see if they are acceptable; **trial period** = time when a customer can test a product before buying it; **trial sample** = small piece of a product used for testing; **free trial** = testing of a machine *or* product with no payment involved **(c) trial balance** = draft adding of debits and credits to see if they balance

tribunal [traɪˈbjuːnl] *noun* official court which examines special problems and makes judgements; **adjudication tribunal** *or* **arbitration tribunal** = group which adjudicates in industrial disputes; **employment appeal tribunal (EAT)** = tribunal which deals with appeals against the decisions of industrial tribunals; **industrial tribunal** = court which can decide in disputes about employment

trim [trɪm] *verb* to cut short; *staff costs have been trimmed*

triplicate [ˈtrɪplɪkət] *noun* **in triplicate** = with an original and two copies; *the application form should be completed in triplicate*

trouble [ˈtrʌbl] *noun* problem *or* difficult situation; *we are having some union trouble or some trouble with the union; there was some trouble in the warehouse after the manager was fired*

◊ **troublemaker** [ˈtrʌblmeɪkə] *noun* difficult employee, who is always causing problems for management

◊ **troubleshooter** [ˈtrʌblʃuːtə] *noun* person whose job is to solve problems in a company

trust [trʌst] *noun* duty of looking after goods *or* money *or* property which someone has passed to you as trustee

◊ **trustee** [trʌsˈtiː] *noun* person who has charge of money in trust *or* person who is responsible for a family trust; *the trustees of the pension fund*

TUC [ˈtiːjuːˈsiː] = TRADES UNION CONGRESS

turn down [tɜːnˈdaʊn] *verb* to refuse; *he turned down the job he was offered; the board turned down the proposal;* **she was turned down for the post** = she was not offered the post

turnkey operation [ˈtɜːnki ɒpəˈreɪʃən] *noun* deal where a company takes all responsibility for constructing, fitting and staffing a building (such as a school *or* hospital *or* factory) so that it is completely ready for the purchaser to take over

◊ **turnover** [ˈtɜːnəʊvə] *noun* **staff turnover** *or* **turnover of staff** = changes in staff, when some leave and others join; *the lack of any clear career prospects is the reason for our high staff turnover or turnover of staff*

turn round [ˈtɜːn ˈraʊnd] *verb* to make (a company) change from making a loss to become profitable; **he turned the company round in less than a year** = he made the company profitable in less than a year

twilight shift [ˈtwaɪlaɪt ˈʃɪft] *noun* evening shift, just before it gets dark

two-tier [ˈtuː ˈtɪə] *adjective* **two-tier board** = system where a company has two boards of directors, an executive board which runs the company on a day-to-day basis, and a supervisory board which monitors the results and deals with long-term planning

type [taɪp] *verb* to write with a typewriter; *he can type quite fast; all his reports are typed on his portable typewriter*

◊ **typewritten** [ˈtaɪprɪtn] *adjective* written on a typewriter; *he sent in a typewritten job application*

◊ **typing pool** [ˈtaɪpɪŋ ˈpuːl] *noun* group of typists, working together in a company, offering a secretarial service to several departments; *she found it difficult to get used to the noise in the typing pool*

◊ **typist** [ˈtaɪpɪst] *noun* person whose job is to write letters using a typewriter; *the personnel department needs more typists to deal with all the correspondence*

Uu

ultimatum [ˌʌltɪˈmeɪtəm] *noun* statement to a someone that unless he does something within a period of time, action will be taken against him; *the union officials argued among themselves over the best way to deal with the ultimatum from the management the management has given the union an ultimatum* (NOTE: plural is **ultimatums** or **ultimata**)

ultra vires [ˌʌltrə ˈvaɪriːz] *Latin phrase* meaning 'beyond powers'; **an ultra vires contract** = contract which the parties are not competent to sign

umpire [ˈʌmpaɪə] *noun* independent person who is asked to decide in a dispute in cases where the adjudicators cannot come to a decision

unacceptable [ˌʌnəkˈseptəbl] *adjective* which cannot be accepted; *the terms of the contract are quite unacceptable*

unanimous [juˈnænɪməs] *adjective* where everyone votes in the same way; *there was a unanimous vote against the proposal; they reached unanimous agreement*

◊ **unanimously** [juˈnænɪməsli] *adverb* with everyone agreeing; *the proposals were adopted unanimously*

unauthorized [ʌnˈɔːθəraɪzd] *adjective* not permitted; *unauthorized access to the company's records; unauthorized expenditure;* **unauthorized absence from work** *or* **absence without leave** = being away from work without permission and without a good reason; **unauthorized person** = person who has not received permission to do something; *no unauthorized persons are allowed into the laboratory*

uncommitted [ʌnkəˈmɪtɪd] *adjective* (worker) who is not happy and does not feel involved in the organization he works for; *there is a drive on to weed out employees who are uncommitted to the objectives of the company*

unconditional [ʌnkənˈdɪʃənl] *adjective* with no conditions *or* provisions attached; *after the interview he got an unconditional offer of a job*

◊ **unconditionally** [ʌnkənˈdɪʃənli] *adverb* without imposing any conditions; *the offer was accepted unconditionally by the trade union*

underachiever [ʌndəəˈtʃiːvə] *noun* person who achieves less than he or she is capable of

underemployed [ʌndərɪmˈplɔɪd] *adjective* with not enough work; *the staff is underemployed because of the cutback in production*

◊ **underemployment** [ʌndərɪmˈplɔɪmənt] *noun* **(a)** situation where workers in a company do not have enough work to do *or* are not used to their full capacity; *top management realized that underemployment was a terrible waste of manpower resources* **(b)** situation where there is not enough work for all the workers in a country (NOTE: no plural)

undergo [ˈʌndəgəʊ] *verb* to go through *or* to take; *the managers have to undergo a period of retraining; she has to undergo a fitness test*

undermanned [ʌndəˈmænd] *adjective* with not enough staff to do the work; *the department will be undermanned during the Christmas period*

◊ **undermanning** [ʌndəˈmænɪŋ] *noun* having too few workers than are needed to do the company's work; *the company's production is affected by undermanning on the assembly line; undermanning is caused by lack of available skilled workers in the area*

undermine [ʌndəˈmaɪn] *verb* to make something less strong; *the leaking of the secret report has undermined confidence in the management*

underpaid [ʌndə'peɪd] *adjective* not paid enough; *our staff say that they are underpaid and overworked*

underrepresent [ʌndərepri'zent] *verb* to give one group fewer representatives than another; *women are underrepresented at senior management level*

understaffed [ʌndə'stɑːft] *adjective* with not enough staff to do the company's work

understanding [ʌndə'stændɪŋ] *noun* private agreement; *the management and union came to an understanding about the demarcation problems;* on the understanding that = on condition that *or* provided that; *the union has accepted the terms of the contract, on the understanding that it has to be ratified by the union's executive;* to come to *or* to reach an understanding = to agree

understudy ['ʌndəstədi] 1 *noun* person who is learning how to do a job which is currently being done by someone else, so as to be able to take over the job if the present incumbent retires or is ill; *they have planned to put understudies into each of the key managements posts; the production manager made sure his understudy could run the factory if called upon to do so* 2 *verb* to learn how to do a job by working alongside the present incumbent, so as to be able to take over if he retires or is ill; *he is understudying the production manager*

undertake [ʌndə'teɪk] *verb* (a) to carry out; *they are undertaking a study on union reactions to pay restraint* (b) to agree to do something; *the union has undertaken not to call a strike without further negotiation with the management* (NOTE: **undertaking - undertook - has undertaken**)

◊ **undertaking** [ʌndə'teɪkɪŋ] *noun* (a) business; *commercial undertaking* (b) (legally binding) promise; *they have given us a written undertaking not to strike before negotiations have been completed*

underutilization [ʌndəjuːtɪlaɪ'zeɪʃn] *noun* situation where members of a social group are underrepresented in a particular job category; *the underutilization of women in top management posts*

◊ **underutilized** [ʌndə'juːtɪlaɪzd] *adjective* not used enough

underworked [ʌndə'wɜːkt] *adjective* not

given enough work to do; *the directors think our staff are overpaid and underworked*

unearned income ['ʌnɜːnd 'ɪnkʌm] *noun* money received from interest or dividends, not from salary or profits of one's business

unemployed [ʌnɪm'plɔɪd] 1 *adjective* not employed *or* without any work; **unemployed office workers** = office workers with no jobs 2 *noun* the unemployed = people with no regular paid work; *as prices rise, life gets harder for the unemployed;* the long-term unemployed = people who have had no regular paid work for over twelve months *or* people with no jobs and no prospect of ever being employed

◊ **unemployment** [ʌnɪm'plɔɪmənt] *noun* not having any work; *the unemployment statistics show no signs of falling; with rising unemployment, more people are starting up small businesses;* falling unemployment = unemployment rates which are falling because more people are finding jobs; **high unemployment** = level of unemployment which is high compared to previous figures; **mass unemployment** = unemployment of large numbers of workers; **rising unemployment** = unemployment rates which are rising because more people are being made redundant; **seasonal unemployment** = unemployment which appears at certain times of the year; **unemployment benefit** *or* **unemployment pay** *or US* **unemployment compensation** = government payment made to an unemployed person; **unemployment rate** *or* **rate of unemployment** = number of people out of work, shown as a percentage of the total number of people available for work

---

QUOTE unemployment fell by 33,000 in February to 2,531,000, the lowest figure for six years

Employment Gazette

QUOTE it must be a major priority to improve our adult training system so that more unemployed people can acquire the skills to fill the vacancies

Employment Gazette

QUOTE tax advantages directed toward small businesses will help create jobs and reduce the unemployment rate

Toronto Star

unequal value [ʌnˈiːkwəl ˈvæljuː] *noun* **unequal value jobs** = jobs done by men and women which are not equal in value

unfair [ʌnˈfeə] *adjective* not just *or* reasonable; *the manager's treatment of the clerk was unfair and completely unjustified;* **unfair competition** = trying to do better than another company by using techniques such as importing foreign goods at very low prices or by wrongly criticizing a competitor's products; **unfair contract term** = term in a contract which a court holds to be unjust; **unfair dismissal** = removing someone from a job for reasons which are not legally fair (as, for example, when a female employee who has had maternity leave and wishes to return to work is refused a job by the company she was working for); *an employee can complain of unfair dismissal to an industrial tribunal;* **unfair labour practices** = illegal activities by workers *or* employers

COMMENT: unfair dismissal cannot be claimed where a worker is dismissed for incapability, gross misconduct or in cases of genuine redundancy

◊ **unfairly** [ʌnˈfeəli] *adverb* in an unfair way; *she complained that she was treated unfairly by her manager*

unfilled [ʌnˈfɪld] *adjective* (vacancy) which has not been filled; *there are still six unfilled places on the training course; many specialized jobs remain unfilled because of a lack of qualified candidates*

unfreezing [ʌnˈfriːzɪŋ] *noun* getting accustomed to a new organization and its procedures; *unfreezing can be stressful in new employees who are used to more bureaucratic organizations*

unilateral [juːnɪˈlætərəl] *adjective* on one side only *or* done by one party only; **unilateral decision** = decision taken by one party alone; *they took the unilateral decision to cancel the contract*

◊ **unilaterally** [juːnɪˈlætərəli] *adverb* by one party only; *they cancelled the contract unilaterally*

union [ˈjuːnjən] *noun* **trade union** *or* **trades union** *or* *US* **labor union** = workers' organization which represents its members in discussions with management about wages and conditions of work and defends their interests; *all union members are asked to pay their dues promptly; he has a lot of experience in union politics;* **to join a union** = to become a member of a union, and pay one's subscription; **general union** = union which recruits usually semi-skilled workers in all industries; **house union** = union representing workers in one company only; **union agreement** = agreement between a management and a trade union over wages and conditions of work; *the union will soon start discussions on a new union agreement;* **union dues** *or* **union subscriptions** = payment made by workers to belong to a union; **union leader** = head official of a union; **union member** = person who belongs to a trade union; **non-union member** = person who does not belong to a trade union; **union official** = paid organizer of a union; **union recognition** = act of agreeing that a union can act on behalf of staff in a company; *the management wanted to avoid union recognition as it would weaken their bargaining position US* **union shop** = place of work where it is agreed that all workers must be members of a union

◊ **unionism** [ˈjuːnjənɪzm] *noun* having trade unions; being a member of a trade union; **dual unionism** = being a member of two trade unions; *dual unionism is common in industries where the workers want to be as well represented as possible*

◊ **unionist** [ˈjuːnjənɪst] *noun* member of a trade union

◊ **unionized** [ˈjuːnjənaɪzd] *adjective* (company) where the members of staff belong to a trade union

> QUOTE the blue-collar unions are the people who stand to lose most in terms of employment growth
>
> **Sydney Morning Herald**

> QUOTE after three days of tough negotiations, the company reached agreement with its 1,200 unionized workers
>
> **Toronto Star**

unit ['juːnɪt] *noun* group of people set up for a special purpose; **bargaining unit** = group of employees who negotiate with their employer to reach a collective agreement; **production unit** = group of workers which produce an item

unitarism ['juːnɪtərɪzm] *noun* belief that the management and workforce are working together for the good of the company (as opposed to pluralism)

unite [juːˈnaɪt] *verb* to join together; *the three unions in the factory united to present their wage claims to the management*

unjustified [ʌnˈdʒʌstɪfaɪd] *adjective* which is not justified; *the union claimed the sackings were quite unjustified*

unofficial [ʌnəˈfɪʃəl] *adjective* not official *or* done without authority; **unofficial industrial action** = industrial action (strike, go-slow, etc.) taken by workers without the approval of a trade union; **unofficial sanctions** = sanctions imposed by an employer on union members who are working to rule; **unofficial strike** = strike by local workers which has not been approved by the main union

◊ **unofficially** [ʌnəˈfɪʃəli] *adverb* not officially; *the personnel manager told the union negotiators unofficially that their claim would be accepted*

unpaid [ʌnˈpeɪd] *adjective* not paid; **unpaid holiday** *or* **unpaid leave** = holiday where the worker does not receive any pay

unpunctual [ʌnˈpʌŋktjʊəl] *adjective* (worker) who is not punctual *or* who does not arrive on time

◊ **unpunctuality** [ʌnpʌŋktjuːˈælɪti] *noun* not arriving on time (for work *or* for an appointment); *he was warned that he would be sacked for further unpunctuality*

unrest [ʌnˈrest] *noun* state of protest because of dissatisfaction with conditions; **industrial unrest** = action by workers (protest meetings, strikes, walk-outs, etc) against pay or working conditions

unskilled [ʌnˈskɪld] *adjective* (workers) who have no particular training; *using unskilled labour will reduce labour costs; with so much specialization in industry, there is little work for an unskilled workforce or for unskilled workers*

unsocial [ʌnˈsəʊʃəl] *adjective* **to work unsocial hours** = to work at times (i.e. in the evening *or* at night *or* during public holidays) when most people are not at work

unstructured interview [ʌnˈstrʌktʃəd ˈɪntəvjuː] *noun* interview which is not built round a series of fixed questions and which encourages open discussion; *an unstructured interview can help a nervous candidate to express himself*

> QUOTE the traditional unstructured interview does not give you enough information. You might as well toss a coin
>
> **Sunday Times**

unsuccessful [ʌnsəkˈsesfʊl] *adjective* not successful; *he made six unsuccessful job applications before he finally got a job*

◊ **unsuccessfully** [ʌnsəkˈsesfəli] *adverb* with no success; *he unsuccessfully applied for the job of marketing manager*

unsuitable [ʌnˈsuːtəbl] *adjective* not suitable; *we send all candidates a short written test, so as to weed out those who are clearly unsuitable for the job*

untrained [ʌnˈtreɪnd] *adjective* (person) who has had no training; *she came into the office straight from school, and completely untrained; the company has a policy of not recruiting untrained staff*

unwaged [ʌnˈweɪdʒd] *adjective* **the unwaged** = people with no jobs (NOTE: is followed by a plural verb)

up [ʌp] *verb* to increase; *management upped their offer to 7%*

upgrade [ʌpˈgreɪd] *verb* to increase the importance of someone *or* of a job; *his job has been upgraded to senior manager level*

◊ **upgrading** [ʌpˈgreɪdɪŋ] *noun* action of increasing the importance of someone *or* of a job

uphold [ʌpˈhəʊld] *verb* **to uphold a decision** = to reject an appeal against a decision

upper [ˈʌpə] *adjective* higher; **upper age limit** = highest age limit; **upper earnings limit** = top level of earnings above which tax or other financial levies do not apply

upward [ˈʌpwəd] *adjective* towards a higher position; **upward communication** = communication between the lower level of staff in an organization and senior management

utmost [ˈʌtməʊst] *adjective* **utmost good faith** = state which should exist between parties to certain types of legal relationship (such as partnerships or insurance)

Vv

vacancy ['veɪkənsi] *noun* job which is to be filled; *there are two vacancies in the personnel department; we advertised the vacancy both internally and in the local press; we have been unable to fill the vacancy for a skilled machinist; they have a vacancy for a secretary;* **casual vacancy** = job which has become vacant because the previous employee left unexpectedly; **job vacancies** = jobs which are empty and need people to do them

◊ **vacant** ['veɪkənt] *adjective* (job) which needs to be filled; **situations vacant** *or* **appointments vacant** = list (in a newspaper) of jobs which are available

> QUOTE the official statistics on the number of vacancies at job centres at any one point in time represent about one-third of total unfilled vacancies. The majority of vacancies are in small establishments
> *Employment Gazette*

vacate [və'keɪt] *verb* **to vacate a post** = to leave a job

◊ **vacation** [və'keɪʃən] *noun US* holiday *or* period when people are not working; *he was given two weeks' vacation to get over his wife's death; the job comes with a month's annual vacation; the CEO is on vacation in Florida*

valence ['veɪləns] *noun* degree to which a person's actions are important to him or her, and therefore an important ingredient in motivation

valid ['vælɪd] *adjective* true *or* which can be used lawfully; *the contract is not valid if it has not been signed by both parties; the intelligence test is not valid since it does not accurately measure basic mental skills*

◊ **validate** ['vælɪdeɪt] *verb* **(a)** to check to see if something is correct; *the document was validated by the bank* **(b)** to make (something) valid

◊ **validation** [vælɪ'deɪʃən] *noun* confirmation of how valid *or* effective something is; *the validation of the intelligence test was based on the results of research in the university psychology department; validation of the interview techniques will help to determine how useful they are in assessing candidates objectively*

◊ **validity** [və'lɪdəti] *noun* effectiveness *or* usefulness; *the validity of these tests is questionable since applicants have also managed to pass them who have been unsatisfactory in subsequent employment;* **face validity** = degree to which a test seems to be valid; **predictive validity** = assessing the validity of selection tests, by comparing the employee's performance in tests with his subsequent job performance

◊ **value** ['vælju:] *noun* amount of money which something is worth; **added value** *or* **value added** = amount added to the value of a product or service, being the difference between its cost and the amount received when it is sold (wages, taxes, etc., are deducted from the added value to give the profit); *see also* VALUE ADDED TAX **value added evaluation** = calculating the worth of a training programme by measuring the difference between the competence or skills of trainees at the beginning and the end of the programme

◊ **Value Added Tax (VAT)** ['vælju: 'ædɪd 'tæks] *noun* tax imposed as a percentage of the invoice value of goods and services

variance ['veərɪəns] *noun* difference between what was planned and the actual results; *taking on more staff than planned has caused a variance of several thousand pounds in the staff budget;* **budget variance** = difference between the cost as estimated for the budget, and the actual cost

◊ **variation** [veərɪ'eɪʃən] *noun* amount by which something changes; **seasonal variations** = changes which take place because of the seasons; *there are marked seasonal variations in unemployment in the hotel industry*

VAT ['viːeɪ'tiː *or* væt] = VALUE ADDED TAX

verbal ['vɜːbəl] *adjective* using spoken words, not writing; **verbal agreement** = agreement which is spoken (such as over the telephone); **verbal warning** = first stage of disciplinary measures, where a worker is told by the supervisor or manager that his or her work is unsatisfactory and must be improved; *after being given one verbal warning, he knew he would be sacked if he was absent from work again*

◊ **verbally** ['vɜːbəli] *adverb* using spoken words, not writing; *he was warned verbally that his work was not up to standard*

vertical ['vɜːtɪkəl] *adjective* upright *or* straight up or down; **vertical communication** = communication down from senior managers via the middle management to the workers on the shop floor; **vertical integration** = joining businesses together which deal with different stages in the production or sale of a product; **vertical job enlargement** = expansion of a job to include new activities *or* responsibilities; **vertical staff meeting** = meeting between managers and two or more levels of subordinate staff; *vertical staff meetings can help management to understand some of the grievances of workers on the shop floor*

vested ['vestɪd] *adjective* **vested interest** = special interest in keeping an existing state of affairs; *stakeholders have a vested interest in a company;* **vested benefit** = benefit attached to a pension scheme to which the contributor has a right; **vested right** = right such as a benefit, retirement pension, etc., to which a pensioner is entitled

vestibule training ['vestɪbjuːl 'treɪnɪŋ] *noun* form of in-service training which takes place in special rooms built to copy exactly the actual place of work

vet [vet] *verb* to examine something carefully; *all candidates have to be vetted by the managing director;* **positive vetting** = close examination of a person working with secret information who may not be reliable (NOTE: **vetting - vetted**)

veteran ['vetərən] *noun* employee who has been in the same post for many years; *there are so many veterans in some departments*

that it is difficult to introduce new working practices

vicarious [vɪ'keəriəs] *adjective* not direct; **vicarious liability** = legal responsibility of a person for actions committed by someone else when he or she is officially under one's control, especially the liability of an employer for acts committed by an employee in the course of his or her work

vice- [vaɪs] *prefix* deputy *or* second in command; *he is the vice-chairman of an industrial group; she was appointed to the vice-chairmanship of the committee*

◊ **vice-president** [vaɪs'prezɪdənt] *noun* US one of the executive directors of a company; **senior vice-president** = one of a few main executive directors of a company

victimization [vɪktɪmaɪ'zeɪʃn] *noun* unfair *or* unreasonable treatment of one employee by the employer *or* by other employees; *victimization can come from senior employees' fear of losing their jobs to juniors, or from racial and sexual prejudice*

◊ **victimize** ['vɪktɪmaɪz] *verb* to treat an employee unfairly; *the worker felt he was being victimized because of his religion*

> QUOTE the Swedish model defines victimization at work as 'recurrent, reprehensible or distinctly negative actions which are directed against individual employees in an offensive manner'
>
> *People Management*

violate ['vaɪəleɪt] *verb* to break a rule *or* law *or* agreement; *the union has violated the terms of the agreement*

◊ **violation** [vaɪə'leɪʃn] *noun* act of breaking a rule; *the strike is a violation of the no-strike agreement signed last year;* **in violation of a rule** = which breaks a rule; *the management made six managers redundant, in violation of the agreement which they had signed with the union*

vocation [və(ʊ)'keɪʃən] *noun* type of job which you feel you want to do; calling to be in a certain type of job; *he followed his vocation and became an accountant*

◊ **vocational** [və(ʊ)'keɪʃənl] *adjective* referring to a choice of career *or* occupation which a person wishes to follow; **vocational**

guidance = professional help for people in choosing a suitable career; *vocational guidance can also prove valuable to employees in mid-career who want to change jobs;* **vocational qualifications** = a person's competence in an occupation, as shown in certificates or other documents; **vocational training** = training for a particular career which a person wants to take up; *he wanted to have some vocational training instead of going to university, as he felt it would give him more practical skills*

volenti non fit injuria [vəˈlentiː nɒn fɪt ɪnˈdʒuəriə] *Latin phrase meaning* 'there can be no injury to a person who is willing': rule that if someone has agreed to take the risk of an injury he cannot sue for it (as in the case of someone injured in a boxing match)

voluntary [ˈvɒləntəri] *adjective* **(a)** done willingly *or* without being forced; **voluntary redundancy** = situation where a worker asks to be made redundant; **voluntary unemployment** = unemployment because people do not want to take existing work; *voluntary unemployment can largely be put down to the excessively low wages offered by employers in the area* **(b)** done without being paid; **voluntary organization** = organization which has no paid staff; *many voluntary organizations are involved in organizing famine relief;* **voluntary service overseas (VSO)** = organization which sends volunteers (young people and older specialists alike) to work overseas, sharing skills and experience with workers in developing countries; **voluntary work** = unpaid work (such as work for a charity *or* club); **voluntary worker** = person who does unpaid work; *we can use voluntary workers to help in fund raising for charity*

◊ **voluntarily** [ˈvɒləntərəli] *adverb* without being forced or paid

◊ **volunteer** [vɒlənˈtiːə] **1** *noun* person who offers to do something; *the shop is run entirely by volunteers* **2** *verb* to offer to do something; *he volunteered for redundancy because he wanted to retire early*

QUOTE British Executive Service Overseas' register of 1,700 volunteers covers almost every type of work
British Business

vote [vəut] **1** *noun* marking a paper, holding up your hand, etc., to show your opinion *or* to show who you want to be elected; **to take a vote on a proposal** *or* **to put a proposal to the vote** = to ask people present at a meeting to say if they do or do not agree with the proposal; *the union put the strike proposal to the vote;* **block vote** = casting of a large number of votes in the same way and at the same time (such as those of a trade union delegation at a conference); **casting vote** = single vote (usually by the chairman) which decides the result, when the numbers voting for and against a motion are the same; **deciding vote** = vote which decides an issue; **majority vote** = vote where one side has a majority of votes cast; **one man one vote** = system where each member or delegate has only one vote (so avoiding block votes); **postal vote** = election where the voters send in their voting papers by post; **vote of confidence** = vote taken to show that the meeting approves the actions of someone **2** *verb* to show an opinion by marking a paper *or* by holding up your hand at a meeting; *the meeting voted to close the factory; 52% of the staff voted for a strike;* **to vote for a proposal** *or* **to vote against a proposal** = to say that you agree *or* do not agree with a proposal

VSO = VOLUNTARY SERVICE OVERSEAS

Ww

wage [weɪdʒ] *noun* money paid regularly (usually in cash each week) to a worker for work done; *she is earning a good wage or good wages in the supermarket;* **basic wage** = normal pay without any extra payments; *the basic wage is £110 a week, but you can expect to earn more than that with overtime;* **hourly wage** *or* **wage per hour** = amount of money paid for an hour's work; **minimum wage** = lowest hourly wage which a company can legally pay its workers; **weekly wage** = amount of money paid per week; **wage adjustments** = changes made to wages; **wage administration** *or* **administration of wages** = planning a wage system and putting it into practice; *wage administration has been made much easier by the new computer system;* **(collective) wage agreement** = agreement between management and a trade union about wages; **total wage bill** = all the money paid by a company in salaries and wages; **wage ceiling** = highest legal wage for a particular class of worker; **wage claim** = asking for an increase in wages; *management considered the union wages claim to be unreasonable and rejected it;* **wages clerk** = office worker who deals with the payment of wages; **wage compression** = narrowing the difference between the highest and lowest paid jobs; *wage compression has been a key factor in reducing discontent among lower-paid workers;* **wage controls** = statutory controls over wage increases, by which governments try to keep wage inflation low; **wages councils** = organizations made up of employer and employee representatives which fix basic employment conditions in industries where places of work are too small or too scattered for trade unions to be established; **wage differentials** = differences between one worker's wage and another's in similar types of jobs; *wage differentials must be justified by differences in experience and ability;* **wage drift** = situation where a wage increase paid is greater than an officially negotiated one; **wages floor** = lowest legal wage for a particular class of worker; **wage formula** = basis on which a worker is paid; *the most common wage formula for salesmen is a combination of a basic salary plus commission;* **wage freeze** *or* **freeze on wages** = official ban on wage increases in a country; *the wage freeze has led the personnel department to compensate by increasing fringe benefits;* **wages inspector** = inspector employed by a wages council to inspect businesses and check on their wage levels; **wage levels** = rates of pay for different types of work; **wage negotiations** = discussions between management and workers about pay; **wage packet** = envelope containing money and pay slip; **wages policy** = government policy on what percentage increases should be paid to workers; **wage-price spiral** = situation where price rises encourage higher wage demands which in turn make prices rise; *the government decided to implement a wage freeze to avoid a wage-price spiral;* **wage restraint** = keeping increases in wages under control; **wage review** = examination of wages paid in an organization to see if workers should get an increase; **wage scale** = table showing different rates of pay for different job grades in the same company, with possible variations at each level; **wage settlement** = agreement on wages reached after negotiations; **wages sheet** = list of employees with the wages they are earning; **wage survey** = study of wages paid by organizations in the same industry to help determine wage levels; *the company had not carried out a thorough wage survey and so was found to be paying much lower wages in some areas and above-average wages in others* (NOTE: **wages** is more usual when referring to money earned, but **wage** is used before other nouns)

◊ **wage-earner** ['weɪdʒɜːnə] *noun* person who earns money paid weekly in a job

◊ **wage-earning** ['weɪdʒɜːnɪŋ] *adjective* **the wage-earning population** = people who have jobs and earn money

QUOTE European economies are being held back by rigid labor markets and wage structures
Duns Business Month

QUOTE real wages have been held down dramatically: they have risen at an annual rate of only 1% in the last two years
Sunday Times

waiting ['weɪtɪŋ] *noun* **waiting days** = the first three days during which a person is sick and cannot claim statutory sick pay; **waiting time** = lost working time caused by a breakdown in machinery, lack of supplies, etc.

waive [weɪv] *verb* to give up (a right); **to waive a payment** = to say that payment is not necessary

◊ **waiver** ['weɪvə] *noun* giving up (a right) *or* removing the conditions (of a rule); *if you want to work without a permit, you will have to apply for a waiver;* **waiver clause** = clause in a contract giving the conditions under which the rights in the contract can be given up; **waiver of breach of contract** = situation where an employer dismisses someone a long time after an offence was committed

walk ['wɔːk 'ɪn] *noun* person who approaches an organization for a job, without knowing if any jobs are available; *most walk-ins never get beyond the receptionist, because the personnel department asks for full written applications for any job*

◊ **walk off** ['wɔːk 'ɒf] *verb* to go on strike *or* to stop working and leave an office *or* factory; *the builders walked off the site because they said it was too dangerous*

◊ **walk out** ['wɔːk 'aʊt] *verb* to go on strike *or* to stop working and leave an office *or* factory; *the whole workforce walked out in protest*

◊ **walk-out** ['wɔːkaʊt] *noun* strike *or* stopping work; *production has been held up by a workers' walk-out*

want [wɒnt] *noun* thing which is needed; **want ads** = advertisements listed in a newspaper under special headings (such as 'property for sale', or 'jobs wanted'); *she went through the want ads every day, looking for a clerical job near her home; Tuesday's want ads are mainly for engineering jobs*

warm-up ['wɔːmʌp] *noun* first informal part of an interview where the interviewer tries to put the interviewee at ease; *every interview should start with a warm-up*

warn [wɔːn] *verb* to say that there is a possible danger; *he was warned that any further instances of absenteeism would be punished by stopping his pay* (NOTE: you warn someone **of** something, or **that** something may happen)

◊ **warning** ['wɔːnɪŋ] *noun* **verbal warning** = oral message to an employee, threatening punishment or dismissal if performance or behaviour is not improved; **written warning** = written message to an employee, threatening punishment or dismissal if performance or behaviour is not improved; *management must always give both an oral and written warning before dismissal; the union complained that their member had been sacked without any warning being given*

wastage ['weɪstɪdʒ] *noun* **natural wastage** = losing workers because they resign *or* retire, not because they are made redundant or are sacked

watchdog body ['wɒtʃdɒg 'bɒdi] *noun* body which watches something (especially government departments *or* commercial firms) to see that regulations are not being abused

weed out ['wiːd 'aʊt] *verb* to remove unsuitable candidates *or* employees; *the test is designed to weed out candidates who have low mathematical skills; the new management has weeded out some of the dead wood in the sales department*

week [wiːk] *noun* period of seven days (from Monday to Sunday); **to be paid by the week** = to be paid a certain amount of money each week; *he earns £500 a week or per week; she works thirty-five hours per week or she works a thirty-five-hour week;* **week's pay** = total gross earnings per week, including bonuses

◊ **weekday** ['wiːkdeɪ] *noun* normal working day (not Saturday or Sunday)

◊ **weekly** ['wiːkli] *adjective* done every week; **weekly wage** = amount of money paid per week; *the weekly rate for the job is £250*

weighted ['weɪtɪd] *adjective* **weighted**

average = average which is calculated taking several factors into account, giving some more value than others; **weighted checklist** = list of factors used for evaluation, which each have a different weighting or importance in the final assessment; **weighted index** = index where some important items are given more value than less important ones

◊ **weighting** ['weɪtɪŋ] *noun* additional salary *or* wages paid to compensate for living in an expensive part of the country; *the salary is £15,000.00 plus London weighting*

welfare ['welfeə] *noun* (a) looking after people; *the chairman is interested in the welfare of the workers' families;* **welfare services** = benefits and assistance provided by an employer to his staff (help with funeral expenses, counselling, legal advice, health checkups, etc.); **welfare state** = country which looks after the health, education, etc., of the people (b) money paid by the government to people who need it; *with no job and no savings, he was forced to live on welfare*

QUOTE California has become the latest state to enact a program forcing welfare recipients to work for their benefits
Fortune

well-paid ['welpeɪd] *adjective* earning a high salary; *he has a well-paid job in an accountancy firm*

◊ **well pay** ['wel 'peɪ] *noun* payment to an employee for having been off sick less often than a specified amount of time; *well pay can be regarded as a reward for good health*

well-qualified [wel'kwɒlɪfaɪd] *adjective* (person) who has good qualifications for a job; *six of the candidates are very well-qualified, which will make the choice difficult*

whistleblower ['wɪsəlbləʊwə] *noun* (*informal*) person who reveals dishonest practices

white-collar ['waɪtkɒlə] *adjective* referring to office workers; **white-collar crime** = crimes committed by business people *or* office workers (such as embezzlement, computer fraud, insider dealings); **white-collar union** = trade union representing white-collar workers; **white-**

collar worker = worker in an office, not in a factory; *there were separate canteens for white-collar and blue-collar workers*

QUOTE the share of white-collar occupations in total employment rose from 44 per cent to 49 per cent
Sydney Morning Herald

whizz-kid ['wɪzkɪd] *noun* brilliant young person who quickly becomes successful in business; *she was a whizz-kid who reached head of department in five years*

wildcat strike ['waɪldkæt 'straɪk] *noun* strike organized suddenly by workers without the approval of the main union office

withdraw [wɪθ'drɔː] *verb* to take back (an offer); *when he found out more about the candidate, the personnel manager withdrew the offer of a job; when the workers went on strike, the company withdrew its revised pay offer*

◊ **withdrawal** [wɪθ'drɔːəl] *noun* taking back; *withdrawal of an offer*

withhold [wɪθ'həʊld] *verb* to keep back (money, information); *to withhold a percentage of wages*

◊ **withholding tax** [wɪθ'həʊldɪŋ 'tæks] *noun* (i) tax which removes money from interest or dividends before they are paid to the investor (usually applied to non-resident investors); (ii) any amount deducted from a person's income which is an advance payment of tax owed (such as PAYE); (iii); *US* income tax deducted from the paycheck of a worker before he is paid

without prejudice [wɪˈθaʊt 'predʒʊdɪs] *phrase* phrase spoken or written in letters when attempting to negotiate a settlement, meaning that the negotiations cannot be referred to in court or relied upon by the other party if the discussions fail; **without prejudice communication** = written offer of compensation, which does not include or imply responsibility or admission of guilt and which cannot be used in evidence in court

wording ['wɜːdɪŋ] *noun* series of words; *did you read the wording on the contract?*

work [wɜːk] **1** *noun* (a) carrying out of jobs

or tasks; **casual work** = work where the workers are hired for a short period; **clerical work** = work done in an office; **factory work** = work on the production line in a factory; **manual work** = heavy work done by hand; **nightwork** = work done at night; **office work** = work done in an office; **piecework** = work for which workers are paid for the products produced *or* the piece of work done and not at an hourly rate; **seasonal work** = work which is available at certain times of the year only (such as in a ski resort); **shift work** = system of work in a factory with shifts; **teamwork** = group effort applied to work; **temporary work** = full-time work which does not last for more than a few days *or* months **(b)** job *or* something done to earn money; *it is not the work itself that the employees are complaining about, but the conditions in the workshop; he goes to work by bus; she never gets home from work before 8 p.m.; his work involves a lot of travelling; he is still looking for work; she has been out of work for six months;* **work-based learning** = learning and the assessment of learning done at the place of work; **the Anglo-Saxon work ethic** = feeling in Britain and the USA that work is the most important task for an adult; **work experience** = part of a training course, where trainees learn what it is like to work in a real job by actually working; *as part of their work experience, the schoolchildren had to spend two days working in a bank;* **work flow** = sequence of jobs which results in a final product *or* service; *a flow chart on the wall showed the work flow for the coming month;* **work group** = group of people who work together in a formal way; **work in progress** = value of goods being manufactured which are not complete at the end of an accounting period; **work measurement** = establishing the time necessary for the performance of certain tasks by a trained worker; **work overload** = having too much work (a frequent cause of stress); **work permit** = official document which allows someone who is not a citizen to work in a country; *many of our workforce are immigrants without work permits;* **work practices** = way in which work is done in an organization; *work practices have been changed in order to improve efficiency; a survey of work practices in the whole industry led to radical changes in the company;* **work sampling** = random observation of work processes in order to improve efficiency and economy; **work schedule** = timetable of jobs to be done; **work simplification** = removing unnecessary tasks in order to make a job simpler; *work simplification can save time which will then be used for other tasks;* **work standard** = output which is considered normal as the basis for a work study; *the work standard had to be lowered since very few workers could meet it;* **work study** = analysis of all aspects of a job affecting efficiency or performance; **work team** = group of workers who perform tasks together; *work teams have led to much greater flexibility and cooperation* **2** *verb* **(a)** to do things with your hands *or* brain, for money; *the factory is working hard to complete the order; she works better now that she has been promoted to work freelance;* **to work a machine** = to make a machine function; **to work to rule** = to work strictly according to rules agreed between the company and the trade union, and therefore work very slowly **(b) to work as a driver** = to have a paid job as a driver; *she works in an office; he works at Smith's; he is working as a cashier in a supermarket*

◊ **workaholic** [wɜːkəˈhɒlɪk] *noun* person who works all the time, and is unhappy when not working

◊ **workday** [ˈwɜːkdeɪ] *noun* day when work is done, as opposed to a holiday

◊ **worker** [ˈwɜːkə] *noun* **(a)** person who is employed; **blue-collar worker** = manual worker in a factory; **casual worker** = worker who can be hired for a short period; **clerical worker** = person who works in an office; **factory worker** = person who works in a factory; **foreign worker** = worker who comes from another country; **freelance worker** = self-employed worker, who works for himself; **immigrant worker** = worker who has entered the country as a potential immigrant, before finding work; **manual worker** = worker who works with his hands; **migrant worker** = worker who moves from place to play, looking for work; **office worker** = worker who works in an office; **semi-skilled workers** = workers who have had some training; **skilled worker** = worker who has special skills *or* who has had long training; **unskilled worker** = worker who has no particular training; **white-collar worker** = office worker; **worker's compensation** = liability of an employer to pay compensation to an employee or his or her family, when the employee has been injured or killed while working; **worker director** = director of a company who is a representative of the workforce; **worker instructor scale** = chart which lists the responsibilities of a job in terms of both set procedures and use of personal judgement; **worker participation** = sharing by workers in management decisions; **worker representation on the board** = having a representative of the workers as a director of the company **(b)** person who works hard; *she's a hard worker*

◊ **workfare** ['wɜːlfeə] *noun* system where people have to do work for the community in order to qualify for welfare payments

◊ **workforce** ['wɜːkfɔːs] *noun* total number of workers in a country, industry or organization; *the company cannot keep to its production schedules with half the workforce sick*

◊ **working** ['wɜːkɪŋ] *adjective* **(a)** (person) who works *or* who performs tasks; *how large is the working population of the country?*; **working partner** = partner who works in a partnership; **working supervisor** = worker who controls the work of others as well as doing manual work himself **(b)** referring to work; **working conditions** = general state of the place where people work (if it is hot, noisy, dark, dangerous, etc.); *working conditions are very bad in the factory;* **working day** *or* **working hours** *or* **working week** = normal time which is worked during a day *or* normal number of hours worked during a day *or* week; **the normal working week** = the usual number of hours worked per week; *even though he is a freelance, he works a normal working week;* **working lunch** = lunch where business matters are discussed; **working practices** = way in which work is done in an organization; *working practices have been changed in order to improve efficiency; a survey of working practices in the whole industry led to radical changes in the company*

◊ **workload** ['wɜːkləʊd] *noun* amount of work which a person has to do; *he has difficulty in coping with his heavy workload see also* WORK OVERLOAD

◊ **workman** ['wɜːkmən] *noun* man who works with his hands

◊ **workmanship** ['wɜːkmənʃɪp] *noun* skill of a good workman; **bad** *or* **shoddy workmanship** = bad work done by a workman

◊ **workmate** ['wɜːkmeɪt] *noun* person who works with another

◊ **work out** ['wɜːk 'aʊt] *verb* **he is working out his notice** = he is working during the time between resigning and actually leaving the company

◊ **workplace** ['wɜːkpleɪs] *noun* place where you work

◊ **works** [wɜːks] *noun* factory; *an industrial works; an engineering works; the steel works is expanding;* **works committee** *or* **works council** = committee of workers and management which discusses the organization of work in a factory (these are obligatory in some EU countries); **the works manager** = person in charge of a works (NOTE: not plural, and takes a singular verb)

◊ **work-sharing** ['wɜːkʃeərɪŋ] *noun* **(a)** system where two or more part-timers share one job, each doing part of the work; *work-sharing is encouraged as a way of reducing overall unemployment figures; managements feel that work-sharing can lead to lack of control and coordination of staff* **(b)** agreed sharing of work between employees, when there is less work available (so as to avoid redundancies)

◊ **workshop** ['wɜːkʃɒp] *noun* small factory

◊ **workshy** ['wɜːkʃaɪ] *adjective* lazy, afraid of doing any work

◊ **workspace** ['wɜːkspeɪs] *noun* memory *or* space available on a computer for temporary work

◊ **workstation** ['wɜːksteɪʃn] *noun* desk with a computer terminal, printer, telephone, etc., where a word-processing operator works

◊ **work-to-rule** [wɜːktə'ruːl] *noun* working strictly according to the rules agreed between the union and management and therefore very slowly, as a protest

◊ **workweek** ['wɜːkwiːk] *noun US* the usual number of hours worked per week

QUOTE the quality of the work environment demanded by employers and employees alike
Lloyd's List

QUOTE every house and workplace in Britain is to be directly involved in an energy efficiency campaign
Times

wreck [rek] *verb* to damage badly *or* to ruin; *the negotiations were wrecked by the unions*

writ [rɪt] *noun* **writ (of summons)** = legal document which begins an action in the High Court; *the company obtained a writ to prevent the trade union from going on strike;* **to serve someone with a writ** *or* **to serve a writ on someone** = to give someone a writ officially, so that he has to obey it

write [raɪt] *verb* to put words *or* figures on to paper; *she wrote a letter of complaint to the manager;* **written warning** = warning in writing sent to an employee by the employer or supervisor, saying that unless work improves he or she will be dismissed; *the written warning preceded dismissal by only a few weeks*

◊ **write-in** ['raɪtɪn] *noun* written enquiry from outside an organization, asking if there are any jobs available; *we have received several write-ins about jobs since it became known that we were setting up a new factory and sales office*

◊ **writing** ['raɪtɪŋ] *noun* something which

has been written; *to put the agreement in writing; he had difficulty in reading the candidate's writing*

wrong [rɒŋ] *adjective* not right *or* not correct; *the accounts department checked his expenses claim and found it was wrong*

◊ **wrongdoer** ['rɒŋduːə] *noun* person who commits an offence

◊ **wrongdoing** ['rɒŋduːɪŋ] *noun* bad behaviour *or* actions which are against the law

◊ **wrongful** ['rɒŋful] *adjective* unlawful; **wrongful dismissal** = removing someone from a job for a reason which does not justify dismissal and which is in breach of the contract of employment

| COMMENT: an employee can complain of wrongful dismissal to the County Court

◊ **wrongfully** ['rɒŋfəli] *adverb* in an unlawful way; *he claimed he was wrongfully dismissed*

◊ **wrongly** ['rɒŋli] *adverb* not correctly *or* badly; *he wrongly invoiced Smith Ltd for £250, when he should have credited them with the same amount*

Xx Yy Zz

X = EXTENSION

year [jɜː] *noun* period of twelve months; **base year** = year on which calculations are based; **calendar year** = year from January 1st to December 31st; **financial year** = the twelve month period for a firm's accounts; **fiscal year** = twelve month period on which taxes are calculated (in the UK it is April 6th to April 5th of the following year); **year to date** = the period between the beginning of a calendar or financial year and the present time

◊ **yearbook** ['jɜːbʊk] *noun* book which is published each year by an organization containing new or updated information about its activities; *there are articles in the company's yearbook about workers who have achieved particularly high levels of productivity*

◊ **yearly** ['jɜːli] *adjective* for each year; *for the past few years he has had a yearly pay rise of 10%*

yellow dog contract ['jeləʊ dɒg 'kɒntrækt] *noun US* agreement between an employer and employee that the latter will not join a union or engage in union activities

yes-man ['jesmæn] *noun* person who always agrees with what his boss says

youth [juːθ] *noun* young people; **Youth Employment Officer** = government official who tries to find employment for young people; *the Youth Employment Officer was kept busy trying to reduce unemployment among school-leavers in his area;* **Youth Training (YT)** = scheme run by the Training and Enterprise Councils which aims to provide young people with both off-the-job training and work experience in a particular area

zero ['zɪərəʊ] *noun* nought, the number 0; **zero-based budgeting** = planning budgets on the basis the no funds are allocated automatically, and that every piece of projected expenditure has to be justified; **zero-hours contract** = contract of employment where the worker is not guaranteed any work, but must wait on standby until required, and is only paid for hours actually worked

QUOTE the new zero-houred staff, employed as part of the plan to double the company's UK labour force and paid only when they are working, will help to meet the company's marketing commitment to service customers' cars free for three years

Times

ZIP code ['zɪpkəʊd] *noun US* letters and numbers used to indicate a town or street in an address on an envelope

zipper clause ['zɪpə 'klɔːz] *noun US* clause in a contract of employment which prevents any discussion of employment conditions during the term of the contract

A SEVEN-POINT PLAN

Requirements for a job
1. Physical: health, appearance, general manner
2. Qualification: Educational background and professional qualifications needed by someone taking up the job
3. Intelligence: intellectual demands of the job
4. Special skills: types of skills needed to do the job, such as skills with the hands, writing skills, ability to use numbers
5. Interests: hobbies, sports, recreations, membership of clubs
6. Character needs: impression on others, ability to take decisions independently, ability to delegate, response to stress
7. Special circumstances: unsocial hours of work, travelling away from home, dangerous job

A FIVE-FOLD GRADING SYSTEM

Personnel requirements for the job
1. Impact on others: appearance, general manner, way of speaking
2. Qualifications: education, technical qualifications, work experience
3. Intelligence: rapidness to understand, ability to learn new skills quickly
4. Motivation: track record, ability to set goals and achieve them
5. Personal needs: stable character, ability to make independent decisions, ability to delegate, response to stressful situations

A. Specimen Co. Ltd.

JOB DESCRIPTION

Job Title:

Production Manager

Main purpose:

supervising the work of the production
department

Duties:

1. agreeing product specifications with sales
   departments and time schedules with stock
   control department
2. ensuring product is manufactured according
   to agreed specifications and within time
   schedules
3. ensuring quality of finished product
4. negotiating with suppliers
5. supervising on-the-job training for staff
   and trainees

Responsible to:

Production Director

Responsible for:

1 sub-manager
10 machinists
3 trainees
2 cleaners
equipment valued at £500,00.00

A. Specimen Co. Ltd.

JOB APPLICATION FORM

Application for employment as: ....

Surname: ....

Other names: ....

Address: ....
....
....
....

Telephone number: ....

EDUCATION & TRAINING

Schools attended since age 11: ....
....
....

Examinations taken: ....
....
....

Diplomas, degrees, qualifications:
....
....

EMPLOYMENT HISTORY

Present employer   Previous employer

Name:........................   ....
Address:.....................   ....
....
....

Job title:...................   ....

Duties:......................   ....

Pay/Salary:..................   ....

Dates of employment:
From: To: From: To:

Reason for wanting to leave: Reason for leaving:

....

No approach will be made to your present employer before an offer of
employment is made to you.

I confirm that the above information is correct to the best of my
knowledge. I accept that deliberately providing false information could
result in my dismissal.
Signed: Date: